FAIR TRADE COFFEE:
THE PROSPECTS AND PITFALLS OF
MARKET-DRIVEN SOCIAL JUSTICE

Studies in Comparative Political Economy and Public Policy

Editors: MICHAEL HOWLETT, DAVID LAYCOCK, STEPHEN MCBRIDE, Simon Fraser University.

Studies in Comparative Political Economy and Public Policy is designed to showcase innovative approaches to political economy and public policy from a comparative perspective. While originating in Canada, the series will provide attractive offerings to a wide international audience, featuring studies with local, subnational, cross-national, and international empirical bases and theoretical frameworks.

Editorial Advisory Board

For a list of books published in the series, see page 349.

GAVIN FRIDELL

Fair Trade Coffee

The Prospects and Pitfalls of Market-Driven Social Justice

UNIVERSITY OF TORONTO PRESS
Toronto Buffalo London

© University of Toronto Press Incorporated 2007
Toronto Buffalo London
Printed in Canada

ISBN 978-0-8020-9238-0

Printed on acid-free paper

Library and Archives Canada Cataloguing in Publication

Fridell, Gavin
   Fair trade coffee : the prospects and pitfalls of market-driven social
justice / Gavin Fridell.

   (Studies in comparative political economy and public policy)
   Includes bibliographical references and index.
   ISBN 978-0-8020-9238-0

   1. Competition, Unfair.   2. Anti-globalization movement.
   3. Coffee industry – Developing countries.   I. Title.   II. Series.

   HD9199.D442F75 2007   382′.41373091724   C2006-906949-2

This book has been published with the help of a grant from the Canadian
Federation for the Humanities and Social Sciences, through the Aid to
Scholarly Publications Programme, using funds provided by the Social
Sciences and Humanities Research Council of Canada.

University of Toronto Press acknowledges the financial assistance to its
publishing program of the Canada Council for the Arts and the Ontario
Arts Council.

University of Toronto Press acknowledges the financial support for its
publishing activities of the Government of Canada through the Book
Publishing Industry Development Program (BPIDP).

For Kate

Contents

Tables and Figures

Tables

Figures

Acknowledgments

I have received important institutional assistance from a variety of sources that have aided me in my research. From the Social Science and Humanities Research Council of Canada (SSHRC) and York University I have received valuable financial assistance. The Centre for Research on Latin America and the Caribbean (CERLAC) at York has provided a stimulating venue for intellectual discussion along with references which can be so important for opening doors during field-work. Thanks are owed to Laure Waridel and McClelland & Stewart for permission to use copyrighted materials. I am particularly grateful to the fair trade organizations in Mexico, the Netherlands, and Canada, without whose assistance and welcome this work could not have been written. This includes the staff at Max Havelaar, TransFair Canada, and Planet Bean, as well as all members of the Union of Indigenous Communities of the Isthmus Region (UCIRI), who very generously hosted me at their cooperative facilities in Oaxaca, Mexico, in October 2002.

I have been extremely fortunate to have had the intellectual and emotional support of many people throughout the years, including colleagues, friends, faculty, and staff at the universities of York and Manitoba. Thanks are due my former teachers, Lionel Steiman, who guided me through the exciting and tumultuous years of my MA in history, and John Saul, who once wisely suggested that a degree of 'strategic naiveté' towards the seemingly endless number of 'must-read' books is required to finish a dissertation. CERLAC Fellows Ricardo Grinspun and Marshall Beck have both been central to creating the collegial atmosphere that has made CERLAC such a valuable focal point of my, and many others', academic pursuits. Marlene Quesenberry, the graduate program assistant in the Department of Political

Science, has been a beacon of light amidst the dense procedural fog at times created by university bureaucracies. Donald Carveth has provided invaluable guidance, both intellectually and personally. I have also benefited significantly from the seemingly countless seminars, academic panels, organizing committee meetings, conversations over beer and coffee, and even picket-line chats, that I have shared with my colleagues and friends, including John Cameron, Aileen Cowan, Megan Dombrowski, Lola Figueroa, Miguel Gonzalez, Mark Hostetler, Alex Latta, J.J. McMurtry, Sabine Neidhardt, Olga Sanmiguel, and Susan Spronk.

Several people have offered invaluable council in refining my dissertation and transforming it into a book. Darryl Reed offered insightful remarks at my defence as well as immeasurable help throughout the years in my academic efforts, and, as a fellow member of the fair trade campaign at York, in my activist endeavours. I am indebted to David McNally for his thoughtful reflections as well as for his own intellectual works, which figure prominently throughout this study, and his dedicated social justice activism, both of which have been key sources of inspiration for me. Anthony Winson, as the external member of my dissertation committee, offered incisive commentary and advice and has assisted me greatly in the publication process. Gratitude is also owed to Virgil Duff, editor at the University of Toronto Press, and to the anonymous reviewers, whose comments I hope I have made good use of here.

The members of my dissertation advisory committee have provided essential guidance, both in my work on fair trade and academic life in general. Gregory Albo's academic work and tireless activism have been a great source of inspiration since my arrival in Toronto, as has been his enthusiasm and support for my research. Viviana Patroni, the director of CERLAC, has offered me a great deal of sage advice on my work and academic life in general, which I hope to continue to draw upon in the coming years. Liisa North, my former supervisor, deserves a very special thanks for suggesting the theme of this study in the first place and then providing sound counsel, intellectual insight, and unwavering support to help see it through to its completion. Even while teaching in Ecuador during a period of political turmoil, she managed to find time to send me invaluable instruction and advice, a testament to her dedication as a supervisor, which I hope to replicate with my own students.

The difficulties of balancing graduate work with other, equally important needs in life is never easy, and I have been very fortunate throughout my life to be able to rely on the support and assistance of my parents, Jerry and Cynthia Fridell. Thanks is owed to them, as well as to the rest of my family, in particular my dearly departed uncle, Martin Spigelman, who unfortunately did not live to see the book completed but no doubt would have pored over it eagerly if he had. I have also relied a great deal on the support of good friends, whose humour and intellectual camaraderie have been immensely helpful in the dissertation struggle and beyond. With Kelly Reimer, I have enjoyed the fruits of countless chats about development theory and politics. David Sarai has assisted me in a variety of ways, not the least of which includes offering a seemingly endless bibliography of useful academic sources for me to draw upon. Martijn Konings has provided invaluable commentary and advice on revisions to my manuscript. The encouragement and council of David Friesen has been central to my personal and intellectual development since we first studied together at the University of Manitoba. My friend, mentor, former MA advisor, and de facto member of my PhD committee, Mark Gabbert, has provided wisdom and critical insight, without which my work may never have been completed. Lastly, I would like to thank Kate Ervine, who has provided immeasurable emotional and intellectual support in my academic pursuits and life in general. The anxiety-ridden, bumpy road that so often accompanies this sort of work has been significantly paved by her presence, and I very much look forward to all of our future endeavours.

The most interesting parts of my work have been those that have drawn from the wisdom and reflection of those mentioned above. As is often said, any shortcomings in this study are entirely my own.

Abbreviations

ACP	African, Caribbean and Pacific Group of States
AG	Andean Group
ANACAFE	Asociación Nacional de la Industria del Café / National Association of Coffee Exporters
ARIC	Asociación Rural de Interés Colectivo / Rural Collective Interest Association (Mexico)
ATO	alternative trade organization
CACM	Central American Common Market
CAN	Conservation Agriculture Network
CAW 3000	Canadian Auto Workers, Local 3000
CBA	collective bargaining agreement
CEC	Centro de educación campesina / Farmer Education Centre (UCIRI)
CEPCO	Coordinadora Estatal de Productores de Café de Oaxaca / Statewide Coordinating Network of Coffee Producers of Oaxaca
CFS	compensatory finance schemes
CI	Conservation International
CIDA	Canadian International Development Agency
CNC	Confederación Nacional Campesina / National Peasants' Confederation (Mexico)
CNOC	Coordinadora Nacional de Organizaciones Cafetaleras / National Coordinator of Coffee Organizations (Mexico)
CSR	corporate social responsibility
CUP	Caring Unites Partners
DFID	Department for International Development (UK)

DWSR	Dollar–Wall Street Regime
ECLA	United Nations Economic Commission for Latin America / Comisión Económica para América Latina
EEV	ecologic enterprise ventures
EFTA	European Fair Trade Association
EOI	export-oriented industrialization
EU	European Union
EUREP-GAP	Euro-Retailer Produce Working Group – Good Agricultural Practices
EZLN	Ejército Zapatista de Liberación / Zapatista Liberation Army
FAC	Fondo de Ahorro y Crédito / Savings and Credit Fund (UCIRI)
FINE	FLO/IFAT/NEWS/EFTA
FLO	Fairtrade Labelling Organisations International
FNC	Federación Nacional de Cafeteros / National Federation of Coffee Farmers (Colombia)
FOB	free on board
FTAA	Free Trade Area of the Americas
FTF	Fair Trade Foundation
GATT	General Agreement on Tariffs and Trade
GCA	German Coffee Association
GCC	global commodity chains
GDP	gross domestic product
GTZ	Deutsche Gesellschaft für technische Zusammenarbeit / German Development Agency
IACA	Inter-American Coffee Agreement
IADB	Inter-American Development Bank (World Bank)
IBC	Instituto Brasileiro do Café / Brazilian Coffee Institute
IBRD	International Bank for Reconstruction and Development (World Bank)
ICA	International Coffee Agreement
ICP	International Coffee Partners
IFAT	International Federation for Alternative Trade
IFI	international financial institutions
IFOAM	International Federation of Organic Agriculture Movements
IISD	International Institute for Sustainable Development
ILO	International Labour Organization

IMF	International Monetary Fund
INI	Instituto Nacional Indígenista / National Indigenous Institute (Mexico)
INMECAFÉ	Instituto Mexicano del Café / Mexican Coffee Institute
IOAS	International Organic Accreditation Service
IPC	Integrated Programme for Commodities
ISEAL	International Social and Environmental Accreditation and Labelling Alliance
ISI	import-substituting industrialization
ISMAM	Los Indígenas de la Sierra Madre de Motozintla / Indigenous Peoples of the Sierra Madre de Motozintha (Mexico)
ISO	International Standards Organization
IUF	International Union of Food, Agricultural, Hotel, Restaurant, Catering, Tobacco and Allied Workers Associations
ITTA	International Institute of Tropical Agriculture
KWS	Keynesian welfare state
LAFTA	Latin American Free Trade Area
LAIA	Latin American Integration Association
MCC	Mennonite Central Committee
MERCOSUR	Mercado Común del Sur / Southern Common Market
MSC	Marine Stweardship Council
MSN	Maquila Solidarity Network
NAFTA	North American Free Trade Agreement
NCA	National Coffee Association
NCRA	National Coffee Roasters Association
NEWS	Network of European Worldshops
NGO	non-governmental organization
NI	National Initiative (FLO)
NIEO	New International Economic Order
NIC	newly industrialized country
NSM	new social movement
OAS	Organization of American States
OECD	Organization for Economic Cooperation and Development
OPEC	Organization of Petroleum Exporting Countries
OWCF	Ontario Worker Co-operative Federation

PACB	Pan American Coffee Bureau
PPP	purchasing power parity
PRI	Partido Revolucionario Institutional / Institutional Revolutionary Party (Mexico)
PRN	Partido Republicano Nacional / National Republican Party
PROCAMPO	Programa de Apoyo Directo al Campo / Direct Rural Support Program (Mexico)
PRONASOL	Programa Nacional de Solidaridad / National Solidarity Program (Mexico)
PSD	Partido Social Demócrata / Social Democratic Party (Costa Rica)
RA	Rainforest Alliance
SANSAD	South Asian Network for Secularism and Democracy
SAPs	structural adjustment policies
SERRV	Sales Exchange for Refugee Rehabilitation (U.S.)
SOFA	Small Organic Farmers Association
STABEX	export earnings stabilization system
SYSMIN	System for Stablisation of Export Earnings for Mining Products
TBT	Technical Barriers to Trade (agreement)
TCO	Trabajo Común Organizado / Organized Communal Work (UCIRI)
TNC	transnational corporation
TRIPS	Trade-Related Aspects of Intellectual Property Rights
TTV	Ten Thousand Villages
TWIN	Third World Information Network (UK)
UCIRI	Unión de Comunidades Indígenas del Región del Istmo / Union of Indigenous Communities of the Isthmus Region (Mexico)
UDT	underdevelopment and dependency theory
UEPC	Unidades Económicas de Producción y Comercialización / Economic Units for Production and Marketing (Mexico)
UN	United Nations
UNAM	Universidad Nacional Autónoma e Mexico / National Autonomous University of Mexico
UNCTAD	United Nations Conference on Trade and Development
UNDP	United Nations Development Program

UPZMI	Unión de Puebles Zapotecas del Istmo / Union of Zapoteco and Mixe Towns of the Isthmus
US/LEAP	US/Labor Education in the Americas Project / US/Guatemalan Labour Education Project
USAID	United States Agency for International Development
USAS	United Students Against Sweatshops
WHO	World Health Organization
WRC	Worker Rights Consortium
WTO	World Trade Organization

FAIR TRADE COFFEE:
THE PROSPECTS AND PITFALLS OF
MARKET-DRIVEN SOCIAL JUSTICE

Introduction:
Fair Trade and Global Capitalism

Everybody knows that the dice are loaded.
Everybody rolls with their fingers crossed.
Everybody knows the war is over.
Everybody knows the good guys lost.
Everybody knows the fight was fixed:
The poor stay poor, the rich get rich.
That's how it goes.
Everybody knows.

Everybody knows that the boat is leaking.
Everybody knows the captain lied.   ·
Everybody got this broken feeling
Like their father or their dog just died.

Everybody talking to their pockets.
Everybody wants a box of chocolates
And a long-stem rose.
Everybody knows.

...

Everybody knows that it's now or never.
Everybody knows that it's me or you.
Everybody knows that you live forever
When you've done a line or two.
Everybody knows the deal is rotten:
Old Black Joe's still picking cotton

For your ribbons and bows.
Everybody knows.*

This excerpt from a song by well-known Canadian artist Leonard Cohen says much about the competitiveness, inequality, and injustice pervasive in modern life. While Cohen touches on many issues, one key underlying theme is how goods are produced and consumed by society. These activities have been central to the social, political, economic, and cultural organization of disparate societies throughout history. This includes societies of the present day where production and consumption are driven by the capitalist imperatives of competition and profit maximization. The overall result of these imperatives, as depicted by Cohen, is a world of alienation, injustice, and exploitation. Consumers, feeling alienated and isolated from other human beings, turn to the consumption of 'ribbons and bows' to buffer their self-esteem and drown their sorrows. Producers, on the other hand, toil in the fields like 'Old Black Joe' to create these commodities under highly exploitative conditions. The outcome – the poor stay poor, the rich get rich – is a sad reality that 'everybody knows.' Yet, the manner in which everybody knows is not through direct, personal ties between producers and consumers. Instead, it is a 'broken feeling' and an overarching sense that 'the deal is rotten.' People's *particular* knowledge of the lives of those who consume what others produce and those who produce what others consume remains obscure. In fact, it is in seeking some temporary escape from a world which Cohen compares to a leaking boat that consumers turn towards buying commodities like chocolate and long-stem roses, indirectly participating in the exploitation of others.

The reason for this situation is that, under capitalism, social relations between producers and consumers are not based on direct contact but are mediated by the market. Individual consumers purchase abstract commodities from the shelves at Wal-Mart and Starbucks. These commodities appear to be without connection to the workers who actually produced them, a situation that nineteenth-century political philosopher Karl Marx referred to as the 'fetishism of commodities' (Marx 1978: 319–29). In our contemporary world of international capitalism, this fetishism obscures vast inequalities and social injustices, especially

*Excerpt from 'Everybody Knows' from *Stranger Music* by Leonard Cohen. Used by permission of McClelland & Stewart Ltd.

between wealthy consumers in the advanced capitalist North and poor workers and small farmers in the underdeveloped South.

Sadly, an abundance of statistics exists to demonstrate the extent of these global inequalities. In 2002, among the high-income countries in the Organization for Economic Cooperation and Development (OECD) (population: 0.9 billion) the average life expectancy at birth was 78.3 years and the average gross domestic product (GDP) per capita was $29,000. This stands in stark contrast to the developing countries in the South (population: 4.9 billion), which had an average life expectancy at birth of 64.6 years and an average GDP per capita of $4,054. The contrast is even greater when we look at the poorest region in the world, sub-Saharan Africa, which had an average life expectancy at birth of an astonishingly low 46.3 years and an average GDP per capita of $1,790, only 6 per cent of that of the rich countries in the North (UNDP 2004: 142). These massive global inequalities are pervasive not only between nations but within them. In poor Southern countries such as El Salvador, Nicaragua, Ghana, Rwanda, and Mozambique, the percentage of the population living below the 1990–2002 income poverty line of $1 per day ranged between 30 and 45 per cent. Wealthier Southern nations, while comparatively better off, still have equally disturbing inequalities. In 2002, Mexico and Brazil, relatively affluent Southern nations with respective GDPs per capita of $8,970 and $7,770, had 26.3 per cent and 22.4 per cent of their populations living below the income poverty line of $2 per day (140, 147–9).

It is these gross inequalities that fair traders seek to combat through a system of ethical trade standards and an international solidarity network composed of certified Southern producer organizations and Northern importers, processors, and distributors. According to the rules of Fairtrade Labelling Organisations International (FLO), the world's largest independent certification body for fair trade primary commodities – such as coffee, tea, cocoa, and bananas – fair trade goods are produced by poor communities in the South under the principles of democratic organization (of cooperatives and unions), no exploitation of child labour, environmental sustainability, and the standards of the International Labour Organization (ILO) Conventions for all paid employees. They are exchanged under the terms of a minimum guaranteed price and include an additional 'social premium' for Southern partners to construct such things as hospitals, schools, roads, and processing facilities. Moreover, to confront the alienation and atomization of consumerism, according to sociologist Laura Raynolds (2002a: 415), fair trade goods 'arrive at the point of consumption

replete with information regarding social and environmental conditions under which they were produced and traded.'

Exploring the political-economic and historical impact and meaning
of the fair trade network and assessing its developmental potential is
the focus of this book. The network began as a loose system of alternative trade organizations (ATOs) in the 1940s and 1950s. In the late
1980s, the fair trade labelling system was introduced, with the goal of
expanding the fair trade market by encouraging conventional corporations to purchase a limited quantity of goods under fair trade–certified
conditions to tap into 'ethical consumer' markets in the North. Since
then the fair trade network has experienced rapid growth and has
emerged as an important international development project. The most
significant growth has occurred in European markets, but in recent
years sales of fair trade products have also increased rapidly in North
America. When I first began my research in Toronto in 2000, I started
asking employees on duty at Starbucks if they sold any fair trade coffee (an action encouraged by fair traders). As an answer, I invariably
received the query, 'What is "fair trade" coffee?' A year later, the
answer had changed to a direct 'No,' at times followed by an explanation about such a product being too expensive for consumers. In 2002,
the answer became 'Yes' when Starbucks started offering limited quantities of fair trade coffee at all their stores in Canada (brewed as a cup
of the day once a month and available in whole bean bags). Fair trade
coffee had emerged as a noteworthy, if still tiny, niche market product
in Canada.

The above anecdote draws attention to more than just the growth of
fair trade sales and increasing consumer consciousness around such
'ethical products' over the past few years. It also reveals a central component of this expansion: the growing participation of conventional
corporations like Starbucks. Over the past two decades, the fair trade
vision has changed from an alternative trading network composed of
small ATOs dealing exclusively in fair trade products, to a market
niche driven by the interests of giant conventional corporations
with minor commitments to fair trade given their overall size. (Only 1
or 2 per cent of Starbucks coffee beans are currently certified as fair
trade.)

While the emerging works on fair trade have been quick to celebrate
the sales growth that this transformation has ushered in, little has been
done to examine critically the political-economic impact of this change
and the historical context within which it emerged, and what they

reveal about the developmental prospects and limitations of the fair trade network. Most of the new works have focused on assessing fair trade's impact on local poverty alleviation and community development (primarily in the South), while leaving basically unexamined the broader political-economic and historically rooted structures that frame the context within which the network has evolved. Yet, while local-level analysis is essential to assessing the network's direct effects, and such work certainly needs to be conducted, examining the impacts of broader structures on the network, and vice versa, are of equal if not greater importance in determining its long-term developmental potential. Thus, whereas most works on fair trade take as their starting point local-level analysis, this study begins with an eye towards the power structures of global capitalism, and seeks to provide a framework for situating fair trade within the 'big questions' of historically informed development theory.

The Fair Trade Network and Development Theory

While there have been some attempts to develop an analysis of fair trade that is situated within the political and historical parameters of development theory (see Jaffee, Kloppenburg, Jr., and Monroy 2004; Raynolds 2002a; Barratt Brown 1993), in general little has been done in this regard, leaving a great deal of open terrain for developing a theoretically informed analysis. This is not to say that the existing works on fair trade do not draw from key assumptions and questions raised by development theory, but most often these are dealt with only implicitly and are not central to the analysis provided. As a result, in situating the present work within the literature, it is less significant to ask where *to locate one's analysis in relation to other works on fair trade* (a theme dealt with in detail in chapters 1 and 2) than it is to ask *where to begin a theoretically informed work on fair trade and why.*

One common starting point for much of the recent literature dealing with local-level development projects is new social movement (NSM) theory, which was originally developed by scholars in the 1960s to assess a variety of emerging movements in Europe. Since the late 1980s, NSM theory has been increasingly applied to the South and has emerged as a key strand in development theory, promulgated in particular by postmodern thinkers such as Arturo Escobar, Sonia Alvarez, and Evelina Dagnino (Alvarez, Dagnino, and Escobar 1998; Escobar 1995; Escobar and Alvarez 1992). Due to the perceived failure of all post-1945 development models to provide for the needs of the majority, and these models' neglect of issues of democratic participation, gender, race, and ecology, NSM theorists argue that 'new social movements' have emerged in the South. These movements have abandoned 'traditional' statist political objectives and instead pursue 'new' issues of gender equality, environmentalism, indigenous and minority rights, gay and lesbian rights, human rights, and local autonomy (Alvarez, Dagnino, and Escobar 1998; Slater 1994; Wignaraja 1993; Escobar and Alvarez 1992; Laclau and Mouffe 1985).

While there is a great deal of diversity in the ways that NSM theory has been applied to the South, most theorists share a few broad assumptions. First, they argue that the goals of NSMs, in contrast to traditional working-class parties and unions, do not centre on class but rather on all aspects of everyday life and a plurality of identity-based rights. Second, they assert that the social struggle carried out by NSMs in the South, rather than being focused on materialist aspirations, is primarily a cultural and symbolic battle over local 'collective identity,' autonomy, and the protection of diversity. Third, they argue that the political terrain of NSMs is not the traditional sphere of formal politics and does not involve a contestation for state power, but rather is located within the realm of civil society and entails a plurality of local acts of resistance that seek to open more cultural space for autonomous political action specific to their own situation (Edelman 1999: 15–20; Carroll 1997) .

While NSM theory draws attention to the need to consider how and why collective identities (such as those of fair trade cooperatives) are formed, it does not provide an adequate basis for a broad assessment of the fair trade network and development projects in general. This is due to a variety of shortcomings raised by NSM theory's critics, which can be touched on here only briefly. First, one of the main shortcomings of NSM theory is its emphasis on the purported 'newness' of contemporary social movements. In fact, many social movements are similar to movements in the past and often draw from a historical legacy, such as the Enlightenment values of social justice and human rights (Carroll 1997: 22; Adam 1997; Nederveen Pieterse 1992). This is certainly the case with the fair trade network, which has significant historical roots, internationally and locally, that are central to the analysis offered in this book. Second, NSMs in the South are not as classless as some theorists have suggested, but often have significant class components that cannot so easily be separated from demands for democracy, gender and racial equality, and environmental sustainability. In this vein, anthropologist Marc Edleman (1999: 20) asserts:

> Just as unions' demands for occupational health and safety are pro-
> foundly environmentalist, calls for equality, affirmative action, and non-
> discrimination clauses in union contracts are profoundly economic, as are
> those for converting war industries to peaceful uses, moving toxic dump
> sites, or closing nuclear power plants ... Many of the most significant
> recent struggles, especially in poorer countries, have occurred 'precisely
> at the point of intersection between' class- and identity-based movements
> ... And for the impoverished inhabitants of today's crisis-ridden Third
> World (or the scholars who work with them), the 'postmaterialist,' 'class-
> less' arguments of NSM theorists ring particularly hollow.

Third, the focus of postmodern NSM theorists on local autonomy and cultural struggle obscures the extent to which contemporary social movements aspire for internationalist, universal goals and materialist objectives to meet basic needs for food, shelter, and clothing. While Southern social movements are frequently portrayed by postmodernists as being opposed to 'Western' development projects, in most cases what they oppose is not being *included* in such development projects in a beneficial way (Edelman 1999: 10; Shuurman 1993: 27). This is certainly the case with fair traders, who aspire not to fight against globalization, but to attain a greater share of its purported benefits.

Finally, the argument that NSMs seek primarily to fend off the growing intrusion of the state – a 'defensive' battle – downplays the extent to which these movements continue to battle 'offensively' with the state to demand not withdrawal but a different type of state action over such things as human rights guarantees and social benefits (Adam 1997; Hellman 1994). Barry Adam argues: 'The state is a primary and unavoidable agent in the reproduction of relations of domination in race, gender, sexuality, and environment, and the new social movements struggle actively to block *and remake* these mechanisms of subordination' (1997: 50; emphasis added). Moreover, to the extent that contemporary social movements have in fact retreated from the goal of gaining state power in favour of struggles for local autonomy and diversity, this is not necessarily something to be celebrated as local 'resistance.' Such a retreat significantly weakens the potential for the alliance building required to take on broader structures of power and cedes the most important political decisions at the national and international level to increasingly undemocratic neoliberal states, transnational corporations (TNCs), and international institutions like the World Bank, the International Monetary Fund (IMF), and the World Trade Organization (WTO) (Edelman 1999: 18–19; Vilas 1997; Hellman 1994). For this reason, the potential of the fair trade network to be part of a broader movement to challenge global power structures is central to the analysis offered in this work.

The historically rooted, universalist (combined with locally specific), and materialist objectives of the fair trade network make for a poor fit between it and NSM theory. More useful avenues for exploring fair trade are provided by theories that better address the needs and objectives of fair traders by assessing development on the basis of the classical Enlightenment ideal of *emancipation*, which includes *liberty* (from structural hierarchies), *equality* (of material, political, and ideological resources), and *fraternity* (through meaningful citizenship and international solidarity) (Shuurman 1993). These ideals have been interpreted throughout modern history in different ways depending on peoples' social, economic, and cultural context and political orientation – for example, the liberal notion of 'equality of opportunity' versus the socialist notion of 'equality of outcome.' In their particular context, Southern fair traders have drawn on Enlightenment values and interpreted them in their own specific way, although in a manner consistent in many regards with the history of peasant radicalism in modern times: equality of property within the community; liberty from outside sources of oppression, such as local and international intermediaries; and fraternity within the community, as well as with Northern partners and consumers (Moore 1966: 497–505). The prospects and limitations of this vision are assessed in this book on the basis of two approaches to development that draw effectively from the Enlightenment legacy: the capability expansion approach, which is employed to assess the local short- and medium-term impact of fair trade, and a historical materialist approach, which is used to examine fair trade's impact on broad structures of power.

The capability expansion approach was first formulated by economist Amartya Sen (1999, 1990) in the 1990s in response to much mainstream thinking which places undue emphasis on assessing development primarily on the basis of economic growth and income expansion. While these indicators are important, Sen argues that they are 'intermediate goals' whose ultimate effectiveness can only be determined by their impact on the actual 'end' of development, the enhancement of human life. To assess this, he has developed the capability approach which evaluates 'quality of life in terms of valued activities and the capability to achieve these activities' (Sen 1990: 43). This method, which merges materialist concerns, such as economic growth, with questions of social and cultural outcomes, provides an effective tool for measuring the short- and medium-term impact of local development projects. For this reason, capability expansion approaches have become widely used and have also become the development methodologies most often employed by academics and institutions in assessing fair trade.[1]

The capability approach is used in this work to assess the ability of fair trade organizations to attain valued activities that have enhanced the quality of life of their members. Nonetheless, while capability expansion is useful for assessing the gains of fair traders *within* the existing social structures of global capitalism, it tells us very little about their ability to confront these structures. This limit is inherent in the capability approach, which constrains its vision of development to working within the constraints imposed by neoliberal globalization.[2] Yet, the ultimate goal of fair trade organizations, as is argued throughout this book, is not just to enhance the capabilities of Southern producers to survive within the existing order, but to enhance their abilities to confront and change it. In consequence, a framework of analysis is required which not only evaluates the short and medium-term gains of fair trade at the local level, but one which identifies broader, historically rooted structures of power and can assess the potential of fair trade to articulate and help advance demands to alter them. Political scientist Colin Leys (1996: 196) argues that multi-levelled and historical analysis needs to be central to formulating effective development strategies, and he cautions against 'a discourse of "complexity" in which everything is dissolved into its details, and the possibility of abstracting and trying to act on the main elements and forces at work in the world is obscured (if not actually denied) ... for all its shortcomings the great merit of development theory has always consisted in being committed to the idea that we can and should try to change the world, not just contemplate it – which means, in practice, being willing to abstract from the detail, to identify structures and causal relationships and to propose ways of modifying them.'

For this reason, a historical materialist approach to development is employed in this book to identify macro-structures of power and their historical, social, and political-economic roots. Historical materialism, a concept formulated by Karl Marx, is premised on the assertion that historically specific 'modes of production' – an abstract concept used to identify how a society mobilizes social labour – are central to determining the distribution of political-economic power and socially produced wealth in society. Thus, in the current context, we live in a world dominated by the capitalist mode of production (the alienating effects of which were described above by Leonard Cohen), and the distribution of wealth and power in the world system is largely determined by the structural imperatives of capitalism at the local and global level.

In the 1960s and 1970s, the dominant historical materialist approach to development theory was a body of diverse works referred to here as underdevelopment and dependency theory (UDT) (see Leys 1996: 46–7). Composed largely of the works of Latin American structuralists (Prebisch 1950, 1980; Cardoso and Faletto 1979; Furtado 1976; Hirschman 1961) and neo-Marxist dependency and world systems theorists (Amin 1977; Wallerstein 1974; Rodney 1972; Frank 1972), UDT was highly influential among radical and some mainstream development circles that sought to identify macro-structures of power. Despite the wide-ranging diversity within the UDT literature, in general most authors argued that underdevelopment occurred as a result of the exploitative structures of the world capitalist system which was divided into 'First World,' imperialist nations in the North, and 'Third World,' colonial and neocolonial nations in the South. The normal operations of the world system resulted in a transfer of surplus wealth produced in the Third World to the First World where it was consumed or invested in production. This occurred due to 'unequal exchange' stemming from the legacy of colonialism which had compelled Third World nations to develop in a manner dependent on the export of a few primary commodities to markets in the North. As a result, Third World nations were reduced to a state of dependence on First World countries for technology, capital, and markets, which restricted and distorted their national development and resulted in what Andre Gunder Frank (1972) has termed 'the development of underdevelopment.' Most UDT authors argued that the gap between North and South was insurmountable under the existing conditions, and that Third World countries needed either to develop highly interventionist state projects and demand changes to the terms of trade within the capitalist world system (as argued by structuralists), or break with the capitalist system entirely and construct a state socialist project (as advanced by neo-Marxists) (Hunt 1989: 121–223).

UDT's broad, systemic analysis reveals much about the highly unequal global distribution of wealth and resources, and, significantly, draws attention to the structural causes of underdevelopment – as opposed to depicting underdevelopment as being due to the 'backward' nature of Southern political cultures, a view common to much traditional and current mainstream development thinking (Leys 1996: 47). For this reason, UDT had significant influence on the fair trade network in its formative years and has also influenced several fair trade analysts, either directly (Ransom 2001; Barratt Brown 1993), in modified form through the study of global commodity chains (GCC) (Taylor 2005; Renard 2005; Jaffee, Kloppenburg, and Monroy 2004; Raynolds 2002a), or implicitly (Waridel 2002; Lappé and Lappé 2002). This influence is analysed in detail throughout this study. For now, a few points need to be raised about the weaknesses of the UDT approach advanced by historical materialists who assert that UDT has neglected the importance of the historically specific social relations of capitalism, an insight that was central to the foundational works of Marx.

Beginning in the 1970s, some Marxist development theorists began criticizing UDT for, among other things, advancing a 'neo-Smithian,' trade-based depiction of capitalism that neglected the *historically specific social relations of production* that underlay modern economic growth under capitalism (Wood 1999; Leys 1996; Brenner 1985, 1977). Adam Smith, they argued, had placed undue emphasis on exchange relations as the primary dynamic behind capitalism, and UDT theorists had replicated this emphasis with their depiction of the capitalist world system as being driven by unequal exchange between the North and South. The shortcomings of this perspective, they pointed out, was that exchange relations of various kinds had existed throughout human history, long before the development of capitalism, and thus could not by themselves account for the unprecedented pace of modern economic growth. This situation could only be explained by the historically unique social relations of production, based on private property and the commodification of labour, that underpin exchange relations under capitalism. As a result of these social relations, workers, who had been 'freed' from pre-capitalist ties to the land, had to sell their labour power on competitive labour markets in order to survive, and property owners had to compete on markets with other property owners in order to maintain their ownership. It is these competitive pressures that have historically given way to modern economic growth and the exploitation and inequality that has accompanied it (McNally 2002,

1993; Wood 1999; Brenner 1985, 1977). This historically specific under-standing of capitalism, which has been advanced not just by Marxists but also importantly by economic historian and anthropologist Karl Polanyi (1944), whose work is drawn on significantly in chapter 4, is central to the analysis offered in this book.[3]

The Marxist and Polanyian critique of a neo-Smithian understand-ing of capitalism has significant implications for assessing the develop-ment projects that UDT analysts have generally offered. Due to their emphasis on trade as the primary dynamic behind capitalist growth, UDT prescriptions have focused on correcting unequal trade relations at the international level while neglecting the capitalist social relations at the local and national level that gave rise to these inequalities in the first place. Latin American structuralists, for example, have called for states and international agencies to carry out radical reforms to the international trade and development regime, without addressing the need to radically change the unequal relations of class power that underpin these institutions. Thus, often elite-dominated Southern states have been called upon to promote 'development' at the interna-tional level. The result, as Leys (1996: 52) states, is that 'the solution always turns out to be part of the problem.' In contrast, neo-Marxist dependency and world systems theorists have acknowledged the need to transform radically domestic social relations, but their analysis – focused on the unequal transfer of surplus wealth internationally – has failed to provide the sort of local level class analysis required to assess the prospects and difficulties of this happening. Directing attention to this weakness, Leys (1996: 52) argues: 'It is no less utopian to appeal to "revolution" and "socialism" to solve the problem as radical [neo-Marxist] structuralism formulates it than to appeal to the existing Third World governments or the US Agency for International Develop-ment (USAID), since a structural analysis doesn't disclose the potential class forces on which a revolutionary struggle can be based or the con-tradictions that condition and are developed by the struggle.'

Drawing from the Marxist critique of the neo-Smithian conception of capitalism, it is clear that the fair trade network has inherited many of the problems associated with UDT. The fair trade network as it is cur-rently articulated is premised on the belief that global inequality and injustice can be combated with radical reforms to trade, at the level of both individual firms and the international trade regime, without a fundamental transformation of political power, class relations, and property ownership within the states that constitute the capitalist world system. This raises two significant questions that are addressed throughout this book.

First, can the fair trade network sufficiently challenge the imperatives of capitalism – competition, accumulation, profit maximization – with its market-based strategy without radically challenging the social relations of production that underlie these imperatives? Most fair traders tend to downplay the *imperatives* of the capitalist market and focus on the market as a place of *opportunities* for those willing and able to take advantage of them. In line with a neo-Smithian understanding of political economy, they depict capitalism less as a particular set of social relations than as a specific *attitude* towards commercial exchanges (McNally 2002, 1993; Wood 1999). Exploitation is not viewed as a result of the structural imperatives of the capitalist market, but as a distortion of the market stemming from the acts of 'unscrupulous' market agents (FLO 2001: 2). To most fair traders, the goal is to correct these distortions by promoting more ethical trading values which they hope will allow everyone, rich or poor, to reap the rewards of the market. Yet, this moral emphasis runs the risk of overlooking the weight of structural imperatives. According to social justice activist and political theorist David McNally (2002: 86), in seeking to combat exploitation under global capitalism: 'To be sure, moral outrage is necessary and laudable. But a purely moral response ignores the fact that capitalism *requires* its dominant participants to behave in an exploitative and destructive fashion. No amount of moral lecturing or enlightenment will change the behaviour of capitalists, since only by doing what they do will they survive *as* capitalists. If they do not exploit the poor, grab land and resources, commodify the globe, and act in environmentally destructive ways, they will not persevere in the war of capitalist competition. The imperatives of cost-minimization and profit maximization compel capitalists to do these things.'

As described in the chapters that follow, the imperatives of the capitalist market have had and continue to have a major impact on the fair trade network. These imperatives have compelled fair traders to abandon their original vision of an alternative trading system based on state regulation and instead adopt a voluntarist, market-driven model designed to reform the existing system. They have also imposed limits on what the new, market-driven model of fair trade entails. For example, while the network has rigorous social standards for Southern fair trade partners, no such standards exist for Northern corporate partners who otherwise would be unwilling to participate in fair trade. This neglect of social relations of production has also been accompanied by a neglect of unequal gender relations. This has frequently been the case for development projects in general, which have often sought to allow women greater access to the male-dominated 'public' sphere of production, even while unequal gender relations have resulted in women attaining more exploitative working conditions under an increased 'double burden' as they have remained primarily responsible for 'private' household work (Scott 1995; Pearson 1994). These trends are also apparent in the fair trade network through patriarchal voting structures and gendered divisions of labour on Southern cooperatives.

The second fundamental question addressed throughout this book is: can the fair trade network challenge the 'fetishism of commodities' and bring producers and consumers together, without a transformation of capitalist social relations of production which lie at the heart of commodification? Most fair traders and fair trade analysts believe that the network challenges the alienation and individualization that characterize capitalist market exchanges by providing information of how goods are produced and by forging bonds of solidarity between consumers and producers. To Marx, this alienation is a result of the commodification of goods and labour which stems from capitalist social relations of production. Under capitalism, all market agents (workers, small producers, large capitalists) must sell either their labour or their goods as abstract commodities on the market in exchange for money, which they then use as consumers to purchase other abstract commodities; as stated by economist A. Hussain (1987: 85), 'Each economic agent produces goods which he himself does not consume, and, in turn, consumes goods which he has not produced.' The result is that people, rather than directly engaging with one another over the production and distribution of goods, engage the market as atomized agents deprived of information on how goods are produced and use their own individual needs as the sole criterion for determining market choices (McNally 1993: 199–200; Marx 1978: 319–29).

As discussed in the chapters that follow, the fair trade network does provide an important symbolic critique of the fetishism of commodities, although always with important contradictions. Fair trade goods do reveal the conditions under which they are produced and traded, and important bonds of solidarity between fair trade partners in the South and North have been forged, which have helped to somewhat shorten the symbolic distance between producers and consumers. At the same time, however, the capitalist market remains the ultimate coordinator of economic life, and the survival and growth of the network are ultimately *entirely dependent* on the decisions of Northern consumers. These consumers are not engaged in a democratic process with Southern producers, but rather remain atomized individuals directly unaffected by the social and political outcomes of their market decisions. They are themselves driven by the imperatives of capitalism, which determines their disposable income and market options, and, at the same time, they are the primary dynamic behind the imperatives that impose certain prospects and limitations on fair trade producers in the South.

Assessing the impact of capitalist imperatives on the developmental potential of the network is the focus of this book, which examines the historical dimensions of the fair trade network in general, followed by a more specific assessment of fair trade coffee, traditionally the highest-selling fair trade commodity, at both global and local levels.

The Global and Local Dimensions of Fair Trade Coffee

Unlike most of the contemporary works on the fair trade network, this book is focused on broad political and developmental questions and as such draws significantly from secondary sources. This includes academic works dealing generally with development and development theory, such as those mentioned above, as well as the rapidly expanding body of literature dealing specifically with fair trade. Significant use is also made of written primary materials produced by small fair trade ATOs in North America; international fair trade groups such as Fairtrade Labelling Organisations International (FLO), the European Fair Trade Association (EFTA), Oxfam International, and Global Exchange, and international organizations such as the United Nations Conference on Trade and Development (UNCTAD), the International Institute for Sustainable Development (IISD), and the World Bank.

This written material is supported with interviews I carried out with fair traders in the Netherlands, Mexico, and Canada. In the winter of 2002 in Utrecht, the Netherlands, I interviewed Hans Bolscher, then director of Max Havelaar Netherlands, the founding organization of fair trade labelling, who had worked for the organization for over nine and one-half years. The following spring, I visited the fair trade coffee cooperative Unión de Comunidades Indígenas de la Región del Istmo (Union of Indigenous Communities of the Isthmus Region, UCIRI), in Oaxaca, Mexico, for a few weeks. There I was given a tour of UCIRI's coffee-processing, health, and education facilities, and was granted access to a small archive that included various UCIRI reports produced over the past two decades. I conducted informal interviews with various members who ran the cooperative. Of particular importance was a lengthy interview with Francisco VanderHoff Boersma, an advisor to UCIRI and one of the founders of Max Havelaar Netherlands and the international fair trade network in general. The interview with Vander-Hoff, as well as the one with Bolscher, is drawn upon extensively throughout this book.

In Canada, my investigation on fair trade draws on my own activist experience as a member of the 'Fair Trade @ York' campaign, which has sought to compel York University in Toronto, Canada, to adopt a fair trade purchasing policy – a demand the university has thus far rejected. Of particular relevance was my role in helping to organize various fair trade events, especially the Fair Trade Workshop for Academic and Fair Trade/No Sweat Practitioners, held at York in June 2004. The workshop, initiated by political philosopher Darryl Reed, brought together representatives from some of the major fair trade ATOs in Canada – including TransFair Canada, Ten Thousand Villages, Oxfam, Équiterre, Planet Bean, and La Siembra – to discuss fair trade and the major issues that ATOs confront in expanding the network. Along with this, in May 2004, I conducted an interview with Bill Barrett, the director and marketing manager of the fair trade coffee cooperative Planet Bean, in Guelph, Ontario, which is the subject of chapter 6.

The chronology of my research, moving from the Netherlands, to Mexico, to Canada, is replicated in the organization of the chapters of this book. Chapter 1 examines the historical and theoretical origins of the fair trade network, from its emergence in Europe and North America in the 1940s and 1950s to its reorientation beginning with the development of Max Havelaar Netherlands in 1988. Little has been done to explore these historical roots, which reveal a great deal about the current orientation of the fair trade network. Through a historical examination, I demonstrate that the current vision of the fair trade network, based on reforming the existing international market by gaining voluntarist commitments from giant, profit-driven TNCs, is substantially different from the old vision of the network, which sought to play a role in laying the groundwork for a broader movement that aspired, ultimately, to create an alternative trading system based on significant international and national market regulation. In moving away from its original vision, the network has made a significant departure from

UDT, which placed a central role on state market intervention, while at the same time maintaining UDT's neo-Smithian understanding of the market.

Chapter 2 examines the history of the fair trade network from 1988 to the present, during which time it has experienced rapid sales growth and has gained the growing support of neoliberal institutions, like the World Bank, and conventional corporations. I argue that the key aspect of the network's success has been its neo-Smithian conception of the market, which, shed of its statist orientation, has proven to be highly compatible with the goals of neoliberal reformers who seek market-friendly, non-state interventionist programs to address the widespread negative social and environmental effects of neoliberal globalization. Within this context, significantly different interpretations of the fair trade network and its ultimate political objectives have emerged: does the network represent a challenge to neoliberal globalization and an alternative model of development (as argued by Oxfam International), or does it represent a complementary project designed to assist poor workers and farmers in more actively participating in neoliberal globalization (as depicted by the World Bank) (Lewin, Giovannucci, and Varangis 2004: 116–27; World Bank 2002b; Oxfam International 2002a, 2002b)? The contemporary perspectives on fair trade are assessed through an examination of three broad groups: the *shaped advantage perspective*, which depicts fair trade as assisting poor producers in participating in neoliberal globalization; the *alternative globalization perspective*, which views fair trade as an alternative model to the neoliberal paradigm; and the *decommodification perspective*, which depicts fair trade as a challenge to the commodification of goods under capitalism. I argue that while the latter two groups effectively express the broad vision of most fair traders, the shaped advantage group more accurately captures the actual impact of the network in its current neoliberal orientation.

What these different views reveal is a growing disparity between the transformative goals that fair traders aspire to accomplish and what the network seems ultimately capable of attaining. The extent to which this is true is examined in the remaining chapters of the book, which assess the developmental potential of fair trade labelling through an examination of the fair trade coffee sector. Chapter 3 provides a short history of the conventional coffee industry and explores the structural roots of exploitation and inequality within the context of the emergence of the capitalist world system. I argue that any attempt to promote human development within the coffee industry in the long-term must address the historical dimensions of exploitation – unequal distribution of land, resources, and political power – and the structural dimensions of exploitation – the capitalist imperatives of competition, accumulation, profit maximization, and increasing labour productivity, which are imposed on all market agents, large or small. With these dimensions in mind, chapter 4 explores various strategies designed to promote development in the coffee industry in the twentieth century – the International Coffee Agreement (ICA), instant coffee and 'forward integration,' the Federación Nacional de Cafeteros (National Federation of Coffee Farmers, FNC) in Colombia, the Costa Rican social welfare state – and compares them to the fair trade network. This comparison reveals that the network has built upon previous projects and has developed some innovative strategies of its own, but ultimately its non-governmental-organization (NGO)-led, voluntarist program falls short of the most successful model, the state-led development strategy in Costa Rica.

Chapter 5 shifts the analysis from broad historical and international political-economic dimensions to the local level and examines the developmental achievements and prospects of the Mexican cooperative UCIRI, one of the most successful Southern fair trade partners in the world. As a result of fair trade criteria and bonds of solidarity with Northern partners, UCIRI has been able to acquire its own coffee processing, transportation, education, and health care facilities and to provide its members with better access to credit, organic agricultural inputs, and technology. All of this has enhanced its members' capabilities to carry out valued activities and improve their quality of life. At the same time, without accompanying reforms at national and international levels, I argue that the impact of UCIRI's project, as well as the potential to replicate it broadly, has been significantly limited by the imperatives of global capitalism and the continuing expansion of neoliberal policies. These macro-level policies continue to be promoted by the very same institutions that give micro-level support to local organizations like UCIRI.

Chapter 6 examines the role of Northern institutions and consumers in the fair trade network in Canada. While strict social and environmental criteria exist for Southern fair trade partners, no such criteria exist in the North. The result is that the network in Canada is driven by the actions and interests of both small-scale ATOs like the worker-owned cooperative Planet Bean and giant TNCs like Starbucks Coffee Company. Through a comparison of the two significantly different organizations, it is demonstrated that Planet Bean is driven by a moral mission that focuses on international solidarity, educating consumers, and promoting local development in Canada, whereas Starbucks is purely profit-driven. As such, Starbucks makes only minimal commitments to protect its corporate image, exploits low-wage, non-unionized workers in the North, and has in fact done more to develop watered-down alternatives to the fair trade network than participate in it. Moreover, when 'ethical consumers' purchase fair trade coffee from a giant TNC like Starbucks, they are not connecting with Southern producers in a substantially different manner than when they purchase any other conventional commodity: consumer and producer remain abstract, anonymous individuals with no real knowledge of each other or their communities. The local development model promoted by Planet Bean is much more in line with the traditional values and vision of fair trade. Unfortunately, over the past few years the network has become increasingly corporate in its orientation, which raises serious concerns about the future of fair trade and its developmental vision.

The prospects and limitations of the fair trade network and its political meaning are analysed in the final chapter. This analysis is made difficult by the complex contradictions in the network's developmental program and its historical progression over time. Since its reorientation in the late 1980s, the network's voluntarist, non-statist program has been viewed by public institutions and corporations as being fundamentally compatible with neoliberal reforms, a fact which has been key to its rapid growth. Yet, the values and a vision promoted by its members are generally premised on a critique of neoliberal globalization, and the network is often portrayed by supporters as 'a response to the cultural impoverishment of capitalism – its erosion of social solidarities and its materialist rather than transcendent motivational structure' (Simpson and Rapone 2000: 55). The effect of these clashing values, visions, and expectations – of being both within and against the market, both in opposition to and compatible with neoliberal globalization – has been a contradictory and at times opaque political platform, one which I argue is best captured by the concept of an international 'moral economy.'

1 Historical and Theoretical Origins of the Fair Trade Network

It is well known that for many years I have fought in ECLA and UNCTAD for the basic elements of [a] new international economic order. I have regarded these as the means not simply of maintaining the existing order, but of fundamentally transforming it.

Raúl Prebisch, The Dynamics of Peripheral Capitalism[1]

Few people in the South believe in market liberalization under WTO-patronage. At the very least, such liberalization has to be transparent from producers to consumers, in open markets with sound competition.

Paola Ghillani, FLO Report 2000–2001[2]

The increasing popularity of fair trade over the past decade has given rise to a small but growing body of literature on the subject produced by fair traders, fair trade analysts, and non-governmental organizations (NGOs). While approaching the topic from a variety of perspectives, few of these works have attempted to provide a thorough historical assessment of the fair trade network. Most analysts have focused on the network since the emergence of fair trade labelling in 1988 and have given only brief mention to its historical development in earlier decades.[3] From this starting point, authors have generally depicted the fair trade network as having developed over the past decade and a half in direct opposition to the emergence of neoliberal globalization. When viewed historically, however, a more complicated picture emerges of the relationship between the fair trade network and neoliberalism. From a historical perspective, the development path initiated by fair traders in the late 1980s marked a significant departure from the more radical vision of the network formulated from the 1940s to the 1970s, and it did not emerge in direct opposition to neoliberal globalization but in partial capitulation to its imperatives.

The historical analysis that follows is based on a careful distinction between the 'fair trade network' and the 'fair trade movement,' terms that are generally used interchangeably in most works on fair trade. Here, the 'fair trade network' is used to refer to a formal network of NGOs that connects peasants, workers, and craftspeople in the South with partners in the North through a system of fair trade rules and principles – what authors typically refer to when they speak of fair trade commodities or handicrafts. In contrast, the 'fair trade movement' refers to a broader movement, which has had significant influence in international development circles since the end of the Second World War. This movement has no official existence, but rather is a term used here to encapsulate a variety of initiatives headed by Southern governments, international organizations, and NGOs with the purpose of radically altering the international trade and development regime in the interest of poor nations in the South. Broadly speaking, the groups involved in this movement have shared two central objectives. First, to pressure Northern countries to eliminate what has been perceived as 'unfair' protectionist regulations in the North. Second, to demand the creation of international cooperative mechanisms to regulate the world market and ensure 'fair' prices and labour conditions for commodity producers and workers in the South.

The fair trade *network* has historically been just one initiative among many others in the broader fair trade *movement*, which includes such things as international commodity agreements, price stabilization schemes, and appeals at international forums for fairer global trade rules. The history of the movement is one of expansion from the 1940s to the 1970s, during the era of embedded liberalism, followed by decline from the 1980s onward, when neoliberal reforms ushered in a new era of state downsizing and market liberalization. Within this broader historical context, the fair trade network has undergone its own specific history, which is divided here into two phases. During the first phase of the network (1940s–80s), fair trade NGOs were significantly influenced by the arguments advanced by Latin American structuralist, dependency, and world systems theorists. Like other organizations in the movement, they emphasized the goal of obtaining 'trade not aid,' and had a commitment to a vision of an alternative world trading system with strong international market regulation. During the second phase of the network (1980s to the present), as other projects in the movement lapsed into decline, the network abandoned its earlier vision and reoriented itself towards more market-friendly goals, such as gaining access to conventional markets and dealing directly with mainstream transnational corporations (TNCs). This sparked a period of unprecedented sales growth for the network. Thus, as most of the projects of the fair trade movement lapsed into decline, the fair trade network boomed, becoming one of the only initiatives of the movement to survive and thrive in the era of neoliberal globalization.

The picture presented here raises important issues about the fair trade network and its relationship to neoliberal globalization. From a historical perspective, the success of the fair trade network has been paralleled by the decline of most of the other projects in the fair trade movement, which raises serious questions about the extent to which the growth of the network can been seen, in a broad context, as indicative of a triumph against neoliberal reforms. In fact, the fair trade network is frequently upheld by international financial institutions like the World Bank as a *neoliberal alternative* to the other, statist projects of the fair trade movement, which are deemed to be a thing of the past.

From a theoretical perspective, the origins of the network's development vision lie in the structuralist, dependency, and world systems theories which were prominent within the fair trade movement in the 1960s and 1970s. In recent years, however, fair traders have abandoned the statist emphasis of these theories while maintaining their neo-Smithian understanding of the capitalist market. This neo-Smithian conception, which privileges *exchange relations* over *relations of production*, is essential to understanding the current prospects and limitations of the fair trade network. The relevance of these issues is examined in the following assessment of the origins of fair trade, which begins with a history of the broader movement followed by the history of the network during its first phase, from the 1940s to the 1980s.

Embedded Liberalism and the Rise of the Fair Trade Movement

The modern fair trade movement rose to prominence in the post–Second World War era, and it has sought to readjust the terms of North–South trade and use international market regulation to support development efforts in the South. Contrary to the claims of many free trade proponents, capitalist markets have always been regulated to some extent, generally in the interests of the rich and powerful

(Polanyi 1944). The most powerful Northern nations in the world today – the United States, Germany, and Japan – as well as the newly industrialized countries (NICs) in East Asia and Latin America all emerged historically behind a protective wall of import controls, tariffs, levies, quotas, and preferences designed to protect domestic industry and enhance export industry (Stiglitz 2003; Baer 1972). Market regulation has, in particular, been employed by powerful nations to protect their dominant position in the global division of labour. What makes the fair trade movement unique is that it has aspired to use market regulation to protect the weak, not the strong, and, ideally, to create a more equal international trading system (Barratt Brown 1993: 79–83).

The origins of the fair trade movement can be found in various attempts to control international commodity markets during the interwar period, 1918 to 1939. These emerged to combat a rapid decline in the price of primary commodities – copper, tin, rubber, coffee, wheat, sugar, and cotton – in relation to secondary, manufactured goods produced in advanced capitalist countries in the North. They were pursued by colonial companies and the colonial states of western Europe, who sought to stave off the possible collapse of the international trading system, as well as to protect the profits of colonial companies and the stability of colonial economies overseas. The drop in commodity prices was due to an overall decline in demand for such goods in the industrialized North caused by a global economic recession in the 1920s followed by the Great Depression in the 1930s, the development of substitutes for primary products, and an expansion of productive capacity in the South for goods whose markets were already saturated (Barratt Brown 1993: 79–87; Furtado 1976: 50–7).

Throughout the 1920s and 1930s a series of control schemes were established for primary commodities which generally involved restricting output and stockpiling to keep commodities off the market, which in turn would artificially raise prices. In most cases, these schemes failed because the higher prices which resulted sparked intensified efforts to develop more substitutes in the North or encouraged new Southern producers to enter the market. The latter had the effect of increasing total production, which merely escalated competitive pressures among producing states (Barratt Brown 1993: 79–87).

The Second World War (1939–1945) brought some relief to commodity producers in the South. The war reduced primary production in Europe, East Asia, and parts of Africa, resulting in a rise in the price of primary commodities in relation to manufactured goods throughout the 1940s. Of greatest importance, however, was the end of the war and the emergence in its wake of an era of state-managed capitalist development at national and international levels. Much of the impetus for this development stemmed from the desire of state elites and national capitalist classes to mitigate the escalating social class conflict sparked by the poverty and uncertainty caused by the Great Depression and the Second World War. This conflict was further fuelled by the apparent success of the Soviet Union, which had emerged from the war as the world's second greatest military power and appeared to many to offer a feasible alternative to capitalist development. This inspired fear among capitalist classes in the North and South of the 'spectre of communism.' In addition, national elites also determined that the state had a key role to play in rebuilding the capitalist world system after the devastation caused by the war (Teeple 2000: 1–21; Hobsbawm 1994).

The result of this new consensus was the emergence of state-led capitalism at the national and international levels. At the national level, the Keynesian welfare state (KWS) became the dominant capitalist model in the North, which entailed previously unheard of state expenditure on public services, infrastructure, and investment, all of which underpinned post-war economic growth (Teeple 2000). In the South, most countries in Latin America and parts of Africa pursued import-substituting industrialization (ISI). This involved the state intervening in the market through the provision of infrastructure, price controls, protective tariffs, the nationalization of key industries, and capital controls to promote the development of domestic industry for manufactured goods historically imported from the North (Hoogvelt 2001: 242–4; Furtado 1976: 107–23, 172–7; Baer 1972). In East Asia, especially South Korea and Taiwan, the state intervened to promote export-oriented industrialization (EOI) by regulating foreign investment and trade and providing infrastructure, research and development, and financing to domestic industry (North and Cameron 2000; Chibber 1999; Evans 1987).

Of greatest significance for the fair trade movement was the development of an international economic order based on an 'embedded liberal' framework which allowed for a degree of restrictive economic practices in order to maintain the stability of the world system (Helleiner 1994). In 1944, the Allied powers met in the United States at Bretton Woods, New Hampshire, to initiate negotiations for agreements which would lay the basis for the post-war order. Most of the participants at the negotiations viewed the interwar system, driven by protectionism and commercial warfare, as having been responsible for the economic chaos of the 1930s, along with the rise of fascism and militarism (Teeple 2000: 53–4). Consequently, they sought to create a new international order premised on the objective of establishing a *regulated international monetary system* to provide a stable basis for a *liberal international trading system* (Helleiner 1994: 4).

The Bretton Woods system that emerged from the negotiations was based on a payment system and exchange rate mechanism pegged to the American dollar, a fixed American dollar-gold convertibility, and international cooperation to control short-term financial flows (Gowan 1999: 16–17; Helleiner 1994: 1–6). Two key public institutions were formed to oversee the system: the International Monetary Fund (IMF), designed to provide short-term loans for countries with balance of payment difficulties; and the International Bank for Reconstruction and Development (IBRD, commonly referred to as the World Bank), designed to provide long-term financing for development projects. In addition, the General Agreement on Tariffs and Trade (GATT) was established to achieve the reduction of trade barriers through a series of negotiated rounds.

Despite the official goal of attaining 'free trade,' various mechanisms for regulating international trade were also developed to ensure a degree of stability for Southern economies. These mechanisms became a key component of the fair trade movement in the post-war era. Among the most significant of them were international commodity control schemes, which, under the terms of the Havana Charter (1948), were to be managed internationally by the newly formed United Nations (UN). Unlike the previous commodity control schemes of the interwar period, which sought to restrict production, the Havana Charter proposed an interventionary use of buffer stocks that could be built up in times of surplus production and run down in times of shortages. The charter stated that, at the request of member states, the UN was to establish study groups for each commodity to formulate international control schemes that aspired to create reasonable prices while ensuring that world demand was met and that the most efficient producers were afforded increases in output (Barratt Brown 1993: 89).

The 1950s witnessed a major decline in the price of nearly all primary commodities on the international market. This sparked a turn towards new commodity control schemes under the principles of the Havana Charter. Study groups previously established for tin, rubber, and wool were reactivated; new study groups for lead, zinc, coffee, and cocoa were initiated; and existing international councils for cotton, sugar, and wheat were reorganized. International agreements were reached for nearly all of these commodities, except for lead and zinc. For a variety of political-economic reasons, these agreements failed to increase the export earnings of nations in the South. The wheat agreement, which was renewed continually from 1949 to 1970, failed to provide higher prices and market opportunities for Southern nations due to the protectionist policies and dumping practices of North America and western Europe. The International Sugar Agreement, signed in 1954, collapsed in the 1960s when the United States unilaterally boycotted Cuban sugar. After that, protectionist and preferential trade policies by the United States, Europe, and the USSR, reduced the international market for sugar and kept prices low. An international agreement on tin, which was renewed continually from 1956 to 1985, brought higher prices in the 1970s and then collapsed in the 1980s due to an overall decline in world demand for tin. An international agreement on coffee (International Coffee Agreement, ICA) was reached in 1962 and lasted until 1989, when a group led by Brazil, the world's largest coffee-exporting nation, and one led by the United States, the world's largest coffee-consuming nation, could not agree on prices and export quotas (Barratt Brown 1993: 89–92; Furtado 1976: 215–18).

In addition to promoting international commodity schemes, the UN also provided important forums for representatives from Southern countries to meet and develop proposals for a new international economic order. Post-war decolonization in Africa, Asia, and the Caribbean in the 1960s and 1970s gave way to dozens of newly independent states in the South, which resulted in a major readjustment of international politics. The majority of Southern states, under pressure from Northern powers, pursued state-led capitalist development strategies, but an important minority pursued Soviet-style Communist models (including China, Cuba, Vietnam, and North Korea). Either way, a certain consensus existed on the necessity of 'state action and state control' (Hobsbawm 1994: 350, 344–71). These Southern states, taken together, represented the bulk of the world's population, held a substantial majority of seats in the UN General Assembly, and attempted to use their new political weight to pressure Northern countries for major readjustments to the international economic order (Bello 2004: 32–58).

One important UN body which sought to advance the interests of Southern states was the United Nations Economic Commission for

Latin America (ECLA), formed in 1948, with its headquarters in Santiago, Chile. Unlike the founding in the same year of the Organization of American States (OAS), dominated by the United States with its headquarters in Washington, DC, ECLA developed a distinctly Latin American development program. Throughout the 1950s and 1960s, ECLA was particularly devoted to promoting ISI, and, to this end, directed significant efforts towards the development of common markets to address the narrowness of Latin American domestic markets for ISI goods. ECLA played a key role in the formation of a Central American Common Market (CACM) in 1958 and the Latin American Free Trade Area (LAFTA) in 1960 (Baer 1972; Hirschman 1961; Mikesell 1961). This was followed by the formation of the Andean Group (AG), composed of Colombia, Venezuela, and Ecuador, in 1969.

In general, the common markets promoted by ECLA failed to bring the intended benefits to their participants, most of whom resisted real measures to lower tariff barriers between members (Bulmer-Thomas 2001; Devlin and Estevadeordal 2001). An exception to this was CACM in Central America, which sparked a considerable increase in intra-regional exports, prompting significant industrial growth and infrastructural development. Nonetheless, CACM was plagued by major weaknesses. The decline in import duties and tax exemptions for local industry, combined with excessive tax evasion by wealthy domestic elites, resulted in significant shortcomings in public revenues at a time when increased spending on public infrastructure was required. In addition, the lack of effective mechanisms to ensure a relatively equitable distribution of benefits between more and less developed members led to conflict between participants which played a significant role in derailing CACM in 1970 (Bulmer-Thomas 1987: 175–199).

A decade and a half after the founding of ECLA, the fair trade movement picked up increasing steam with the first United Nations Conference on Trade and Development (UNCTAD) in 1964. This was organized due to the widely perceived failure of commodity schemes to bring increased export earnings to Southern producers (Furtado 1976: 221). At the conference, resolutions were passed by a substantial majority of mostly Southern nations in favour of constructing a new relationship between the North and South. Southern nations wanted a greater transfer of wealth from the North to the South through aid, compensation, and most importantly 'fairer trade.' The strategy for attaining fairer trade focused on two key demands which lie at the heart of the fair trade movement and continue to bear significant influence on the prescriptions of fair trade organizations: the elimination of 'unfair' protectionist regulations in the North, and the creation of interventionist mechanisms to ensure 'fair' prices for commodities produced in the South.

Regarding the first key demand, Southern nations wanted the rich nations in the North to weaken their protectionist policies – tariffs, import controls, levies – which they asserted prevented primary commodity producers from developing the value-added, processing stages of primary production (Barratt Brown 1993: 92). A particularly glaring example of this was the system of escalating tariff rates in the North, which were and continue to be applied unequally to processed and unprocessed primary products. For example, the tariff rate of coffee beans entering the European Union from 2001 to 2003 was zero for unprocessed green beans, 7.5 per cent for roasted beans, 8.3 per cent for decaffeinated green beans, 9 per cent for decaffeinated roasted beans, and 11.5 per cent for substitutes containing coffee such as instant coffee (UNCTAD and IISD 2003: 4).

The second key demand made by Southern nations was for UNCTAD members to ensure fair prices for primary commodities by developing a system of direct subsidies to producers to replace the grants and financial aid provided by the IMF. The slogan that accompanied this demand was 'Trade not Aid' – which would become the unofficial slogan of the fair trade movement.

In the end, both demands proved to be too great a threat to the interests of the world's dominant powers. Representatives from the eight richest countries in the world, along with twenty-five neutrals and 'Second World' Communist countries in eastern Europe, voted against or abstained from every key resolution. Since UNCTAD was required to work by consensus, nothing substantial was accomplished. UNCTAD itself, however, was established as a key forum and research body for information and ideas on fairer trade for Southern nations (Bello 2004: 34–5; Barratt Brown 1993: 92; Furtado 1976: 221–4).

A key fair trade concept which both ECLA and UNCTAD were central to developing was the idea of 'unequal exchange.' The theoretical foundations for this concept were first laid out by economist Raúl Prebisch, the executive secretary of the ECLA (1948–62) and the founding secretary general of UNCTAD (1964–9), who is generally considered a founder of the Latin American structuralist school. Prebisch's work was a challenge to theories of international trade based on the 'comparative advantage' concept of classical economic theorist and millionaire stockbroker David Ricardo (1772–1823). These theories asserted that each nation had an economic advantage over other nations for the production of some goods. If each nation were to focus on producing the goods for which it had a comparative economic advantage, it would be to the relative benefit of all nations in the world. It followed that the South should continue to produce primary goods, for which these countries allegedly had a comparative advantage, while the North would continue to produce manufactured goods and everyone would benefit from North–South trade. Against these notions, Prebisch (1980, 1950) argued that all nations of the world could not benefit from the existing international trade system because North–South trade was highly unequal and systematically benefited the North at the expense of the South through the mechanism of unequal exchange.

According to Prebisch, unequal exchange between the North and South stemmed from the gradual deterioration over time in the prices of primary products in relation to manufactured goods. This was because, unlike manufactured goods, primary products had a relatively *inelastic demand*, which meant that decreasing prices did not necessarily lead to consumers buying more primary goods. The main reasons for this were the physiological limits on the quantity of primary goods that individuals could consume, the increasing development of industrial substitutes for primary materials, and the declining productivity of raw material output compared to industrial output due to technological advances. In addition, Prebisch argued that the relative emancipation of labour movements in the North had pushed up the prices of Northern manufactured goods in relation to Southern goods where labour was generally not emancipated. Prebisch and other structuralist thinkers generally argued that these obstacles could be overcome through capitalist development and without severing ties with Northern TNCs. To do so, however, required strong state-protected ISI initiatives designed to free Southern states from their over-reliance on primary products, as well as united efforts on the part of Southern states to put political pressure on the North to adopt fairer trade practices (Bello 2004: 34–5; Hoogvelt 2001: 40–1, 242–3; Hunt 1989: 47–51; Prebisch 1980, 1950; Furtado 1976; Baer 1972; Hirschman 1961).

The concept of unequal exchange was further developed by the proponents of dependency theory and world systems theory, which dominated radical development thinking in the 1960s and 1970s. These theorists argued that a world capitalist system which was divided into First World imperialist nations in the North and Third World colonial and neocolonial nations in the South, had existed since the sixteenth century. The normal operations of the world capitalist system resulted in a transfer of surplus wealth produced in Third World nations to First World nations where it was consumed or invested in production. This situation, they asserted, was due largely to unequal exchange relations stemming from the legacy of colonialism, which had compelled Third World nations to develop in a manner dependent on the export of a few primary commodities to markets in the North. As a result, Third World nations were reduced to a state of dependence on First World countries for technology, capital, and markets, which restricted and distorted their national development. Most of these theorists viewed the gap between North and South as insurmountable under the existing terms of trade, and argued that Third World countries needed to make a radical break with the world capitalist system through a highly interventionist state project. Many of the foundational thinkers of dependency and world systems theory, such as Andre Gunder Frank (1972), Immanuel Wallerstein (1974), and Samir Amin (1977), were neo-Marxists who asserted that such a project should be oriented towards constructing state socialism and include 'de-linking' from the world capitalist system entirely. While these theorists have differed significantly from structuralists regarding their views on the potential for Southern states to develop within the capitalist world system, the major foundational theorists from all three traditions share several overarching common assumptions, and can be grouped, as Colin Leys has done, into a broad school of thought on '"underdevelopment" and "dependency" theory' (UDT) (Leys 1996: 45–6; Prebisch 1980).

In the 1970s, the ideas advanced by the promoters of UDT had a significant influence on Southern governments (Leys 1996: 63), many of which pursued policies based on economic nationalism, self-reliance, autonomous development, and delinking, and continued to pressure for changes to the international trading system. In numerous negotiating forums, Southern nations demanded more secure prices for primary commodities, preferential access to domestic markets in the North for infant industries in the South, reforms to the international monetary system, new aid flows, and codes of conduct for TNCs. These demands became enshrined in the UN Programme of Action for the Establishment of a New International Economic Order (NIEO) (1974) and the UN Charter of Economic Rights and Duties of States (1976) (Bello 2004: 38–41; Hoogvelt 2001: 41–2, 177).

Of key importance for the fair trade movement, at the 1976 UNCTAD meeting, Southern countries continued to push the fair trade agenda developed at the 1964 meeting by proposing an Integrated Pro-gramme for Commodities (IPC). The program called for a variety of changes to the international trade and development regime, including the creation of international commodity stocks to control price fluctua-tions financed by a common fund, compensatory finance for com-modities for which stockpiling could not assure adequate prices, and an end to unfair Northern protectionist barriers. Northern nations rejected all of the proposals of the IPC except the plan to develop a common fund, which they agreed to in principle although they stalled for years in providing the actual financing it required (Bello 2004: 39; Barratt Brown 1993: 93).

In addition to advocating commodity agreements, UNCTAD also promoted the development of compensatory finance schemes (CFS). Under such schemes, producers receive compensation from Northern donors for deviations in the market price if it drops below an agreed upon level. The rational behind CFS is that the market is allowed to find its own prices so that artificially high prices do not encourage excess production, and compensation is then paid in the form of direct grants or loans to producers. The most notable example of this was the export earnings stabilization system (STABEX) agreement adopted by the European Community in the early 1970s and designed to compen-sate its ex-colonies – known as the African, Caribbean and Pacific Group of States (ACP Group) – as part of the Lomé Conventions. Under the terms of the agreement, target prices were established for over fifty products and the European Community pledged to make up the difference when prices fell below the target.

In general, STABEX funds were frequently inadequate and in some years failed to meet even 40 per cent of the agreed upon obligations. Moreover, while it was hoped that STABEX funds would be used to promote diversification, in general its grants and loans were used to raise output in existing sectors, thus reinforcing Southern nations' long-term dependence on the production of a few primary commodi-ties. Nonetheless, STABEX did provide much-needed price subsidies to poor producers in the South (LeClair 2002). Perceptions about its rel-ative benefits led to the adoption in 1980 of a similar CFS agreement for mining products under the Lomé Conventions called the System for Stablisation of Export Earnings for Mining Products (SYSMIN).

The establishment of the NIEO, the UN Charter of Economic Rights

and Duties of States, the IPC, and STABEX and SYSMIN proved to be
the pinnacle of the fair trade movement. In the 1980s and 1990s, the
movement was derailed by the emergence of neoliberal globalization
as states and international organizations abandoned 'embedded liberal' policies of government intervention and turned towards neoliberal policies bent on market deregulation and the removal of national
and international capital controls (Bello 2004: 42–4; Leys 1996: 1–44).

Neoliberalism and the Decline of the Fair Trade Movement

The reasons for the emergence of neoliberal globalization are manifold
and complex. Many authors place the greatest emphasis on new technological changes, which have allowed TNCs to shift capital around
the world with unprecedented speed, and declining national growth
rates in the North, which have compelled capitalists to expand their
global operations in search of new markets and cheap labour (Hoogvelt 2001; Teeple 2000; Friedman 2000; Held et al. 1999; Greider 1997).
However, while new technological changes can tell us how TNCs have
been able to operate effectively at an international level and market
forces can explain why Northern capitalists have seen the need for
some sort of response to declining growth rates, the nature of the specific
response that has emerged – neoliberal globalization – must ultimately
be seen as a consequence of political decision made by the world's
most powerful states, in particular the United States (Harvey 2003;
McNally 2002; Gowan 1999; Helleiner 1994).

As Peter Gowan has effectively argued, neoliberal globalization
emerged in the 1970s as a result of the political actions of the U.S. government which moved to initiate a Dollar–Wall Street Regime (DWSR)
in response to its declining position in international trade. First, in 1971
the U.S. government abandoned the dollar-gold convertibility, which
allowed it to freely determine the price of the dollar, entrenched as *the*
international currency, in its own interests. Second, in 1974 the United
States unilaterally abolished its capital controls, which led to an inflow
of foreign investment into Wall Street, already the world's financial
centre, and helped to finance the United States' growing trade deficit
(Gowan 1999: 1–38). Throughout the 1980s, nation-states in the North
and the South were compelled to remove their own capital controls
in order to remain attractive to investors and halt capital flight to
the United States, initiating a process of 'competitive deregulation'
(Helleiner 1994: 12).

The removal of capital controls brought an end to the Bretton Woods system and rolled back the post-war consensus on state-managed capitalism, which required capital controls to preserve the policy autonomy of states. This effectively led to the decline of the fair trade movement, whose momentum from the 1950s to the 1970s had relied on two main pillars: 'developmental' states in the South who formed the basis for the political support for fair trade in international forums like UNCTAD; and international mechanisms designed to regulate trade in the interest of poor states, such as commodity control schemes and CFSs. By the end of the 1980s, these two pillars had been toppled by neoliberal reforms.

The decline of the interventionist state was imposed on the South not just through competitive deregulation but through the direct political mechanism of neoliberal structural adjustment policies (SAPs), which were forced on highly indebted nations as a condition for the refinancing and rescheduling of loan repayments. While the fair trade movement was pushing for 'trade not aid,' a crisis had emerged in the South in the 1970s in the form of unserviceable amounts of foreign debt acquired as development 'aid.' In response to a series of oil shocks throughout the 1970s, many Southern nations dramatically increased their foreign borrowing to cover the unprecedented increase in the price of oil. When these debts were acquired, they appeared to be an economically rational response on the part of Southern leaders as interest rates were low or negative. However, in 1979 the United States, amidst the deepest economic recession since the 1930s, increased its interest rates to stave off inflation and attract the return of capital from the South. This, in turn, increased the interest rates on loans to Southern countries at a time when the global recession had caused real prices for primary commodities to tumble. Finding themselves squeezed between high oil prices, high interest rates, and low commodity prices, many Southern nations were forced to default on their debt repayments, the most notable cases being Mexico in 1982, followed by Brazil and Venezuela in 1983 (Stiglitz 2003; Gowan 1999: 48–51; Cobridge 1993).

In response to the defaults, the IMF moved in to protect the stability of commercial banks in the North and the interests of TNCs with export industries based in the South. The IMF offered highly indebted nations a 'rescue package' which included refinancing and the rescheduling of some loan payments, on the condition that they agreed to implement a series of neoliberal SAPs. These included severe cuts to public spending; reducing or eliminating capital controls, protectionist barriers, and market regulations; and devaluing local currencies to make exports more competitive. By the early 1990s, over 100 highly indebted Southern nations had SAPs imposed on them. SAPs proved to be ineffective in solving the debt crises – indebted countries had an estimated net outflow of resources to the North of more than $200 billion in the 1980s – and caused growing poverty and inequality as a result of such things as cuts to public health care and education and the collapse of internal purchasing power (Stiglitz 2003; Weisbrot et al. 2001; Chossudovsky 1997: 33–4; Cobridge 1993). What they did accomplish was to reorganize debt-ridden countries in the interest of the United States and other Northern countries, whose banks and corporations have benefited significantly from debt repayments, unchecked capital flight from the South, and greater access to Southern markets (Bello 2004: 42–4; Gowan 1999).

In Latin America and parts of Africa, the imposition of SAPs brought about a dismantling of state-led ISI projects, the impact of which had varied significantly from country to country depending on the extent to which state officials were willing or able to carry out a redistribution of wealth and check the penetration of foreign capital (North and Cameron 2000: 1753; Evans 1987; Bulmer-Thomas 1987: 175–99; Furtado 1976: 172–7, 298; Baer 1972). In general terms, however, despite many contradictions, ISI brought about decades of previously unprecedented economic growth in most countries which was accompanied by overall progress in most major indicators of human development – life expectancy at birth, GDP per capita, infant and child mortality rates, education, and literacy. This is in sharp contrast to the impact of neoliberal reforms since the 1980s which have been accompanied by a clear decline in progress for most of these indicators, including economic growth which neoliberal pundits claim lies at the heart of their development policies – GDP per capita in Latin America grew by 75 per cent from 1960 to 1980 compared to only 6 per cent from 1980 to 1998 (Stiglitz 2003; Weisbrot et al. 2001; Weisbrot et al. 2000). In Southeast Asia, where state-led EOI had combined economic growth with a significantly better distribution of wealth than in the NICs in Latin America, many states relied significantly less on foreign 'aid' and were less vulnerable to demands from rich nations to initiate neoliberal reforms. In the late 1990s, however, consistent political pressure from the United States, along with the Asian financial crises compelled some states, in particular South Korea, to adopt neoliberal reforms to gain access to IMF funds. This marked an important turning point in the history of state-led capitalist development in the region (although, importantly, the economies of China, Taiwan, Vietnam, and India continue to employ a state-led model, and, to varying degrees, resist neoliberal reforms) (Bello 2004: 44–50; Stiglitz 2002: 89–132, 2000; Gowan 1999: 60–127).

For the fair trade movement, the decline of state interventionist models in the South led to an erosion of political support for the post–Second World War consensus on the necessity of international market regulation. This effectively halted the fair trade movement and eroded its gains. The political support upon which the NIEO and the Charter of Economic Rights and Duties of States had been constructed dissolved and the doctrines became defunct. The common fund for the IPC never came close to realizing its original intentions. It took UNCTAD thirteen years to gain the required support of 100 nations and attain the necessary financial pledges amounting to over $330 million to initiate the fund. By the time it came into existence in 1989, there were few international commodity organizations that were still in operation. In consequence, much of the IPC's funds were redirected away from commodity price control schemes and towards non-interventionist strategies such as promoting crop diversification, quality improvements, and better marketing strategies (Bello 2004: 39; Barratt Brown 1993: 93–5).

The assault on strategies of national and international market regulation continued throughout the 1990s, spurred on by the sudden collapse of the USSR in 1991. The disappearance of the 'Communist threat' – so long a major factor in inspiring social reform in the capitalists world – boosted the momentum of neoliberal globalization. At the end of 1994, the GATT agreements were ratified and the World Trade Organization (WTO) was formed. The WTO is charged with policing and promoting deregulation and market liberalization among its more than 120 member states. Its formation was accompanied by moves on the part of Northern countries to successfully oppose any linkages between the WTO and UNCTAD and to erode the latter's negotiating role, essentially limiting its formal functions to providing consultation and technical assistance. In light of this development, Walden Bello (2004: 51), the founding director of the policy research institute Focus on the Global South, comments that 'UNCTAD continues to survive, but the truth of the matter is that it has been rendered impotent by the WTO.' In 2000, the WTO, spurred on by the United States, succeeded in pressuring the EU and the ACP Group to replace the Lomé Conventions with the Cotonou Agreement which promises to gradually phase out all preferential trade arrangements, including STABEX and SYSMIN, by 2008 (BRIDGES 2001, 2000; ACP Group 2000).

The expansion of market liberalization in the 1990s also gave way to the emergence of a 'new' regionalism in the South that differed significantly from the 'old' regionalism in the 1960s and 1970s which had sought to promote state-led ISI and combat dependence on the North (Baer 1972). In Latin America, the debt crisis in the 1970s led to a collapse of intra-regional trade, which effectively derailed the efforts of CACM, the AG, and LAFTA. In their place emerged a new regionalism that has sought to further integrate Latin America into the world system by promoting private sector growth; the withdrawal of the state from direct economic activity; and the penetration of foreign investment, trade, and services. This neoliberal reorientation began with the transformation of LAFTA into the Latin American Integration Association (LAIA) in 1980, and was followed by the re-launching of CACM in 1990, the founding of the MERCOSUR (Mercado Común del Sur / Southern Common Market) customs union in 1991 (consisting originally of Argentina, Brazil, Paraguay, and Uruguay, with Chile and Bolivia incorporated in 1996 as associate members), the transformation of the AG into the Andean Community in 1996, and the ongoing negotiations for the thirty-four-member Free Trade Area of the Americas (FTAA) (Bulmer-Thomas 2001; Devlin and Estevadeordal 2001: 22).

By the turn of the millennium, the fair trade movement's various calls for the international regulation of prices, aid flows, trade rules, and labour rights in the interest of the poorer states in the South had collapsed. In recent years, there have been some mild signs of a revival of the fair trade movement as Southern governments have grown increasingly resistant to the demands of Northern governments and international financial institutions. One of the most important examples of this has been the emergence of a coalition of developing countries, the G20, headed by India, Brazil, China, and South Africa, which derailed the fifth ministerial meetings of the WTO in Cancún, Mexico, in September 2003. The G20 has demanded the elimination of Northern protectionist barriers to Southern commodities and an end to Northern agricultural export subsidies, long-standing goals of the fair trade movement (Bullard 2004). These demands, however, represent an attempt by Southern states to attain only those concessions that are compatible with a neoliberal discourse of 'free trade' – the elimination of 'unfair' protectionist policies in the North. Absent from the G20 agenda are the other demands that have, historically, been central to the fair trade movement – the development and expansion of interventionist mechanisms to ensure 'fair' prices and living standards for Southern producers and workers. As such, the emergence of the G20, while a positive sign, does not significantly detract from the overall decline of the fair trade movement.

The rise and decline of the broad fair trade movement has had an important impact on the history of the fair trade network, the latter being a specific development project that connects peasants, workers, and craftspeople in the South with partners in the North through a system of fair trade rules and principles. During the heyday of the fair trade movement, from the 1950s to the 1970s, the fair trade network was developed and its original objectives greatly influenced by the broader movement's emphasis on forging a new international economic order. During the 1980s and 1990s, when the fair trade movement lapsed into decline, the fair trade network boomed and attained unprecedented sales growth and recognition. While the goals of the fair trade movement, focused on state-managed development and a radical readjustment of international trade, have been incompatible with those of neoliberalism, the fair trade network adjusted its strategy in the 1980s, placing a new emphasis on market-driven development and voluntarist reforms to the existing international economic order. The remainder of this chapter discusses the first phase in the history of the fair trade network, from its formative decades to its readjustment in the late 1980s.

The Fair Trade Network, Phase 1: Promoting Alternative Markets (1940s–1980s)

The fair trade network was significantly influenced by the broader fair trade movement. From the movement, the fair trade network drew an emphasis on combating unfair commodity prices, on attaining 'trade not aid,' and on the necessity of promoting national and international market regulation to support its efforts. Moreover, during the first phase of its history, from the 1940s to the 1980s, fair traders were influenced by UDT, with its critique of world capitalism and unequal exchange and its emphasis on the need to develop an entirely new international economic order. Many fair traders were particularly influenced by the assertion of radical thinkers that the world capitalist system was incapable of providing developmental benefits to the poor majority in the South. Consequently, they sought not only to promote radical reforms to the existing trade system but also aspired, in the long term, to lay the basis for a parallel trading system that would open alternative markets for Southern products. In these alternative markets, prices would not be determined by the vagaries of supply and demand but would be formed through a process of negotiation between producers in the South and consumers in the North, based on the premise of fairness to all parties (Waridel 2002: 93–5; Simpson and Rapone 2000). Conceptually, the notion of a fair price would go beyond the unrealized aspiration of mainstream classical economists for a degree of 'procedural fairness,' such as free and consistent access to information for all trading parties, and include the goal of 'outcome fairness' designed to ensure that no trading partners are exploited or deprived in comparison to others (Blount 1997: 244–7).

The fair trade network took root in the 1940s and 1950s when NGOs in Europe and North America began selling goods produced by disadvantaged Southern artisans in direct-purchase projects. In Europe, Oxfam UK was at the head of the fair trade network. Oxfam was formed during the Second World War when a group of Quakers in Oxford founded a committee to raise funds for famine relief for victims of the war. When the war ended, Oxfam turned its attention towards combating poverty in the South. In 1950, it began selling crafts made by Chinese refugees, and in 1964 it created its first alternative trade organization (ATO) to import crafts and commodities directly from artisans and producers in the South. These initiatives were paralleled by similar actions in continental Europe. In 1959, S.O.S. Wereldhandel (whose name was later changed to Fair Trade Organisatie) was founded by a group of youth members of a Catholic political party in the Dutch town of Kerkrade. At first, the group focused on providing vocational training to poor communities in southern Europe, and it was not until 1967 that it established itself as a fair trade organization and began purchasing products from groups in the South for sale in the Netherlands. This step was followed in 1969 by the founding in the Netherlands of the first 'world shop' by Cane Sugar Groups, which sought a better deal for Southern sugar farmers. The shops were originally devoted to the sale of cane sugar and Southern handicraft products and later expanded to include a broad variety of fair trade goods (Waridel 2002: 94; EFTA 2001a: 22–4; 2001b: 42–4; 1995).

Throughout the 1970s and 1980s, fair trade importing organizations and world shops continued to spring up throughout Europe, due significantly to the promotional efforts of Oxfam and Fair Trade Organisatie. In 1973, Fair Trade Organisatie first introduced coffee into fair trade markets in Europe. The turnover of fair trade coffee soon exceeded that of handicrafts and sparked further growth for the network. By the early 1990s, there were over sixty fair trade importing organizations and thousands of world shops throughout Europe. Oxfam Trading had developed into an organization with 625 shops in the United Kingdom and a retail turnover of $15.4 million in 1994. Fair Trade Organisatie had grown even larger with a retail turnover of $24 million in 1994 (EFTA 1995).

The origins of the fair trade network in North America, like those in Europe, can be traced to the actions of religious groups. In 1946, the Mennonite International Development Agency (later renamed the Mennonite Central Committee, MCC), began importing embroidered textiles produced in Puerto Rico and Jordan for sale in Mennonite churches and among Mennonite women's groups in the United States. The MCC was driven by its religious philosophy which considers service to others and meeting human need as central to Christian life. In the 1950s, the MCC escalated its efforts by developing an Overseas Needlepoint and Crafts Project in Jordan for Palestinian refugees. This project was renamed SELFHELP Crafts in 1968, and in 1972 the first SELFHELP retail store was opened in the United States. By the end of the 1970s, there were over 60 SELFHELP stores across the United States and Canada, which doubled to over 120 by the late 1980s (Littrell and Dickson 1999: 61–88).

Other organizations that were key to the formation of the fair trade network in North America were the Sales Exchange for Refugee Rehabilitation (SERRV) program of the Church of the Brethren and the coffee roaster/distributor Equal Exchange. SERRV emerged out of efforts by the Church of the Brethren to import handmade clocks and other crafts made by refugees in Europe after the Second World War for sale in parishes in the United States. In the 1950s, SERRV turned its attention towards assisting Southern artisans. Throughout the 1960s and 1970s, SERRV gained broad ecumenical appeal through a close partnership with Church World Services, the development arm of the National Council of Churches. By the late 1980s, SERRV had annual sales of over $3 million (Littrell and Dickson 1999: 89–112). Equal Exchange was formed in 1983 by a group of social justice activists who aspired to bring fair trade coffee into markets in the United States.

Facilitated by financial support from Protestant and Catholic religious groups, Equal Exchange developed into a key ATO in the North American fair trade market, with sales over $3 million per annum in the mid-1990s (Simpson and Rapone 2000).

The ATOs that developed the fair trade network in North America and Europe from the late 1940s to the early 1980s aspired to create an alternative trading network composed of alternative producer and artisan groups in the South and alternative importers and distributors in the North. Unlike conventional trading companies, Northern ATOs did not seek to make a profit that would accrue to private pockets, but instead sought to cover operating costs and direct all remaining profits into the hands of Southern producer groups (Renner and Adamowicz 1998: 3). Their definition of fair and/or alternative trade was vaguer than the more highly codified definitions of fair trade which have been developed since the late 1980s by fair trade umbrella groups. They focused on job creation for disadvantaged artisans and rural workers; helping to protect and reinforce cultural traditions in the South; developing direct and honest trading relationships aimed at paying the highest price possible for handicrafts and commodities; dealing with groups in the South that are concerned about member participation and safe working conditions; and generally putting the needs of people before profits (Littrell and Dickson 1999: 61–112). In addition, most of the fair trade ATOs in this period hoped to forge a new international trading system derived from the vision expounded by the broader fair trade movement and the work of UDT theorists. This was especially true of Oxfam International, which, in addition to being a key fair trade ATO, was and continues today to be one of the world's most important promoters and lobbying organizations for regulated international trade, a return to commodity control schemes, and a fairer distribution of global wealth (Oxfam International 2002a, 2002b, 2001).

One of the clearest examples of the ideas that were prominent in the fair trade network during its formative decades is presented in the work of Michael Barratt Brown (1993), the founding chair and trustee of Third World Information Network (TWIN) and Twin Trading Ltd., a fair trade organization headquartered in London which has played an important role in promoting fair trade in the United Kingdom. Barratt Brown draws explicitly on the concepts of UDT – especially the more radical vein – and argues for the need to expand the fair trade network to combat underdevelopment in the South, which he asserts stems primarily from unequal exchange. He states that unequal exchange occurs as a result of a variety of factors that work against primary producers in the global market: food products are often perishable and cannot be held off markets to manipulate price levels; Southern producers do not have the facilities for processing, packaging, and storing, which add value to the final product; Southern countries are vulnerable to the ups and downs of global commodities markets due to the colonial legacy of dependence on only a few export crops; the millions of small producers who exist in the South are far too numerous to form cartels to manipulate market prices like manufacturing companies do; and primary producers lack access to technology and infrastructure required to raise productivity and efficiency (Barratt Brown 1993: 23–43). In Barratt Brown's view, fair trade can provide important solutions to the causes of unequal exchange by giving Southern producers greater access to technology, education, credit, and value-added processing and storage facilities, while at the same time protecting them from the whims of the global market through guaranteed prices, strict labour standards, and bonds of solidarity between producers and consumers.

Yet, while asserting that the fair trade network is key to confronting underdevelopment in the South, Barratt Brown argues that its benefits can only be broadened and sustained if it is combined with strong international market regulation. In an unregulated global market, he asserts, giant TNCs will always be able to profit through speculation and market manipulation, while small producers will always suffer the most as a result of the unpredictable market swings caused by these actions. Consequently, Barratt Brown proposes a model for a new economic order composed of democratically controlled state marketing boards, with grassroots control at all levels, and direct links between Northern consumers and Southern producers. Central to his vision is an alternative trade clearing union, designed to address Southern countries' lack of access to hard currency and credit needed to diversify and develop trade. The clearing house would make multiple deals between Southern countries in cases where direct exchanges would not satisfy any one country.[4] Exchanges would be based on credit notes (not money) which could also act as an exchange reserve like gold or hard currency. In Barratt Brown's model, fair trade standards, green consumerism, and consumer-producer unions are essential to promote workers rights, as well as the rights of consumers to have an input in and information on how goods are produced. The final outcome would be a decentralized economy based on 'a parallel trading system and an alternative trade network within that system growing up side by side with the present organisation of world trade by giant companies' (Barratt Brown 1993: 134).[5]

Since the late 1980s, the fair trade network has undergone a significant reorientation and most fair traders have, to varying degrees, departed significantly from Barratt Brown's vision of a new economic order. Two key aspects of Barratt Brown's work have been left behind. First, most fair traders have abandoned his focus on the nation-state as a primary agent in development, which derives from UDT's focus on the goal of national self-sufficiency. To Barratt Brown, a democratically run, interventionist state is required to regulate the economy both internationally and domestically; to provide much needed infrastructure, credit, and technology to domestic producers; and to coordinate various sectors within a national economy to ensure diversification and a degree of self-reliance. In contrast to this, most fair traders now focus on NGOs, in both the North and South, as the primary agents of development. The state is viewed as having the potential to provide benefits to fair traders through the provision of such things as basic social welfare, protection for weak sectors of the domestic economy, and labour and environmental legislation; but its role is generally viewed as subsidiary, not central, to the fair trade network (Bolscher, interview 2002; VanderHoff Boersma 2001).

The second key aspect of Barratt Brown's analysis that most fair traders have sidelined is his focus on creating a parallel trading network that presents itself as a distinct alternative to the existing international capitalist market. Barratt Brown argues against the concept of de-linking promoted by some dependency theorists because he thinks that Southern nations require access to Northern technology. However, he is convinced of the need to break away to some degree from the world capitalist system and develop an alternative model for a new international trade system that, in the long run, aspires to be free from the pressures imposed by profit-driven TNCs and the imperatives of the capitalist market. In contrast to his vision, over the past two decades, fair traders have moved increasingly towards attempting to reform the existing trade system rather than forging an alternative to it. This reorientation has been led by the emergence of fair trade labelling in the late 1980s and 1990s under the aegis of a variety of national organizations (Max Havelaar, TransFair, the Fair Trade Foundation) coordinated since 1997 under the umbrella group Fairtrade Labelling Organisations International (FLO). The FLO system has been designed to reorient fair trade towards reforming the existing international trading system by allowing conventional corporations to participate in the fair trade network on a voluntary basis. Corporations are presented with the option of tapping into 'ethical consumer' markets in the North by meeting FLO's fair trade standards and qualifying for certification labels. These labelling initiatives are described in greater detail in the following chapter.

There are two main factors that account for the emergence of fair trade labelling and the reorientation of the fair trade network that began in the late 1980s. First, the reorientation stemmed from the imperatives of the capitalist market and the material realities faced by the network. Constrained by the goal of forging an alternative trade network, the fair trade market in the North remained relatively small until the late 1980s and proved unable to provide the access to consumer markets that its Southern partners required to survive. The growth of the network was hindered by lack of access to consumers who do most of their shopping at major supermarkets, the limits of volunteer labour, poor marketing formulas, and public perceptions about the poor quality of fair trade goods. In response to these limitations, fair trade organizations abandoned the goal of an alternative trading system and instead sought to gain access into mainstream markets which they hoped would help them meet the needs of Southern partners (Waridel 2002: 93–6; Ramírez Guerrero, interview 2002; Ransom 2001: 20–2; Simpson and Rapone 2000: 47, 54; Renard 1999: 493–6). To do this, fair traders not only developed fair trade labelling initiatives, but they also stepped up their efforts in consumer research, marketing strategies, and quality control.

Second, the impetus for the reorientation of the fair trade network stemmed also from the dramatically altered political-economic and ideological conditions ushered in by the rise of neoliberal globalization. Fair traders' original vision of an alternative trading system was a reflection of the rise of state-managed capitalism at both national and international levels and of calls for a new international economic order in the post-war era. When neoliberal reforms imposed the decline of interventionist policies globally and derailed the broader fair trade movement, the political-economic realities under which the fair trade network had to operate were significantly changed. No longer able to pressure for such things as international commodity agreements or domestic state policies to manage prices and provide some market stability, fair traders felt compelled to turn towards conventional corporations and seek some form of non-governmental (and therefore non-binding) arrangements to try and meet the needs of Southern partners.

This has been a growing trend among social justice groups in general. As states have increasingly signed on to neoliberal agreements like those of the WTO, which impose strict limits on their ability to intervene in the market for social and environmental considerations, activist groups have responded by focusing their campaigns on private corporations whose hands are not officially tied by such agreements.[6]

Nonetheless, while neoliberal globalization has imposed new political realities on the fair trade network, it is also important not to lose sight of the ideological dimension of globalization, which can be equally as inhibiting. The political and economic pressures that Northern states (in particular the United States), the World Bank, the IMF and the WTO have used to impose neoliberal reforms on the South have been part of a broader neoliberal hegemonic project that has advanced the idea that the decline of state-managed development is both inevitable and necessary. Neoliberal pundits employed by Northern states, IFIs, NGOs, and the media have repeatedly argued that state-managed development models are inefficient and unproductive compared to the allegedly superior model of neoliberalism. Their efforts have led to the widely held perception of the failure of state-intervention strategies at national and international levels – a perception granted further fuel by the collapse of the statist command economies of the former Soviet Bloc. This has given way since the 1980s to an 'impasse' in development thinking as academics and NGOs have sought to develop new, non-statist projects that conform to neoliberal hegemony (Leys 1996: 1–44). The reorientation of the fair trade network in the 1980s and 1990s occurred within this broader context and in part reflects an acceptance by fair traders of the vision of the state promoted by neoliberal reformers. This new vision is reflected in the following statement by Francisco VanderHoff Boersma (2001), one of the founders of fair trade labelling: 'We are not against market liberalization. Fiscal barriers, protectionism, international commercial prejudices, etcetera, do not favour a peaceful coexistence between people. They have caused local and global wars and a poor international distribution of social wealth. State intervention in economic areas has demonstrated inefficiency, corruption, and even social disasters.'[7]

Conclusion: The Theoretical Foundations of the Fair Trade Network

One need not romanticize the state-interventionist models of the Bretton Woods era to see that the neoliberal vision of such models accepted by many fair traders and development practitioners in general is deeply flawed. While the weaknesses mentioned by VanderHoff were often apparent, the fact remains that the era of state-managed capitalism was accompanied by unprecedented progress in most major indicators of human development in the South.[8] At the national level, despite their various shortcomings, the ISI and EOI models brought about unprecedented economic growth and industrialization (Stiglitz 2003; Weisbrot et al. 2000; Gowan 1999: 48–51; Evans 1987). At the international level, the international commodity agreements promoted by the fair trade movement, while generally subject to eventual collapse due to competitive pressures between states, brought about some degree of price stability on otherwise highly unstable markets (Oxfam International 2002a, 2002b). Similarly, CFS programs like STABEX, while frequently lacking appropriate funding, did provide much-needed price subsidies to poor producers (LeClair 2002). As a result of interventionist programs such as these, the 1960s and the 1970s witnessed rapid progress in income per person, life expectancy, infant mortality, and education and literacy rates throughout the South. If the various proposals advanced by the fair trade movement for a more equal distribution of global wealth, reforms to the international trading system, enforced ILO labour standards, and codes of conduct for TNCs had been put into effect, they likely would have contributed to continued progress in these areas. Instead, neoliberal reforms were adopted, dismantling state-led development models and derailing the fair trade movement, leading to two decades of declining progress in most major social and economic indicators (Stiglitz 2003; Weisbrot et al. 2001; Weisbrot et al. 2000).[9]

Due to the benefits that accrued to the majority of the inhabitants in the South as a result of state-interventionist programs, the reorientation within the fair trade network away from the state-led development promoted by the broader fair trade movement represents an overall setback for the network and its vision. This is true regardless of the extent to which the reorientation was driven by changing political-economic realities or the power of neoliberal hegemony. Either way, forces more powerful than the fair trade network have proven capable of pulling the network away from its more radical vision influenced by UDT and towards one with an increasingly neoliberal flavour. The most important contribution that UDT has made to developmental debates has been its recognition of the limits imposed on small producers, workers, and poor countries in the South by the structures of the capitalist world system and how these limits cannot be overcome through the market, which is systematically biased against them, but must ultimately be challenged through political mechanisms that seek to confront it. While fair traders have increasingly abandoned this emphasis on the state, however, the vision of the network can still be located within the broad UDT paradigm. This is because fair traders have maintained UDT's neo-Smithian, trade-based depiction of capitalism, which is the weakest aspect of the UDT approach.

Writing in the second half of the eighteenth century, Scottish philosopher Adam Smith (1713–90) depicted capitalism as primarily a market-driven phenomenon that emerged out of people's alleged natural 'propensity to truck, barter, and exchange one thing for another' (Smith 1776: 117). The decline of feudal relations, Smith asserted, unleashed this propensity by removing barriers to the free exchange of goods and labour. This led to a tendency to transform production towards greater efficiency as individual economic actors pursued their own self-interest on the market, resulting in the rapid and continuous economic growth characteristic of modern capitalism. Marxist (and Polanyian) theorists have criticized Smith for focusing on market exchanges, which have existed throughout history, and neglecting the historically specific social relations of production that underlie market relations under capitalism (McNally 2002, 1993; Wood 1999; Brenner 1985, 1977; Polanyi 1944). It is these specific social relations, in particular the emergence of private property and the commodification of labour, that have led to the dynamics of capitalist growth that Smith depicted as 'natural.' Under capitalism, workers, who have been 'freed' from traditional ties to the land, must sell their labour power on competitive labour markets in order to survive, and property owners must compete on competitive markets with other property owners in order to maintain their ownership. Historian Robert Brenner (1985: 34) states: 'It is only where capitalist property relations prevail, that all the economic actors have no choice but to adopt as their rule for reproduction the putting on the market of their product (whatever it is) at the competitive, i.e., lowest, price. It is only in such an economy that all economic actors are perpetually *motivated* to cut costs. It is only in such an economy that there exists a *mechanism of natural selection* (i.e., competition on the market) to eliminate those producers who are not effectively cutting costs. It is for these reasons that only under capitalist property relations can we expect a pattern of modern economic growth.'

This critique of Smith's theories has also been applied to UDT, which has been accused of presenting a neo-Smithian understanding of the capitalist world system. Like Smith, most UDT theorists have depicted capitalism as being driven primarily by exchange relations. With the expansion of European colonialism beginning in the sixteenth century, a capitalist world system developed in which surplus wealth was systematically transferred from the South to the North, resulting in capitalist development in the North and underdevelopment in the South. Yet, as Brenner has convincingly argued, the historical development of capitalism in the North cannot stem merely from the transfer of surplus wealth from the South – the transfer of wealth from one region to another has many precedents in history prior to the development of capitalism. What was essential was the transformation of the social relations of production in the North from feudal relations to capitalist relations, beginning in the seventeenth century. This assured that the surplus was employed to spark further accumulation and economic growth as opposed to being invested in warfare, state building, or conspicuous consumption as was typically the case under feudalism (Leys 1996: 52–4; Brewer 1990: 161–99; Brenner 1985, 1977). Thus, it is the social relations of production that underlie the dynamics behind capitalist growth, not the mere escalation of market exchange relations.

This issue has great significance for the fair trade network and its development program. Most fair traders and fair trade analysts have adopted UDT's neo-Smithian conception of capitalism which emphasizes exchange relations (trade, the market) over social relations (private property, commodified labour). Thus, fair traders have focused on the market as the primary site of struggle, but have neglected the imperatives of capitalism which stem from the historically specific capitalist social relations that underlie it. According to Marxist political theorist Ellen Meiksins Wood (1999: 6–7), this specificity involves the following:

> ... first, that material life and social reproduction in capitalism are universally mediated by the market, so that all individuals must in one way or another enter into market relations in order to gain access to the means of life; and second, that the dictates of the capitalist market – its imperatives of competition, accumulation, profit maximization, and increasing labor productivity – regulate not only all economic transactions but social relations in general. As relations among human beings are mediated by the process of commodity exchange, social relations among people appear as

relations among things, the 'fetishism of commodities,' in Marx's famous phrase.

The characteristics of the capitalist market described by Wood lie at the heart of the exploitation that emerges in a capitalist system. All market agents – whether workers, small scale farmers, or giant TNCs – must compete in a sink or swim environment where they must continually exploit others (such as a TNC forcing down workers' wages) or themselves (such as small-scale farmers selling their crops at near starvation prices) in order to remain competitive and survive.

It is this drive towards exploitation inherent in the capitalist system that fair traders seek to confront and ultimately change, which raises important questions about the fair trade network's ability to do so with its market-driven approach. The aspirations of fair traders, of course, entail more modest aims than confronting exploitation on a global scale and challenging the international trading system. Central to the fair trade network is the goal of providing immediate and tangible benefits to Southern partners to assist them in developing the capabilities to better survive *within* the existing system. Assessing fair trade as a development project requires an eye towards this immediate and necessary goal, while at the same time not losing sight of the need to determine if the network's benefits can be broadened and sustained in the long term within the context of global capitalism in its neoliberal form. To focus only on the immediate, tangible benefits of fair trade for specific local groups would be to fall prey to a 'small is beautiful' discourse, which, as Liisa North and John Cameron (2000: 1751–2) effectively argue, neglects to assess the extent to which a given development project can generate widespread, long-term benefits. They state: 'One project or program benefits, at most, a small segment of the socially and economically disenfranchised population. The developmental question is whether the general conditions that can ensure the success of very large numbers of local initiatives are present or being created.'

In the chapters that follow, two key aspects of the historical origins of the fair trade network are essential to understanding its current orientation. First, the fair trade network as originally conceived was significantly different than its current form and placed far greater emphasis on the role of the state and on creating a distinctly alternative market. Adjusting to the imperatives of the international market and political pressure from neoliberal reformers, however, fair traders abandoned their more radical goals in favour of a more market-friendly approach. For this reason the network has been able to survive and thrive while the other projects of the fair trade movement, whose statist goals are incompatible with neoliberalism, have staggered and declined.

Second, the neo-Smithian theoretical origins of the fair trade network have had and continue to have a significant impact on the evolution of the network and its reorientation. Stripped of the market interventionist aspects promoted by UDT, the neo-Smithian conception of the market has in recent years become more pronounced within the network. This has set the stage for fair traders' growing embrace of the ideology of 'free trade' and the belief that their goals are compatible with the ideals (if not, often, the actual practices) of neoliberal institutions like the World Bank and the WTO.

Taken together, these two aspects reveal that the reorientation of the fair trade network initiated in the late 1980s has not been a minor adjustment on a relatively continuous development path. Instead, it has entailed the emergence of a distinctly different development model for the fair trade network based on the abandonment of its statist orientation and the strengthening of its neo-Smithian market orientation to conform to the demands of neoliberal globalization. While frequently depicted as being in direct opposition to neoliberal globalization, the fair trade network in its current form in fact represents a *neoliberal version* of its earlier model, and has been adopted by many international organizations and conventional corporations as a *neoliberal alternative* to the other, statist projects of the fair trade movement. Thus, it is the fair trade network's relative *compatibility* with neoliberal reforms that has been key to its rapid growth over the past decade and a half.

2 Neoliberal Globalization and the Fair Trade Network

We repudiate a state economy, as well as a neoliberal economy, and we propose a socially sustainable economy. In place of an economy of exclusion and death we propose an economy of inclusion, of life.

Francisco VanderHoff Boersma, 2001[1]

As a core philosophy, fair traders believe in as little market intervention as possible.

Paul Rice[2]

When discussing the fair trade network and neoliberal globalization, fair traders and fair trade analysts tend to offer varying perspectives which are at times ambiguous or contradictory. In some instances, fair traders describe the network as a sort of third way project focused on 'sustainability' that is neither state-driven nor neoliberal, and purportedly neither capitalist nor socialist. At other instances, fair traders (frequently the same ones) draw attention to the compatibility between fair trade and 'free trade' and the overall ideals of neoliberal institutions like the World Bank and the World Trade Organization (WTO) (Bolscher, interview 2002; VanderHoff Boersma, interview 2002). In other cases, some fair traders, still devoted to the older version of the network described in the previous chapter, refer to it as an incipient alternative trading system that is explicitly at odds with neoliberalism and global capitalism – a view that is increasingly marginalized within the network in general (Planet Bean 2004c; Barrett, interview 2004; Ransom 2001). In a broad sense, these different perspectives tend to collide around one central question: is the fair trade network a *challenge to* or *compatible with* neoliberal globalization? The varying responses to this question can be collected into two general views: the fair trade network is an explicit challenge and an alternative model to neoliberalism; or, the fair trade network is compatible with neoliberal globalization and seeks to enhance the ability of Southern partners to more actively participate in its 'opportunities.' The argument advanced in this chapter is that the fair trade network has the potential to provide some basis for both of these views but that its success in recent years has been due to its growing conformity with the latter.

The relative success of the fair trade network since its reorientation in 1988 has been due to its emphasis on voluntarism and mainstreaming. While not necessarily incompatible with the statist goals of the other projects in the fair trade movement, this new emphasis has proven to be highly compatible with neoliberal reforms and key to the network's ability to gain the support of international institutions and transnational corporations (TNCs). The ultimate effect that this has had on the network is assessed below. The first part describes the history of the fair trade network during its second phase, beginning with the development of fair trade labelling initiatives. The second part analyses the emerging perspectives on fair trade and describes how various authors have attempted to account for the network's relationship to neoliberal policies and global capitalism. I argue that, in the final analysis, the success of the fair trade network has been significantly due to its compatibility with the pro-market policies of neoliberal reformers, which raises serious doubts about the network's ability to ultimately challenge these policies.

The Fair Trade Network, Phase 2: Reforming Conventional Markets (1988 to the Present)

The second phase in the history of the fair trade network began with the establishment of Max Havelaar, the first fair trade labelling initiative, in the Netherlands in 1988. This event emerged out of discussions between Solidaridad, an ecumenical foundation that administered grants to peasant cooperatives obtained from religious groups, and the Unión de Comunidades Indígenas de la Región del Istmo (Union of Indigenous Communities of the Isthmus Region, UCIRI), a fair trade coffee processing cooperative in Oaxaca, Mexico (the subject of chapter 5). Seeking to break the cycle of poverty and attain higher prices for their beans, UCIRI members started selling fair trade coffee in 1985 to

Fair Trade Organisatie in the Netherlands and the fair trade organization GEPA in Germany. In 1988, UCIRI members were invited to visit the Netherlands and meet with members of Solidaridad. According to the Hans Bolscher, the former director of Max Havelaar Netherlands, at these meetings UCIRI members pushed for access to 'real markets,' which they felt they could attain by dealing directly with transnational corporations (TNCs) in the North. In response, Solidaridad initiated a series of discussions with major coffee TNCs in the Netherlands and asked them if they would be willing to pay a higher price for coffee produced by fair trade cooperatives. The TNCs rejected this request, stating that higher prices would only hurt their competitiveness and that consumers in general were not willing to pay more for coffee (Bolscher, interview 2002; Lappé and Lappé 2002: 198–9; Ramírez Guerrero, interview 2002; Simpson and Rapone 2000).

Realizing that TNCs would not be willing to participate in fair trade without a profit incentive, UCIRI and Solidaridad adjusted their strategy and turned their attention towards consumers. According to Bolscher: 'Without consumers willing to pay more, and without consumers putting pressure on companies, fair trade could never work' (cited in Lappé and Lappé 2002: 199). The result was the founding of the labelling initiative Max Havelaar, named after the hero in a famous Dutch novel who denounced the treatment of Indonesian coffee farmers under Dutch colonial rule (Multatuli 1987). The objective was to promote the label and its mission and offer it to conventional importers who met Max Havelaar's fair trade standards in exchange for a certification fee. Conventional importers would be encouraged to participate in fair trade because of the 'added value' the fair trade label – injected with symbolic social meaning – would give them on the market (Renard 2005: 421, 1999: 484; Bolscher, interview 2002).

After the founding of Max Havelaar in the Netherlands, the fair trade labelling movement spread quickly: by the late 1990s there were seventeen National Initiatives (NIs) throughout Europe, North America, and Japan. In countries where the name of Max Havelaar did not have popular recognition – such as in Germany, Austria, Italy, Canada, and the United States – the new labelling initiatives were called Trans-Fair or – in the case of Britain and Ireland – the Fair Trade Foundation (FTF). Since 1997, these NIs have been coordinated under the umbrella group Fairtrade Labelling Organisations International (FLO), headquartered in Bonn, Germany (FLO 2001).

FLO is run by a board of directors composed of twelve representatives, six of whom are elected every three years by its NIs at their 'Meeting of Members,' and six of whom are elected every three years by producer and trader licensees at their 'Fairtrade Forum.' The board, in turn, elects a director who is responsible for FLO's everyday operations, in particular its financial and personnel matters. According to FLO, the organization has three main tasks. First, FLO certifies and audits fair trade licensees in-line with the standards of the International Standards Organization (ISO). This includes the development of an operating manual for FLO certification and a training methodology for FLO inspectors, as well as the provision of detailed information on FLO's certification and auditing procedures, policies, and terms of reference. Second, FLO facilitates business contacts between licensed fair trade producers and traders. Third, through its Producer Support Facilitator, FLO promotes the provision of organizational and technical support for smallholders and workers. In order to maintain a necessary distance between FLO's role as an independent certification body and its role in actively assisting fair traders through business and technical support, in 2002 FLO established its certification unit as a separate limited company called FLO Certification Ltd. (FLO 2003b).[3]

As of the start of 2003, FLO had on its certification register 315 producer organizations (representing almost 500 small producer organizations and around 900,000 families of farmers and workers in Africa, Asia, and Latin America), 249 traders (including exporters, processors, importers, and manufacturers), and 443 retailers in Europe, North America, and Japan. FLO has international fair trade standards and labels for a variety of goods, including coffee, tea, cocoa, bananas, honey, cane sugar, oranges, rice, mangos, pineapples, a variety of fruit juices, and even sportsballs. They are currently in the process of developing new standards for other fruits (both fresh and dried), herbal teas, wine, nuts, seeds, and oils (FLO 2003b). Depending on the historical development of property relations within particular industries, these goods are produced either by small producers organized into marketing and processing cooperatives (as is the case with coffee, cocoa, honey, and cane sugar) or by large plantations with hired labour (as is frequently the case with such commodities as tea, bananas, and orange juice) (Zonneveld 2003; FLO 2001).

FLO-certified goods are exchanged under the terms of a minimum guaranteed price and include 'social premiums' paid by the buyer to producer communities for the development of social and physical infrastructure such as hospitals, schools, and roads. Southern partners

can request an advance, partial payment of up to 60 per cent of the contract price prior to harvest to assist them in their work and limit their
need for short-term loans. The minimum guaranteed price is determined taking into account both the demands of Northern markets and
the requirements of Southern producers to recoup their production
costs and make sufficient profit to cover their daily needs (Waridel
2002: 65; Simpson and Rapone 2000: 47). Thus, while prices must be
high enough to ensure fair trade's objectives, they cannot be so high as
to scare off 'ethical consumers' in the North, confined by what sociologist Marie-Christine Renard (1999: 497) refers to as the 'difficult compromise between ethical principles and the market.'

FLO has strict labour standards, based on International Labour Organization (ILO) Conventions, to which all of its Southern licensees must
adhere. Small producers and plantations must abide by principles pro-
hibiting child labor and forced labor, and guaranteeing freedom of association, collective bargaining for workers, environmental sustainability
programs, occupational health and safety standards, minimum wage
requirements, and non-discrimination policies. On plantations, workers
are required to be represented by a trade union, or, if no union exists in
the region, to develop a certified collective bargaining agreement (CBA)
in consultation with the International Union of Food, Agricultural,
Hotel, Restaurant, Catering, Tobacco and Allied Workers' Associations
(IUF). In addition, every fair trade plantation must form a joint body
composed of management and worker representatives to decide on
how to use the social premium paid to them by their trading partners.
The joint body must reflect the gender and cultural makeup of the workforce, must strive to make decisions by consensus (failing which the
consent of the majority of worker representatives is required), and cannot spend the premium on the costs of running the plantation. Small
producer cooperatives certified by FLO must be run by a general assembly which decides how the social premium is spent and elects a board to
handle the daily operations of the cooperative. The general assembly
must have a democratic structure with voting rights for all members
and a transparent administration (FLO 2003a).

FLO's fair trade standards do not just include 'minimum criteria,'
which all Southern partners must meet for initial certification, but they
also include 'process criteria' designed to encourage continuous development and improvement. For example, while a minimum criterion is
a policy of no official discrimination based on race or gender, process
criteria involve special programs designed to improve the positions of

disadvantaged groups and affirmative action in recruitment, staff hiring, and committee membership on cooperatives. Another minimum criterion that producers must meet is the regional minimum wage for plantation labour, while process criteria involve gradually increasing salaries above the minimum wage and progressively diminishing the differences in salaries and employment benefits that typically exists between casual, seasonal, and permanent workers (FLO 2003a).

To ensure that FLO's licensees are adhering to the criteria for certification, FLO inspectors pay periodic visits to their partners in both the North and the South. FLO currently has close to forty local inspectors trained in accordance with ISO standards in forty-five countries (FLO 2003b). In the case of fair trade coffee, inspectors visit Southern cooperatives every one or two years, depending on the volume of production and the needs of the cooperative. In May 2001, FLO had 363 coffee cooperatives from twenty-two Southern countries on its fair trade registry. Of these cooperatives, 110 were approved only provisionally and needed to demonstrate that they could meet their fair trade and commercial agreements for two coffee seasons before they could attain permanent status on the FLO registry. Inspections of Northern partners vary depending on the available finances of the national labelling initiative. In Switzerland, Northern partners are inspected every six to twelve months, whereas in Canada and the United States, Northern partners are inspected less frequently. The cost of certification, which for coffee runs between $0.08 and $0.13 per pound depending on the country, is primarily paid for by the roaster/importer in the North. This is in contrast to organic certification, which is paid entirely by the producers themselves (Calo and Wise 2005: 12–13; Waridel 2002: 96–9).[4]

In addition to rules governing commercial exchanges, labour rights, and democratic participation, FLO has a policy of political neutrality to which its Southern partners must adhere. FLO requires that licensed partners are 'politically independent, and there are sufficient guarantees that the organisation will not become the instrument of any political party or interest' (FLO 2003a). According to Bolscher, this policy means that FLO does not care if a cooperative is pro-Sandinista or pro-Contra, for the Zapatistas or against them, as long as profits are not used to buy arms, and the cooperative works in the interest of the 'people' (Bolscher, interview 2002). This aspect of FLO's criteria stems from two considerations. First, official neutrality is frequently needed in order to attempt to stave off the threat of political violence from the state and local elite. Unfortunately, such a strategy is often not good enough: from 1985 to 1992, thirty-nine members of UCIRI were assassinated by local elite coffee traders who correctly viewed UCIRI as a threat to their local monopoly (Waridel 2002: 71).

Second, official neutrality stems from FLO's 'producerist' political philosophy, which places the greatest emphasis on the short- and medium-term needs of fair trade producers. According to Bolscher, fair trade licensers focus on where their interests lie: with their producers. FLO will either ignore or cooperate with a given state, depending on its willingness to assist fair traders in their immediate development aims. FLO does not promote any particular vision of what a state should look like, but it tries to get companies, governments, small producers, and workers together – essentially a neo-corporatist strategy – with the common goal of reaching the standards of ILO Conventions (Bolscher, interview 2002).

FLO's eagerness to do business with conventional importers and distributors and gain access to conventional markets has caused some commentators to view fair trade as a subset of ethical business practices, which include such things as 'corporate citizenship,' 'codes of conduct,' and 'corporate social responsibility' (Klein 2000: 428–36; Blowfield 1999: 753–70; Bird and Hughes 1997: 159–67). FLO licensers argue, however, that the goals of fair trade transcend those of ethical business practices, which are generally little more than window dressing and are limited by the desire of corporations to protect themselves from public criticism. Whereas corporate initiatives are 'money-driven,' fair trade is 'mission-driven' and is defined, in the words of Paola Ghillani, former FLO president and current director of Max Havelaar Switzerland, 'by the overall aim of sustainable livelihoods for the affluent North and the disadvantaged in the South' (FLO 2003b: 3; Bolscher, interview 2002; FLO 2001: 3). Unlike ethical business practices, which are profit-driven and top-down, fair trade is focused on long-term developmental aims and the organization and empowerment of marginalized workers and small farmers from below.[5]

Over the past decade and a half since its formation, FLO's strategy has proven to be successful and the fair trade label has gained growing popularity among consumers, small-scale importers, and mainstream supermarkets in Europe and, to a lesser extent, North America. Sales of FLO-certified goods grew by 35 per cent from 1997–2000. The total retail turnover of FLO-certified goods in 2000 was worth over 220 million Euros, of which more than 55 million Euros went directly to producers. This is about 40 per cent more than would have been justified by conventional prices. Consumers in Switzerland have purchased the greatest quantity of FLO-labelled goods (34.8 per cent of the total from 1997–2000), followed by the Netherlands (24.7 per cent), Germany (17.6 per cent), the United Kingdom (9.8 per cent), and the remaining fair trade countries (13.1 per cent). Canada and the United States each account for only 0.2 per cent of the total of FLO-certified goods during this period (FLO 2001).

In addition to retail turnover, public awareness of fair trade and the points of sale for FLO-certified goods in Europe also grew substantially in the 1990s. According to market research, public awareness of the Max Havelaar label in Switzerland grew from around 36 per cent of the Swiss population in 1994 to over 60 per cent in 2000. Public awareness during this same period grew in the Netherlands from 70 to 74 per cent, in Germany from 17 to 41 per cent, and in the United Kingdom from 13 to 16 per cent. The total points of sale for fair trade-labelled products for all of Europe grew from 45,000 retail channels (including fair trade specialty shops, small commercial shops, and supermarkets) in 1994 to over 63,800 in 2000. FLO's greatest success in this regard has been in the Netherlands, where Max Havelaar–labelled products in 2000 were available for sale in 2,200 supermarkets, representing nearly 90 per cent of all the Dutch supermarkets. In Switzerland, fair trade products were available for sale at over 75 per cent of all commercial retailers in the country in 2000 (EFTA 2001b, 1995). While similar statistics do not exist for Canada and the United States, it is fair to say that these numbers would be substantially lower because fair trade products have been excluded from mainstream retail channels in North America until very recently.

There are several possible factors that can help explain the broader acceptance and popularity of fair trade goods in Europe as opposed to North America. Many European nations have relatively stronger labour-based political parties which have been essential in gaining the support of public institutions for fair trade. From a culturalist perspective, another important factor might be the idea, inherited from western Europe's feudal past, of noblesse oblige, wherein 'beneficent, charitable, and honourable behaviour' is considered the moral duty of the upper classes (Olsen 2002: 111). This cultural tradition is frequently evoked by analysts to partly explain the relatively more extensive and paternalistic social welfare policies that have evolved in Europe compared to North America, which was colonized by middle-class British colonists with strong, liberal values that emphasized individualism and competition over charity and reciprocal obligations (111–14). These values might partially explain the relative popularity of fair trade in Europe, derived from a greater sense of moral obligation by middle- and upper-class consumers towards poorer Southern producers.

Perhaps most importantly, from a historical perspective, timing and geography are key in accounting for these disparities: the FLO-system and the concept of mainstreaming fair trade was initiated in Europe in the late 1980s and it took several years until it was replicated in North America. Since the introduction of the FLO system into Canada and the United States in the late 1990s, however, fair trade sales have grown rapidly, as has typically been the case in previously untapped markets, and it is possible that sales figures over the next few years could reach levels more appropriate to North America's economic weight (Waridel 2002: 99–100).

In terms of specific commodities, FLO has had its greatest success in the promotion of fair trade coffee, tea, and bananas. In 2000, sales of FLO-certified coffee, traditionally the largest fair trade sector, accounted for 3 per cent of the coffee market in Switzerland, 2.7 per cent in the Netherlands, 1.8 per cent in Denmark, and 1.5 per cent in the United Kingdom. In the remaining fair trade countries, sales were 1 per cent or lower. To meet this demand, FLO had 163 coffee coopera- tives on its register, representing 516,544 coffee-producer families out of a total of over 20 million coffee-producer families worldwide. These cooperatives were situated mainly in Latin America but were also present in parts of Africa and Asia. Fair trade tea, although not as big a seller as coffee, accounted for 4 per cent of the tea market in Switzer- land, 2.5 per cent in Germany, 1.8 per cent in Denmark, and 1 per cent or less in the remaining fair trade countries. At the end of 2000, FLO had registered thirty-seven tea plantations and nine small producer organizations from various parts of Asia and Africa. The sale of fair trade bananas has recently emerged as a major area of growth for FLO, with total sales increasing by 25 per cent from 1999 to 2000. In 2000, sales of FLO-certified bananas accounted for 15 per cent of the banana market in Switzerland, 4.2 per cent in the Netherlands, 2 per cent in Denmark, 1.8 per cent in Sweden, and 1 per cent or less in the remain- ing fair trade countries. FLO had registered twelve banana-producer organizations in Latin America, the Caribbean, and Ghana (FLO 2001).

FLO's rapid growth since the 1980s has been accompanied by the emergence of other fair trade organizations which have also played a key role in promoting fair trade and its new mainstream orientation.

The International Federation for Alternative Trade (IFAT) was formed in 1989 to serve as a forum for ATOs in both the North and South to exchange information on product development and marketing strategies, jointly promote fair trade among Northern consumers, lobby governments for changes in the international trade system, and provide better access to financing and professional training for its members. IFAT members agree to adhere to a broadly worded code of conduct, which includes meeting workers' basic needs, no exploitation of child labour, transparency, environmental sustainability, and a commitment 'not to maximize profits at the producer's expense.' The majority of IFAT's members concentrate on the production and sale of handicrafts, making IFAT the world's largest fair trade certification body for handicraft products, but many of its members are also involved in trading commodities like coffee and tea. Currently, IFAT consists of 148 member organizations from 48 countries in Africa, Asia, Europe, North America, and South America (IFAT 2001).

In 1990, the European Fair Trade Association (EFTA) was formed, consisting of eleven of the largest fair trade organizations in Europe, including Oxfam UK and GEPA, the organization with the largest turnover of fair trade goods in the world (EFTA 2001b: 30). Similar to those of IFAT, EFTA's core objectives are to make fair trade importing more efficient and effective by promoting the exchange of information on product development and marketing strategies, and to lobby European institutions to address the imbalances in international trade and support fair trade. In 2001, EFTA members imported fair trade products from over 400 trading partners in Africa, Asia, and Latin America, and their combined turnover easily accounted for a majority share of the total retail turnover of all fair trade products in Europe. EFTA members' combined turnover in 2001 was nearly $134 million, up over 23 per cent since 1999. Of the total sales, handicrafts represented 25.4 per cent and commodities represented 69.4 per cent (EFTA 2001c).

Following the formation of IFAT and EFTA came the establishment of the Network of European Worldshops (NEWS) in 1994. The objective of NEWS is to facilitate cooperation and the exchange of information between fair trade 'worldshops' in Europe on such matters as shop management, promotion, and media work. Currently, NEWS is composed of approximately 2,500 worldshops from fifteen national associations in thirteen European countries (NEWS 2004). In 1998, NEWS joined with FLO, IFAT, and EFTA in creating an informal umbrella network called FINE (composed of the first letter of each organization's acronym), which seeks to advance a common definition of fair trade, develop similar criteria and monitoring systems, and coordinate advocacy and campaign strategies (EFTA 2001a: 35–6).

Like FLO, the umbrella organizations IFAT, EFTA, and NEWS have all been central to the fair trade network's reorientation towards conventional markets. However, they have focused on a different role than FLO in this reorientation. FLO's main objective has been to gain the participation of new players – conventional importers, processors, and distributors – in the fair trade network. In contrast, IFAT, EFTA, and NEWS have focused on enhancing the marketing skills and efficiency of fair trade ATOs so that they are better able to compete against conventional corporations and gain a greater share of mainstream markets.[6] These organizations have been at the head of the 'professionalization' of fair trade ATOs as they have adopted marketing and managerial strategies common to mainstream businesses. Beginning in the 1990s, ATOs have placed greater emphasis on efficiency through staff training and computerization. New, stylish magazines and catalogues have been developed, and Northern fashion designers have been consulted on how to develop fair trade goods that reflect market trends. Better promotional strategies for the use of radio and television have also been adopted. Worldshops have moved from obscure shopping areas to the centre of busy shopping districts and have developed new window designs, interior layout, and staff training to attract more customers. In addition, greater attention has been paid to attractive packaging, and many worldshops have created common names, logos, and styles to make them more easily recognizable to consumers (EFTA 2001a: 35).

The professionalization of fair trade ATOs has stemmed not just from a desire to expand the fair trade market but from the need to adjust to market imperatives to remain competitive and survive. For example, in the 1990s organizers at both SELFHELP and SERRV (both IFAT members) realized that they needed to shift from a mission-directed focus to one with a greater emphasis on conventional business practices if they wished to stave off fierce competition from large conventional corporations. SELFHELP renamed itself Ten Thousand Villages, deemed to be more appealing to consumers, and established its first national board of directors, which included many members with extensive experience in business and retail. SERRV downsized its permanent staff by 20 per cent, from thirty-one personnel to twenty-five, resulting in fatigue and overwork for many of the remaining employees. In addition, both organizations changed their purchasing and product development strategy by abandoning their tradition of limited product intervention in favour of suggesting changes to meet market trends, and by refocusing their efforts on larger Southern partners who could more efficiently develop a single product into an entire line. Due in part to these reforms, Ten Thousand Villages was able to increase its annual sales from $5.3 million in 1992 to $6.8 million in 1997. SERRV, which had fallen into the red in the early 1990s, was able to pull itself back into the black by the end of the decade, with total sales increasing from $4.8 million in 1992 to around $5 million in 1997 (Littrell and Dickson 1999: 61–112).

Despite the fact that ATOs and their umbrella organizations (EFTA, IFAT, NEWS) have a different focus than labelling initiatives (FLO), they share the same essential principles and goals. Often their efforts are intertwined. For example, many fair trade ATOs, such as Oxfam UK (a member of IFAT and EFTA), Equal Exchange (IFAT), and GEPA (IFAT and EFTA), import, process, and distribute commodities certified by FLO. Similarly, worldshops in Europe and North America sell both handicrafts and commodities certified by IFAT or FLO. Thus, it is best to view all these actors as part of the same international fair trade network. In October 2001, FINE established one single definition of fair trade which was accepted by all of the key actors in the network. It states:

> Fair Trade is a trading partnership, based on dialogue, transparency and respect, that seeks greater equity in international trade. It contributes to sustainable development by offering better trading conditions to, and securing the rights of, marginalised producers and workers – especially in the South.
>
> Fair Trade organisations (backed by consumers) are engaged actively in supporting producers, awareness raising and in campaigning for changes in the rules and practice of conventional international trade. (EFTA 2001a: 24)

Expanding the Fair Trade Market

The combined efforts of all actors in the fair trade network resulted in substantial growth throughout the 1990s. EFTA estimates that the net retail value of all fair trade products (handicrafts and commodities) in

Europe in 1998 was over 200 million Euros, representing an increase of over 400 per cent since the early 1990s.[7] In 2001, EFTA put this figure at over 260 million Euros (approximately U.S.$232 million), an increase of 30 per cent over a three-year period (EFTA 2001a: 33). Of this figure, the net retail value of fair trade commodities certified by FLO represented around 80 per cent of the total net retail value.[8] These numbers are dwarfed when compared to conventional international trade: in 2001 fair trade represented around 0.01 per cent of all global trade (EFTA 2001a: 23). They do, however, represent substantial and unprecedented growth within the network itself.

Despite the rapid growth of the fair trade network since its reorientation, there are several indications that significant limitations still exist to its current market size and its prospects for long-term expansion. First, while sales figures have been impressive, they have not increased fast enough to meet the needs of the network's Southern partners. In many cases, Southern organizations can only find enough room in the fair trade market to sell a small proportion of their total production. For example, by one estimate, fair trade coffee cooperatives certified by FLO on average are currently selling only 20 per cent of their coffee on fair trade markets, with the remainder being sold on conventional markets at significantly lower prices (Renard 2005: 427; Raynolds 2002b: 11). A similar situation exists in other fair trade sectors. The FLO annual report for 2000–1 draws attention to one of its seven fair trade cocoa partners, Kuapa Kokoo Union, a smallholder cooperative in Ghana with over 30,000 members that was able to sell only 3 per cent of its total production on fair trade markets (FLO 2001: 9).

Second, while growth in previously untapped national markets has been impressive in recent years, there are indications that a glass ceiling may well have been reached in more mature fair trade markets (Lewin, Giovannucci, and Varangis 2004: 123–5; Giovannucci 2003; EFTA 2001a). This raises the prospect of a growth ceiling for the entire fair trade network in the longer term. According to EFTA, while the average annual growth rate in total retail value for its members from 1995 to 1999 was 3.3 per cent, this varied greatly from country to country. In European countries where the concept of fair trade was relatively recently introduced, annual growth rates of EFTA members were very high. This was the case in Spain, where EFTA members recorded a growth rate of 31 per cent from 1995 to 1999, as well as in Italy (17 per cent), France (13.6 per cent), and Belgium (8 per cent). In these countries, fair trade sales started from a very small base and expanded rap-

Figure 2.1 Roasted fair trade coffee sales growth

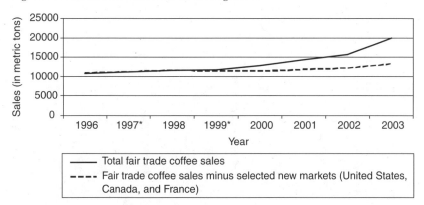

*Figures for 1997 and 1999 are drawn partially from estimates based on average growth rate.
Sources: FLO web site (2005): http://www.fairtrade.net/sites/products/coffee/why.html; Laura Raynolds et al. (2004: 1112).

idly. However, in countries where the concept of fair trade was well established and fair trade products had been available for forty years – such as in the Netherlands, Switzerland, Germany, the United Kingdom, and Austria – EFTA members registered sluggish growth, and sometimes even decline and crises (see figure 2.1). According to EFTA (2001a: 33–6), 'This reflects the attainment of a certain threshold level of sales or market shares which then seems very difficult to surpass.'

Third, not only have traditional national markets shown indications of flagging sales growth, but some traditional fair trade commodities have also experienced similar trends. The overall sale of fair trade–certified products has grown at an average of 20 per cent per year from 1999 to 2002 (Giovannucci 2003: 19). This growth, however, varied significantly, depending on the specific commodity. Fair trade bananas, a relatively new commodity, have been a major growth leader, with average sales increasing by 20 per cent per year since they were first introduced in 1997. Fair trade fruit juices, introduced over the past few years for an increasing variety of fruits, have also demonstrated rapid growth, with a sales increase of 43.5 per cent in 2002 (see figure 2.2). Fair trade cocoa, a traditional fair trade product that has historically attained relatively small sales, has also experienced rapid growth over

Figure 2.2 Fair trade sales, selected commodities, 1999–2003

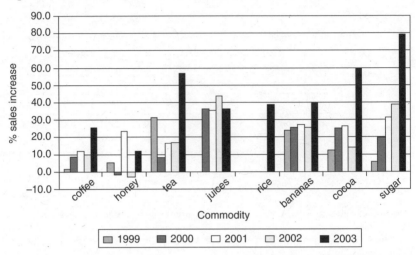

Source: FLO web site (2005), http://www.fairtrade.net/sites/products/products_02.html.

the past few years, which comes close to the average growth for fair trade products overall (FLO 2003b, 2001) (see figure 2.3 and table 2.1).

Such has not been the case for other traditional fair trade commodities. Sales of fair trade tea have fluctuated significantly, but have generally remained well below the overall average for fair trade products (see figure 2.4 and table 2.2). Sales of fair trade honey, following a trend in declining sales for conventional honey worldwide, declined by 3.5 per cent from 1999 to 2000. In 2001, conventional honey sales picked up and many cooperative members have since chosen to sell their honey to conventional intermediaries who can offer higher prices than fair trade cooperatives in the short term.[9] As a result, fair trade buyers in the North have been unable to meet their honey supply needs and the fair trade honey market has stagnated (see figure 2.5 and table 2.3). This threatens the market's ability to meet the needs of fair trade honey farmers in the future when conventional prices drop again (FLO 2003b, 2001). Perhaps the most alarming trend has been the declining growth of the fair trade coffee market. Sales of fair trade coffee have averaged an annual growth rate of around 8 per cent from 1997 to 2002, well below the overall fair trade average and much less than is necessary to meet the needs of Southern farmers. The sales figures for the most-

Figure 2.3 Sales volume of fair trade cocoa, by country, 2002–2003

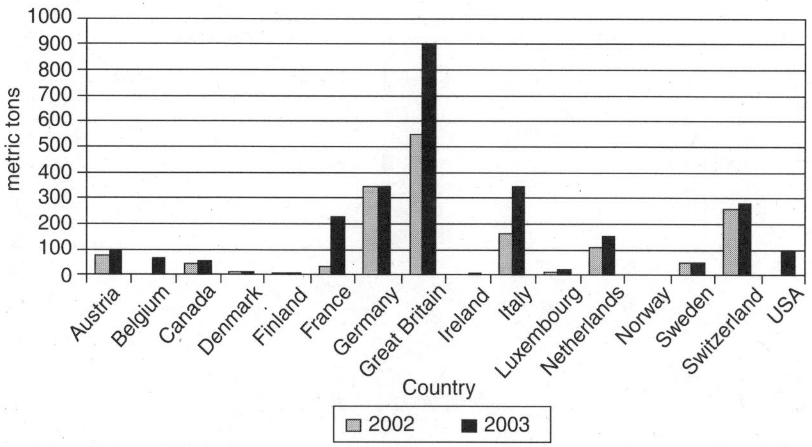

Source: FLO web site (2005), http://www.fairtradenet/sites/products/cocoa/markets.html.

Table 2.1 Sales volume of fair trade cocoa, by country, 2002–2003

	Sales (in metric tons)		% Increase or decrease (2002–3)
	2002	2003	
Austria	76.7	94	22.6
Belgium	2.9	61	2003.4
Canada	42.7	54	26.5
Denmark	13	13	0.0
Finland	6.5	9	38.5
France	32.6	227	596.3
Germany	339.4	343	1.1
Great Britain	550.6	903	64.0
Ireland		5.7	
Italy	162.8	346	112.5
Luxembourg	17.1	21	22.8
Netherlands	105.9	147	38.8
Norway	0.4	0.5	25.0
Sweden	49.7	52	4.6
Switzerland	253.8	275	8.4
USA	2.1	92.2	4290.5
TOTAL	1,656.20	2,643.40	59.6

Source: FLO web site (2005), http://www.fairtradenet/sites/products/cocoa/markets.html.

Figure 2.4 Sales volume of fair trade tea, by country, 2002–2003

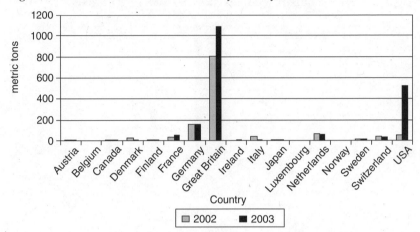

Source: FLO web site (2005), http://www.fairtradenet/sites/products/tea/markets.html.

Table 2.2 Sales volume of fair trade tea, by country, 2002–2003

	Sales (in metric tons)		% Increase or decrease (2002–3)
	2002	2003	
Austria	8.1	8.1	0.0
Belgium	0.8	2	150.0
Canada	4.3	5.6	30.2
Denmark	22	7	−68.2
Finland	4.8	4.8	0.0
France	31	52	67.7
Germany	154.8	156	0.8
Great Britain	806	1,089.50	35.2
Ireland	1	10.7	970.0
Italy	41.6	10.1	−75.7
Japan	7.9	8.5	7.6
Luxembourg	1	0.9	−10.0
Netherlands	67.5	59.6	−11.7
Norway	2.2	3.1	40.9
Sweden	16.6	14	−15.7
Switzerland	41.7	36.5	−12.5
USA	54.6	521	854.2
TOTAL	1,265.80	1,989.30	57.2

Source: FLO web site (2005), http://www.fairtrade.net/sites/products/tea/sales.html.

Figure 2.5 Sales volume of fair trade honey, by country, 2002–2003

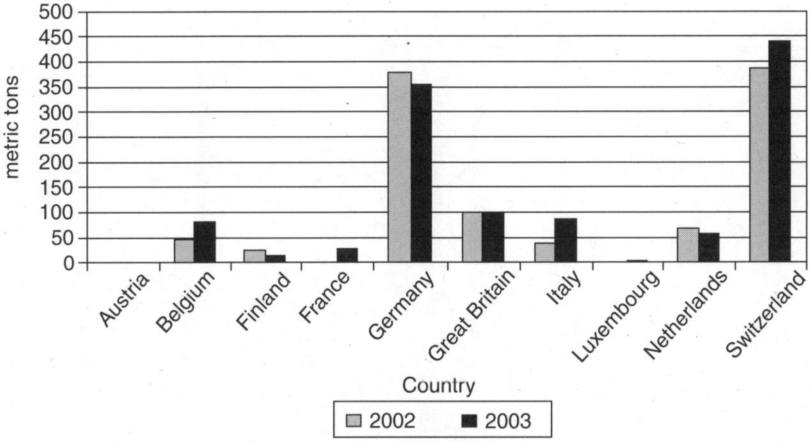

Source: FLO web site (2005), http://www.fairtradenet/sites/products/honey/markets.html.

Table 2.3 Sales volume of fair trade honey, by country, 2002–2003

	Sales (in metric tons)		% Increase or decrease (2002–3)
	2002	2003	
Austria	1.5	00.4	−73.3
Belgium	46	83	80.4
Finland	25	14.6	−41.6
France		27	
Germany	377.5	354	−6.2
Great Britain	99.6	101.3	1.7
Italy	37.6	85.1	126.3
Luxembourg	0.5	2.1	320.0
Netherlands	66.3	57.9	−12.7
Switzerland	384.5	438.3	14.0
TOTAL	1,038.40	1,163.70	12.1

Source: FLO web site (2005), http://www.fairtradenet/sites/products/honey/markets.html.

established national fair trade coffee markets are even more telling: from 1999 to 2001, fair trade coffee sales remained stagnant in the Netherlands, and declined by 2 per cent in both Germany and Switzerland (Lewin, Giovannucci, and Varangis 2004: 123–5; FLO 2003b; Giovannucci 2003: 14–26; FLO 2001; Renard 1999: 498). As a result of these trends, in 2001 FLO stated that it was reluctant to register any new coffee cooperatives (FLO 2001) (see figure 2.6 and table 2.4).

Figure 2.6 Sales volume of roasted fair trade coffee, by country, 2001–2003

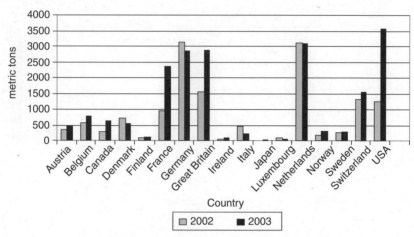

Source: FLO web site (2005), http://www.fairtradenet/sites/products/coffee/markets.html.

Table 2.4 Sales volume of roasted fair trade coffee, by country, 2001–2003

	Sales (in metric tons)			% Increase or decrease (2001–3)
	2001	2002	2003	
Austria	332.3	409.1	463.1	39.4
Belgium	582.2	632.2	762.5	31.0
Canada	277.0	425.0	625.1	125.7
Denmark	712.0	655.0	543.0	−23.7
Finland	97.0	109.0	113.2	16.7
France	950.0	1386.0	2368.4	149.3
Germany	3128.6	2942.0	2864.8	−8.4
Great Britain	1553.9	1953.9	2889.1	85.9
Ireland	62.0	60.0	99.9	61.1
Italy	453.0	243.2	229.6	−49.3
Japan	6.5	9.6	21.5	230.8
Luxembourg	77.3	68.0	64.9	−16.0
Netherlands	3104.7	3139.7	3096.1	−0.3
Norway	178.9	232.0	312.5	74.7
Sweden	253.6	289.2	294.0	15.9
Switzerland	1306.4	1246.0	1550.0	18.6
USA	1263.0	1854.0	3574.0	183.0
TOTAL	14338.4	15653.8	19830.6	38.3

Source: FLO website (2005), http://www.fairtradenet/sites/products/coffee/markets.html.

According to FLO, fierce competition from outside the fair trade network has been a major cause of these trends. Since 2000, the fair trade network has been hit hard by unprecedented declines in the prices of tropical goods and by price wars among giant supermarket chains, which have further increased the gap between the prices of fair trade and mainstream goods, thus damaging fair trade's competitiveness (FLO 2001). This has particularly been the case of the conventional coffee sector, which has experienced a global crisis due to a staggering dive in world export prices for specialty coffee from 2000 to 2002 from around a dollar to as low as 41 cents per pound, tying a record low set in 1882. The primary cause of this has been global oversupply caused by stepped-up production in existing coffee countries as well as the recent entrance of newcomers into the coffee industry, especially Vietnam, which rose from being an insignificant coffee exporting nation to the world's second largest by the end of the 1990s. A major factor driving these catastrophic actions have been the policies of the World Bank and IMF, which have encouraged Southern countries to increase commodity exports to earn foreign exchange to meet their debt payments (Talbot 2004: 75–7, 127–8). Throughout the crisis the fair trade minimum price has remained at $1.26 per pound, which has damaged fair trade's competitiveness but has also saved many fair trade producers from the bankruptcy, mass migration, and hunger experienced by tens of thousands of small-scale coffee farmers worldwide (Ross 2002; Global Exchange 2001; Oxfam International 2001).

In response to these global market pressures, fair traders have sought to escalate their efforts to promote fair trade and expand the fair trade market. In recent years, particular attention has been paid to the United States (the largest consumer market in the world) and Canada, which together represent a relatively insignificant proportion of fair trade sales globally. From 1997 to 2000, 34 per cent of the total number of FLO-certified goods were sold in Switzerland (population 7.3 million) and 24.7 per cent were sold in the Netherlands (population 16.1 million). This is in stark contrast to the United States (population 280.6 million), which was responsible for only 0.2 per cent of total sales in this period; and Canada (population 31.9 million), which also posted a figure of 0.2 per cent of the total (FLO 2001). Since the introduction of the FLO system into North America in the late 1990s, fair trade sales have grown rapidly from a very small original base, as has typically been the case in previously untapped markets, and fair trade activists have made a concerted effort to keep sales growth from levelling off (Waridel 2002:

99–100). These efforts have generally focused on the promotion of fair trade coffee, traditionally viewed as the flagship commodity for penetrating new markets. From 2000 to 2002, the average annual sales growth for fair trade coffee was around 48 per cent in the United States and 78 per cent in Canada (Lewin, Giovannucci, and Varangis 2004: 123–5).

Social justice activists have pursued two main strategies to promote the expansion of fair trade markets: 'buycotting' campaigns targeting large-scale corporations, and campaigns to gain the support of public institutions through their procurement policies. Buycotting campaigns have been particularly prevalent in North America and entail fair trade activists raising awareness among 'ethical consumers' to create demand for fair trade products. The *buycotting* strategy is counterpoised to a consumer *boycott* strategy. Whereas boycotting campaigns involve pressuring corporations to adopt more socially just standards by refusing to buy their goods, fair traders assert that buycotting campaigns offer corporations a positive alternative that allows them to increase their profits by tapping into 'ethical' markets. The goal of activists is to demonstrate that ethical demand exists, and then to pressure corporations to meet this demand for reasons of both moral imperative and corporate profitability (Waridel 2002: 107–9; Lappé and Lappé 2002: 207–8). In this way, fair traders aspire to tap into the 'power' of consumers. Laure Waridel, the co-founder of Équiterre, a Montreal-based NGO that promotes ecological and socially responsible choices and has actively promoted fair trade, sums up a widely held view among fair trade activists when she states: 'Once organised, consumers have much more power over companies than they think. They are the *raison d'être* of all companies. Without consumers, there is no business' (Waridel 2002: 109).

Perhaps the most notable buycotting campaign has been the one headed by Global Exchange, a San Francisco–based human rights NGO, which compelled Starbucks Coffee, the world's largest speciality coffee roaster, to agree to sell fair trade coffee in its 2,300 stores across the United States in April 2000. After a series of protests and letter-writing campaigns, Starbucks agreed to sell fair trade coffee just three days before Global Exchange had planned to initiate a nationwide protest targeting Starbucks in thirty U.S. cities. Starbucks agreed to sell whole bean fair trade coffee but has so far refused to sell brewed fair trade coffee. The decision of the giant coffee TNC nearly doubled the number of fair trade sales outlets in the United States, which had previously numbered approximately 2,500 (a number that includes all 1,600 Safeway stores in the United States, which willingly agreed to sell fair trade coffee at the start of 2000) (Waridel 2002: 108–9; Global Exchange 2000). It also had spillover effects in other nations, and in 2002 Starbucks began offering limited quantities of fair trade coffee in its stores in the United Kingdom and Canada (CBC 2002). In the wake of these successful buycotting campaigns, more major coffee corporations have got on board with much less pressure than was initially required for Starbucks. Over the past few years, for example, Sara Lee (owner of Douwe Egberts) and Procter & Gamble (owner of Folgers and Millstone), two of the largest coffee TNCs in the world, have begun offering limited quantities of fair trade coffee (Oxfam America 2003; Global Exchange 2003).

The growing involvement of giant TNCs in the fair trade network has generally been celebrated by fair trade activists who view corporate involvement as essential to the further expansion of the fair trade market (Waridel 2002: 105–6). This corporate-driven expansion, however, does not come without a cost. As FLO (2003b) acknowledges in its critique of corporate social responsibility, most corporate ethics initiatives are driven not by the genuine moral concerns of consumers, but by the desire of TNCs to protect their public image for the sake of profitability (see also Renard 2005). This cynicism is indeed well warranted. As Michael Dawson has well documented in his book *The Consumer Trap*, giant TNCs have systematically and consciously employed sophisticated marketing strategies to manipulate, rather than meet, the demands of consumers. In pursuit of their 'profit-über-alles' objectives, big-business marketers have considered the genuine ethical, health-related, or ecological concerns of consumers to be 'less than peripheral' to their corporate activities (Dawson 2003: 8,165). As Dawson states: 'If you bother to look at what corporate marketers actually do in their jobs, you find them talking of managing demand by concocting ways of shifting attention, pushing emotional buttons, spreading misinformation, and otherwise engineering prospective buyers' perceptions, choices, and actions. You also confirm, in spades, the truth of the advertising executive Gordon Webber's admission: "Oh sure, we're interested in the *people* who use the product, but only, to be candid about it, in relation to how we can influence them to buy it"' (7).

As is typically the case with corporate marketing strategies, big-business support for fair trade no doubt has at its heart the desire to 'shift attention' and 'engineer consumers perceptions.' For making relatively minor commitments to fair trade (Starbucks sells only around 1 to 2 per cent of its beans certified fair trade); TNCs attain 100 per cent positive publicity, which masks their devotion to 'exploitation-as-usual' in most of their operations. Moreover, the relatively minor commitment of these TNCs is a major one for the fair trade network – Starbucks is now among the largest fair trade roasters in North America – which promises to give TNCs immense influence on the future direction of the network (Renard 2005: 430). For example, in 2003 FLO began to seriously discuss making amendments to its generic fair trade standards for coffee to allow for the certification of coffee plantations (Giovannucci 2003: 38n13). Currently, only smallholder cooperatives can be certified to produce fair trade coffee, and fair trade plantations are permitted only in industries where few smallholders exist. This proposed change has likely been considered to appease TNCs that have long-term trading relations with large-scale plantations and generally consider them more stable and reliable trading partners than small producers (Renard 2005: 427; Lewin, Giovannucci, and Varangis 2004: 123–5; Wong, presentation 2004).

In addition to influencing the future direction of fair trade, the growing involvement of TNCs in the network may pose a significant threat to the viability of existing small-scale fair trade ATOs that have struggled to maintain their competitiveness through the cooperative efforts of IFAT, EFTA, and NEWS. These ATOs, which generally sell 100 per cent of their products fair trade, now find themselves in an increasingly competitive environment against giant TNCs with massive financial and marketing resources. These realities have given way to growing controversy within the network. Recently, a handful of smaller fair trade coffee roasters in the United States have broken with TransFair USA and aspire to form a new association composed entirely of 100 per cent fair trade coffee roasters, the details of which have yet to be worked out (Rogers 2004).

In addition to buycotting campaigns, fair traders have also sought to expand the fair trade market by gaining the support of public institutions, whose procurement policies can be a significant avenue for increasing sales. This has proven to be the case in Europe. From 1991 to 2000, the EU passed a series of resolutions in support of fair trade and EFTA has been allowed to organize five Fair Trade Days and a Fair Trade Lunch at the European Parliament. Currently, all European Union institutions use fair trade coffee, although not exclusively, and some also use fair trade tea (EFTA 2001a: 34). In Switzerland, Max

Havelaar has received significant financial support from the federal department for external affairs, and fair trade coffee is used in several government departments, the Swissair airline, and the International Committee of the Red Cross. In Britain, thirty local authorities have passed fair trade resolutions, and fair trade beverages are offered in many government offices, including the Scottish Parliament and its House of Commons. In Germany, fair trade coffee is consumed at many conference centres and university canteens, the City Council of Hamburg, the regional Parliaments of Bavaria and Thuringia, the national Parliament (Bundestag), and the office of the President of the Republic (EFTA 2001b). Similar examples can be found throughout Europe.

In North America, the support of public institutions for fair trade has lagged far behind Europe, and procurement policies have only recently become a focus for fair trade activists in the United States and Canada. This has been the case in particular on university campuses, where student groups have organized information tables, teach-ins, fair trade coffee tastings, petitions, and letter writing campaigns to gain the support of campus food services (Fridell 2004b). In the United States, these campaigns have yet to result in a university or college adopting an official fair trade purchasing policy, although student activists have succeed in convincing various vendors to offer some fair trade products at over 300 campuses, including Georgetown, Yale, Harvard, New York University, and UCLA (Oxfam America 2003; FLO 2003b). Moreover, there are hopes that the recent success of campus 'no-sweat' campaigns, which have compelled over 100 colleges and universities to adopt anti-sweatshop codes of conduct for trademark licensees, can be extended to include fair trade purchasing policies in the near future. An important precedent for public procurement policies and fair trade in the United States has been the Berkeley City Council's adoption of an organic and fair trade coffee policy for all city purchases in 1999. In Canada, in 2002, McMaster University in Hamilton, Ontario, became the first university in North America to adopt a 'no-sweat' code of conduct *and* a fair trade purchasing policy which forces all retailers on campus to offer the choice of fair trade coffee. This was followed by the adoption of a similar fair trade code at Trent University in Peterborough, Ontario, in early 2004, and activists hope to compel other universities to follow suit (Fridell 2004b; Curwin 2002).

Due to the growing emphasis on expanding the public procurement of fair trade products, concern has been raised among fair traders over the potential barriers posed to the network's further expansion by the WTO and its Technical Barriers to Trade (TBT) agreement. Under the TBT agreement, many social and environmental regulations are considered obstacles to free trade, and, according to Waridel, it is possible that 'voluntary, nongovernmental eco-labelling schemes may be judged to discriminate against "like" products on the basis of how they are produced rather than what they are.' In response to this threat, some of the world's leading international accreditation and labelling organizations in social and environmental standards have formed the International Social and Environmental Accreditation and Labelling Alliance (ISEAL). The primary goal of ISEAL is to gain recognition and credibility for its members' initiatives in the eyes of international trade bodies, and demonstrate that they do not pose a barrier to free trade and neoliberal restructuring. Its members include FLO, as well as the Conservation Agriculture Network (CAN), the International Federation of Organic Agriculture Movements (IFOAM), the International Organic Accreditation Service (IOAS), the Marine Stewardship Council (MSC), and Social Accountability International (Waridel 2002: 113–114).

Despite these concerns, the fair trade network's voluntarist development strategy has in fact proven to be a digestible pill for many of neoliberalism's fiercest promoters. This has not gone unnoticed by fair traders. According to Hans Bolscher, fair trade is appreciated by socialists for its cooperative aims, by Christian charities for its efforts to help the poor, and by neoliberals for its accordance with 'free trade' and 'free competition.' One of the strengths of fair trade, asserts Bolsher, is that it is transparent and imposes no official limits on free trade (Bolscher, interview 2002). For this reason, it has been possible to gain the support and participation of neoliberal institutions. This includes the World Bank, a primary architect of neoliberal restructuring, which has begun taking increasing notice of fair trade due to the bank's growing interest in promoting 'private (market driven) standards that encourage employers to adopt desirable labour practices' (World Bank 2001: 74; Golub 1997).

The World Bank's growing interest in market-driven social justice projects like fair trade stems from its desire to combat an escalating crisis of legitimacy in the wake of global justice protests against the negative impact of neoliberal globalization (McNally 2002: 197). The World Bank has decided that its purported objective of 'making markets work better for poor people' may be highly compatible with FLO's stated desire 'to make international trade and globalisation work for the poor' (FLO 2003b: 18; World Bank 2001: 61). In consequence, the World Bank has met several times with fair trade representatives, has begun promoting the fair trade network, and has even started serving fair trade coffee at its head office in Washington, DC (Zonneveld 2003; World Bank 2002b). Many fair traders have responded favourably to these moves, and some have felt compelled to disavow the radical aims of the Global Justice Movement, whose participants they have pejoratively referred to as 'globaphobes,' in an attempt to present themselves as responsible stakeholders worthy of further consideration at meetings of the World Bank and the WTO.[10] In the eyes of international organizations like the World Bank, as well as TNCs and public institutions in Europe and North America, the fair trade network is increasingly viewed as a legitimate project precisely because it is not seen as a radical challenge to the central tenets of neoliberal globalization.

The efforts made by fair traders to gain the support of public institutions and conventional corporations have thus far led to a continuation of the steady growth experienced by the network throughout the 1990s. This growth, however, while resulting in greater numbers of Southern producers gaining access to fair trade standards, must be qualified in several ways. First, from a marketing standpoint, much of the new growth experienced in the network has been a result of the promotion of new commodities and the expansion of relatively untapped markets. Recently introduced commodities such as bananas and tropical fruits have been the major growth leaders in the network for the past few years, while traditional leaders, in particular coffee, have experienced stagnant growth rates (see figure 2.2). This suggests that the current high-growth rates could well level off once the new commodities reach their market peak, as has been the case with coffee. Similarly, much of the recent growth of the network has been due to rapid sales in previously small, relatively untapped national markets, including the United States and Canada, as well as France, Norway, and Sweden. In all likelihood, these initial bursts of national sales growth will level off once a certain threshold of sales has been attained, as has been the case in more mature fair trade markets in Germany and the Netherlands (Renard 2005; Lewin, Giovannucci, and Varangis 2004: 123–5; Giovannucci 2003; EFTA 2001a; Giovannucci 2001). Thus, the current impressive growth rates experienced in the fair trade network do not provide an adequate indication of the network's long-term growth, which will likely slow down once various fair trade niche markets are saturated.

Second, even if the market for ethical goods proves to have greater potential for continued expansion than argued above, this does not necessarily mean that the FLO system and its partners will be the main beneficiaries of this future growth. Over the past several decades, fair traders have made significant gains in developing fair trade niche markets, and, as a result, have attracted the attention of conventional corporations which have shown growing interest in tapping into 'ethical consumer' markets. These corporations have shown initial interest in relatively small quantities of fair trade, but have recently begun showing greater interest in other 'sustainable' products, such as organic, eco-friendly, bird-friendly, shade-grown, and 'fairly' traded goods. Consumer research indicates that most ethical consumers make little distinction between various 'sustainable' initiatives, which gives corporations considerable flexibility in determining their strategies to carve out territory in ethical niche markets (Giovannucci 2003: 21–2, 55–9; 2001). Consequently, conventional corporations have been quick to turn their attention towards those initiatives which lack FLO's rigorous social and environmental standards or its third-party verification, or both.

Within the sustainable coffee sector, for example, some increasingly popular alternatives to fair trade coffee include eco-friendly or shade-grown labelling. These initiatives are generally conducted by corporate-friendly third parties (such as Conservation International or the Rainforest Alliance), lack FLO's rigorous social criteria, and offer a significantly lower price premium (Giovannucci 2003: 21–3, 61–71). Eco-friendly and shade-grown labelling made their first significant appearance in Northern markets in the late 1990s and currently have smaller sales than the more established fair trade network. Nonetheless, they have been rapidly gaining the acceptance of conventional corporations, and as a result could well overtake fair trade sales in the near future. According to Bryan Lewin, Daniele Giovannucci, and Panos Varangis (2004: 125) in their sustainable coffee report for the World Bank, eco-friendly and shade-grown coffee 'could have the greatest potential for mainstream market success because it appeals to larger-established producers because it does not require strict organic production and, unlike fair trade, is not limited to smallholders. These larger producers often have the market contacts and volumes to more quickly establish a relationship with larger buyers.'

Along with corporate-friendly labels, a variety of private sustainable coffee initiatives have also emerged in recent years. These initiatives lack independent third-party certification, although some have been developed with the cooperation of various NGOs. Starbucks has recently adopted its own sustainable coffee guidelines with the advice of the Consumer's Choice Council; Neumann Kaffee Gruppe and Nestlé have begun developing their own guidelines through their Sustainable Agricultural Initiative; Kraft and Sara Lee are piloting their own small sustainable coffee projects in Vietnam; and the German organic wholesaler Rapunzel Naturkost has developed its own 'fairly' traded standards through its Hand in Hand program. The International Coffee Partners (ICP), consisting of several of Europe's top roasters, have developed various sustainable initiatives, and the German Coffee Association (GCA) is working in cooperation with the German Development Agency (GTZ) to develop a common sustainability code for its members. The Rabobank Foundation has developed its Progreso Coffee Fund to promote sustainable guidelines, and the Euro-Retailer Produce Working Group has initiated its Good Agricultural Practices (EUREP-GAP) to encourage corporations to voluntarily adopt its principles. On the basis of the EUREP-GAP criteria, the transnational retail food giant Ahold NV recently established its own sustainable coffee certification body called Utz Kapeh, which is managed as its own foundation and has the participation of other roasters. Utz Kapeh does not directly interfere in negotiations between buyers and sellers, but makes 'strong recommendations' for price premiums which are generally well below those of fair trade (Renard 2005: 426–30; Giovannucci 2003: 36–40, 55–71; 2001).[11]

All of the above private initiatives lack FLO's rigorous social standards and genuinely independent third-party verification, and offer price premiums well below those of the fair trade network. Their emergence and growth represent attempts by corporations to 'free ride' off the promotional efforts of FLO and other fair trade organizations in developing the sustainable coffee market in the first place. It is quite possible that these corporations will be successful and that their private initiatives will become dominant players in ethical markets in the future. According to agricultural marketing expert Daniele Giovannuci in his assessment of the sustainable coffee market, 'These private initiatives could easily become much larger than today's accepted sustainable certifications' (Giovannucci 2003: 36) This poses a significant threat to the future of certified fair trade, which could well be overcome by competition from private and corporate-friendly initiatives with greater marketing resources.

Finally, the impressive growth of the fair trade network must also be assessed within the political context of the decline of the other projects of the fair trade movement and the emergence of neoliberal globalization, as described in the previous chapter. To most fair trade organizations, the fair trade network represents a challenge to neoliberal reforms, and its growth is viewed as a stepping stone towards achieving the broader structural reforms proposed by the fair trade movement (see Oxfam International 2002a). For example, fair trade organizations recently played an active role in the UNCTAD XI meetings in June 2004, where they put forward a Fair Trade Declaration, signed by over 90 fair trade organizations from 30 countries, which affirmed their support for the development of international mechanisms to regulate commodity markets (Hamerschlag, Ferrari, and Monteiro 2004; Fair Trade Declaration – UNCTAD XI 2004). Yet, despite these proclamations, many fair traders have at the same time increasingly adopted the neoliberal discourse of 'free trade,' and the network's voluntarist model has proven to be as compatible with the goals of neoliberal reformers as it is with the fair trade movement. Consequently, its growing acceptance does not automatically represent a movement towards the state-driven, macro-economic structural reforms traditionally sought by organizations like UNCTAD. UNCTAD itself is aware of this, and in a recent report, published jointly with the International Institute for Sustainable Development (IISD), stated: 'A key challenge facing the FLO system stems from its reliance upon supply chain relations alone for the administration and management of its "sustainability criteria." Although fair trade attempts to provide a mechanism for "economic" sustainability at the producer level, *it does not offer a response to the macro-economic conditions of the market fundamentally responsible for price and credit behaviour.* The solution to such market problems, on the fair trade model, is sought through the development of a consumer market for fair-trade labelled coffees' (UNCTAD and IISD 2003: 12; emphasis added).

In contrast to the consumer-driven model of the fair trade network, UNCTAD and IISD believe that fair trade criteria need to be developed that are based on 'multi-stakeholder and multilateral cooperation at the international level' – in other words, on the centrality of state-enforced market regulation. (Although it must be pointed out that both UNCTAD and the IISD have also been significantly effected by neoliberal hegemony, as is apparent in their growing emphasis on 'multi-stakeholder' negotiations that would involve corporations playing a central, as well as voluntary, role.) Proposals such as this, that still place an emphasis on international market regulation, are certainly theoretically compatible with the needs of the fair trade network. They are not, however, compatible with the political objectives of most of the TNCs, public institutions, and international organizations that have thrown their support behind the fair trade network over the past few years. To these organizations, the fair trade network represents not a step towards a regulated international market but an *alternative to it*.

While organizations in Europe and North America have shown increasing support for the fair trade network, they have also continued to reject the other, statist initiatives of the fair trade movement and have pushed forward with neoliberal reforms. This suggests that to these institutions, the fair trade network is being employed as an 'ethical fig leaf' designed to mask their devotion to a broader neoliberal agenda. Thus, while the World Bank, the EU institutions, and many national and local governments in the North have thrown their support behind the fair trade network, they have at the same time continued with neoliberal restructuring and have refused to eliminate unfair protectionist barriers to Southern commodities and agricultural export subsidies, long-standing demands of the key organizations of the fair trade movement (Bullard 2004; Bello 2003). The same can be said for conventional TNCs that have pressured governments to adopt neoliberal reforms. The coffee giants Procter & Gamble and Sara Lee, for example, successfully lobbied the U.S. government to abandon the International Coffee Agreement (ICA) in 1989 and are currently making huge profits as a result of the collapse of coffee bean export prices that has occurred in its wake (Oxfam International 2002a, 2001). At the same time, these TNCs have shown growing support for fair trade coffee. This reveals that the support of major institutions and corporations for the fair trade network has been paralleled by continuing support for neoliberal policies, suggesting that the former are, in fact, being adopted to mask the negative impact of the latter.

The increasing employment of fair trade as an ethical fig leaf by public institutions and TNCs reveals a growing disparity over the political meaning of fair trade and its relationship to neoliberal globalization. To NGOs such as FLO, IFAT, EFTA, Oxfam International, and Global Exchange, the fair trade network is viewed as a challenge to neoliberal globalization that seeks to promote an *alternative globalization* that puts the needs of poor workers and farmers ahead of the whims of the international market. From their perspective, the fair trade network remains only one component of the broader fair trade movement and continues to promote its essential values and vision. Oxfam Canada programmer Tina Conlon (presentation 2004b) has argued that support for the fair trade network is a form of 'direct action' that is only one part of a broader strategy to reform the international trading system.

In sharp contrast to this, international organizations, public institutions, and corporate fair trade partners have a distinctly different vision of the fair trade network. From their perspective, the network's voluntarist, market-driven approach is compatible with neoliberal reforms, and their support of fair trade is seen as assisting poor workers and farmers in more actively participating in neoliberal globalization. This is expressed, for example, in a report on fair trade prepared in 2000 for the UK government's Department for International Development (DFID):

> Market liberalisation and associated reforms have generally been favourable to most export commodity producers, but there are significant problems with the way in which these markets operate. Newly liberalised markets, while often highly competitive, exhibit pervasive market failures and have a limited capacity to support the emergence of the type of contractual arrangements that will improve quality, enable credit to be mobilised and used through the marketing chain, and enable producers and traders to manage the price risks they face ... [Fair trade] initiatives, through providing support to producer organisations, may therefore have a significant role in a strategy to improve the functioning of markets for small producers. (Oxford Policy Management 2000: vi)

Unlike most fair trade NGOs, conventional institutions support the fair trade network as a neoliberal alternative to the other, statist proposals traditionally advanced by the fair trade movement. These competing visions reveal the highly contentious nature of the fair trade network since its reorientation, and point towards what will likely be heightened conflict about the political meaning of the network in the near future. While little open, explicit debate has yet to emerge among NGOs, activists, and academics on this issue, the growing literature on fair trade contains the seeds of implicit disagreements. These debates, whose relevance extends to the core of what the network is, are described and discussed below.

Contemporary Perspectives on the Fair Trade Network

In recent years, a small but growing body of literature on fair trade has emerged, composed of works by academics and activists who have sought to assess fair trade's potential for combating the negative effects of neoliberal globalization on poor communities in the South. As discussed in chapter 1, most of these analysts have, to varying degrees, departed significantly from the statist vision of the fair trade network dominant during its formative decades and as represented by the work of Michael Barratt Brown (1993). Following neoliberal trends within the fair trade network and the international political economy in general, these authors have abandoned Barratt Brown's focus on the nation-state as a primary agent in development and his focus on creating a parallel trading network that poses itself as a distinct alternative to the existing global capitalist system. Yet, despite these broad similarities, distinct positions have emerged within the new literature that offer significantly different interpretations of fair trade and its relation to neoliberal globalization. These positions are not immediately clear, as few authors have attempted to explicitly define their own theoretical roots, to locate themselves in relation to one another, or to define broad debates within the literature. It is, however, possible to extract the main theoretical underpinnings that are *implicit* to most of the arguments. On this basis, I have grouped the various arguments into three broad perspectives on the basis of similar overarching assumptions, which are contrasted with those of the old vision (see table 2.5).[12] These perspectives, rather than being ideally represented by any one specific author, are general, overarching views that various fair trade analysts tend to focus on to different degrees. Some authors present multiple perspectives in their work, whereas others tend to focus more intensely on a specific perspective.

The first grouping, which I have termed the *shaped advantage* perspective, depicts fair trade as a project that assists local groups in developing the capacities and infrastructure required to somewhat offset the negative impact of globalization. The second grouping, which I have termed the *alternative globalization* perspective, depicts fair trade as an alternative model of globalization, which, unlike the neoliberal paradigm, seeks to 'include' the poorest sectors in the South, which it asserts has thus far been 'excluded' from the benefits of international trade. The third grouping, which I have termed the *decommodification* perspective, asserts that fair trade represents a challenge to the com-

Table 2.5 Contemporary perspectives on the fair trade network

	Old vision	Shaped advantage	Alternative globalization	Decommodification
Focus	Micro & macro-economic	Micro-economic	Micro & macro-economic	Values of capitalism & commodification
Method	Skills training & cooperation Alternative trading system Promote market regulation	Skills training & cooperation Social & cultural capital, capacity building, & market-ing skills	Skills training & cooperation Promote 'true' free trade or 're-embed' markets	Raise awareness Bridge gap between producer & consumer
International context	international capitalism: unequal exchange Alternative exchange required	Neoliberal globalization: unprecedented liberalization Limits fair trade niche & price	Neoliberal globalization: rigged against poor countries Market must be reformed	Varies: in all cases, market lacks transparency
Development objective	Shield participants from negative effects of market New international economic order Central role for democratic state regulation Grassroots producer and consumer groups	Shield participants from negative effects of market Mitigate impact of neoliberal globalization Non-governmental approach	Shield participants from negative effects of market Include socially excluded in new model for globalization Part of broader political project State regulation in some areas	Decommodification Challenge capitalist moral economy
Shortcomings	Insufficient sales	Neglects broader objectives	Neglects compatibility with neoliberalism & the limits of market	Neglects limits of consumer solidarity & eroding powers of market

modification of goods under global capitalism. These three perspectives represent central views on the network as expressed in academic, developmental, and popular circles, and they reveal much about the long-term prospects of fair trade.

Fair Trade as Shaped Advantage

The first perspective, that of *shaped advantage*, comes from authors that variously describe fair trade as an exercise in enhancing 'social and cultural capital,' 'institutional capacity,' and marketing skills designed to allow poor producers to enter the global market under more favourable conditions by taking advantage of a socially conscious 'market niche' in Europe and North America (Page and Slater 2003; LeClair 2002; Simpson and Rapone 2000; Oxford Policy Management 2000; Blowfield 1999; Renard 1999; Sick 1999; Littrell and Dickson 1999; Renner and Adamowicz 1998; Bird and Hughes 1997). Fair trade is viewed as shielding its participants from the worst effects of neoliberal globalization by providing a non-governmental approach to price subsidies and a degree of social welfare in the wake of the death of the 'developmental state.' From this perspective, fair trade is depicted as mitigating the inevitability of globalization, which imposes firm limits on the network's ability to grow and expand its benefits. This is similar to the view expounded by promoters of the 'third way,' who depict neoliberal globalization as irreversible and advocate the role of government as being limited to removing specific constraints that have impeded certain groups from attaining the greatest possible benefit from the global market.[13] Along this line of thinking, those writing from the shaped advantage perspective assert that fair trade producers can improve their position in the global economy through training and the development of networks based on trust and cooperation.

The shaped advantage perspective's emphasis on the limits imposed on fair trade by neoliberal globalization is the source of both its greatest strength – a critical assessment of the limits of the fair trade market niche – and its greatest weakness: an overemphasis on micro-economic tinkering at the expense of altering macro-economic relations of power. With regard to the former, those writing from the shaped advantage perspective tend to argue that the fair trade network's reliance on the individual purchasing decisions of Northern consumers has resulted in significant limitations on the size of the fair trade market niche and the price of fair trade goods. These limits are significant and tend to be

neglected or downplayed by commentators writing from other perspectives (e.g., Raynolds, Murray, and Taylor 2004; Waridel 2002: 113–
21; Lappé and Lappé 2002: 197–210, 280–315; VanderHoff Boersma
2001).

Pointing to trends in the international economy in general and fair
trade sales in particular, such as those described above, authors from
the shaped advantage group assert that strict limits to the further
expansion of the network likely exist (LeClair 2002; Renard 1999; Bird
and Hughes 1997). As for the prices for fair trade goods, these authors
point out that prices are significantly limited by consumer demand
and the imperatives of the market. While fair trade prices are higher
than conventional market prices, they cannot be so high as to scare off
ethical consumers, confined by what Renard calls 'the difficult compromise between ethical principles and the market' (LeClair 2002;
Blowfield 1999; Renard 1999: 497). This compromise also has an impact
on the social justice message promoted by the fair trade network, as it
must be radical enough to attract a core group of ethical consumers but
not so radical as to alienate a broader base of 'semi-ethical' consumers
(Bird and Hughes 1997: 164). Moreover, authors that emphasize the
shaped advantage perspective assert that fair trade purchasing decisions are not based solely on ethical considerations but are also determined by levels of disposable income which fluctuate depending on
the status of Northern economies and their relative distribution of
wealth (LeClair 2002: 956–7; Bird and Hughes 1997: 159). Through the
discipline of the market, these factors impose strict limits on a 'fair'
price.

In evidence of the validity of these claims, one need only look at the
current basic minimum price for fair trade arabica coffee beans, which
at $1.26 per pound is more than twice as high as current conventional
coffee prices due to the global coffee crisis (Oxfam International 2002a).
While this price is high compared to current conditions, when viewed
historically the fair trade price is relatively low and consistent with
conventional prices. From 1976 to 1989 and from 1995 to 1998, a total of
sixteen years, the international price for conventional Brazilian arabica
beans was generally close to or well above $1.26 per pound (see figure
2.7) (UNCTAD 2004).[14] It would be untenable, given the historically
exploitative conditions under which coffee producers have lived and
worked (described in chapter 3), to make the claim that during these
years the price of coffee beans was fair. This reveals that the price of
fair trade coffee beans is not determined solely on the basis of social

Figure 2.7 Comparison of green coffee bean export prices, Brazilian arabicas versus fair trade beans, 1960–2000

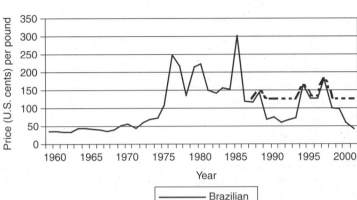

Source: UNCTAD (2004), *UNCTAD Handbook of Statistics On-Line*, http://stats.unctad.org.

justice (which would warrant a price much higher than the conventional one), but is limited to a price that is '(as) fair (as possible)' given the demands of Northern consumers (Renard 1999: 496).

While the authors of the shaped advantage group are correct in pointing out the market limits of fair trade, they are incorrect in viewing these limits as an inevitable outcome of globalization, which is frequently depicted in fairly mainstream terms as the unprecedented growth of international trade, the liberalization of markets, and the inevitable decline of the nation-state. Although many of the authors that emphasize this perspective do not necessarily view neoliberal globalization as a positive occurrence for the world's poor (in particular see LeClair 2002; Simpson and Rapone 2000; Renard 1999), they do nevertheless tend to depict it as inevitable and as such view the network as primarily aspiring to protect a select group of producers from its worst effects while enhancing their competitiveness on global markets through micro-economic tinkering. Through the fair trade network, Southern partners develop economically efficient, community-based organizations; gain experience in sales, accounting, machine maintenance, and basic education; and construct their own processing, storage, and transportation infrastructure so that they can better capture profits previously lost to intermediaries (Page and Slater 2003;

LeClair 2002: 951–4; Simpson and Rapone 2000: 46–7; Renard 1999: 493–6; Bird and Hughes 1997: 165–6).

While shaping advantage in favour of Southern producers is indeed an important component of fair trade, there are three main weaknesses to this perspective. First, it is premised on a flawed depiction of globalization. As much recent empirical analysis has revealed, neoliberal globalization does not involve unprecedented levels of world trade or freer trade: while tariffs on exports and imports have declined over the past twenty years, quotas and non-tariff trade barriers have increased substantially over the same period of time. What globalization has involved is removing capital controls and limiting the rights of states to intervene in the operations of TNCs for the sake of social, environmental, or developmental concerns (McNally 2002: 29–59; Hoogvelt 2001: 67–93). However, the decline of the nation-state is neither inevitable nor irreversible. While the imperatives of competition on a world market have lessened the ability of individual states to act autonomously, this situation is to a significant extent self-imposed by nation-states which have actively developed and pursued the neoliberal political-economic agreements to which they claim to be subservient (Albo 1996; Helleiner 1994). This is especially true of the rich nations in the North, in particular the United States, which have shaped neoliberal globalization in their own interest and continue to selectively employ its concepts to the benefit of the North (Gowan 1999). A telling example of this is Northern countries' refusal to adhere to the tenets of 'free trade' by lowering Northern protectionist barriers to Southern commodities and eliminating Northern agricultural export subsidies despite the demands of Southern states in international forums like the WTO (Bullard 2004).

A second weakness of the shaped advantage perspective, which derives from the belief in the inevitability of globalization, is its emphasis on micro-economic adjustment at the local level at the expense of confronting highly unequal macro-economic relations of power at the international level. Economist Ben Fine's critique of the notion of social capital is instructive in this regard. According to Fine, social capital moved to the fore of development thinking and the social sciences in the late 1990s, promoted by the World Bank, which sought a non-state solution to the growing social inequalities caused by the global economy. In line with the World Bank's agenda, Fine asserts that social capital promotes the idea that capital is a thing – as opposed to a social relation premised on class exploitation – and directs development strategies away from altering highly unequal macro-relations of class power and towards correcting 'micro-imperfections in economic and non-economic relations' (Fine 1999: 2). This critique can be broadly applied to the authors of the shaped advantage perspective, whether their focus is on developing social and cultural capital, 'institutional capacity,' marketing skills, or 'sustainable' business practices (LeClair 2002: 951–4; Simpson and Rapone 2000; Blowfield 1999: 745; Bird and Hughes 1997). The effect is to limit their interpretation of the developmental prospects of fair trade to one which, in the words of James Petras (1997: 26), confines itself to working 'within the niches of the free market imposed by the World Bank and structural adjustment.'

An overemphasis on shaping advantage at the local level results in neglecting the international political-economic forces which continue to mould the everyday lives of fair traders, as well as the tens of millions of Southern producers who are not members of the fair trade network. Under the auspices of neoliberal reforms, the most important decisions concerning the welfare of citizens have been moved out of national democratic control and into the hands of international financial organizations, such as the WTO, the IMF, and the World Bank, whose short-sighted policies have had devastating effects on the world's poor (Stiglitz 2003, 2002; Weisbrot et al. 2001; Weisbrot et al. 2000).

The global coffee crisis is a telling example of this. The neoliberal policy prescriptions of international financial institutions have played a key role in the collapse of the ICA, which has led to an extreme downward spiral in coffee prices. This situation has been made worse by the debt crisis and the neoliberal policies of the World Bank and IMF, who have used their leverage over indebted poor countries to promote the expansion of commodity exports. Faced with the need to earn foreign exchange to service their debt payments, countries like Vietnam have responded by stepping up the export of commodities like coffee, leading to further global oversupply and declining prices (Talbot 2004: 75–7, 127–8).[15] The impact has been bankruptcy, mass migration, and starvation for tens of thousands of small coffee farmers throughout the globe (Ross 2002; Oxfam International 2002a; Global Exchange 2001). The greatest immediate impact on the fair trade network has been the growing gap between conventional coffee prices and fair trade prices, which has been a major factor in the levelling off of fair trade coffee sales globally (FLO 2001).

The third weakness of the shaped advantage perspective is that it does not adequately reflect the broad aims of the NGOs most actively involved in the fair trade network. To fair trade organizations and solidarity groups such as FLO, IFAT, EFTA, Oxfam International, and Global Exchange, the fair trade network is not just about enhancing the abilities of fair traders to survive and compete in the global economy, but is part of a broader movement that seeks to confront and change the unfair structures of world trade (VanderHoff Boersma, interview 2002; Oxfam International 2002a; FLO 2001; IFAT 2001; EFTA 2001a; James 2000). To these organizations, the fair trade network is a political project that offers an alternative globalization model to the neoliberal paradigm expounded by the rich countries in the North, the World Bank, and the WTO. Shaping advantage at the local level is only one part of a broader strategy aimed at reforming the international trading system. These broader aims are generally overlooked by authors that emphasize the shaped advantage perspective. An important exception to this is the work of Renard (2005: 426), who points out that fair traders do have a long run vision to 'transform global production,' but questions whether or not fair trade's market-driven model is truly capable of attaining this goal, resulting in a 'contradiction between philosophy and practice, between principles and political economy.' These contradictions are key to understanding and assessing the perspectives that follow, as well as the prospects of the fair trade network in general.

Fair Trade as Alternative Globalization

The second perspective expressed by various authors is that of fair trade as a model for an *alternative globalization* to the neoliberal paradigm (Taylor 2005; Jaffee, Kloppenburg, and Monroy 2004; Fisher 2004; Waridel 2002; Lappé and Lappé 2002; Raynolds 2002a; VanderHoff Boersma 2001). These authors depict fair trade as an alternative model for the international trade and development regime that comes closer than the shaped advantage group to the vision of fair trade prior to its reorientation and as expressed in the work of Barratt Brown. However, in line with fair trade's new orientation, the state is not seen as a primary agent in development, and the goal of the fair trade network is depicted as providing an alternative to neoliberal policies, but not an alternative to the global capitalist system in general. Many authors writing from this perspective depict fair trade as a true 'free trade' movement, in neo-Smithian terms, that counters the neoliberal version of free trade, which they assert is merely a hypocritical mystification that obscures protectionism and monopoly in the interest of rich countries in the North and their TNCs (Waridel 2002; Lappé and Lappé 2002; VanderHoff Boersma 2001). Others, drawing from the work of Karl Polanyi, see fair trade as a way to socially 're-embed' international trade relations and challenge the neoliberal logic and rules for 'how markets are constructed and administered, how they deliver and apportion economic benefits to participants' (Taylor 2005; Jaffee, Kloppenburg, and Monroy 2004: 192; Raynolds, Murray, and Taylor 2004; Raynolds 2002a).[16] In general, authors in the alternative globalization group do not depict fair trade as a project that seeks to break with the global capitalist market, but as one which seeks to challenge neoliberal policies and reform the market so that it 'serves people, and not the other way around' (Jaffee, Kloppenburg, and Monroy 2004: 192; Fisher 2004; Waridel 2002: 121–2; Lappé and Lappé 2002: 299; VanderHoff Boersma 2001: 4).

The authors that emphasize the alternative globalization perspective share many of the assumptions of the shaped advantage group concerning the immediate benefits of the fair trade network to Southern producers. They depict fair trade as a mechanism through which peasants and workers can overcome obstacles to marketing their products in the global economy by taking advantage of a socially conscious market niche in the North (Raynolds, Murray, and Taylor 2004). By developing marketing and processing skills and through cooperative organization, fair traders can add value to their goods, shelter themselves from the worst effects of the global market, and construct much-needed social infrastructure such as roads, schools, and hospitals. However, they also assert that benefits such as these are not enough in and of themselves. They argue that the network, if it is to survive and expand in the long term, cannot just address poverty and marginalization at the local level, but it must address the structural causes of these effects and the international relations of power that underlie them. In this sense, fair trade is depicted as part of a broader political project that seeks to confront and change the current neoliberal political-economic order.

To many authors in the alternative globalization group, the model offered by fair trade is derived from a radical interpretation of Adam Smith which posits that true free trade – the unrestricted flow of goods and services across national and regional boundaries – will work in the best interest of all producers and consumers, big and small, as long as the state intervenes to prevent monopoly and collusion and to provide basic social services to its citizens (Waridel 2002: 11; Lappé and Lappé 2002: 299–300; VanderHoff Boersma 2001: 4).[17] Due to their promotion of the ideals of free trade, the vision for an alternative order presented by these authors does not involve a heavily regulated global economy with strong state intervention. The authors do, however, envision a certain amount of market regulation, which they believe is required to expand the benefits of fair trade and ensure its long-term feasibility. At the state level, they argue forcefully for basic state-provided social welfare, some protectionist measures for weak sectors of the domestic economy, and labour and environmental legislation (VanderHoff Boersma 2001: 4). At the level of the international trading system, they argue for such things as the Tobin Tax on currency exchanges to impose some controls on financial speculation; extra taxes on TNCs designed to make them pay a monetary sum for the social and environmental costs of their corporate decisions; and compulsory labelling systems that force TNCs to give information about the social and environmental impacts of their products. Such mechanisms would, they argue, give a competitive advantage to fair traders at the expense of TNCs (Waridel 2002: 24–7; Lappé and Lappé 2002).

The greatest strength of the alternative globalization perspective is that it more accurately reflects the broader aims of fair trade NGOs who tend to view neoliberal globalization as a conscious political project driven by the interests of rich states and TNCs that can be confronted, and, ultimately, changed (Fried, presentation 2004; Vander-Hoff Boersma, interview 2002; Noticias 2002; Oxfam International 2002a; FLO 2001; IFAT 2001; EFTA 2001a; James 2000). Authors from this perspective employ fair trade as a critique of the hypocrisy of Northern states that use neoliberal reforms and the rhetoric of free trade to open up Southern markets while maintaining their own protectionist measures (Taylor 2005). These authors are correct to point out that international trade rules are, in the words of Oxfam International, 'rigged' against poor states and poor producers and workers in the South (Fried, presentation 2004; Oxfam International 2002b). Despite the decades-long demands of the fair trade movement, rich Northern nations continue to subsidize their agriculture to the tune of $1 billion a day, and they dump their surpluses on world markets to the detriment of poorer Southern producers. And developing countries continue to face unfair trade barriers for their exports to the North, which are four times those encountered by rich countries (Stiglitz 2003, 2002: 59–64; Oxfam International 2002b).

The 'free trade' agreements of the WTO have failed to address these inequalities, as they are inherently structured in favour of rich and powerful nations. For example, it is commonly accepted that during negotiations for the Uruguay Round in 1994, Southern nations abandoned their opposition to Trade-Related Aspects of Intellectual Property Rights (TRIPS) in order to gain concessions on greater access to Northern markets for their agriculture and textile products. Yet, while this may have been the case on paper, in practice rich Northern countries have employed a variety of exemptions and selective liberalization policies to ensure that increased market access for most Southern countries has been minimal or non-existent, while poor countries have been hit hard by increasing rent payments for Northern technology as a result of TRIPS. According to Ronald Mendoza and Chandrika Bahadur (2002), analysts for the United Nations Development Program (UNDP), the resulting situation has not been a win-win scenario for the North and the South, but one in which 'developing countries suffer annual losses of US$20.8 billion' as a result of these unfair trade rules and their implementation.

Authors writing from the alternative globalization perspective also criticize neoliberal globalization for entailing the *exclusion* of vast sectors of the globe from any productive role in development, which runs contrary to much mainstream thinking that depicts globalization as the further *integration* of previously neglected sectors. For example, while national and international capital controls have been severely curtailed due to neoliberal reforms, the majority of capital flows are increasingly concentrated in the rich countries in the North and a handful of newly industrialized countries (NICs) in the South, resulting in the growing exclusion of vast sectors of the South from the investment dollars required to create productive industries, generate employment, and develop social and physical infrastructure (McNally 2002: 29–59; Hoogvelt 2001: 67–93). For authors from the alternative perspective, fair trade represents a rejection of neoliberal globalization in favour of new vision of globalization that seeks to include the socially excluded majority in the South (Jaffee, Kloppenburg, and Monroy 2004: 192; VanderHoff Boersma 2001).

Yet, while proposing a vision of fair trade that goes beyond the microeconomic tinkering of the shaped advantage perspective and is more in line with the goals of fair traders, the alternative globalization perspective does not necessarily provide a more accurate depiction of what fair trade ultimately is capable of attaining (Renard 2005). A key flaw in the alternative globalization view is its portrayal of the fair trade network as a direct challenge to neoliberalism. Yet, as discussed in this chapter and the previous chapter, the success of the fair trade network after its reorientation has not been achieved because it is an *alternative* to neoliberalism, but because it is highly *compatible* with neoliberalism. The rapid growth of the fair trade network since the late 1980s can be attributed to its non-statist development strategy which has focused on voluntarism and mainstreaming. It is owing to this strategy that the network has survived and thrived while the other projects of the fair trade movement have staggered and declined. This has been part of a broader transformation in the international trade and development regime which has involved the decline of state intervention and market regulation and the rise of NGO-led development projects. Throughout the 1980s and 1990s, thousands of new NGOs emerged to fulfil the social welfare and developmental role once played by the state. Many of these NGOs receive funding from official institutions, such as the World Bank, which view NGOs as a non-statist solution to the negative social and environmental consequences of neoliberal reforms (Petras 1997). In the view of the World Bank and the other public institutions and private corporations that have been central to the network's growth, the fair trade network is *part* of this neoliberal transformation. In the era of neoliberalism, the fair trade network, with its voluntary non-statist program, has moved to the fore over the other, statist prescriptions of the fair trade movement for such things as commodity control schemes and state-enforced ILO labour standards.

In addition to neglecting the extent to which the fair trade network is in effect highly compatible with neoliberal globalization, authors from the alternative globalization group also tend to overlook the limits of their own market-friendly vision of fair trade. As a result of their neo-Smithian depiction of capitalism, these authors maintain that the market, with the proper macro-economic reforms, can be made to work in a 'win-win' fashion for all market agents: small farmers, rural workers, consumers, and giant TNCs. Rather than see exploitation as inherent in the market under capitalism, these authors see exploitation as a distortion of true market principles (McNally 1993). The goal, then, becomes that of correcting these distortions to allow everyone to reap the rewards of the market. The effect is a tendency among these authors to focus on the market as a place of *opportunities*, while overlooking the structural *imperatives* of capitalism and the negative impact these imperatives have had and continue to have on the fair trade network.

The impact of capitalist imperatives on the network raises serious concerns about its ability to continually expand, and, ultimately, provide a feasible alternative macro-economic model for the international trade and development regime. As argued above and supported by authors in the shaped advantage group, consumer demand and the imperatives of the market impose significant limits on the price of fair trade goods, the content of fair trade's social justice message, and the size and growth of fair trade niche markets. These limits have compelled fair traders to abandon their original vision of a state-regulated alternative trading system and instead deal increasingly with giant TNCs that are concerned only with the need to protect their public image for the sake of profitability. The growing involvement of these TNCs threatens to erode the fair trade network's principles and may well prove to be the greatest single barrier to the future growth of the network. While the alternative globalization group tends to depict fair trade as an alterative model pointing the way forward to more radical, macro-economic reforms, the history of the network reveals that the imperatives of the capitalist market continue to limit and erode the network's vision and raise concerns about its long-term viability. In consequence, the more limited vision of the fair trade network expounded by the shaped advantage perspective likely provides a more accurate assessment of its ultimate potential (Renard 2005).

Fair Trade as Decommodification

The third perspective on fair trade is generally not expressed independently of the other two but is put forward, in varying ways, by most of the authors of the previous groups. Whether depicting fair trade as shaped advantage or as alternative globalization, most authors also assert that fair trade is more than a challenge to the social inequalities in global trade, and that its ethical values and educational mission represent a significant challenge to the core values of global capitalism and its imperatives of competition, accumulation, and profit maximization. To some authors, while fair trade's ability to directly challenge the global trading system is limited, its greatest potential lies in its ability to raise awareness among Northern consumers of global inequalities by revealing the conditions under which Southern goods are produced (Fisher 2004; LeClair 2002: 956; Simpson and Rapone 2000: 54; Blowfield 1999: 767; Bird and Hughes 1997: 166).

Others go beyond this and assert that fair trade challenges the very nature of capitalist culture and the atomization, individualism, and anonymity characteristic of market exchanges under capitalism. In this vein, Charles Simpson and Anita Rapone (2005: 55) argue that fair trade challenges 'the cultural impoverishment of capitalism – its erosion of social solidarities and its materialist rather than transcendent motivational structure.' Laura Raynolds asserts that 'fair trade networks socially re-embed commodities, so that items arrive at the point of consumption replete with information regarding social and environmental conditions under which they were produced and traded' (Raynolds 2002a: 415; Jaffee, Kloppenburg, and Monroy 2004: 170). Laure Waridel and Francis Moore Lappé and Anna Lappé, in their respective works, maintain that fair trade frees consumers from the 'mental colonialism' or 'thought traps' that hide the truth behind how goods are produced in a capitalist system (Waridel 2002: 23; Lappé and Lappé 2002: 27–31).

Although most do not directly draw on Marxists concepts in their analysis, these authors are essentially arguing that fair trade challenges the 'fetishism of commodities,' where social relations among people appear as relations among things (Marx 1978: 319–29). As described in the introductory chapter, commodity fetishism is a necessary outcome of the capitalist mode of production, which compels people to engage the market as self-interested individuals, either as atomized consumers or as workers alienated from the commodities they have produced. According to Diane Elson (1988: 16–17), the capitalist market, 'does not encourage me to relate to others as fellow-citizens, members of the same community, who have a multiplicity of goals besides buying products.' Elson, as well as Marxist political economists Ian Hudson and Mark Hudson (2003), directly argue that fair trade represents an initial attempt to challenge the fetishism of commodities. Elson even depicts fair trade labelling, and other similar projects, as key to her vision of a future socialist society based on a 'socialized market' (Elson 2002). From their work, and from the work of the authors above, two essential arguments about how fair trade is purported to challenge the fetishism of commodities can be extracted: (1) Fair trade reveals the social and environmental conditions under which goods are produced, which challenges the commodification of these goods into items with an independent life of their own; (2) Fair trade affirms non-economic values of cooperation and solidarity which challenge the capitalist imperatives of competition, accumulation, and profit-maximization (Fisher 2004; Hudson and Hudson 2003; Waridel 2002: 24–7, 100–13;

Lappé and Lappé 2002: 199–203, 293–6; Elson 2002, 1988; Raynolds 2002a: 415–20; Simpson and Rapone 2000: 47–55).

The extent to which these two assertions are accurate and the fair trade network represents a significant challenge to the commodification of goods is dealt with in greater detail in chapters 5 and 6, which explore fair trade from the perspective of coffee producers in the South and consumers in the North. At this point, some brief comments about these propositions can be made. First, it is argued that fair trade bridges the gap between producer and consumer by revealing the conditions under which goods are produced. Thus, in purchasing fair trade goods, Northern consumers are not merely buying a commodity for sale, but are relating directly with Southern producers through an 'associative' network based on ethical values (Elson 2002). This relationship goes beyond a market exchange and involves political acts of solidarity, such as the 'buycotting' campaigns described earlier (Waridel 2002: 106–109).

While bonds of North/South solidarity promoted by fair trade are indeed positive and represent a challenge to the *principles* of market exchange under global capitalism, this challenge is strictly limited by existing capitalist relations of property and labour. Truly disrupting the fetishism of commodities involves not just making information on how a good is produced available to consumers, but it requires carrying out production in a democratic and consciously regulated process in which *both* producers and consumers are involved and are accountable for the decisions they make. As the authors writing from the shaped advantage perspective remind us, in the fair trade network the role of consumers is entirely voluntary and they are not responsible for the outcomes of their decisions. Thus, market choices that can be a matter of life and death for fair trade producers are merely ethical shopping options for Northern consumers who make their decisions based on a variety of factors, including cost, convenience, image, and level of disposable income. In this sense, fair trade appears to be less about challenging the fetishism of commodities than it is about reinforcing the commodification of our daily lives, as it now becomes possible to *purchase ethics* at the local supermarket.

Second, it is argued that the fair trade network's non-economic values of cooperation and solidarity are a challenge to the capitalist market imperatives of competition, accumulation, and profit-maximization. Indeed there is much evidence to demonstrate how fair trade, like any democratic, cooperative project, challenges the principles of capitalism. A portion of the profits that accrue to fair trade cooperatives are used to construct social infrastructure needed by the community, rather than reinvested for further capital accumulation or distributed to private pockets. Fair trade producers and importers work together to attain the fairest trading relationship possible, and large producer cooperatives at times provide assistance to other, smaller, fair trade cooperatives (Taylor 2002: 7; Simpson and Rapone 2000: 53). These actions can best be interpreted as an incipient international moral economy, which attempts to assert the notion of people's right to live taking precedence over the competitive and ethically impoverished values of capitalism (Simpson and Rapone 2000).

Yet, while fair trade represents a challenge to capitalism's moral economy, capitalism is about much more than a set of ethical values (McNally 2002). Competitive and exploitative behaviour under capitalism is not primarily a result of greed or lack of scruples, as many fair trade analysts, influenced by a neo-Smithian understanding of capitalism, would assert. Rather, this behaviour is a result of the imperatives of the capitalist market which compel all producers to compete, accumulate, and maximize profits in order to remain competitive and survive. While the ethical aspirations of fair trade have been able to somewhat mitigate the worst effects of these imperatives, the fair trade network has not been able to escape the power of the global capitalist market which has imposed strict limits on the network and how it has evolved over time. These imperatives threaten to erode the fair trade network's culture of solidarity and cooperation. For example, the limited size of the fair trade coffee market has in recent years given way to growing competition between fair trade coffee producers seeking to expand their market access (Raynolds 2002b: 11; Taylor 2002: 35–6).

In the final analysis, while fair trade does represent an important symbolic challenge to the principles of market exchanges under capitalism, the extent to which the network is capable of truly confronting the commodification of goods is limited by its market-based approach. While fair trade goods do formally reveal the social and environmental conditions under which goods are produced, consumers in the North remain alienated individuals who are disconnected from producers and are unaccountable for their market decisions. Moreover, while fair trade does affirm non-economic values of cooperation and solidarity, in the end the capitalist imperatives of competition, accumulation, and profit-maximization are not a matter of choice, but are a necessity for all economic enterprises that wish to survive under global capitalism. As is the case with the alternative globalization perspective, the decommodification perspective offers a vision of the fair trade network that appears to go beyond the network's actual impact and potential.

Conclusion: The Fair Trade Network and Neoliberalism

The above comparison of different views of the fair trade network and its potential to initiate both micro- and macro-level reforms raises several important considerations for assessing the network's developmental achievements and long-term prospects. Authors writing from the shaped advantage perspective have correctly pointed out the manner in which fair traders aspire to mitigate the negative impact of neoliberalism within the constraints of the existing international order, but they have failed to address the aspirations of fair traders to go beyond this and radically reform the international trading system. Authors writing from the alternative globalization perspective have more accurately captured the political aims of fair traders to challenge neoliberalism, but have failed to account for the extent to which the network's success has in fact been due to its compatibility with neoliberal reforms. Along a different line of thinking, the decommodification perspective has captured how the network can provide a symbolic challenge to the commodification of goods, while neglecting the extent to which the network remains ultimately confined by the imperatives of capitalism which have limited and threaten to erode its cooperative values. In the end, what these different views reveal is a growing disparity between the transformative goals that fair traders *aspire to accomplish* and what the network seems *ultimately capable of attaining* – the latter of which is more accurately captured by the limited vision of the shaped advantaged perspective (Renard 2005).

The extent to which the above statement is true is the focus of the remainder of this book, which moves from an analysis of fair trade generally to a specific assessment of fair trade coffee at global and local levels. Three key issues are raised by the discussion above which are central to the analysis that follows. First, shaping advantage for small producers and workers at the local level is a key consideration when assessing the impact of the fair trade network. Nonetheless, the assessment cannot stop there, as tends to be the case among authors in the shaped advantage group. Equal attention must be paid to the ability of fair traders to attain their broader, transformative political goals: an alternative model to neoliberal globalization. Second, the fair trade network's ability to contribute to a broader movement against neoliberalism cannot just be assumed, as tends to be the case among the alternative globalization group, but must be carefully and soberly assessed. There is, in fact, a powerful contradiction between the fair trade network's compatibility with neoliberal reforms and the belief that the network is a fundamental challenge to neoliberalism. This contradiction does not mean that the fair trade network does not have the potential to be part of a broader challenge to the current international order. It does mean, however, that the ability of the fair trade network to either confront or concede to neoliberalism is contingent and based on a variety of considerations, including the political decisions of fair traders as well as the impact of pressures asserted on the network by its new corporate and institutional partners and by the imperatives of the capitalist market in general. Finally, an assessment of the developmental potential of the fair trade network must not just focus on micro and macro political and economic impacts, but, as pointed out by the decommodification perspective, it must also address the network's potential to challenge capitalist culture and the commodification and alienation characteristic of market exchanges under global capitalism.

The assessment of fair trade coffee provided in the following chapters reveals that the network has been more successful at shaping advantage for specific groups to enter the international market on relatively better terms than it has been at providing a radical challenge to neoliberalism and conventional trade in general. This is because the very success of the fair trade network's market-driven social justice project has been due to its compatibility with the pro-market policies of neoliberal reformers, which has severely limited fair traders' ability to challenge these policies without losing the institutional and corporate support that their success has been based on. The result has been increasing devotion within the network to the principles of 'free trade' and a growing dependence on neoliberal institutions and giant, profit-driven TNCs. Yet these same institutions and TNCs promote macroeconomic policies that run contrary to the needs of poor farmers and workers and pose the greatest threat to the moral mission and marketing success of the fair trade network in the long term. This raises questions about the future of the network and its voluntarist, market-driven project and its potential to continue to survive and thrive without the sort of macro-economic, state-led reforms that were central to the vision of the fair trade network and the other projects of the fair trade movement prior to the 1980s.

3 Coffee and the Capitalist Market

On seeing the immense quantity of Javanese products auctioned in the Nether-lands, one must be convinced of the effectiveness of [Dutch colonial] policy, even though one cannot consider it noble. For, if anyone should ask whether the man who grows the products receives a reward proportionate to the yields, the answer must be in the negative. The Government compels him to grow on *his* land what pleases *it*; and *it* fixes the price it pays him. The cost of transport to Europe, via a privileged trading company, is high. The money given to the Chiefs to encourage them swells the purchase price further, and ... since, after all, the entire business *must* yield a profit, this profit can be made in no other way than by paying the Javanese just *enough* to keep him from starving, which would decrease the producing power of the nation.

Multatuli, *Max Havelaar*[1]

During the past year Oxfam has been monitoring the impact of falling coffee prices on communities across Africa and Latin America, talking to those most affected by the crisis. The picture that emerges is uniformly bleak ... While the coffee economy generates bumper profits for Nestlé and Starbucks, it is also intensifying poverty and fuelling social dislocation in the world's poorest countries.

Oxfam International (2001)

As the previous chapters demonstrate, the historical evolution of the fair trade network has been greatly influenced by fair traders' under-standing of the capitalist world system, which has been derived from neo-Smithian political economy. The vast majority of fair traders and fair trade analysts have tended to ignore the specific structural imperatives that drive exploitation in a capitalist system. From their perspective, whether or not exploitation occurs through the market is largely dependent on the unethical or excessively *capitalist attitude* of 'greedy' or 'unscrupulous' market agents (Ransom 2001: 4–26; FLO 2001: 2; Sick 1999: 91–2). Yet, the structural imperatives of capitalism – not unethical attitudes – are the primary dynamic behind exploitation in the coffee industry (McNally 1993: 3, 30–1). This is not to say that ethical values, good or bad, do not play an important role in allowing or preventing gross social injustices. But, values within a given society do not exist as independent casual factors. They have emerged in response to, and are limited by, a set of concrete social and historical circumstances. Along these lines, Barrington Moore Jr. (1966: 487) argues that 'to take values as the starting point of sociological explanation makes it very difficult to understand the obvious fact that values change in response to circumstances. The perversion of democratic notions in the American South is an all too familiar example, incomprehensible without cotton and slavery.'

In the final analysis, the extent to which ethical values can impact on the decisions of wealthy capitalists, large and small farmers, rural and urban workers, and consumers, is limited by the *necessity* under capitalism to exchange goods and labour power on the market, and to do so as competitively as possible (Wood 1999; Brenner 1985). It is this necessity which has been the primary dynamic behind both the unprecedented pace of modern economic growth and the preponderance of widespread global inequality and exploitation. Consequently, the developmental potential of the fair trade network must be assessed within the context of these historically grounded structural imperatives, which ultimately set the broad political and economic parameters for the networks' prospects and limitations.

With this in mind, the following chapters shift the analysis from a general examination of a fair trade and the international political economy, to an historically grounded assessment of fair trade coffee and the political economy of the coffee industry.

This chapter initiates this shift with a short history of the political economy of the coffee industry, which is essential to analysing fair trade due to coffee's importance in both international commodity markets and the fair trade network. Coffee is the second most valuable legally exported commodity of the South, after oil, and it provides a livelihood for around 25 million coffee-producing families worldwide.[2] Nearly 70 per cent of the world's coffee comes from farms of less than ten hectares, and of this the vast majority are small family plots of between one and five hectares. On average, a coffee farmer receives around $0.14 per kilogram for unprocessed, green coffee beans, which are then transported, processed, and sold by importer/roasters on markets in the North for upwards of $26.40 per kilogram, representing a price inflation of more than 7000 per cent (Oxfam International 2002a: 7, 22–4).

Due to these gross inequalities, fair trade coffee has become the flagship of the fair trade network and is the largest and historically the fastest-expanding fair trade sector. During the network's period of rapid expansion in the 1990s, fair trade coffee imports certified by the Fairtrade Labelling Organizations International (FLO) rose from 4,500 tons in 1991 to 12,818 tons in 2000, an increase of over 280 per cent (Raynolds 2002b: 27; Renard 1999: 498). Currently, of the 800,000 producer families on the FLO register, 550,000 of them, almost 69 per cent, are coffee-producing families (Zonneveld 2003; Raynolds 2002b: 8).

The analysis that follows provides a historical basis for an assessment of fair trade coffee at the global and local level. Particular attention is paid to three sub-themes: (1) the tendency towards monopoly among coffee transnational corporations (TNCs) in the North; (2) the extended cycles of boom and bust which pervades the coffee industry; and (3) the role of class, ethno-racist, and gender exploitation within the industry. I argue that the unpredictability, inequality, and exploitation pervasive in the coffee sector are primarily driven not by ethical values but by deeply rooted historical and structural dimensions. Any attempt to combat exploitation and promote human development within the coffee industry – several examples of which, including fair trade coffee, are explored in the following chapter – must ultimately seek to address and challenge these roots if they are to attain broad and long-term developmental outcomes.

A Short History of Coffee and Capitalism

Coffee emerged as a significant world trade commodity alongside the development of the world system that first took root in the late fifteenth and early sixteenth centuries on the heels of European colonial expansion. Many foundational thinkers in underdevelopment and dependency theory (UDT) have depicted the historical emergence of the world system as being from the beginning a distinctly *capitalist* world system.[3] Due to their neo-Smithian, trade-based depiction of capitalism, they have asserted that capitalism began with the emergence of an international trading system in which surplus wealth was transferred unequally from the South to the North. In fact, at the time of European expansion, the dominant modes of production – how a society mobilizes social labour – throughout the world were not capitalist, but were tributary and kinship modes. The major agricultural areas were dominated by tributary states which extracted surplus from primary producers by direct political or military rule. More peripheral areas tended to be dominated by kin-ordered modes wherein labour was organized on the basis of appeals of filiations, marriage, and other forms of symbolic affinity. The expansion of tributary states gave birth to the modern world system, which was then significantly altered by the outward expansion of industrial capitalism in the nineteenth century (Wolf 1997).[4]

A crisis in western Europe's dominant tributary mode, feudalism, was the spark that ignited European expansion. This crisis emerged as a result of the limited productive capability of feudal agriculture, which led to growing scarcity and epidemics, combined with the actions of competitive, expanding feudal states which sought to extract more surplus from the peasantry to pay for their wars. The result was a rising tide of peasant resistance and rebellion. Eventually, the feudal elite sought to solve the crisis by moving beyond European frontiers and seizing new resources – agricultural land, gold, silver, and slaves – to meet their expansionist needs. In the process, highly concentrated mercantile states, based on political coalitions between political elites and the merchant classes, were formed, which would come to dominate the evolving world system (Wolf 1997: 73–109).

Prior to the emergence of a world system, coffee was generally a minor crop traded by Arab merchants for use as medicine or for ceremonies for the wealthy. The exception to this was in Abyssinia, now Ethiopia, the birthplace of coffee, where coffee was cultivated for hundreds of years for a variety of purposes and was integral to Abyssinian culture. It was not until the fifteenth century, when coffee houses began to spring up throughout the Islamic world – Persia, Egypt, Turkey, and North Africa – that coffee gained some notoriety as a popular commodity. Due to Islamic law, which prohibited the use of alcohol, coffee gained a reputation as a desirable stimulant among merchants and intellectuals, and its popularity continued to grow into the sixteenth century despite attempts by various Islamic rulers, who saw coffee houses as places of sedition, to stifle its use (Pendergrast 1999: 3–13; Dicum and Luttinger 1999: 6; Topik 1998: 38–41).

It was not until after the 1650s that coffee gained some popularity in markets in western Europe. This was a result of the efforts of Dutch mercantilist traders, who dominated world trade in the seventeenth century. Dutch traders first began growing coffee in the Dutch colony of Ceylon in 1658. In 1699, they expanded their efforts to the colony of Java, followed by Sumatra, Celebes, Timor, Bali, and other islands of the East Indies. To find labour to produce the coffee beans, the Dutch brutally enslaved the native populations of their conquered territories. Coffee became increasingly more available and more affordable on European markets. It ceased to be used exclusively as an exotic medicine, although it remained a luxury good beyond the reach of the vast majority. Coffee houses sprung up throughout Italy, Britain, France, Holland, and Scandinavia, and coffee became a desired drink for the emerging middle classes of merchants, intellectuals, army officers, lawyers, actors, clergy, and musicians (Pendergrast 1999: 3–13; Dicum and Luttinger 1999: 9–10, 27; Topik 1998: 41).

Throughout the eighteenth century, the growing demand for coffee and other commodities boosted the Atlantic slave trade, which had been initiated by the Portuguese in the fifteenth and sixteenth centuries primarily to provide highly exploitable labourers for the production of sugar in the Caribbean. From 1701 to 1810, the colonial powers of Europe forcibly exported over six million slaves from Africa, over three and a half times the number exported during the previous two and a half centuries. England was the leading slave trader during the eighteenth century, transporting over two million slaves (Wolf 1997: 195–201; Mintz 1985: 19–74). The substantial profits that accrued to English merchant and banking interests as a result of this highly exploitative trade led Eric Williams, in his book *Capitalism and Slavery* (1964), to argue that the slave trade had provided the capital that gave birth to industrial capitalism. Although the Atlantic trade certainly provided a 'principal dynamic element' for English industrialization in the form of colonial markets and cheap raw materials, this assertion neglects the important role played by English and European markets and overestimates the role played by American and African capital (Wolf 1997: 199–200).

Of greater importance, however, is that the extraction of surplus wealth from Latin America and Africa could not in and of itself spark industrialization in England, any more than it did in other colonial empires. Imperial Spain, for example, despite more than three hundred years of direct colonial domination in Latin America, was still a feudal society (Weeks 1985: 11–12). To ignite industrialization, what was required was a fundamental transformation in the relations of production, from a feudal mode of production to a capitalist one. Under feudalism, the elite extracted surplus wealth from the peasantry and conquered territories through direct political coercion, requiring massive expenditure in state building and war. This reduced the amount of wealth invested in consumption and production, which led over time to a fundamental lack of productivity and crisis. Under capitalism, competitive pressures push market agents towards increasing labour productivity, technological innovation, and a more efficient investment of surplus wealth, resulting in a pattern of modern economic growth (Brenner 1985). This distinction is key to understanding why England employed surplus wealth to initiate industrialization. Otherwise, argues historian Robert Brenner (1977: 67), 'we are left to wonder why any wealth transferred from the core to the periphery did not result merely in the creation of cathedrals in the core and starvation in the periphery.'

The unique conditions for the transformation from a feudal to a capitalist mode of production first took root in England in the sixteenth century, when a new system of land tenure emerged that allowed for peasants, who were formerly tied to the land, to be disposed if they failed to meet their new rent payments. This sparked new competitive pressures as tenant farmers, who had previously focused the majority of their efforts on subsistence farming, sought to sell their goods on the market to gain currency to make their rent payments and survive. In the long term, land became increasingly concentrated in the hands of the most efficient farmers and the number of dispossessed peasants increased to unprecedented levels, and many flocked to the cities in search of work. Forced to sell their labour power in order to survive, the dispossessed masses became the new industrial working class for the capitalist revolution under way in England by the eighteenth century. Thus, contra the neo-Smithian understanding of capitalism upheld by many fair traders, competitive market behaviour did not emerge primarily as a result of a new set of *values*, or as the outcome of peasants seeking new market *opportunities*. Rather, changing political economic realities forced peasants to act in an increasingly competitive, accumulative, and profit-maximizing way in order to survive. This occurred in response to structural *imperatives*, imperatives which continue to drive the highly competitive capitalist world system today (Wood 1999).

In the realm of consumption, the new industrial working class became the basis for a new mass consumer market in cheap everyday goods, such as textiles and food. Among these goods, coffee was particularly well suited for the new factory setting and became part of the daily meal for much of the working classes. Under the new factory system, men, women, and children were employed outside the home for long hours and had little time to prepare and eat meals. Coffee could be prepared quickly, would not spoil easily, provided calories (at the time many thought nutrients), and could serve as a replacement for alcohol, something welcomed by capitalists concerned about a sober, controllable labour force. As a result, coffee consumption in Europe grew tenfold from 1739 to 1789 (Pendergrast 1999: 16–17; Topik 1998: 41–2; Mintz 1985: 74–150).

The development of industrial capitalism in England would eventually compel other countries, starting in Europe and North America, to pursue economic development in a capitalist direction as they sought to keep up with England's new competitive advantage (Wood 1999: 102). However, the process through which capitalism expanded in the eighteenth and nineteenth centuries was complex, as the capitalist mode interacted with and penetrated other modes of production in a variety of ways which were neither immediate nor total. As described by anthropologist Eric Wolf (1997: 296–7), 'the outcome of this process was a complex hierarchical system controlled by the capitalist mode of production, but including a vast array of subsidiary regions that exhibited different combinations of the capitalist mode with other modes.'

The emergence of a growing mass consumer market for coffee in England had the effect of giving further impetus to the African slave trade in Europe's colonial holdings in the South. In the eighteenth century, the coffee industry was dominated by the French, who, beginning in 1730, imported approximately 30,000 African slaves each year to accommodate the needs of the rapidly expanding sugar and coffee plantations in French colonial holdings. The French colony of Saint Domingue, today Haiti, was at the heart of the coffee expansion, and by 1771 it supplied half the world's coffee and had nearly 500,000 slaves (Dicum and Luttinger 1999: 30). French domination in coffee production was brought to an abrupt end in 1791 by a massive slave revolt that, after years of intense warfare, ended with the abolition of slavery and the proclamation of an independent Haiti under black leadership in 1804. Haitian slaves had brought about the first modern war for national liberation, but the costs of resistance were great. The necessity of waging war, of destroying the colonial socio-economic structure, and of the severing of ties with colonial markets, ruined the island's export-dependent economy and set it on the road of long-term decline (Topik 1998: 42; Knight 1990: 193–221).

Despite the setbacks experienced by imperial France, the nineteenth century was the century of coffee as production continued to expand. Coffee became a key export crop in Brazil, Central America, and Venezuela, along with much of India and Ceylon. Brazil, which gained independence from Portugal in 1822, was the leader of this expansion. The sugar plantations (*fazendas*) which developed in colonial Brazil in the seventeenth and eighteenth centuries had left the country with a pattern of huge plantations and masses of highly exploited African slaves. The slaves worked in appalling conditions and lived an average of seven years after being imported as it was considered cheaper to buy new slaves than to maintain the health of existing ones. With sugar prices on the decline, Brazilian slave-owning planters turned their energy towards the production of coffee beans in the Paraiba valley. As coffee production increased, so did the import of slaves, and from 1800 to 1850 Brazil imported African slaves at a historically unprecedented rate. By the end of the 1820s, there were over one million slaves in Brazil, representing one-third of the total population. This number had risen to over two million by 1850, the year in which Brazil, under pressure from the British, who had abolished the slave trade in 1808, was compelled to ban the import of slaves (Pendergrast 1999: 19–25; Topik 1998: 42–3). By this time, Brazil produced nearly half of the world's 294,000–ton coffee supply (Dicum and Luttinger 1999: 31).

With Brazil at the head, coffee production in Latin America grew fifteen-fold during the nineteenth century (Topik 1998: 42). This massive growth not only occurred in response to consumer demand in Europe, but actually helped increase demand by producing quantities of coffee large enough to drive prices down and boost the market for coffee among the working classes in the North (62). The production boom originally caused a glut on coffee markets so that prices dropped to eleven cents per pound in 1825 from a previous high of twenty-one cents per pound. For the next thirty years, coffee prices remained low at around ten cents per pound, as Brazil, Java, and Ceylon picked up the pace of production and Central America entered the game. Workers in the North, especially in the United States, responded to these lower prices. Per capita consumption of coffee in the United States increased from three pounds per year in 1830, to five and a half pounds in 1850, and eight pounds by 1859 (Pendergrast 1999: 46–47).

The cultivation and primary processing methods Brazilian planters adopted in the nineteenth century are still dominant in much of the coffee sector in that country today. The cultivation process involves 'full sun' growing, which entails removing all forest cover through clear-cutting and then planting coffee trees in rows up and down hills. This method generally encourages soil erosion, and it results in the depletion of soil nutrients, due to the rapid growth of sun-exposed trees, which leads to a reliance on artificial fertilizer. The result is a pattern where Brazilian planters have continually exhausted existing lands and then abandoned them to clear new areas in the country's tropical rainforests, which do not regenerate like northern arboreal forests.

The dominant type of coffee bean grown in Brazil is *arabica*, which until the end of the nineteenth century was the only coffee bean produced for export. Arabica coffee grows best on land located between 3,000 and 6,500 feet above sea level in areas that are frost-free and have a mean average temperature of between 17 and 25 degrees Celsius (Talbot 2004: 31). In Brazil, 95 per cent of the country is located below 3,000 feet, so that Brazilian beans have generally been considered low-quality, lacking 'acidity' and 'body,' and the country suffers from periodic frosts, which has ruined annual harvests on many occasions. In addition, arabica beans are highly susceptible to a variety of diseases, fungi, bacteria, and pests because their trees historically have come from a limited genetic stock. The two greatest threats to arabica trees are 'coffee leaf rust' (a fungi) and the 'coffee berry borer worm' or '*la broca*' (a pest), both of which at times have put an entire region's coffee industry in jeopardy (44–45).

The primary processing technique adopted in Brazil and still in use today is the 'dry method.' In this method, ripe and unripe coffee cherries are stripped from branches, spread onto huge patios, and turned several times a day. The husks shrivel, get hard and black, and are then removed by pounding them. Originally, the beans were left in the remaining 'parchment' (or skin) for export, but by the end of the nineteenth century it was possible to use machines to pound off the parchment, size the remaining 'green beans,' and polish them before export. This is advantageous as green beans are lighter and significantly less bulky than parchment beans, and therefore easier and cheaper to transport. The dry method is generally considered to produce poor-quality coffee, as both ripe and unripe beans are harvested together and the beans can get mouldy and absorb earthy flavours while lying on the patios. Today, about 40 per cent of the world's arabica beans are

'Brazilian arabicas' that are processed through the dry method and generally come from Brazil, Paraguay, and Ethiopia (Talbot 2004: 31–4; Pendergrast 1999: 25–7; Topik 1998: 62).

As a result of the full-sun cultivation method, by the middle of the nineteenth century most of the natural resources in the coffee lands of Brazil's Paraiba valley had been exhausted and planters were forced to move to the southern and western regions of the state of São Paulo to begin anew. In the 1860s and 1870s global coffee prices boomed and so did the development of monoculture coffee plantations. Rail lines connecting the coffee regions to the main ports at Santos and Rio de Janeiro were constructed, and the amount of track grew from 800 miles in 1874 to 6,000 miles in 1889. In 1871, the 'law of free womb,' making the children of all slaves in Brazil legally free, was passed and planters turned towards debt peonage to meet their labour needs. Under the peonage system, European immigrants were given paid passage to Brazil and a piece of land, but they had to work off the cost of transportation and other advances under conditions of near-slavery until all debts were paid. From 1884 to 1914 more than one million immigrants, mostly Italians, came to Brazil under these harsh conditions. In 1890 Brazil produced 5.5 million 132–pound bags (the industry standard), which nearly tripled to 16.3 million bags in 1901 (Pendergrast 1999: 29).

Through the development of coffee production, Brazil became increasingly integrated into the capitalist global economy. The key aspect of this was not the conditions under which coffee was produced, which involved pre-capitalist forms of slavery and debt peonage, but the growing dependence on the production of goods for sale on the market. Previous forms of agricultural production, which involved largely self-sufficient economic units, large or small, were replaced by monoculture plantations that relied on the imperatives of the international capitalist market.

A similar situation developed in other emerging coffee regions where distinctly pre-capitalist social relations were employed in laying the groundwork for the development of a capitalist mode of production and its integration into the global capitalist economy. In Central America, which emerged as a key coffee-producing region by the end of the nineteenth century, while wage labour did develop in certain regions, indigenous populations frequently were forced into slavery, debt peonage, or onerous tenant relations, and communal Indian lands, as well as Church property, were confiscated to make way for large-scale, agro-export production. In Guatemala, El Salvador, Nicaragua, and also Chiapas in the south of Mexico, many pre-Columbian indigenous groups were self-sufficient and had to be forced to work for the local elite (Topik 1998: 66–7; Paige 1997: 70; Samper 1994: 17–24, 58–92; North 1985: 17–28; Weeks 1985: 13–17). In Guatemala, for example, under the leadership of liberal dictator Justo Rufino Barrios (1873–85), all of the land not planted in coffee, sugar, cocoa, or pas-   ture – mostly indigenous land – was declared '*tierras baldías*' (idle land) and confiscated by the state. As the self-sufficient indigenous Mayan peasants refused to work on the new plantations, Barrios revived the colonial-era forced-labour system and compelled them to do so under the barrel of a gun (McCreery 2003: 193–5; Weeks 1985: 13–17; Handy 1984: 65–9).

While forced labour was revived by the growth of the coffee economy in Latin America, outside of Brazil smallholder cultivation also emerged as a major source of coffee production. The existence of widespread communities with claims to the land prior to the coffee boom gave way to a mixture of smallholder farms and large-scale plantations, with the former often providing a major source of forced or 'semi-proletarian' labour for the latter (Samper 1994: 60–71).[5] In Costa Rica, small and medium-sized coffee farms emerged as the dominant form of coffee production, although land concentration was still highly unequal – 71 per cent of the peasantry was landless by 1883 (Topik 1998: 64). The relative unavailability of large stretches of land, and the relative lack of capital and cheap labour (the indigenous population had been largely wiped out by the second half of the nineteenth century) combined with terrain and transportation difficulties, made smallholder producers more efficient as they used family labour and provided for their own subsistence needs. Costa Rica's elite found it more profitable to dominate the processing and marketing of coffee. A similar situation also existed in the coffee regions of Colombia, where the relative lack of land, labour, and capital gave way to coffee production being dominated by smallholders, tenant farmers, and sharecroppers (Topik 1998: 61–7; Weeks 1985: 111–22).

The methods adopted to cultivate and process arabica coffee beans in Central America and Colombia differed significantly from those employed in Brazil. In these regions, beans have traditionally been 'shade-grown' under the protection of the existing forest canopy with the branches trimmed to allow in sunlight. This method protects the soil from nutrition loss and erosion. Today, the shade-grown method remains the choice of many small farmers throughout Central America and southern Mexico who cannot afford the costly chemical-intensive full-sun method, although many of the more highly developed coffee countries, such as Costa Rica and Colombia, have adopted full-sun cultivation on a massive scale (Pendergrast 1999: 36–7; Rice 1998; Samper 1994: 72–8).

Lacking the social infrastructure and economies of scale to compete with large, well-established Brazilian planters in terms of mass production, farmers in Central America and Colombia eked out their competitive advantage on the basis of quality. While the cultivation method (full-sun or shade-grown) has a significant impact on the social and ecological effects of coffee production for growers and their communities, it is the chosen processing method that has the greatest impact on the quality of the coffee bean. In Central America and Colombia, the 'wet' processing method was developed, which is generally considered to produce a bean of superior taste. Beans are hand-picked and then 'depulped' by machines, which are typically either hand-cranked or gas-powered. The beans are then left in water fermentation tanks for up to forty-eight hours. In the tanks, the parchment decomposes and loosens, after which it is washed off. (Often it has been carelessly allowed to float downstream, causing massive pollution problems for nearby communities.)[6] The green beans are then spread out to dry in the sun or placed in huge rotating cylinders heated by fuel. Finally, the dried beans are sorted, and broken, black, mouldy, or over-fermented beans are removed. It is the labour-intensive nature of this method that results in the production of a higher-quality bean (Talbot 2004: 46–7; Topik 1998: 66; Samper 1994: 78–83). Today, two major types of arabica beans are generally processed by the wet method: 'Colombian milds,' which represent around 25 per cent of the world's arabicas and are produced in Colombia, Kenya, and Tanzania; and 'other milds,' which represent about 35 per cent of the world's arabicas and are produced in Central America, Mexico, and various other regions of Latin America, Africa, and Asia (Talbot 2004: 33–4).

By the end of the nineteenth century, Central America had emerged as a major coffee-producing region, along with Java, Sumatra, Ceylon, and Venezuela (Colombia did not become a major coffee-producing state until the twentieth century), but none of them could match Brazil. In 1876, Brazil accounted for nearly three-quarters of all coffee consumed in the United States, which had emerged as the world's leading coffee-consuming country and was importing 340 million pounds of coffee annually. At this time, the United States consumed close to one-third of all of the world's coffee exports, which rose to nearly half by the turn of the century (Pendergrast 1999: 44, 62). The international market for coffee was highly profitable for large importer/roasters in the North and wealthy landowners in the South, but could frequently be highly volatile and exploitative for small-scale farmers and rural plantation workers. Two central characteristics of the international coffee industry had become firmly entrenched by the end of nineteenth century and are essential to understanding the profitable, volatile, and exploitative nature of coffee production on a global scale: (1) the tendency towards monopoly among coffee corporations in the North; and (2) the extended cycles of boom and bust which pervade the coffee industry.

The Tendency Towards Monopoly in the North

Monopoly control over markets in the North is a dominant trend in the history of the coffee industry. During the colonial period, the coffee trade was dominated by large mercantilist companies which were granted official trade monopolies by their imperialist home states in Europe. In the nineteenth century, when most of the colonies in the Americas gained their independence, these mercantilist arrangements were broken up. Much of the impetus for these changes came from industrial capitalists in England who, having attained the competitive advantage of becoming the 'workshop of the world,' now sought to force weaker powers to dissolve their trade barriers and allow the British access to their markets and natural resources (Stavrianos 1981: 169–76).

The mercantilist companies were replaced by private corporations. Rather than eliminating monopoly, however, these corporations soon developed unofficial monopoly control over Northern markets. The reasons for this lay in the imperatives of the international capitalist market, which compelled corporations to seek larger shares of the market and buy up smaller competitors. In this way, corporations sought protection from the volatility and competitive pressures of the market through the use of greater economies of scale, price-fixing, and absorbing the competition. Far from a distortion of market principles, the historical tendency towards monopoly under capitalism stems from market imperatives, a fact recognized by Adam Smith himself, who believed that 'to widen the market and to *narrow the competition*, is always the interest of the dealer' (cited in McNally 1993: 56; emphasis added).

The tendency towards monopoly was already apparent in the coffee industry in the United States in the 1870s. At this time, three private firms – B.G. Arnold, Bowie Dash & Co., and O.G. Kimball & Co. – had formed a syndicate known as the 'Trinity,' which dominated coffee imports into the country. For years the syndicate managed to hold the price of Java coffee beans artificially high by purchasing them in vast quantities and holding them off the market. In 1878, Brazilian beans flooded the American market, and the syndicate began purchasing Brazilian beans to hold them off the market in a similar manner. This time, however, the cost of controlling the market proved to be too high, and in 1880 O.G. Kimball & Co. declared bankruptcy with over $2 million in debt, and Bowie Dash & Co. suspended business with liabilities of $1.4 million. Roasters and exporters had grown so dependent on these three giants that their downfall echoed throughout the industry, resulting in an estimated loss of $7 million for the industry in 1880 (Pendergrast 1999: 64–5).

In the wake of the collapse of the Trinity, the New York Coffee Exchange was incorporated in 1881. Many believed that the exchange would discourage disastrous attempts to corner the market by providing some risk assurance against volatile price swings. On the exchange, a buyer would contract with a seller to purchase a certain amount of coffee at a certain time in the future at a guaranteed price. The exchange would arbitrate disputes and police trade abuses. It was argued that 'real coffee men' would use the contracts as *hedges* against price changes, while speculators would provide *liquidity*. At first, the exchange was slow to be used, but things picked up at the turn of the century when new technologies significantly improved international communication. However, rather than providing a degree of price stability, the exchange merely escalated the instability of the coffee market as speculators sought to profit by predicting or manipulating prices on the exchange (Pendergrast 1999: 66–7).

As the coffee industry developed over the twentieth century, control over the import, processing, and distribution of coffee was concentrated in fewer and fewer hands. Giant trading companies in North America and Europe, which typically traded in a variety of commodities of which coffee was only one, came to dominate the importing, shipping, financing, and often the exporting of coffee beans from key ports. These companies monopolized the international trade of pre-roasted green beans and sold them on the coffee exchanges in New York and London. In Northern markets, the roasting and distribution of coffee became dominated by giant food processing corporations (Talbot 2002). Smaller corporations purchased their green beans from brokers on the coffee exchanges. Large-scale Northern roaster/distributors, in contrast, generally acquired their own brokers and imported their own beans directly, with transnational trading companies hired only to transport the beans. Through their massive buying and selling power, these giant roaster/distributors exercised enormous influence over the coffee exchanges (Waridel 2002: 51–3).

The historical development of the major coffee roaster/distributors in the United States in the twentieth century serves to exemplify the tendency towards monopoly in the coffee industry. In 1915, there were over 3,500 roasters in the United States (Pendergrast 1999: 229). The largest ones were Arbuckle Brothers, Chase & Sanborn, J.A. Folger & Co., Hills Brothers, MJB, Maxwell House, A&P (which owned the coffee brand Eight O'Clock), and the Jewel Tea Company. As these corporations grew in the 1920s and 1930s, competition between them for market shares heated up and they adopted increasingly expensive national advertising strategies or cost-cutting measures to enhance their competitiveness. Such competitive pressures sparked a series of mergers, bankruptcies, and acquisitions. During this period, the Postum Cereal Company (renamed General Foods in 1929) purchased the Cheek-Neal Company (owner of Maxwell House) and Arbuckle Brothers, as well as the rights to market Sanka and Kaffee-Hag, which gave it sole possession of the decaffeinated coffee market. In 1929, Fleischmann Company bought the Royal Baking Powder Company (owner of Chase & Sanborn) and was reincorporated as Standard Brands (Talbot 2004: 51–3; Pendergrast 1999: 124–209).

By 1945, the number of roasters in the United States had dropped to only 1,500, and of them only 4 per cent were roasting over 50,000 bags per year. Smaller companies could not compete with the massive advertising dollars of the major roasters – in 1949, General Foods spent a previously unheard of $2.5 million advertising Maxwell House. In the 1940s, Nestlé, a long-established Swiss firm, entered the coffee market in the United States with its own brand of instant coffee, Nescafé, which emerged to become General Foods' number one competitor in instant coffee sales (Pendergrast 1999: 229–45). The development of new processing techniques, such as those involved in instant coffee, as well as new mechanization and packaging strategies gave a further advantage to the large roasters who had the economies of scale necessary to afford the new technologies. By the late 1950s, the number of roasters had declined to 850, and the five biggest roasters – General Foods, Standard Brands, Folger's, Hills Brothers, and A&P – accounted for well over 40 per cent of the coffee market in the United States (Talbot 2004: 51–3; Pendergrast 1999: 261–2).

In the 1960s and 1970s, the mergers and bankruptcies continued. In 1963, the massive consumer food conglomerate Procter & Gamble bought Folgers for $126 million. In 1964, Coca-Cola (a long-time rival of coffee) merged with Duncan Foods and acquired a handful of smaller roasters to become the fifth largest coffee roaster in the United States. By 1965, there remained only 240 roasters in the United States, and of them the top 8 accounted for 75 per cent of all coffee sales. Many of the new mergers involved increasingly transnational operations as North American and European corporations sought to expand their reach into foreign markets. Throughout the 1960s and 1970s, General Foods purchased roasters in France, Germany, Sweden, Spain, and Mexico, and set up joint operations in Japan. In 1978, Sara Lee purchased the Dutch corporation Douwe Egberts, one of the largest roasters in Europe, to make an aggressive entrance into the global coffee industry (Pendergrast 1999: 282–4). By the end of the 1970s, states John Talbot (2004: 52), 'any new coffee manufacturer who wanted to break into one of the major consuming markets would need deep pockets, and a national strategy to challenge the dominant companies.'

These patterns have persisted until the present day as major coffee roasters have become increasingly transnational, and competition between them has moved from the national to the international level. During the 1980s, Nestlé made a bold move to increase its market share in North America, buying up Hills Brothers, Chase & Sanborn, MJB, Stark's Gourmet Coffee, and Goodhost, a major Canadian roaster. In 1985, the giant tobacco company, Philip Morris, seeking to diversify into the agro-food industry, bought General Foods for $5.8 billion. This was followed by Philip Morris's purchase of Kraft Foods in 1988 (which was later merged with General Foods) and then Jacobs Suchard, the dominant European coffee-chocolate conglomerate, in 1990 for $3.8 billion. Not to be outdone, in 1999 Sara Lee bought Chock Full o' Nuts, the fourth largest coffee company in the United States, as well as Hills Brothers, Chase & Sanborn, and MJB, from Nestlé (Talbot 2004: 103–4; Pendergrast 1999: 345–66; Dicum and Luttinger 1999: 126–7).

At the start of the new millennium, just a handful of roasters dominated the global coffee industry, with the four largest – Kraft General Foods, Nestlé, Sara Lee, and Procter & Gamble – each having coffee brands worth $1 billion or more in annual sales. At the end of 2002, the five largest roasters were responsible for purchasing nearly half of the world's supply of green coffee beans, with Kraft General Foods buying just over 13 per cent of the total, followed by Nestlé (13 per cent), Sara Lee (10 per cent), Procter & Gamble (4 per cent), and Tchibo (4 per cent), which sells coffee mainly in Germany. These giant TNCs have major advantages over smaller competitors due to their 'brand power,' which stems from massive multimillion-dollar advertising campaigns (it is estimated that major roasters spent a total of $65 million in 1999 advertising instant coffee in the United Kingdom alone); access to new technologies and innovations; and large purchasing power and economies of scale which allow them to manipulate prices and minimize market risks (Oxfam International 2002a: 2, 25–8). Similar monopoly trends have also developed in the importing and shipping of green beans. In the early 1990s, just five large coffee importers – Neumann Gruppe, Volcafe, ED&F Man, ECOM Agroindustrial, and Goldman Sachs – controlled over 40 per cent of total world coffee imports (Talbot 2004: 105–17). Through their immense size, these TNCs seek to stave off competition and protect themselves from the extreme swings of the highly volatile international coffee market.

The Extended Cycles of Boom and Bust in the Coffee Market

The international coffee market has historically been highly volatile and subject to repetitive cycles of boom and bust caused by discrepancies between supply and demand. In general, neo-Smithian economists have tended to view these discrepancies, which often result in crises for producers and workers, as distortions of the market, which is assumed to move towards equilibrium if left unhindered. However, these crises are in fact systemic and are common to the exchange of all commodities on the capitalist market due to the need for individual agents to produce goods for the market without certainty that buyers will exist to purchase them, or that competitors will not absorb the demand which earlier appeared to exist (McNally 1993: 162–7). The coffee industry has been particularly susceptible to these uncertainties due to the specific nature of coffee cultivation. Unlike many other crops, such as wheat and corn, arabica coffee beans are grown on a perennial plant that takes three to five years to mature and requires a major commitment of capital (in contrast, poorer-quality robusta beans, discussed below, mature in only two years). The result has been exaggerated boom and bust cycles: during the boom, prices are artificially high as new trees mature; and during the bust, planters are unable to easily switch to other commodities due to relatively large amounts of fixed capital they have invested in coffee. According to Talbot (2004: 35): 'In the absence of any intervention in the market, [the nature of coffee cultivation] tends to produce recurring tree crop price cycles. If world market coffee prices are high, growers will plant more coffee, but the coffee from this new planting will have no effect on the market for three to five years. Growers will tend to over-plant as prices remain high, sowing the seeds of a glut on the market three to five years later.'

The boom and bust cycle reached crisis proportions in the second half of the nineteenth century as coffee farmers, both large and small, moved increasingly towards monocrop production and greater dependency on the international market. In 1896, a major crisis hit the coffee sector in Brazil as planters flooded the international market, causing supply to outstrip demand. The average price per pound of green coffee beans on the New York Coffee Exchange dropped from a previous range of between fourteen to eighteen cents to under ten cents. In 1897, production continued to grow and prices fell to eight cents. The downward slide in prices was given temporary relief in 1899 when Brazil was quarantined due to a serious outbreak of bubonic plague, an event celebrated by coffee brokers in the North as the 'bubonic plague boom.' However, a bumper Brazilian crop in 1901 brought world production up to nearly twenty million bags – of which Brazil was responsible for almost half – at a time when world consumption was only fifteen million bags, re-igniting the downward trend in prices. Prices dropped to six cents per pound. Due to these alarming trends, in 1902 representatives from Latin American coffee-producing countries met at the New York Coffee Exchange to discuss the possibility of a quota system to control prices. However, consuming and producing countries could not agree on target prices, so little was achieved other than an agreement to ban the export of the worst-quality coffee (known as 'triage'), to cut coffee import taxes in Europe and to spend more money on collectively promoting coffee (Pendergrast 1999: 68–80).

In 1906, with the Brazilian coffee sector still in crisis, the government of Brazil's major coffee state, São Paulo, took bold action to protect the interests of the local coffee elite. It initiated a valorization scheme to buy surplus coffee and keep it off the market – a scheme which would later become central to the coffee policies of the national government. In October 1906, the state government formed a syndicate of British and German banks and coffee merchants which began purchasing Brazilian arabica 'Santos' beans at the average price of seven cents a pound. São Paulo nominally owned the beans (as security on their loans) and had to pay 20 per cent of all purchases, as well as the cost of storage in warehouses in North America and Europe. Once the market price went over seven cents, the valorization would stop and the state would be in a position to begin selling off the surplus coffee. By the end of 1906, the syndicate had purchased over two million bags of coffee, which had little initial effect on prices due to a bumper crop that year which produced twenty million bags globally. By 1908, over seven million bags had been purchased but prices remained around 6 to seven cents. Finally, in 1910 prices rose to ten cents per pound, which then increased to fourteen cents in 1911. This was celebrated by Brazilian planters but caused an uproar among politicians and consumer groups in the United States who accused the syndicate of cornering the market. Under intense pressure from the U.S. Secretary of State, Brazil agreed to sell all of its valorized coffee in storage in North America in 1912 (Pendergrast 1999: 82–93).

From the perspective of Brazilian planters and the state, the valorization scheme had been a success. The result was a reorientation of the mindset of state officials towards the efficacy of market regulation, which led to the continuation of state regulation in the coffee sector in Brazil throughout the twentieth century (Talbot 2004: 48). The higher prices attained for Brazilian beans as a result of its first valorization scheme encouraged planters to clear more fields for coffee production, which was given further impetus by the Brazilian government's decision to abandon its tax on new plantings. This set the stage for another glut in the coffee market when the First World War (1914–18) caused a decline in global demand. In response, the Brazilian government headed the country's second valorization scheme and in 1917 bought nearly three million bags of green beans. The following year the war ended which, combined with news of a Brazilian frost, sent prices skyrocketing (Pendergrast 1999: 149–50). The government sold off its valorized coffee for a substantial profit, further demonstrating the effectiveness of valorization schemes in the minds of Brazilian officials.

Prior to the war, Brazil produced nearly 80 per cent of the world's coffee and completely dominated the global coffee industry. However, the increased prices brought about by its valorization schemes, along with growing demand in the North, sparked escalating competition from other coffee-producing countries which began to challenge Brazil's dominance. Central America increased its exports of coffee from 40 million pounds in 1914 to 158 million pounds in 1919. Colombia, which previously had been an insignificant coffee producer, increased its exports of coffee from 500,000 pounds in 1905 to 91 million pounds in 1914 and 121 million pounds in 1919. Haiti, Java, and Sumatra also increased their exports. The escalating competition increased global supply, which placed downward pressure on coffee prices. Thus, in 1921 Brazil initiated its third valorization, financed by a joint British–American loan for £9 million. Millions of bags were purchased and were then sold off at mid-decade when coffee prices doubled. This led to protests from the U.S. Congress which was spurred on by accusations of price-fixing by the National Coffee Roasters Association (NCRA). Brazil refused to abandon its valorization schemes, correctly pointing out that they were similar to protectionist measures that the United States had for cotton, wheat, petroleum, and tobacco (Pendergrast 1999: 149–52, 173–4).

From 1926 to 1929 Brazil continued to purchase more coffee beans to boost sagging prices. Eventually, the Brazilian government ran out of loan-money to keep the valorization afloat and prices began to drop. This was made worse on 29 October 1929, when the U.S. stock market crashed, initiating the Great Depression of the 1930s. The price of coffee plummeted from 22.5 cents per pound in 1929 to eight cents per pound in 1931. Amidst the social unrest caused by the coffee crisis, populist dictator Getúlio Vargas came to power in Brazil in a military coup in October 1930. Vargas banned new coffee planting and burned seven million bags of coffee – worth about $30 million – in an attempt to bolster prices. This was, however, a small portion of the over twenty-six million bags of unsold beans in Brazilian warehouses (Pendergrast 1999: 179–82).

The crisis of the 1930s led to an exacerbation of the already terrible working and living conditions of coffee workers and small farmers globally. Wages, which could be as low as twelve cents for a ten-hour work day, were slashed; workers were fired; and many small farmers went bankrupt and starved. The result was a tide of social unrest throughout the coffee regions which was quashed by the emergence of ruthless dictatorships backed by rural elites (Pendergrast 1999: 182–5). In El Salvador, for example, declining coffee production deprived indigenous peasants of the low-wage, exploitative jobs that they required to survive. These peasants had been forcibly displaced from coffee-producing lands since the 1870s by agents of the state and landed elite. The collapse of the coffee industry provoked an uprising of indigenous rural workers and peasants seeking to regain possession of their land in 1932. In response, the state, under the dictatorship of General Maximiliano Hernández Martínez, and the landed elite ordered the military and the landowners' private 'White Guards' to carry out the indiscriminate slaughter of an estimated 15,000 to 30,000 indigenous people within a matter of weeks, an event which has come to be known as *La Mantanza* (The Massacre) (North 1985: 29–42).

The Great Depression of the 1930s heightened the negative effects of the boom and bust cycles of the coffee industry and revealed the limitations of Brazil's unilateral valorization schemes. First, in sparking a temporary rise in coffee prices, valorization promoted the continued expansion of coffee production both in Brazil and among its growing competitors. The result was increased global oversupply, which escalated the impact of the 'bust' when it invariably occurred. Second, Brazil's unilateral actions provided a secure umbrella under which its competitors could 'free ride' and continue to expand their production while the Brazilian state accepted all of the risk (Talbot 2004: 48–9). Unilateral valorization may have been sustainable for Brazil as long as it alone had been *the* dominant coffee producer in the South (Topik 1998: 54), but this situation changed significantly as competing states increased their production. In consequence, coffee countries were eventually compelled to turn towards multilateral 'collective action' to find effective solutions to the crisis. Rapidly declining coffee prices not only hurt the interests of coffee elites but posed a significant threat to the stability of coffee-producing states as they sparked social unrest among smallholders and cut into state revenues which were drawn significantly from tariffs on the coffee industry (Talbot 2004: 14, 35–7).

In hopes of developing a collective response to the coffee crisis, Brazilian officials called for a conference of Latin American coffee countries, which was held in Bogotá, Colombia, in 1936. Participants agreed to fund a Pan American Coffee Bureau (PACB) to promote coffee in Northern markets, and Colombia and Brazil agreed to boost prices by selling high-quality Colombian beans for no less than 12 cents per pound and lower-quality Brazilian Santos beans for no less than 10.5 cents per pound. In addition to these multilateral agreements, Brazil continued to valorize and burn its own coffee. In 1937, Brazil burned 17.2 million bags at a time when world consumption was only 26.4 million bags, and only 30 per cent of Brazil's harvest reached the market (Talbot 2004: 48–9; Pendergrast 1999: 186–8).

Within a year of the Bogotá conference, Colombia broke the agreement. In response to growing social unrest among the country's small coffee farmers, state officials decided to sell Colombian beans under the twelve-cent limit in hopes of increasing exports and raising smallholder incomes (Thorp 1991: 10). In response, Brazil called for another conference of Latin American coffee producers, this time in Havana, and threatened to stop its valorization schemes unless other countries also took measures to keep their beans off the market. The conference ended without resolution as other countries doubted Brazil's willingness to abandon its valorization scheme. In response, Vargas declared a policy of 'free competition' and opened the floodgates on Brazilian beans with a tax reduction of $2 per bag. At first, Brazilian planters celebrated the decision, until prices rapidly declined to 6.5 cents per pound. In consequence, according to Mark Pendergrast (1999: 188): 'In 1938 Brazil exported 300 million pounds more coffee to the United States than the previous year – but received $3.15 million *less* for the total than in 1937' (see also Talbot 2004: 48–9).

The onset of the Second World War in 1939 created the conditions under which Latin America coffee-producing countries as well as the United States were willing to agree on regulations for the global coffee industry. The war closed off European coffee markets and raised fears in Latin America about a continuing decline in prices. At the same time, the United States feared that worsening coffee prices could drive Latin American countries, especially Brazil, into the Nazi or the Communist camps. The result was the establishment in November 1940 of the Inter-American Coffee Agreement (IACA). Through the IACA the United States agreed to restrict the amount of coffee allowed into the U.S. market to a total quota of 15.9 million bags, nearly one million over the estimated total U.S. consumption at that time. Brazil was granted 60 per cent of the quota, Colombia received just over 20 per cent, and the rest was divided among Latin American countries, with an insignificant 353,000 bags left over for countries in Asia and Africa. The agreement had an immediate effect on the price of coffee, which almost doubled by the end of 1941. Prices increased so rapidly, in fact, that the U.S. government felt compelled to unilaterally increase the quota by 20 per cent in August 1941, and then froze the price at 13.38 cents per pound in December of that year, where it remained until the price ceiling was lifted in 1946 (Talbot 2004: 49; Pendergrast 1999: 217–41).

When the war ended, coffee prices boomed in response to the opening of European markets and the growing demand in the United

States, especially for instant coffee which had gained notoriety as part of the standard food ration in the U.S. Army. Prices rose to fifty cents per pound for Santos green beans in 1947 and then to a high of eighty cents in 1949. Amidst the throes of the new boom, the IACA was quietly allowed to expire in 1948. At first, Brazilian producers were unable to meet the new demand due to the previous decades of overproduction in the São Paulo coffee fields, which had drained the soil of nutrients and left the Brazilian crop vulnerable to *la broca* infestation. In response, in the 1950s thousands of Brazilian farmers flocked to the Paraná region, where the soil and climate conditions were better for coffee, and began planting new trees. The new location, along with new innovations in fertilizers, pesticides, and planting strategies, allowed farmers to produce five times more coffee per acre than in São Paulo. In 1953, a frost hit the Paraná which ruined part of the year's harvest and caused prices to climb even higher, encouraging producers to plant even more trees. The stage was set for another bust in the coffee market (Pendergrast 1999: 237–56).

In 1955, a major glut in the coffee market ensued, caused by increased production in existing major coffee-producing countries and the rapid growth of coffee production in Africa. In 1951, African coffee accounted for 4.8 per cent of U.S. coffee imports. By 1955, this number had more than doubled, to 11.4 per cent. Over 80 per cent of the green beans exported from Africa were *robusta* beans. In contrast to the more widely used arabica beans, robusta beans were resistant to coffee leaf rust, took only two years to produce their first harvest, and grew in greater abundance at lower altitudes and in warmer regions with a mean average temperature of between 20 and 26 degrees Celsius. However, they tended to produce coffee which had a harsh taste and twice as much caffeine as arabica. For these reasons, robusta had remained relatively unpopular until the 1950s. At this time, the growing popularity of instant coffee, in which bean quality was largely irrelevant, and fierce price competition between major roasters, who could blend robusta in with their arabica beans, provided an expanding market for robusta beans. By the end of 1956, robusta beans accounted for 22 per cent of world coffee exports. The major producers were the Ivory Coast, which exported 1.4 million bags of robusta in 1954, and Angola which exported one million bags. Today, around 25 per cent of the world's coffee beans are robusta and are produced throughout western, central and southern Africa, as well as in Indonesia, Vietnam, Thailand, Brazil, and Ecuador (Talbot 2004: 33–4; Pendergrast 1999: 43–4, 152–4, 257–9).

The escalating coffee crisis led to further attempts to develop multi-lateral agreements to regulate the global coffee industry. In 1958, the Latin American Coffee Agreement was signed, under which Brazil agreed to withhold 40 per cent of its annual crop, Colombia agreed to withhold 15 per cent, and other Latin American countries agreed to smaller restrictions. The African coffee-producing countries were in attendance at the meetings for the agreement but refused to limit their production. At this time, world production had reached fifty million bags while world consumption was only thirty-eight million bags. The following year, African producers agreed to join fifteen Latin American countries in a one-year quota system in which each country agreed to export 10 per cent less than its best year in the past decade. The quotas were widely violated, as no enforcement mechanism existed, but the agreement was extended for another year in 1960. These measures failed to address adequately the crises in overproduction that had overtaken the global coffee industry (Pendergrast 1999: 273–7). They did, however, lay the basis for the drafting of the International Coffee Agreement (ICA), which is dealt with in chapter 4.

Class, Race, and Gender Exploitation in the Coffee Industry

Over the centuries the global coffee industry has developed into a complicated international network of production and accumulation which is both highly profitable and highly volatile and exploitative. At the root of the coffee industry is a grossly unequal social class hierarchy in which all participants are driven, directly or indirectly, by the capitalist imperatives of competition, accumulation, profit maximization, and increasing labour productivity. At the bottom of the hierarchy are the rural workers and small-scale farmers in the South. Rural workers have historically been dispossessed of their land and forced into a variety of working relationships, from slavery, to debt peonage, to free labour (Kurian 2003; McCreery 2003; Dore 2003; Rus 2003; Samper 1994; North 1985: 17–28). Today, workers must compete in highly saturated labour markets for seasonal jobs that pay near-starvation wages under generally deplorable conditions. In Guatemala, for example, the government considers the minimum wage to cover only 40 per cent of basic needs. Yet even this low wage is considered too high by the coffee elite: a survey of plantations in Guatemala in 2000 found that none of them paid the country's minimum wage and that a majority did not even pay half the minimum wage. Child labour is also frequently exploited on coffee plantations in some countries. It is estimated that 30 per cent of the coffee pickers on plantations in Kenya are under the age of fifteen (UNCTAD and IISD 2003: 6, 6n16; World Bank 2003b: 54–6).

Small-scale farmers at not much better off and must struggle in highly competitive and volatile markets in which they can barely make enough to survive. In many cases, they are forced into bankruptcy or seasonal migration in search of work. Owning land does provide small farmers with an extra source of survival that landless workers lack, but in general terms both smallholders and rural workers are deprived of access to basic health care, sanitation, and proper housing (UNCTAD and IISD 2003; World Bank 2003a; Oxfam International 2002a, 2001; Dicum and Luttinger 1999: 44–9). David Ransom, journalist and editorial member of the *New Internationalist*, characterizes the life of coffee farmers along the Tambopata river valley in Peru like this:

> If your coffee harvest brings you in less than it costs you, if you have labored for a year without reward, then you will have nothing to pay for treatment for you or your children when sickness strikes, as it invariably does in places such as this – yellow fever is rampant. As a result, there are no doctors or medicines. The prevailing certainty becomes that if you get sick you die – it's as simple as that. Whether or not you will be able to keep your children in school is doubtful. So there are not enough schools. The cumulative effect of all this continuing year after year, and of having to submit your life entirely to the whims of world coffee prices, is what powerless really means. (Ransom 2001: 46)

Moving up the hierarchy, we have a series of local middlemen, who generally monopolize local transportation and credit, and make their profits by buying low from small-scale farmers and selling dear to coffee processors. Coffee processors, many of which are foreign-owned companies, clean, shell, and classify green coffee beans prior to export, 'adding value' to the final product. Some processors export directly to the North while others are linked to giant transnational trading companies. These intermediaries generally get only a small proportion of the total coffee income and make profits through economies of scale that are relatively large compared to small-scale farmers (Talbot 2004: 172–9). As is the case throughout the industry, the workers employed by intermediaries, both historically and today, have generally been highly exploited, low-wage workers. This has especially been the case for women workers, who have often made up the bulk of the seasonal coffee-sorting labour force and have worked under deplorable conditions for substantially less wages than their male counterparts (Fowler-Salamini 2002).

Another significant intermediary is the state, whose role varies from country to country, but it has played a key function in processing and exporting coffee beans, especially since the end of the Second World War. Following the broader trends in the international trade and development regime described in the previous chapters, over the past fifteen years pressures from international and domestic neoliberal reformers have led to a general decline in state coffee agencies, whose position has largely been replaced by private companies (Talbot 2004: 107–9, 115–16).

Along with intermediaries in the South, large-plantation owners generally possess their own transportation and processing infrastructure and employ a variety of workers. Moreover, due to their political influence over the state, they have significantly greater access to rural credit and infrastructure than small-scale farmers (Waridel 2002: 43). They make their profits by extracting surplus value from their workers, which is done by paying workers less in wages than the value of the wealth that is created by their labour power. These powerful landowners must compete on a highly volatile international coffee market, which generally causes them to depress wages in an attempt to lower costs, beat out competitors, and survive. Yet, while vulnerable to the swings of the market, large landowners posses significant economies of scale which generally allow them to make profits even under price conditions that can be destructive for smallholders (Talbot 2004: 172–9).

This latter point is significant, as it draws attention to the fact that the low incomes attained by smallholders relative to large landowners is not due to a lack of efficiency, but is primarily a result of the fact that poor producers lack economies of scale – they simply do not have enough land. In fact, despite many myths to the contrary, in economic terms small-scale farmers in general tend to be more efficient than large-scale farmers in resource utilization and productivity per unit of area (Grinspun 2003: 48–50). Moreover, if we adopt a broader notion of efficiency that takes into consideration environmental and social sustainability, the balance is tipped even further in favour of small producers. Small producers tend to provide more rural employment than large producers, rely less on expensive and environmentally destructive agricultural inputs (such as chemical fertilizers, pesticides, and herbicides), and are more likely to manage the local ecosystem in a more sustainable manner, especially in instances where land is organized communally or cooperatively and local cultural traits promoting environmental stewardship remain strong (Grinspun 2003: 48–50; Sarukhán and Larson 2001; Moguel and Toledo 1999). Thus, the position occupied by large landowners along the coffee chain is not due to their economic efficiency or their social utility, but rather to their political-economic power, which, as the previous historical section demonstrates, they have exercised to their individual and class advantage.

Further up the coffee hierarchy are giant transnational trading companies in the North which typically trade in a variety of commodities and monopolize international importing, shipping, and finance as well as exporting from key ports in the South. These TNCs make their profits by buying low and selling high on a massive scale. At the top of the hierarchy are transnational roaster/distributors with enormous economies of scale that acquire the semi-processed green beans directly or on the coffee exchanges and then roast them and distribute them to retailers throughout the North. These TNCs make their profits in two main ways. First, they use their monopoly control of Northern markets to artificially increase the gap between international green bean prices and roasted bean prices on retail markets in the North (Talbot 2004: 103–7). The effect is to extract surplus from farmers in the South who are forced to sell beans well below their final retail value in the North.

Second, they 'add value' to the final product through the roasting, packaging, marketing, and distribution processes in the North. As is the case with landlords in the South, the core aspect of this process is the extraction of surplus value from low-wage workers. Historically, coffee companies have utilized a variety of methods to keep the wages paid to Northern workers low, such as drawing extensively on piecework and seasonal employment (Pendergrast 1999: 95–112, 138–42). Today, they continue to do so by drawing workers from growing 'flexible' labour markets, which are based on jobs that are low paying, with limited health and pension benefits, and a high risk of unemployment – the average annual employee turnover rate for coffee service-sector workers is around 200 per cent (Jackson 2003b; Pendergrast 2002). To create the conditions for these labour markets, giant coffee TNCs and the corporate sector in general have actively lobbied Northern governments to lower real minimum wages, employment and welfare benefits, and corporate taxes, and have aggressively fought against unionization and workers' rights to collective bargaining.[7]

As discussed in chapter 1, the international trade regime under which the coffee industry operates is one that has been dominated by the rich countries in the North. Some Southern countries, however, such as Brazil which has a large internal market and a relatively high level of industrialization, have been able to resist various pressures from the North and exert significant influence over the international coffee market. An example of this is Brazil's refusal throughout the first half of the twentieth century to abandon its valorization schemes despite immense pressure from the United States. The Southern countries which have been the most vulnerable to the whims of the coffee market have been those which have the weakest economies and are the most dependent on coffee exports. This includes countries such as Burundi, whose coffee exports in 1998 represented 80 per cent of its total national exports but less than 1 per cent of world coffee exports; Ethiopia, whose coffee exports were 67 per cent of its total exports but only 2 per cent of the world total; and Rwanda, whose coffee exports in 2004 were 43 per cent of its total exports but less than 1 per cent of the world total (UNCTAD 2004; Oxfam International 2001: 11).

The vulnerability of smaller, poorer states to an international coffee market upon which they have very little impact can have politically devastating effects, as the Rwandan genocide of 1994 demonstrates. Civil war between Tutsi rebels and the Hutu-dominated government in Rwanda erupted into genocide when militant Hutus massacred over half a million Tutsi and dislocated nearly two million more. The source of the conflict was long-standing, going back to when the Belgian colonial regime had fuelled inter-ethnic rivalry and recruited the minority Tutsi groups to manage the colonial administration. The specific context under which the genocide took place, however, was an economic and social crisis caused in large part by the collapse of international coffee prices in the wake of the failure of the ICA (discussed in the next chapter), along with the effects of neoliberal reforms imposed by the World Bank and the IMF. In a country with 90 per cent of its labour force engaged in agriculture that relied on coffee for 80 per cent of its foreign exchange earnings in 1994, the fall in coffee prices sparked famine and crippled the state, which relied heavily on coffee industry rents. At the same time, World Bank/IMF policies of trade liberalization, state downsizing, and currency devaluations sparked inflation and a decline in purchasing power, along with the collapse of health and education services (Talbot 2004: 117–18; Chossudovsky 1995a, 1995b). The result was a crisis that, while not the sole cause of the genocide, according to economist Michel Chossudovsky (1995a), 'exacerbated simmering ethnic tensions and accelerated the process of political collapse.'

In recent years, some academics have begun to employ the global commodity chain (GCC) approach, pioneered by Gary Gereffi and Miguel Korzeniewicz, to analyse and describe the complex interplay between rich and poor states, corporations, and social groups in the global coffee industry. A GCC is described as 'a network of labour and production processes whose end result is a finished commodity' (Gereffi and Korzeniewicz 1994). The GCC approach has been derived from world system theory and is intended to provide an intermediate unit of analysis between the world system and the nation-state. Its proponents assert that a focus on the world system alone does not provide a unit of analysis small enough for detailed empirical and historical investigation, while a focus on the nation-state suggests that the nation-state is an independent, self-contained unit, as opposed to a component of a unitary social system with a single global division of labour. The GCC provides a unit of analysis within which both the single world economic system and the territorially fragmented international political system can be examined. Along each chain is a series of nodes where the original commodity is transformed, value is added, and profits are generated. Change in the commodity chain occurs as a result of choices pursued by states, enterprises, and households as they battle for control over the nodes where the largest share of surplus flows (Talbot 2004: 5–30; Gereffi and Korzeniewicz 1994).

Using this approach, John Talbot asserts that the global coffee commodity chain is most accurately described as a 'tropical commodity chain' which has two different types of 'governance structures.' Up to the point where green beans enter consumer markets in the North, the coffee chain has an 'international trader-driven' structure wherein giant trading companies exercise a loose and indirect form of governance over suppliers based on price, volume, and reliability. Once in Northern markets, the coffee chain has a 'producer-driven' structure in which roaster/distributors coordinate the production of the finished product and control distribution and retailing (Talbot 2002, 1997).

The GCC approach to the coffee industry provides an instructive understanding of how coffee beans are altered as commodities as they flow from South to North, and of who dominates this process. The GCC approach has been used to exemplify how the 'rent' (or income) derived from value-added activities is distributed highly unequally along the coffee chain – out of the hands of poor Southern producers and into the hands of Southern intermediaries, international traders, and Northern roaster/distributors. These value-added activities can involve applying technology to the coffee bean (through initial processing, roasting, and packaging) or can be derived purely from massive marketing strategies designed to 'differentiate' a given coffee product from others, thereby increasing its market value. Through the lens of the GCC approach, analysts have effectively argued that fair trade coffee represents an attempt to direct more rent into the hands of poor producers by increasing the value of fair trade products through ethical marketing strategies and by encouraging cooperatives to 'integrate forward' into the higher-technology, value-added activities of the coffee chain (this is discussed in greater detail in the following chapter) (Taylor 2005; Renard 2005; Raynolds 2002a).

Nonetheless, while the GCC approach provides an instructive lens for assessing the unequal distribution of rents along the coffee chain, like the world systems theory approaches from which it is derived, as well as the Underdevelopment and Dependency Theory (UDT) literature in general, it tends to emphasise the flow of surplus value from South to North. This can lead to neglecting or downplaying the extraction of surplus value by the dominant social classes within each node of the commodity chain – such as plantation owners extracting surplus value from rural workers, or Northern roasters extracting surplus value from Northern factory workers. The composition of social class relations at the point of production/processing/distribution within the global coffee industry must be central to any understanding of how the industry operates. For example, according to Oxfam International, in 1992 coffee-producing countries in the South earned $10 billion from a coffee market worth around $30 billion – one-third of all the value generated by the coffee industry that year (Oxfam International 2002a: 20). This represents a significant retention of wealth in the South – wealth that for the most part did not see its way into the hands of the rural workers and poor farmers who produced it. Instead, it remained largely in the hands of the dominant classes: wealthy landowners and local intermediaries. Only an understanding of the social class relations of production within the South can fully account for this disparity.

In addition, the highly unequal social class relations in the global coffee industry must be contextualized within systems of ethno-racial and gender exploitation. Historically, ethno-racial discrimination was central to the emergence of colonialism and the world system which brought with it the beginnings of the global coffee industry. In order to justify ideologically the plunder of land, the conquest of societies, and the use of slavery, European colonialists depicted their enemies as savage barbarians and heathens – which essentially meant that they were considered non-human and thus not protected by Christian laws. With the emergence of capitalism in the eighteenth and nineteenth centuries, a new, 'scientific' regime of racial oppression was developed which promoted the notion of the existence of physically distinct races of humans with biologically different characteristics. As capitalists drew heavily on an ideology based on freedom and equality, ethno-racial discrimination was required to justify the forced labour and land theft, which, as we have seen, capitalist penetration brought to the coffee regions in the South (Kurian 2003; McCreery 2003; Rus 2003; McNally 2002: 103–15; Samper 1994: 56–8; North 1985: 17–42).[8]

These ethno-racial structures and attitudes persist today, and are often used by elites in the North and South to justify extreme class exploitation and inequality within the industry. Often this is done under the guise of respect for 'cultural differences.' In 2004, Starbucks Coffee Company commented on the use of child labour by their suppliers on coffee plantations. Washing its hands of the role that it and other giant coffee TNCs have played in creating the conditions under which low-wage workers are compelled to send their children to work, the company stated: 'Starbucks sources coffee from countries that are different culturally and do not have similar labor standards to the U.S. It is very common for young children to accompany parents to the workplace, as infant and toddler childcare is neither feasible nor culturally accepted in many regions. Many migrant workers depend on the work on coffee farms for their livelihood and this includes help from their children' (Starbucks 2004e).

In addition to class and ethno-racial exploitation, gender oppression through the imposition of Western patriarchy has also been central to the historical development of the coffee industry. While patriarchal systems existed prior to European expansion, the spread of colonialism and capitalism had the effect of eroding those matriarchal systems that did exist, and of preserving and compounding non-Western structures of gender oppression, often through 'invented traditions' (Ranger 1983: 257–9). As European patriarchal legal systems and notions of private property were imposed on the South, many women lost traditional access and rights to land as colonizers only recognized male 'heads of household' as legitimate property owners. In addition, as capitalist social relations penetrated the South, women were separated from the economic sphere – deemed to be the domain of men – and assigned the role of reproduction in the private sphere (Dore 2003; McNally 2002: 124–8).[9] Yet, at the same time, women were compelled to enter the economic sphere as lower-paid workers where they frequently faced sexual harassment and oppressive working conditions. This resulted in a 'double burden' for women, who remained primarily responsible for household labour but also worked as wage labourers. As their income was considered 'subsidiary' to those of males, women were paid significantly less than their male counterparts and often had to hand their wages over to their husbands (Kurian 2003; McCreery 2003: 200–1; Dore 2003: 229; McNally 2002: 124–8; Fowler-Salamini 2002; Samper 1994: 85, 92–6). These disparities existed in both the South and the North. For example, female plantation workers in Ceylon in the nineteenth century and female factory workers employed by Hills Brothers in the United States during the First World War were both paid around half as much as their male co-workers (Kurian 2003: 181; Pendergrast 1999: 138–42).

These patriarchal conditions of work and property ownership continue to pervade the coffee industry and the international political economy in general, and are particularly onerous for women from discriminated-against ethnic groups who must confront gender inequalities with the additional burden of racism. In general terms, women farmers and workers throughout the South still confront lower pay, less stable employment, widespread sexual harassment at work, and the double burden (Oxfam International 2004). Women coffee workers in Honduras in 2002 were paid up to 30 per cent less than male coffee workers for the same work, a situation common throughout the industry (Oxfam International 2002a: 12). A recent report on sustainable coffee by UNCTAD and the IISD (2003: 7) states that 'the coffee sector, like other agricultural sectors, exhibits traditional gender distinctions that can place women at a social and economic disadvantage. In addition to outright gender discrimination observed in plantation settings, there is evidence that the role of women in household decision-making is often disproportionate to the work they devote to actual coffee production.'

Conclusion: The Historical and Structural Roots of Exploitation

The above overview of the global coffee industry reveals it to be highly exploitative and volatile for those at the bottom of the class, race, and gender hierarchy upon which it is constituted. For those higher up the hierarchy, in contrast, the coffee industry can be highly lucrative, especially for giant TNCs at the top of the chain, whose monopoly control of distribution, marketing, and roasting in the North places them in the best position to manipulate markets in the interest of corporate profitability. These gross inequalities persist as a result of the structural mechanisms of international capitalism, which have been the primary dynamic behind the coffee industry since the eighteenth century. The implications of this for those who seek to combat exploitation and promote human development in the coffee industry are many, but two broad propositions are particularly salient.

First, there is a historical dimension to exploitation in the coffee industry, and any attempt to promote human and democratic development in the current context must address the legacy of past injustices. For example, in the coffee regions of countries such as Guatemala, El Salvador, and Brazil, combating exploitation would require more than ensuring higher coffee bean prices and higher wages (although this would certainly be a good start), and would necessitate a radical readjustment of the highly unequal distribution of land and resources inherited from the past. Similarly, combating gender inequality in coffee communities would require more than micro-projects to ease women's work, but would necessitate challenging local or 'traditional' (or invented) notions of the peasant family being run by property-owning, male 'heads of households.'

Second, there is a structural dimension to exploitation in the coffee industry, which is driven not primarily by ethical values but by the capitalist imperatives of competition, accumulation, profit maximization, and increasing labour productivity. The emergence of ever-larger, monopolistic coffee TNCs have been due primarily to fierce competitive pressures as corporations have beat out or bought up one another in order to survive. The exaggerated boom and bust cycles of the coffee industry have emerged out of the decisions of millions of large and small coffee farmers, rational on an individual level, to respond to temporary upswings in coffee prices by increasing production. The result has been repetitive crises in overproduction, leading to fierce competition for market shares. Responding to these competitive pressures, wealthy landlords have struggled to force down wages and step up exploitative mechanisms to extract as much wealth from workers as possible, and small farmers have been forced into a variety of survival strategies to cope with near-starvation coffee incomes. To address the exploitation and inequality that pervades the coffee industry, a variety of development projects were initiated in the twentieth century which sought to dampen the coffee cycle and provide workers and small-scale farmers in the South with a greater share of the total wealth garnered by coffee production. This is the subject of the following chapter, which explores the strengths and weaknesses of some of the most important attempts to promote greater social justice within the industry, including fair trade coffee.

4 Coffee and the 'Double Movement'

The people in the World Bank were extreme reactionaries who came to Costa Rica and listened to what the oligarchy here, which we had just overthrown, was saying, and repeated all the arguments for us. They were against the nationalization of the banks. They were against taxing capital after the war. They were against anything that meant social progress ... I have had many dealings with the World Bank in the University of Stanford in San Francisco. I had my first quarrel in the very early fifties about prices, stability international [sic], the founders of the World Bank said it was heresy, that prices should be allowed to get established by offer and demand.

José Figueres Ferrer[1]

It was only under pressure from the Japanese that the World Bank had undertaken the study of economic growth in East Asia ... and then only after the Japanese had offered to pay for it. The reason was obvious: The countries had been successful not only in spite of the fact that they had not followed most of the dictates of the Washington Consensus, but *because* they had not. Though the experts' findings were toned down in the final published report, the World Bank's Asian Miracle study laid out the important roles that the government had played. These were far from the minimalist roles beloved of the Washington Consensus.

Joseph Stiglitz[2]

The uncertainty, social unrest, and exploitation pervasive in the coffee industry described in the previous chapter has historically led to varied 'double movements,' as social groups have mobilized and pressured for certain forms of protection from the market's gravest effects

(Talbot 2004: 26–7). The concept of the double movement was developed by economic historian and anthropologist Karl Polanyi (1944), who asserted that the emergence and extension of industrial capitalism and the 'self-regulating market' have historically been accompanied by a simultaneous – or double – movement that has imposed significant market regulation as a political solution to its destructive impact.

The self-regulating market, argued Polanyi, had emerged with the advent of industrial capitalism and a 'market society' in Europe in the nineteenth century. Prior to the emergence of industrial capitalism, there had been markets, but they had been 'embedded' in society and organized around cultural and political principles. In the nineteenth century, this changed as markets became 'disembedded' from society and placed beyond direct political control. Polanyi asserted that a key aspect for this to occur was the creation of 'fictitious commodities' – such as labour and land – which were subordinated to the market. This was a 'fiction' because labour and land are not creations of the market but are, in fact, the core substance of human society and 'no other than human beings and the natural surroundings in which they exist' (Bernard 1997: 79). Thus, the commodification of labour and land was not a result of a 'natural' development in human society, but, as demonstrated in the previous chapter, the outcome of a variety of complex political-economic and cultural processes that have *assigned* them a role as market commodities (Bernard 1997).

As this situation was ultimately premised on fictions, Polanyi argued that the extension of market relations required the extension of state institutions both to organize society along these lines and to provide some protection against its negative effects – such as unemployment and poverty for landless workers, bankruptcy for companies, and general social and political disorder (Polanyi 1944: 68–76). According to Polanyi: 'Undoubtedly, labor, land, and money *are* essential to a market economy. But no society could stand the effects of such a system of crude fictions even for the shortest stretch of time unless its human and natural substance as well as its business organization was protected against the ravages of this satanic mill' (73). Consequently, as the modern state has moved to impose the 'free' market on society and remove all constraints on the power of capital, the destructive impact of these actions have simultaneously given way to social uprisings and political strife. This, in turn, has historically led the imposition of significant *market regulation* as a political solution to turmoil caused by the *unregulated market* – an occurrence that Polanyi referred to as a 'double movement' (Talbot 2004: 26–7; Bernard 1997; Polanyi 1944).

The history of the coffee industry in the twentieth century is replete with various development projects that exemplify the Polanyian double movement. Many examples involved the emergence of state coffee agencies throughout the South to regulate coffee exports and pro- mote more efficient production. In Africa and Asia a variety of state coffee agencies emerged in the late colonial period in the 1950s and after independence. Most of these agencies held a monopoly of coffee exports, provided some agricultural extension and research services to growers, and artificially held internal coffee bean prices below world market prices to provide rents to the state. In Latin America, most coffee countries also developed state coffee agencies, which did not always directly monopolize exports but did regulate them and set minimum prices for coffee beans while providing varying degrees of extension and research services. In general, many state coffee agencies displayed significant signs of corruption and inefficiency, yet at the same time pro- vided growers with much-needed agricultural services and a degree of protection from the wild swings of the world market. During the 1990s, most of these state coffee agencies were eliminated or had their inter- ventionist role significantly reduced under pressure from the World Bank and other neoliberal institutions (Talbot 2004: 53–4, 107–16).

While the state coffee agencies that emerged in the twentieth century shared some broad commonalities, there were also notable differences among the strategies they pursued and their overall success. In Brazil, the state pursued valorization schemes and instant coffee produc- tion. In Colombia, the quasi-state Federación Nacional de Cafeteros (National Federation of Coffee Farmers, FNC) pursued a price pre- mium strategy based on high-quality coffee. In Costa Rica, state coffee regulation was combined with broader reforms and the construction of a social welfare state. At the same time, in addition to these national state projects, important international development strategies, like the International Coffee Agreement (ICA) and the non-statist fair trade network, also emerged as part of the double movement against the exploitation and social unrest caused by global coffee production. This chapter explores the most successful of these strategies, assesses their strengths and weaknesses, and compares them to the development model offered by fair trade coffee since its reorientation in the late 1980s (see table 4.1).

Table 4.1 Comparing coffee development projects

	International Coffee Agreement (1963–89) (Key players: Brazil & USA)	Forward integration (1960s–) (Instant coffee in Brazil)	Price premium (1927–) (Federación Nacional de Cafeteros)	State regulation & social reform (1948–) (Costa Rican state)
Strategy	Export quotas Stockpiling	Move up instant coffee chain	Promote high-quality coffee Provide services to farmers	Tax revenues directed towards state-led modernization Political reforms
Conditions for emergence	South: Economic crisis & instability North: Cold War fears	Access to technology Supportive state policies	Significant smallholder class Uniqueness of FNC	Significant smallholder class Dominant agro-industrial elite Unique rise to power of Partido Social Democrática
Difficulties	Little impact on national wealth distribution Encouraged oversupply Unpredictable swings Conflict-ridden & fragile	Little impact on national wealth distribution Northern TNCs still dominate Mixed gains for income Highly subsidized	Negative impact of modernization 'Fallacy of composition' Dependence on volatile market Lack of national reforms Instability & civil war	Negative impact of modernization 'Fallacy of composition' Difficult to replicate Threatened by market imperatives & neoliberal reforms
Attainments	Somewhat dampened coffee cycle Greater retention of coffee income in south	Mixed gains for income retention in South Some backward linkages	Higher incomes for farmers One of most advanced coffee industries in world Revenue for infrastructure & services	High overall living standards One of most advanced coffee industries in the world Democratic reforms & relative peace

The International Coffee Agreement (ICA), 1963–1989

According to John Talbot, the emergence of the ICA is an excellent example of the Polanyian double movement in action. The extension of the self-regulating market in the coffee industry on a global scale perpetuated the negative social and political impacts of the boom and bust cycles and led to a movement for regulation at the international level (Talbot 2004: 26–7, 36). The precursor to the ICA was the Inter-American Coffee Agreement (IACA), which, as discussed earlier, was established during the Second World War. Historically, Northern countries had been reluctant to sign international commodity agreements due to opposition from corporations and fears that higher prices would decrease the purchasing power of Northern workers (Talbot 2004: 16). Various political pressures at particular historical junctures could overcome this reluctance. This was the case with the IACA, which the United States signed out of fear that Latin American countries might move towards the Nazi camp in the face of declining coffee prices and wartime barriers to European markets (Talbot 2004: 49). After the war, the IACA was allowed to expire in 1948, when coffee prices were relatively high.

The higher prices experienced after the war did not last long and by the mid-1950s they were once again in rapid decline. This ignited another double movement and countries in Latin America and Africa began placing intense pressure on the United States to enter into a new agreement. After prolonged and fierce negotiations convened by the United Nations in New York in 1962 under the terms of the Havana Charter, the ICA was finally agreed to, with a deadline for ratification for December 1963. A variety of pressures came to bear on producing and consuming states to bring this event about. In the major coffee producing states in the South, declining prices threatened their legitimacy and stability. Economic crisis in the coffee sector caused despair and discontent among millions of small-scale farmers, which sparked social unrest and threatened the legitimacy of the state if it failed to demonstrate its ability to defend prices. In addition, coffee was often a major source of foreign exchange earnings for coffee-producing countries, and therefore a major source of tariff revenues for the state. Declining revenues threatened to shrink state coffers, and, by extension, the very ability of the state to carry out its daily functions (Talbot 2004: 36–7, 41).

In the major consuming countries in the North, in particular the United States, the decision to ratify the ICA was driven by Cold War fears that plummeting prices would drive Southern states into the communist ·camp. Two events of particular importance were the Cuban revolution in 1959, which heightened fear in American officials of the spread of communism in Latin America; and the election of John F. Kennedy as president of the United States in 1960 (Talbot 2004: 58). In 1961, Kennedy proclaimed the 'Alliance for Progress,' which, according to historian Gabriel Kolko, was designed to fight the spectre of communism in Latin America by 'employing a big stick along with what was to prove, despite much verbiage, a quite modest carrot.' This modest carrot entailed increasing economic aid to the South, although much less than originally promised, and led to growing U.S. support for the ICA (Kolko 1988: 150–3). In addition, the ICA also received the support of key U.S. roasters, who had traditionally fought against price controls. They wanted to avoid the highs of the coffee cycle and to ensure a stable supply of coffee, and they were under intense pressure from Brazil and Colombia to approve the agreement. These countries offered massive and lucrative coffee contracts under special terms to the largest Northern roasters and were thus able to bring significant weight to bear on their partners (Talbot 2004: 62–3; Dicum and Luttinger 1999: 87–90).

The ICA was a five-year agreement, due for renegotiation in 1968, that placed a quota of 45.6 million bags on world exports of green coffee beans allowed into the major consuming countries in North America and western Europe. Of the original quota, Brazil received 18 million bags, Colombia received 6 million bags, the Ivory Coast 2.3 million bags, and Angola just over 2 million bags, with the rest distributed to the remaining coffee countries on the basis of previous export years. These quotas were raised by 3 per cent in 1964 under pressure from the U.S. Congress, which, fearing that the ICA would result in high coffee prices, held up the full implementation of the agreement until 1965. Decisions on export quotas required the approval of both two-thirds of the importing and two-thirds of the exporting countries. Each group of countries were allocated 1,000 votes, which were divided among them on the basis of size of exports and imports. Brazil and the United States were each give 400 votes from their respective group, which meant that both countries had effective veto over any quota decisions. Other important terms of the ICA included: a requirement that certificates of origin accompany every coffee shipment; an exemption from quotas for low coffee-consuming countries such as Japan, China, and the USSR; and a guarantee of 90 days notice by any country that wished to withdraw from the agreement (Talbot 2004: 58–9; Pendergrast 1999: 273–9).

Soon after its implementation, problems in the agreement began to emerge. Smaller coffee-exporting countries, such as India and Indonesia, complained that quotas were not readjusted accordingly as they increased production. As a result, the ICA was revised so that quotas were determined by target price ranges. If prices dropped below the target price range a proportional quota decrease was automatically triggered, and if prices rose above the target range a proportional quota increase was automatically triggered. Target prices were determined by a 'selectivity principle' which allocated different price ranges for different qualities of coffee: robusta (primarily from Africa and Indonesia); unwashed arabicas (primarily from Brazil); Colombian Milds (Colombia and Kenya); and 'other milds' (Central America) (Pendergrast 1999: 296).

Other significant problems remained unresolved by ICA members. One such problem was the emergence of 'tourist coffee' – cheaper beans sold to dealers in exempt countries, such as the USSR and Japan, who would then re-export the beans to major consuming countries while avoiding quota restrictions. Another major problem for the industry as a whole was overproduction, which remained entirely unresolved by the ICA. In 1966, world production exceeded demand by 87 million surplus bags, 65 million of which were in Brazilian warehouses. In response, Brazil developed programs to bulldoze or burn billions of older coffee trees. At the same time, the development of new technologies, such as fertilizers and hybrid trees, made it possible to grow increasingly more beans per acre of land (Pendergrast 1999: 295–7). These technologies were designed to help some farmers, mostly wealthy planters, beat out competitors, but from a broader perspective were totally irrational considering that the coffee industry was already supplying millions of bags more per year than global demand could handle.

In 1968, the ICA was renewed for another five years. The goal of the ICA had been to keep the price of average green arabica beans from dropping below its 1962 level of 34 cents per pound, and in 1968 prices hovered around 40 cents per pound. The result was a fairly predictable price range which had significantly cut down on the amount of hedging and speculation on the New York Coffee & Sugar Exchange (formerly the New York Coffee Exchange). In 1969, however, prices dropped to 35 cents per pound, and nine representatives from major coffee-producing regions in Latin America and Africa met in Geneva to demand lower quota levels and higher prices. The fears of the 'Geneva Group' were temporarily allayed the following year when a frost, followed by a drought, hit the Paraná region in Brazil and coffee prices climbed to over 50 cents for Brazilian santos beans. In response, Brazil halted its bulldozing program and began planting 200 million new trees, and the producing countries agreed to raise ICA quotas to avoid angering the United States (Pendergrast 1999: 303).

　In the summer of 1971, disagreements about the ICA quotas came to a head when U.S. president Richard Nixon, amidst the escalating cost of the Vietnam War, abandoned the dollar-gold convertibility, temporarily froze wages and prices, and officially devalued the dollar. As discussed in chapter 1, these moves were part of the U.S. administration's attempt to take advantage of its 'structural power' in financial markets and to initiate a Dollar–Wall Street Regime (DWSR) to compensate for its declining position in world trade (Gowan 1999; Helleiner 1994). The immediate impact on the coffee industry was to lower the real prices of coffee (due to a devalued U.S. dollar), which led anxious producing countries to request a readjustment of quotas to compensate. The United States refused. In response, the Geneva Group was reactivated and its members began holding beans off the market, which undercut the quotas of the ICA. Coffee prices rose steadily, which sparked protests from the U.S. government. Amidst the escalating conflicts between ICA members, the agreement was allowed to lapse in December of 1972, after which the buying and selling of futures contracts on the New York exchange rapidly took off in anticipation of future market swings (Talbot 2004: 71; Pendergrast 1999: 303–4).

The United States was eventually compelled to sign a new ICA. The primary motivating factor for this was Brazil's 'Black Frost,' which hit the coffee region in 1975. For the first time in recorded history, snow fell on the Paraná region, destroying most of the year's harvest and over 1.5 billion trees, well over half the country's total growth. This resulted in a major boom in coffee prices, which was further heightened by a series of global events that drastically curtailed coffee supply: escalating civil wars in Angola and Ethiopia; the ruthless actions of Idi Amin in Uganda, which killed hundreds of thousands of people and ruined the national coffee industry; a dock workers' strike in Kenya; a devastating earthquake in Guatemala in 1976; massive flooding and guerrilla war in Colombia; and the emergence of coffee leaf rust in Nicaragua (Talbot 2004: 74; Pendergrast 1999: 317–21). The price of Brazilian arabicas climbed from 75 cents per pound in 1975, to around $1.50 per pound in 1976, to as high as $3.20 per pound in 1977 (UNCTAD 2004). The sale of coffee futures on the New York exchange exploded and speculation ran rampant, while consumers and retail chains began hoarding coffee, all of which further drove prices up. In the United States, consumer boycotts and congressional hearings were organized to protest the price hikes. Eventually, the U.S. government was forced reluctantly to sign a new ICA in 1976 in hopes of stabilizing coffee prices. For their part, Southern states, although temporarily enjoying high coffee prices, were eager to sign on in anticipation of a downward spiral in prices that would likely soon follow (Talbot 2004: 72–3; Pendergrast 1999: 321).

For the first few years after the signing of the ICA, the agreement was relatively meaningless. The price of Brazilian arabicas was well above the ICA's trigger price of 77 cents per pound, and quotas would not officially kick in until prices dropped below it. This trigger price, however, was very low due to the high rate of inflation in the United States. Southern coffee countries pressured the U.S. government to approve an increase, but it refused. When the price of green beans fell to around $1.50 per pound in mid-1978, conflicts concerning ICA quotas once again re-emerged. In an attempt to combat declining prices, representatives from the major coffee-producing countries in Latin America gathered in closed meetings in Bogotá, Colombia, and formed the unofficial 'Bogotá Group,' which was given $140 million to speculate on the coffee futures market and drive up prices. The Bogotá Group met with great success – prices rose as high as $1.89 per pound in 1979 – and in 1980 it was officially incorporated as Pancafe Productores de Café S.A., a Panamanian trading house. In response, the United States stepped in and forced a new consensus: Pancafe would be disbanded, but the United States agreed to sign a new ICA with a target price for average arabicas of $1.68 per pound (UNCTAD 2004; Talbot 2004: 73; Pendergrast 1999: 331–334).

The ICA continued throughout the 1980s, during which time prices fluctuated from a high of over $2.20 per pound to as low as $1.19 per pound (UNCTAD 2004). The United States, still driven by Cold War fears that Latin America would join the communist camp, reluctantly agreed to new ICAs in 1983 and 1987 even though market regulation ran contra to the 'Washington Consensus' on neoliberal restructuring (Talbot 2004: 74). However, the political consensus upon which the ICA had been constructed was slowly eroding. The United States grew increasingly upset over the actions of Latin American coffee cartels, such as the Bogotá Group, which it viewed as a violation of the 'free market.' The sale of 'tourist coffee' continued to grow, spurred on by ICA members who were producing well beyond their quota allotments. Costa Rica, for example, had become one of the most efficient coffee producers in the world and was forced to sell more than 40 per cent of its coffee on markets outside the ICA, often at less than half the ICA price (Talbot 2004: 78; Dicum and Luttinger 1999: 94). In addition, Northern roasters complained about quotas on mild arabicas, which limited their access to higher-quality beans. With world production continuously outstripping demand, Northern roasters no longer feared the potential of soaring prices, and in 1988 the National Coffee Association (NCA) abandoned the ICA and called for 'free and unrestricted trade in coffee' (Talbot 2004: 80–97; Pendergrast 1999: 347, 361–3).

The decision by the NCA set the stage for the final collapse of the ICA. In 1989, the United States refused to come to agreement with Brazil and Colombia on new quarterly quotas and the ICA was suspended. With the USSR on the verge of disintegration, the Reagan administration no longer saw a strategic need to support the ICA against its own neoliberal aims. Moreover, the United States was involved with Brazil in an increasing number of trade disputes over market access for goods such as computer software and pharmaceuticals. American officials viewed Brazil as having one of the most restrictive trade policies towards U.S. exports, and thus chose a hard line in ICA negotiations. Joining the United States in opposing the agreement was a group of 'other milds'-producing countries – Costa Rica, the Dominican Republic, Ecuador, El Salvador, Guatemala, Honduras, India, Mexico, Nicaragua, Papua New Guinea, and Peru – that believed the ICA imposed unfair limits on higher-quality beans. Brazil, Colombia, most of Africa, and most of Europe supported an extended ICA, but were unable to garner enough support. The agreement was suspended, followed by the United States' official withdrawal from the ICA in 1993 (Talbot 2004: 81–97).

The result of the suspension of the ICA was an almost immediate drop in prices and a speculative boom in futures contracts (Calo and Wise 2005: 5–7). The total volume of futures contracts traded on the New York exchange leapt from five times the volume of physical coffee sold in 1980 to nearly 10 times the physical volume sold in 1994, so that 'by the mid-1990s, the vast majority of trades made on the coffee futures markets were made for purely speculative purposes' (Talbot

2004: 111). The price of Brazilian arabicas dropped from $1.45 per pound in 1989, to 70 cents in 1990, to 62 cents in 1992. Prices recovered somewhat from 1995 to 1998, reaching as high as $1.80 per pound, only to plummet in 1999 down to 99 cents. After this, prices fell at a rapid rate, dropping to 64 cents in 2000 and then as low as 42 cents in 2002 (see figure 2.7). This was the lowest price reached in 30 years, and, according to Oxfam International, probably the lowest *real value* in over one hundred years, taking into account historical rates of inflation (UNCTAD 2004; Oxfam International 2002a).

As has historically been the case, the primary reason for this decline has been oversupply caused by the planting of new coffee trees, technological innovations, and the arrival of newcomers into the coffee market, especially Vietnam, which developed from an insignificant coffee exporter to the world's second largest by the end of the 1990s. This historical cycle has been made worse by the debt crisis and the neoliberal policies of the World Bank and the IMF, which have compelled Southern countries to expand commodity exports to earn much-needed foreign exchange and service their debt payments (Talbot 2004: 75–7, 127–8). The impact of the coffee crisis on farmers and workers has been falling incomes, mass layoffs, bankruptcy, migration, and hunger. At the same time, large Northern roasters have raked in huge profits as the gap between green prices and retail prices has widened significantly (Ross 2002; Oxfam International 2002a, 2001; Global Exchange 2001).

Had the ICA been in operation when the present coffee crisis began, measures likely would have been taken to avoid the extreme lows to which prices have fallen. For this reason, the establishment of a new ICA – along with retention schemes, the destruction of millions of bags of coffee, and a windfall tax on Northern coffee roasters to finance such measures – lies at the heart of the proposed solution to the coffee crisis put forward by Oxfam International, which continues to push for a regulated global economy of the sort traditionally envisioned by the fair trade movement described in chapter 1 (Oxfam International 2002a, 2001). During the decades of its operation, the ICA had somewhat dampened the coffee cycle, which led to a greater retention of coffee income in the South. Throughout most of the 1970s, up to the mid-1980s, the portion of global coffee income retained in consuming countries was around 50 per cent, while approximately 33 per cent was retained in producing countries (with the remainder absorbed by shipping costs or weight loss accrued during roasting). This changed abruptly in the years following the collapse of the ICA in 1989, when the portion of global coffee income retained in consuming countries grew to around 75 per cent, while that retained in producing countries fell to around 15 per cent (Talbot 2004: 163–95). Nonetheless, while a new ICA is certainly a needed component of any emergency plan to deal with the crisis, the history of the ICA reveals that its long-term impact on the highly volatile coffee market was limited and that it is far from a panacea for the problems of coffee production in a highly competitive global capitalist economy.

One of the limits of the ICA was its minimal impact on how the wealth retained in the South through higher prices was distributed. This was determined entirely by internal class relations and inequalities in political power and resources. For example, Mary Bohman, Lovell Jarvis, and Richard Barichello (1996) have examined the distribution of extra rents that accrued to Indonesia as a result of ICA-driven higher prices in the early 1980s, during which time it received around 5 per cent of the global coffee quota. They argue that from 1983 to 1985, the average value of domestic quota rents reached around $171 million, nearly $124 million of which was retained in the hands of exporters and corrupt government officials, while the rest was largely squandered by market inefficiencies. Government bureaucrats, often in exchange for bribes, distributed export quotas on the basis of an ambiguous criterion to specific firms that either used them or sold them on an illicit market. The result was a highly inefficient regulation of coffee quotas, which led to market inefficiencies and to Indonesian export coffee beans selling for less than beans of similar quality from other countries, representing a loss of $50 million annually. In the end, Indonesian producers, the vast majority of whom were smallholders, received little or no benefits as a result of ICA prices. Bohman, Lovell, and Barichello (1996: 389) conclude: 'International Coffee Agreement quotas, given the Indonesia response to their imposition, shifted the distribution of income away from the government treasury and farmers, the two groups that the ICA importers intended to assist, toward exporters and government bureaucrats.'

Not all coffee countries experienced the high degree of corruption of the Indonesian state, and in many cases a significant proportion of extra rents made its way into state coffers or the hands of coffee producers. In these cases, however, wealth retained by the state was often oriented towards public expenditure that disproportionately benefited the wealthy elites who dominated the state apparatus. And wealth retained by growers was unequally distributed on the basis of property ownership. Large-scale property owners who could take advantage of economies of scale received substantial incomes, while rural workers continued to receive relatively low wages and small-property owners received relatively small incomes (Talbot 2004: 163–95). Nonetheless, while the benefits of higher prices were unequally distributed, this is not to say that they did not 'trickle down' at all to the poor and provide improved living standards to broad sectors. Talbot points out that during the decades of the ICA, higher prices meant that 'small coffee growers, while they were not getting rich, were able to live, support their families, and enjoy a standard of living better than many other Third World agriculturalists' (195).

Yet, while the 'trickle down' benefits of the ICA were important, vast inequalities in power and wealth within nation-states served to significantly dampen the impact of these gains and offset their overall developmental impact. Countries that pursued a state-managed project that distributed greater resources to small farmers and workers, such as Costa Rica and Colombia, were able to attain significantly better development gains than countries with a highly unequal distribution of land and resources, such as El Salvador, Guatemala, and Brazil. For this reason, Oxfam maintains that any long-term solution to the coffee crisis must include national government policies to direct more wealth and resources to the rural poor through extensive credit programs, technical and marketing assistance, and the construction of social infrastructure (Oxfam International 2002a: 49–51, 2001). To this must be added the long-standing need for land redistribution, required to address historically unjust property relations, an issue which is currently absent from Oxfam's more modest coffee agenda.[3]

A second limit of the ICA was its inability to deal effectively with the structural causes of global oversupply. In fact, the ICA not only failed to discourage this occurrence, but also actually encouraged it. The formula for determining quarterly export quotas, a highly politically contentious issue, was arrived at on the basis of a given state's 'historic' world market share and its 'demonstrated capacity' to produce and export coffee. The effect of the latter determinant was to provide an incentive to member states to overproduce beyond the level of their export quota. In this way, they had political ammunition to demand an increase in their export quota on the basis of their 'demonstrated capacity' being well beyond their current quota allotment. In effect, Talbot (2004: 75–7) states, 'the regulatory regime attempted to limit total coffee exports while simultaneously creating conditions under which producers would tend to produce coffee in excess of the amount needed to fill the global quota.'

A third weakness of the ICA was its inability to do little more than dampen the unpredictable swings of the coffee cycle (Dicum and Luttinger 1999: 59). For example, in the wake of the Black Frost in Brazil in 1975, the price of green beans rose by nearly 300 per cent from 1976 to 1977, only to then drop by 45 per cent by 1979 (UNCTAD 2004). This situation is a far cry from what Oxfam has referred to as a 'golden era of good and stable prices' (Oxfam International 2002a: 17). In reference to the swings of the 1970s, John Talbot argues that they in fact demonstrate the effectiveness of the ICA, as the greatest movements occurred when the ICA was either not in effect (1973–6) or when it was in effect but with very low trigger prices (1976–80) (Talbot 2004: 67–100). While this was indeed the case, this still must be regarded as a weakness of the ICA. It is the very nature of the ICA and the political difficulties inherent in carrying out such an agreement in a competitive global economy that have led to pauses in its implementation and periods of low trigger prices that have allowed the boom and bust cycles of the coffee industry to continue.

Connected to this last point is a fourth limit of the ICA, its fragile existence and eventual collapse when the political-economic conditions which gave rise to it dissipated. This was not an instance particular to the coffee industry, but, as argued in chapter 1, the outcome of most attempts at multilateral commodity agreements in the twentieth century (Barratt Brown 1993: 79–95). These failures are a result of a competitive global capitalist economy in which multilateral agreements are based on tenuous alliances between competing interests and thus are vulnerable to a variety of partial state and corporate considerations. In the case of coffee, this involved the end of the Cold War, consumer pressure for cheaper coffee, the move by Northern roasters to take fuller advantage of global overproduction, and the decision of more efficient producers to oppose the ICA, which they perceived to be a hindrance to their competitive advantages. In the long term, it is not clear that international commodity agreements, unless supported by radical reforms at the national level, are feasible under global capitalism.

Instant Coffee and 'Forward Integration'

Another important strategy for addressing the inequalities of the global coffee industry has been attempts at 'forward integration' –

promoting movement along the 'commodity chain' to allow Southern producers and states to gain greater access to revenues, investment, and value-added activities (Talbot 2004: 12; Gereffi and Korzeniewicz 1994). Attempts at forward integration in the coffee industry have historically been limited by the nature and geography of coffee processing. After initial processing, green beans can be stored for long periods of time, but roasted beans rapidly go stale. In consequence, it has been necessary to process beans only up to the green bean stage and leave the roasting stage until after beans have been exported to the major consuming countries in the North where they can be quickly distributed. However, the increasing production and sale of instant coffee after the Second World War opened up new opportunities for forward integration because instant coffee could be stored for long periods after final processing and thus could be entirely produced and processed in the South (Talbot 2004: 135–62, 2002, 1997).

Instant coffee sales boomed in the United States in the 1950s, so that by the end of the decade instant coffee consumption accounted for 20 to 25 per cent of total national coffee consumption. During these years, the instant coffee industry became largely dominated by major TNCs: Nestlé, General Foods, Tenco, and Borden. Only these giant corporations had the necessary capital to invest in the research and development, new technologies, and modern facilities required to process instant coffee. The majority of the new plants built by these TNCs were constructed in North America and Europe and essentially replicated the geography of the existing global coffee chain. By the mid-1960s, however, instant coffee processing was far enough advanced in the product life cycle so that the required technology was not changing too rapidly, and it became possible to acquire instant coffee facilities without an insurmountable research and development expenditure. This led to government-promoted attempts to develop instant coffee processing in countries such as Brazil, Colombia, Ecuador, India, and the Ivory Coast.

It was in Brazil that the biggest push towards the development of a national instant coffee industry took place. Beginning in the 1960s, the Brazilian government's Instituto Brasileiro do Café (Brazilian Coffee Institute, IBC) announced measures to encourage national capitalists to invest in the development of instant coffee facilities. This included a commitment by the IBC to sell green beans from its stock to instant coffee entrepreneurs at low prices (many of these beans were below export-quality 'grinders' that were still adequate for instant coffee), a guarantee that the IBC would purchase 80 per cent of the instant coffee produced in the first year of operation, and an exemption from the standard national export taxes applied to green beans. As a result of these measures, the instant coffee industry expanded rapidly. The number of instant coffee factories in Brazil grew from one in 1965 to ten by 1969, by which time Brazilian instant coffee had captured 14 per cent of the total U.S. market for instant coffee (Talbot 2002, 1997; Pendergrast 1999: 296–7).

Brazil's rapid entrance into the instant coffee market was stymied in the 1970s. Under intense pressure from the United States, which stalled on signing the 1968 ICA, Brazil agreed to impose an export tax on all instant coffee destined for U.S. markets and to sell 560,000 bags of green beans per year exempt from regular export taxes to U.S. instant coffee manufacturers (Pendergrast 1999: 296–7). These measures severely weakened Brazil's comparative advantage and compounded the difficulties of penetrating Northern markets dominated by giant TNCs with huge advertising dollars and established distribution networks. As a result, in the 1980s and 1990s Brazil was forced to sell most of its instant coffee in bulk to Northern TNCs in order to gain access to core markets, somewhat replicating the geography of the traditional coffee industry – albeit with some extra 'value-added' wealth being retained in Brazil. The situation has been similar in other emerging instant coffee-producing nations such as Colombia, Ecuador, India, and the Ivory Coast, whose attempts at forward integration through instant coffee have been severely limited by the structure of the global coffee industry (Talbot 2002, 1997). In 2000/1, instant coffee constituted 6 per cent of all coffee exported from developing countries, representing significant initial growth, but limited long-term expansion (Oxfam International 2002a: 33).

According to Talbot, who has examined the instant coffee industry through a global commodity chain (GCC) approach, attempts at forward integration along the instant coffee chain have brought only limited benefits to the South. He states that these attempts have resulted in some backward linkages for manufactured inputs such as roasters, tanks, and valves, much of which have been produced locally, especially in Brazil. Backward linkages for labour have been less apparent as instant coffee production is highly mechanized and creates few local jobs. As a strategy for Southern countries to gain a larger share of total income and profits, Talbot argues that the results have been mixed. In the 1960s, for example, Brazilian instant coffee sold for a higher percentage of the U.S. retail price than did Brazilian green beans, resulting in a higher share of total income for Brazil. However, the instant coffee industry at this time was highly subsidized by the Brazilian government, so that the increase in total income 'represented primarily a transfer of surplus from the state to the private sector' (Talbot 1997: 132). Moreover, due to growing international supply, instant coffee exports have not always gained a higher price than green bean exports: from 1984 to 1990, Japan paid slightly *less* for instant coffee from Brazil than it paid for an equivalent amount of Brazilian green beans. Finally, Talbot concludes that the monopoly control over Northern coffee markets exercised by major TNCs has strictly limited the ability of Southern producers to expand their market share in both established and emerging markets (Talbot 2002, 1997).

While the structure of the global coffee industry has prevented the further expansion of instant coffee production in the South, it is unclear that such a strategy of forward integration in and of itself would bring developmental and social benefits to workers and small-scale farmers. Forward integration can challenge the unequal distribution of wealth between nations, but, as with the ICA, it does not necessarily challenge the unequal distribution of wealth within nations, which is determined by the social relations of production and the balance of class power. Thus, while the development of instant coffee factories in Brazil may result in greater profits accruing to large producers, it does not necessarily result in higher wages for Brazilian workers or higher prices for small farmers, all of which are determined by other factors. This is the essential weakness of both forward integration strategies and the GCC approach. As sociologist William Robinson (2002: 1053) concludes, 'It is not clear that such integration into GCCs leads to development processes rather than to the reproduction of social hierarchies under new circumstances.'

The Colombian 'Price Premium'

Another key attempt at addressing the inequalities of the global coffee industry has been the campaign by the Federación Nacional de Cafeteros (National Federation of Coffee Farmers, FNC) in Colombia to promote its high-quality arabica 'Colombian milds' and attain a price premium on Northern markets. The FNC is a quasi-state organization founded in 1927 as an official private institution but empowered by the state to collect and spend a coffee export tax. Due to a variety of histor-

ical factors, coffee production in Colombia has been conducted primarily by small farmers who have dominated the FNC. Long before
Colombia's twentieth-century emergence as a major player in the global coffee industry, the indigenous population had been forced out of
what became coffee-growing regions by the colonial regime, resulting
in a lack of cheap, available labour for exploitation. Combined with a
relative lack of sufficient capital and a difficult, hilly terrain, these
conditions gave way to a preponderance of small farms that utilized
family labour and grew their own subsistence crops. The prevalence of
smallholders was further consolidated by a wave of protests and
squatting campaigns by tenant farmers and workers in the 1930s that
compelled the state to pass laws making vacant coffee land subject to
expropriation, resulting in a further decline of large-scale coffee plantations. This trend was then further reinforced by the FNC-led development strategy after 1930, which emphasized high-quality coffee that
was more efficiently produced by intensive family labour. These factors set a historical pattern which continues to this day; in 2002, the
FNC had a membership of over 500,000 coffee farmers with an average
farm size of less than two hectares (Waridel 2002: 41; Pendergrast 1999:
185; Topik 1998: 66–7; Thorp 1991: 1–22, 199).

Since its formation, the FNC has played a central role in developing
the nation's coffee export and marketing policies and social and physical infrastructure. Starting in the 1930s, the FNC instituted monitoring
and quality controls, provided credit and extension services, and constructed warehouses and processing facilities to integrate forward into
an export sphere which was monopolized by foreign interests. As a
result, by the 1950s the FNC had become Colombia's major coffee
exporter, and foreign companies handled only 20 per cent of total coffee exports. This meant greater wealth for the FNC, which further
extended its provision of technical services and credit, and expanded
its activities to include the construction of roads, schools, and hospitals
(Dicum and Luttinger 1999: 77–8; Thorp 1991: 9–10, 206).

One of the most important campaigns of the FNC has been its promotion of high-quality Colombian arabicas through the symbol of Juan
Valdez, a 'friendly, mustachioed coffee grower who, with his mule,
trundled his hand-picked beans down from the Colombian mountains'
(Pendergrast 1999: 185). Beginning in 1960, the FNC launched a major
advertising campaign promoting Juan Valdez in ten primary U.S. markets at the cost of $1 million for the first year. Five months after the
campaign began, market researchers reported a 300 per cent increase in

the number of U.S. consumers who identified Colombian coffee as the world's finest. In 1962, the FNC expanded its campaign to Europe and Canada. Motivated by the growing interest created by the FNC's efforts, General Foods changed its high-end Yuban brand to 100 per cent Colombian coffee in 1964. The following year, over forty U.S. brands and twenty European roasters followed suit and developed their own 100 per cent Colombian brands. By the end of the decade, Colombian milds had become established as premium 'value-added' products which could garner higher prices than regular arabicas due to the quality of its bean and the Juan Valdez promotional campaign (Pendergrast 1999: 285–7).

Since the 1960s, the premium price for Colombian arabicas has generally hovered well above the price of other arabicas. From 1960 to 1975, the price for Colombian arabicas fluctuated from around 4 per cent to 18 per cent more than the price of Brazilian arabicas. These trends were reversed for several years beginning in 1976, during which time the price of Brazilian arabicas experienced a major upswing in the wake of the Black Frost and sold anywhere from 3 per cent to 20 per cent more than Colombian arabicas. After 1987, the relative price of Colombian beans recovered and sold from around 10 per cent to 34 per cent more than Brazilians for the next fifteen years (see figures 4.1 and 4.2). Since 2002, with coffee prices plummeting to unprecedented lows, Colombian arabicas have sold from 42 per cent to 50 per cent more than the Brazilian variety (UNCTAD 2004). This growing price differential is due to different national strategies. Whereas Brazil has traditionally focused on increasing production and efficiency, Colombia has paid greater attention to promoting the quality of its beans, which has allowed it to garner relatively higher prices even in times of fierce price competition (Dicum and Luttinger 1999: 105).

The Colombian price premium has provided higher incomes for coffee farmers and has served as a source of greater revenue for the FNC (through export taxes and membership dues), which has been used to construct social and economic infrastructure for coffee communities. In consequence, Colombia has developed one of the most modern and efficient coffee industries in the world; in 2000, Colombia consumed 233,500 grams of fertilizer per hectare of arable land, compared to 139,700 grams in Brazil, 148,900 grams in El Salvador, and 1,190 grams in Nicaragua. In the same year, the percentage of total crop land under irrigation in Colombia was 19 per cent, compared to 4 per cent in Brazil, 5 per cent in El Salvador, and 3 per cent in Nicaragua (World Bank

Figure 4.1 Colombian price premium compared to Brazilian arabicas
(Brazilian prices = 0)*

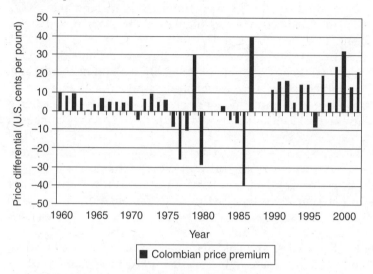

*Data for Colombia for 1981, 1988, 1989 are not available.
Source: UNCTAD (2004), UNCTAD Handbook of Statistics On-Line, http://stats.unctad.org.

2004). These gains in income and developmental infrastructure have
translated into relatively better living standards for Colombian coffee
farmers, even while they continued to live under general conditions of
austerity and insecurity.

Prior to the onset of declining coffee prices in the 1990s, in the 1970s
and 1980s Colombia's central coffee-growing region emerged as the
wealthiest rural region in the country, which meant that internationally
Colombia fared better than most other major coffee-exporting nations.
In the central coffee-growing region in Colombia, the annual increase
in mean household income per capita between 1978 and 1988 was 5.6
per cent, which was faster than the average growth rate in urban areas
of 4.1 per cent (World Bank 2002a: 112–14). In comparison to other
major coffee-growing countries, at the start of the 1990s the percentage
of rural population living in poverty in Colombia was around 61 per
cent, compared to 83 per cent in Nicaragua, 71 per cent in Brazil, and
around 64 per cent in El Salvador (ECLAC 2004: 257–8). The percentage of the rural population with access to adequate water from an
improved source was 84 per cent in Colombia, compared to 54 per cent

Figure 4.2 Comparative green coffee bean prices, Colombian milds and
Brazilian arabicas, 1960–2000

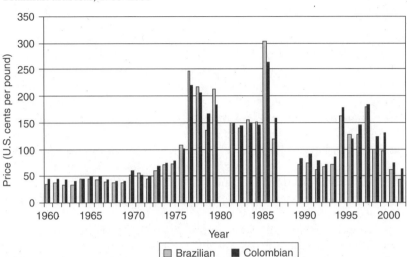

*Data for Colombia for 1981, 1988, 1989 are not available.
Source: UNCTAD (2004), *UNCTAD Handbook of Statistics On-Line*, http://stats.unctad.org.

in Brazil, 48 per cent in El Salvador, and 44 per cent in Nicaragua
(World Bank 2004).

Despite the positive impact of the FNC's production and marketing
scheme, such a program has many weaknesses as a long-term development strategy that can be replicated elsewhere. The first of these
weaknesses is the negative ecological and social impact of the modernization of the coffee sector, which has involved a turn towards
monocrop production, under full-sun conditions, with a massive use
of chemical pesticides, fertilizers, and insecticides. Since the introduction of new 'Green Revolution' high-yielding coffee plants and agro-
chemicals in the 1970s, around 30 to 40 per cent of Latin America's
total coffee land has been transformed from shade-grown to 'technified' full-sun cultivation (Rice 1998: 53). Colombia, along with Costa
Rica, has been at the head of this modernization, and currently has an
estimated 68 per cent of its coffee grown under full-sun, monocrop
conditions (UNCTAD and IISD 2003: 4).

The impact of this method of coffee cultivation has included the
destruction of tropical rainforests required to preserve atmospheric

dynamics, water quality, and wildlife species; major declines in the biodiversity of trees, birds, animals, and insects; and increased soil erosion. The decline of natural predators to coffee pests has left coffee crops vulnerable to outbreaks of *la broca* and coffee leaf rust, which increasing applications of pesticides have been unable to control. Workers and farmers have been exposed to a variety of chemicals which have been implicated in certain cancers, birth defects, developmental problems, and other illnesses. In 1993 and 1994, the use of the insecticide endosulfan on coffee plantations in Colombia was linked to more than two hundred poisonings (UNCTAD and IISD 2003: 4–7; Waridel 2002: 34–5; Dicum and Luttinger 1999: 54, 98–9). In addition, while monocrop production has increased productivity per hectare for individual coffee farmers, on an international scale the turn towards the modernization of coffee production has merely contributed to the current crisis of global oversupply that has sparked downward prices (Talbot 2004: 75–7).

A second weakness of the Colombian strategy has been its continued dependence on the whims of a highly volatile coffee market. Although Colombian farmers have been able to attain a higher price for their beans, they have not been able to avoid the unpredictable swings of the coffee market. For example, when the price of Brazilian arabicas plummeted from $1.79 per pound in 1998 to 42 cents by 2002, the price of Colombia arabicas followed a similar pattern and dropped from $1.84 to 60 cents over the same period (see table 4.3) (UNCTAD 2004). The Colombian price premium is entirely dependent on the whims of Northern consumers, whose shopping preferences are unpredictable and vulnerable to competitive marketing strategies. In recent years, the production and sale of cheap robusta beans has boomed as major Northern roasters have turned increasingly towards competing on the basis of low prices, not quality coffee. This has resulted in a decline in demand for high-priced, high-quality arabicas, which has hit the coffee industry in Colombia hard and forced the FNC to cut back on marketing expenses for Juan Valdez (Oxfam International 2002a: 30, 42).

A third weakness of the Colombian strategy is its inapplicability as a developmental model which can be replicated in other coffee regions. On a national level, the particular history of Colombia's coffee regions has led to a predominance of smallholders, which has ensured that the FNC's resources were employed in a manner which genuinely benefited most coffee farmers (Thorp 1991: 1–22). In countries with a highly unequal distribution of coffee land, such as Guatemala and Brazil, an FNC-style program would simply not work or its benefits would accrue largely to wealthy elites. On an international level, the very existence of Colombia's price premium is derived from the fact that other countries have not adopted a similar approach. According to Oxfam International (2002a: 42): 'Not all poor producers can move into the premium market of specialty arabica coffees. If too many producers try to move into this segment of the market, it would cease to be a niche capable of commanding high prices ... The problem of everyone running for the same exit – known in economics as "the fallacy of composition" – has been a hallmark of commodity production for decades, and one that has been insufficiently tackled by international institutions.'

The final major weakness of the Colombian coffee strategy has been its sectoral focus and the lack of accompanying political-economic reforms on a national level. Outside of the coffee regions, Colombia is characterized by vast disparities of wealth and resources, and the national state has historically been invariably dominated by factions from the agrarian and industrial elite. Conflict over land (for bananas, cut flowers, tropical hardwoods, and cattle), resources (such as petroleum, coal, and hydroelectric power), and control of the state has mired Colombia's twentieth-century history in civil war and militarism. Over the past decade, more than one million Colombians have been displaced and thousands are killed each year as a result of political violence, most of which has been orchestrated by elite groups and executed by the Colombian military and right-wing paramilitary groups (Wirpsa 1997).

The chaos, violence, and uncertainty in Colombia have created conditions which are ripe for the growth of the coca industry (used in the production of cocaine) in areas controlled by paramilitaries and left-wing guerrilla groups, and illegal drugs have become the country's number one export, ahead of both petroleum and coffee. This has led to growing intervention by the United States, which has granted massive amounts of aid and training to the Colombian military, a fact which has merely heightened the violence and instability in the region and has had little effect on stemming the drug trade (Wirpsa 1997; Thorp 1991: 195–216). With coffee prices plummeting, increasing numbers of Colombian coffee farmers are turning towards the production of high-value coca, which is cultivated under conditions similar to coffee beans (Oxfam International 2002a: 12). Ironically, the United States continues to provide ineffective and highly detrimental military aid to

Colombia while at the same time refusing to support the ICA, which likely would have helped in part to stem the growing tide of coca production in the country.[4] All of these factors have resulted in a broad developmental failure on a national scale to establish democracy, respect for human rights, and social welfare in Colombia.

Costa Rica: Regulated Coffee Industry and Social Welfare State

The most successful development project in the coffee world has been the construction of a regulated coffee industry and a social welfare state in Costa Rica, a tiny country with a population of less than four million people located in the historically war-torn and highly militarized region of Central America. Due to a state-led development strategy initiated in the late 1940s, Costa Rica has developed one of the most advanced coffee economies in the world, and many of its citizens enjoy living standards significantly higher than those of most Southern nations and comparable in many regards to rich nations in the North. At the start of the millennium, life expectancy at birth in Costa Rica was 78 years – which matched the average for high-income nations in the North – and the adult illiteracy rate was 4 per cent, compared to 8 per cent in Colombia and 21 per cent in El Salvador. Costa Rica's efficient coffee industry had resulted in an annual GDP per capita purchasing power parity (PPP) of $9,460 (compared to $7,040 in Colombia and $5,260 in El Salvador), and Costa Rica employed over three times as much fertilizer and agricultural machinery per hectare of arable land than Colombia (World Bank 2004).

The benefits of Costa Rica's development have been broadly spread within rural areas, and the World Bank estimates that in 2000 the percentage of the rural population with access to adequate water from an improved source was 92 per cent, and the percentage of the rural population with access to improved sanitation facilities was 97 per cent (World Bank 2004). The average income of agricultural workers between the ages of 20 and 29 in Costa Rica was around 4.8 times the per capita poverty line, compared to 2.7 in Colombia, 2.3 in El Salvador, 1.7 in Nicaragua, and 1.2 in Brazil (ECLAC 2004: 279–80). Perhaps most indicative of Costa Rica's social gains in the rural sector is the percentage of the rural population living below the poverty line, which in 1999 was around 22 per cent. This was only a few percentage points higher than Costa Rica's national urban poverty rate, unheard of in the region, and well below the rural poverty rate of all other major coffee-producing nations and the Latin American average of 64 per cent (ECLAC 2004: 257–8; Quijandría, Monares, and de Peña Montenegro 2001: 31).

Along with these developmental gains, the Costa Rican state has also sought to avoid the militarization and state-orchestrated violence common to several other countries in the region and to promote peace and stability. Its standing army was abolished in 1949, and, while it does maintain a significant national police force, in relative terms it has avoided the costly military expenditure of other coffee-producing nations; in the 1990s the percentage of central government expenditure devoted to military spending in Costa Rica was zero, compared to around 6 per cent per annum in Brazil and over 15 per cent per annum in Colombia (World Bank 2004; Edelman 1999: 56; Booth 1988: 401)

The origins of Costa Rica's welfare state are frequently traced back to its colonial history. Due to its lack of mineral wealth, it is argued, Costa Rica was a peripheral region of the Spanish colonial system; it was sparsely settled and had a significant proportion of its relatively tiny indigenous population wiped out by white colonists. This led to the dominance of small and medium-scale, white family farms, which contrasted sharply with the massive estates and the enslavement of indigenous and black workers throughout the rest of Central America, and laid the basis for the emergence of a more democratic state.

Although it must be qualified in several important ways, this perspective does reveal certain aspects of the historical roots of Costa Rican democracy. The country's relatively tiny indigenous population was heavily exploited during the colonial period and severely decimated, declining from 80 per cent of the total population in 1700 to only 16 per cent in 1800 (Booth 1988). Remaining indigenous communities were forcibly displaced by liberal elites after colonialism in the 1840s (Paige 1997: 14).[5] At the same time, the use of black slave labour in Costa Rica was relatively small compared to the rest of the Caribbean, and was confined mostly to the Atlantic coasts and not the central coffee-producing region of the *meseta central*. The result was a relative shortage of cheap labour, which worked against the widespread consolidation of large-scale haciendas and gave way to the emergence of a significant smallholder class. The existence of this relatively racially homogeneous, smallholder class gave way to a 'somewhat less exclusionist oligarchic state' (Winson 1989: 170), and resulted in a broader distribution of certain social benefits than in the rest of Central America where the coffee elites frequently used racism to justify forced labour and hyper-exploitation. For example, public literacy programs initiated by liberal dictatorships in Costa Rica resulted in nearly half of the population being literate in 1905, a very high percentage for that time (Booth 1988).

At the same time, this picture must be significantly qualified. First, the emergence of the coffee industry in Costa Rica at the end of the nineteenth century gave way to increasing land concentration and the growth of landless rural workers – patterns which continue to this day. This situation was somewhat mitigated by the relative scarcity of labour, and, until the mid-twentieth century, the relative availability of unclaimed arable land in the Pacific lowlands outside of the coffee-growing regions. This resulted in relatively high wages for rural workers and a degree of interclass harmony between rural coffee workers and smallholders (Samper 1994: 17–24, 84–92; Booth 1988; Weeks 1985: 111–22). Second, despite growing land concentration, the prevalence of smallholder coffee farms did persist. These small farms, however, were not predominantly independent family farms, but 'sub-family' farms that had to rely on selling their labour power to make ends meet. Jeffery Paige states: 'Costa Rican coffee farmers were a semi-proletariat of land-starved mini-farmers rather than an autonomous yeoman farmer class' (Paige 1997: 65). Third, large-scale coffee estates persisted in Costa Rica and have up until this day. Nonetheless, unlike in the rest of the region, these agrarian elites did have to share a substantial amount of productive means with a class of smallholders, which played a significant role in the emergence of Costa Rica's welfare state (53–95).[6] These smallholders eventually formed a key basis of political support for the reformist government that emerged in the country in the 1940s (Winson 1989: 169–74).

The Costa Rican elite's relative lack of dominance over coffee land and production led the upper classes towards a greater emphasis on monopolizing coffee processing, marketing, credit, and export activities in the country. The result was a power shift within the elite classes from the agrarian faction (who dominated land and production) towards the agro-industrial faction (who dominated export and processing). According to Paige, this shift is key to explaining Costa Rica's unique development path. In Central America, agrarian factions have tended to be more tied to authoritarian politics due to their dependence on unequal land ownership and control over labour. Thus, in Guatemala and El Salvador, which were largely dominated by agrarian factions dependent on highly unequal land distribution and labour-repressive estate agriculture, authoritarian institutions were developed to control and discipline the labouring masses. In contrast, agro-industrial factions are not dependent on land ownership or the control of large numbers of labourers, making them less tied to authoritarian politics and potentially more open to democratic reforms, as was the case in Costa Rica (Paige 1997: 53–95).

Yet, while less tied to authoritarian politics, Costa Rica's agro-industrial factions were still resistant to democratic change, as has historically been the case with most agrarian elites. To shake this resistance, a particular set of historical events had first to occur in the 1930s and 1940s that threatened elite dominance and compelled them to accept reform for the sake of their own survival. Internationally, the Great Depression of the 1930s followed by the Second World War led to a collapse of coffee prices and insecurity and chaos throughout the coffee industry. This weakened the power of the coffee oligarchy and fuelled growing resentment from small and medium farmers over the formers' monopolization of credit and processing facilities. At the same time, the Partido Republicano Nacional (National Republican Party, PRN), traditionally a party of the coffee elite, formed a Popular Alliance with the Communist Party to fight fascism and promote radical reforms. The PRN had previously supported the coffee elite's low-wage, free trade policies but the party increasingly viewed them as a barrier to the growth of the domestic market and domestic industry. Severely weakened and fearing the overthrow of its power, the coffee oligarchy felt it had no other choice but to throw its support behind the reformist Partido Social Demócrata (Social Democratic Party, PSD), which, under the leadership of José Figueres Ferrer, seized control of the Costa Rican state by force in 1948 (Winson 1989; Booth 1988).

According to Anthony Winson, although ostensibly supported by the desperate coffee elite, Figueres and the PSD emerged in the 1940s as a 'third force' between the radical Popular Alliance and the conservative coffee oligarchy. Once in power the PSD manoeuvred between these two polar forces and created a new national state with a degree of autonomy from both forces and a well-articulated plan for national development. This plan included an agrarian reform that differed from a program of land redistribution, which in Latin America typically met with fierce resistance from the local elite and the United States (Winson 1989: 50–76). In Guatemala, for example, democratic reforms in the 1940s and 1950s required a redistribution of the country's grossly unequal land ownership – 72 per cent of the country's agricultural land was controlled by slightly more than 2 per cent of farms in 1950 (Handy 1994: 82).[7] When radical reformist president Jacobo Arbenz attempted this in 1952, he was overthrown by a CIA-backed coup two years later and replaced by an authoritarian regime that rolled back the redistribution and set the country down a path of decades of brutal dictatorship, underdevelopment, and civil war (Handy 1994; Weeks 1985: 26–8).

In Costa Rica, the urgent need for land redistribution was not as powerful, and the PSD was able to focus on modernizing the coffee sector, which satisfied the elite and solidified the political support of smallholders for the PSD program. The agrarian reform involved state taxation on a greater share of coffee revenues, which was then directed back into spending on rural development through the construction of infrastructure, the formation of new state credit programs, and the promotion of new planting techniques and technologies (Winson 1989: 99–113). It also entailed the formation of the state run Oficina del Café (Coffee Office), which set the prices that processors had to pay producers for coffee beans and required processors to provide loans to smallholders under favourable terms. Similar state-run organizations emerged to regulate domestic food crops, such as grains, and provide guaranteed prices for farmers and subsidized retail prices for consumers. These economic reforms were accompanied by political reforms – which included the introduction of universal suffrage, the abolition of the army, and the strengthening of democratic institutions – designed to provide a popular base for the new interventionist state and its developmental program (Edelman 1999: 44–68; Winson 1989: 67–73).

In addition to direct state involvement, the PSD also promoted, through generous tax advantages, the development of agricultural production and processing, credit and savings, purchasing, transportation, and housing cooperatives. Their number and membership grew steadily, so that by the mid-1980s nearly 30 per cent of the economically active population belonged to some sort of cooperative. They were particularly important in the coffee sector where they channelled public funds and provided research and extension services to members and in doing so played a key role in the modernization of Costa Rica's coffee sector. By the early 1980s, cooperatives accounted for 30 per cent of the nation's coffee-processing output (Edelman 1999: 58–9; Winson 1989: 107–8). This represents a significant dent in a stage of the coffee chain traditionally dominated by the coffee elite. Cooperatives in Costa Rica have not just been important to the nation's economic development, but they have also played an important political role in providing poor and marginalized groups with a collective voice to advance their interests and express their needs (Arias Sánchez 2004; Booth 1988: 407).

At first, the Costa Rican coffee elite were reluctant supporters of the new reforms orchestrated by the PSD, which curtailed their political power and cut into their coffee revenues. However, the modernization of the coffee sector soon revealed its benefits to the coffee oligarchy, who could take advantage of state-provided infrastructure and innovations to enhance their competitiveness in international markets. By the 1970s, Costa Rica had moved from being one of the most backward coffee-producing nations to one of the most advanced and efficient in the world. The transformation of the Costa Rican state also provided benefits to workers, who attained higher state-imposed wages and stronger labour rights, and small- and medium-scale farmers, who received greater access to infrastructure, technology, and credit. The democratic compromise attained in Costa Rica led to the development of a social welfare state which provided average Costa Ricans with such things as public health care, education, and social assistance (Winson 1989). This has resulted in a relatively more egalitarian distribution of social wealth in Costa Rica compared to most other coffee-producing countries, although vast disparities continue to exist (Booth 1988). In the late 1990s the Gini coefficient, a statistical measure of inequality (the lower the coefficient, the greater the equality), in Costa Rica was 46, compared to 54 in Colombia, 61 in Brazil, 41 in the United States, and 32 in Canada (World Bank 2004).

The development of a state-regulated coffee industry and social welfare state in Costa Rica stands in significant contrast to the FNC-led development strategy in Colombia where the majority of coffee farms are also small-scale units. In Costa Rica, the modernization of the coffee sector was accompanied by major political reforms on a national level, which weakened the power of the traditional landed elite and broadened the benefits of the new development strategy. In Colombia, the traditional elite remained in control of the national state; benefits remained limited to the coffee sector; and the country descended into civil war, violence, and militarism which have severely curtailed Colombia's future prospects for a democratic and more egalitarian developmental path.

Nonetheless, the Costa Rican case is not without its weaknesses. One of these has been the ecological and social impact of the modernization of the coffee sector, which mirrors that of Colombia. Nearly 40 per cent of Costa Rica's coffee is grown under chemical-intensive, sun-grown, monocrop conditions which has had widespread negative effects on water quality, biodiversity, soil quality, and the vulnerability of coffee trees to *la broca* and coffee leaf rust (Dicum and Luttinger 1999: 53). It has also had negative effects on workers and rural communities; recently the use of nitrogen fertilizers on modernized farms has been linked to cases of unsafe groundwater pollution (UNCTAD and IISD 2003: 7).

A second weakness of the Costa Rican model lies in the difficulty inherent in its replication. Similar to the strategy of the FNC, the success of the Costa Rican coffee promotion model depends on other countries not having adopted a similar approach. The foundation of Costa Rica's welfare state rests in part on the revenues it gains through its 'competitive advantage': being one of the most efficient coffee industries in the world. From its relatively advantageous position, the Costa Rican state has worked to promote the interests of its coffee producers at the expense of international competitors. For example, Costa Rica actively campaigned for an end to ICA quotas, which were viewed as a major obstacle to the growth of the Costa Rican coffee industry, even though they were essential for the viability of weaker competitors (Dicum and Luttinger 1999: 94). If other major coffee-producing nations were to replicate the Costa Rican model, this would likely lead to an erosion of Costa Rica's competitive advantage, and, in Oxfam's words, to the 'problem of everyone running for the same exit' (Oxfam International 2002a: 43). Such a move would not stem the volatility and insecurity of the international coffee market but would merely intensify competitive pressures between nations.[8]

Connected to this is a third aspect of the Costa Rican model that also calls into question the difficulties inherent in its replication: the historically unique conditions that gave way to its emergence (Winson 1989: 174–7). While Costa Rica's actual history is far more complex than popular myths about an egalitarian, small-farmer democracy, the fact remains that the emergence in the nineteenth century of a semi-proletariat smallholder class did play a significant role in the later development of the welfare state. These smallholders weakened the power of the agrarian faction of the elite and provided political support for the new reformist measures. While severe inequalities of wealth and power remained, the unique situation in Costa Rica allowed for small and medium farmers and the coffee elite to reach a class compromise based on the modernization of the coffee industry. In countries with a more highly unequal distribution of coffee land and resources, such as Guatemala, El Salvador, and Nicaragua, the conditions for such a compromise did not exist. In these countries, modernization, democracy, and even a moderate degree of social justice, required a major redistribution of productive resources, which led not to class compromise but to class conflict resulting in authoritarian politics, genocide, and civil war (Paige 1997; North 1985; Handy 1984).

A final weakness of the Costa Rican model stems from concerns over its inability to remain sustainable in the long term and to withstand the imperatives of global capitalism. As was the case throughout the South, described in chapter 1, Costa Rica was hit hard by the economic crisis of the 1970s. Squeezed between growing indebtedness, high interest rates, and increasing oil prices on the one hand, and declining commodity prices on the other, Costa Rica became the first country in Latin America to declare a moratorium on servicing its $4 billion debt in 1981. The response was a series of 'rescue' packages from the IMF, the World Bank, and the United States Agency for International Development (USAID) throughout the 1980s and 1990s. In exchange for new loans to rollover old ones, Costa Rica was compelled to initiate a series of neoliberal structural adjustments, which included cuts to public-sector spending, downsizing the state, privatizing state assets, removing market barriers to foreign imports, corporate tax breaks, currency devaluation to boost exports and dampen consumption, and various measures to promote export-led growth in non-traditional agricultural products like cut flowers, ornamental plants, coconut oil, and citrus juice. In the agricultural sector, neoliberal reforms have involved the eventual elimination or restriction of crop price supports, subsidized credit provisions, import restrictions, and consumer subsidies on food crops such as maize, beans, and rice (Edelman 1999: 44–90; Booth 1988; Weeks 1985: 185–8). These reforms have also been accompanied by the expansion and growing militarization of Costa Rica's 'Civil Guard,' a process that was first initiated by the United States in the 1980s as part of its war against the Sandinistas in neighbouring Nicaragua. (U.S. military assistance to Costa Rica grew from zero in 1980, to $2.5 million in 1983, to $10 million in 1985 [Booth 1988: 413–18].)

Neoliberal restructuring has put Costa Rica's social welfare and market interventionist policies in jeopardy. The negative social impact of these reforms has, thus far, not been as severe as in other countries, causing many neoliberal ideologues to uphold Costa Rica as a successful example of pro-market reforms. Marc Edelman, however, points out that Costa Rica's relative stability in the face of neoliberal reforms has been largely due to massive amounts of economic aid provided by the United States during the 1980s due to fears of the Sandinista 'threat' in Central America, as well as benefits stemming from Costa Rica's statist legacy, which includes: various export subsidies for non-traditional exports; the decision by many foreign investors to locate in Costa Rica due to its well-developed infrastructure and educated, healthy labour force; and the growth of tourism (the nation's leading source of foreign exchange since 1994), which has relied significantly on Costa Rica's reputation as an international leader in environmental conservation (Edelman 1999: 3–4, 83–4). Costa Rica's cooperative movement, another legacy of its statist era, has also helped to some-what offset the negative impact of neoliberal reforms as some state enterprises selected for privatization, such as the state-owned sugar enterprise, have been strategically sold to the cooperative sector instead of to private corporate interests (Arias Sánchez 2004).

Nonetheless, while Costa Rica has fared better than most in institut-ing neoliberal reforms, the impact of such reforms has still been largely negative and threatens to get worse. Throughout the 1980s and 1990s, per capita GDP, private consumption per capita, and real wages declined or stagnated; social welfare provision declined; and the growth in non-traditional primary exports served to provide mostly low-wage, 'flexible' jobs and a continued reliance on highly volatile international markets (Edelman 1999: 3–4, 44–90). At the same time, these sacrifices have had little impact on the nation's overall debt, which at the start of the millennium was roughly the same as it was in the early 1980s, causing Edelman to conclude: 'With debt still at high levels, many macroeconomic targets unfulfilled, a majority with diminished access to social services, one-fifth of the population stub-bornly mired in poverty, and erratic growth in the most dynamic sec-tors after more than a decade of stablization and adjustment, Costa Rica is hardly an unambiguous free-market success story' (90).

Thus, in the final analysis it is not clear that the Costa Rican welfare state is sustainable under neoliberalism in the long term. And the his-torical specificity of its evolution suggests that it is not easily replica-ble; other coffee countries would have to pursue a more radical redistribution of wealth and resources to attain the democratic and welfarist reforms achieved in Costa Rica. Yet, despite these short-comings Costa Rica does reveal the superiority of a state-led, na-tional development strategy combined with democratic participation through state and local cooperatives, compared to the other major development programs in the coffee industry. This is especially true when one considers Costa Rica's relative lack of political power and resources compared to larger, wealthier Southern states. From 1948 to 1980, the tiny country attained decades of rapid progress in human development despite the fact that, as John Booth (1988: 401) commented in the late 1980s, 'economically, Costa Rica remains a relatively poor country, and suffers from high dependency on price-elastic commodity exports (coffee, bananas), declining terms of trade, and an enormous foreign debt.'

Moving forward and creating new models that are more resilient and broadly replicable than the Costa Rican case requires building on its strengths, not heading in the opposite direction as promoted by market-friendly, neoliberal reformers. As argued in previous chapters, the state-interventionist models of the 1960s and 1970s provided significantly greater progress in most major social and economic indicators than the neoliberal models of the 1980s and 1990s (Stiglitz 2003; Weisbrot et al. 2001; Weisbrot et al. 2000). The history of the Costa Rican welfare state exemplifies this, and it draws attention to the need to place democratic, state, social, and economic management at the front of any future development model.

Fair Trade Coffee in Historical Perspective

Fair trade coffee represents one of the more recent and innovative attempts to deal with the injustices of the international coffee market. As discussed in chapter 2, the sale of fair trade coffee first hit markets in Europe in the 1970s and North America in the 1980s, on the heels of the initiation of the sale of fair trade handicrafts after the Second World War. According to sociologist Marie Christine Renard (1999: 485), fair trade coffee emerged alongside similar issue-based products – health, organic, and ecological – as 'interstices in the midst of prevailing tendencies.' These tendencies involved a global agro-food system increasingly characterized by industrialization, corporate monopoly, mass distribution, and the homogeneous consumption of international brands. Against these tendencies, 'niches and micro markets' emerged in the North to appease a small minority of consumers who distrusted the health, environmental, and ethical standards of TNCs and desired products which expressed cultural diversity, 'old-fashioned' nostalgia, and 'natural' content (Renard 1999).

One of these new products was whole bean specialty coffee (higher-quality, whole bean arabicas) whose sales grew rapidly beginning in the 1970s alongside the boom in European-inspired coffee houses in North America. Specialty coffee has been particularly popular in the United States, where its has grown from being a tiny industry to representing 17 per cent of the total U.S. green coffee imports and 40 per cent of total U.S. retail coffee sales at the start of the millennium (Giovannucci 2003, 2001: 7). The boom gave way to the emergence of hundreds of new specialty coffee roasters and wholesalers, along with attempts by the major coffee TNCs to monopolize the emerging market niche. In 1985, General Foods launched its first whole bean coffee brand, followed by A&P and Procter & Gamble, and in 1987 Nestlé bought Sark's Gourmet Coffee. The true corporate success story of the specialty coffee market, however, was Starbucks Coffee Company, which opened its first store in Seattle in 1971. By 1991, Starbucks owned over 200 stores throughout North America and had made nearly $57 million in sales (Pendergrast 1999: 292–379, 418–21). Starbucks continued to grow, buying up competitors and signing deals with major distributors like Kraft, so that by 2002 it had become firmly entrenched as the world's largest specialty roaster, with over $3.3 billion in revenues, and over 5,800 stores and 62,000 employees worldwide (Starbucks 2004g, 2003; Pendergrast 2002).

The growth of the specialty coffee market resulted in a boom in new, small-scale roasters, even while the industry continued to be monopolized by giant TNCs. The number of coffee roasters in the United States grew from only 240 in 1965 to around 2,000 in 1998, although the largest 4 per cent of them accounted for over 80 per cent of all of the coffee roasted that year (Dicum and Luttinger 1999: 68). Some of these small roasters participated in the processing of fair trade coffee, or were designed exclusively for that purpose, and the specialty coffee market became the primary focus of fair traders. Large specialty coffee roasters like Starbucks, Van Houtte, the Seattle Coffee Company, and Second Cup became the primary target of fair trade activists. Fair trade coffee has been particularly well-suited to making inroads into the specialty coffee market. It is produced primarily from arabica beans which are shade-grown and hand-picked, resulting in higher-quality beans. Most fair trade coffee is organic and is produced with little or no use of chemical fertilizers, herbicides, and pesticides.

As a development project, fair trade coffee merges many of the concepts from previous development strategies, possesses some of their strengths and weaknesses, and in some cases introduces new strategies. Similar to the development of instant coffee-processing facilities in the South, fair trade represents an attempt to establish forward integration along the coffee commodity chain to gain greater access to revenues and value-added activities. Through the construction of their own coffee-processing facilities and transportation networks, fair trade cooperatives seek to free themselves from dependence on local traders and processors and engage directly in trade with Northern partners. In addition, like the FNC in Colombia, fair traders seek to gain a price premium for their coffee beans through a marketing formula designed to promote the special qualities of their product on Northern markets. Fair trade's 'market advantage' is deemed to derive from a mixture of moral, environmental, and quality considerations which allow Southern producers to tap into specialty niche markets in the North (Ransom 2001: 22, 108; Simpson and Rapone 2000: 47–54; Blowfield 1999; Renard 1999: 490, 497).

Despite the similarities between the FNC's and fair traders' price strategies, there are significant differences between the two. Whereas the FNC's marketing formula is based entirely on promoting the quality of Colombian coffee, the fair trade network makes ethical considerations the central component of its marketing formula, although quality remains an important secondary issue. Fair trade coffee does not appeal solely to the tastes of Northern consumers but also to the value of solidarity and the need to assist Southern producers. In this sense, the fair trade price strategy is similar to the *values* expressed by the ICA, which sought to create prices that were more socially just and more stable for Southern producers regardless of the market value of green beans. For this reason, fair trade prices are generally well above the price of Colombian milds. While the prices of Colombian beans have declined from nearly $1.00 per pound in 2000 to their current low of around $0.60, the price of fair trade arabicas has remained constant at a guaranteed minimum of $1.26 per pound (UNCTAD 2004). Should the market price rise above the minimum guarantee, a premium of $0.05 per pound will be added to the market price (Waridel 2002: 65).

Nonetheless, regardless of the important differences in their price strategies, an essential similarity between the FNC and the fair trade network still exists: a complete reliance on the purchasing decisions of Northern consumers. While fair trade coffee includes a minimum guaranteed price, the ability to provide this price depends on fair traders' success at 'selling' ethics to Northern consumers (Renard 1999: 497). As a group, fair trade coffee cooperatives and roasters must compete on the international market against cheaper, mainstream coffee by stealing market shares and winning consumer loyalties (Blowfield 1999: 766). In this context, the market remains the final arbiter of prices: while the price for fair trade goods must be higher than the market norm to justify labelling them 'fair' in the first place, if the prices are too high consumers will not be willing to pay them. As with the FNC strategy, in the final analysis, consumer whims remain the central pivot upon which fair trade coffee must swing.

One important area in which fair trade coffee pushes beyond the developmental aims of the FNC, the ICA, and forward integration strategies, is its emphasis on regulating the local relations of production and the distribution of socially produced wealth. All fair trade coffee certified by FLO has traditionally been produced by small-scale farmers organized into processing co-operatives.[9] Cooperatives must be run by a general assembly that decides how the social premium is spent, and elects a board to handle daily operations. The board must operate under the premise of 'transparent planning,' which involves having annual business plans, cash flow predictions, and longer-term strategies approved by the General Assembly. In addition, all workers hired by the cooperative must be employed under the terms of the ILO Conventions (FLO 2003a).

Yet, while fair trade coffee goes beyond some earlier development projects in regulating relations of production, it still shares some of their major weaknesses and falls short of the most successful coffee economy-development strategy, that of Costa Rica. Similar to the FNC program, fair trade coffee has a sectoral focus and cannot bring about the political-economic reforms on a national level which are required to forge a development path to facilitate and promote a more egalitarian distribution of resources and wealth that the Costa Rican state pursued (North and Cameron 2000: 1763–64). The vast disparities of wealth and political power common to most coffee-producing countries remain largely unchanged by the existence of fair trade. This means that while fair traders promote democracy and egalitarian aims within their own cooperatives, the national and international policies that forge the broader context within which they must operate continue to be outside the meaningful democratic control of poor farmers and workers. In fact, aspirations for broader national reforms often must be sacrificed by fair traders to meet the immediate needs of their cooperatives. For example, in 1988 the fair trade licensed Coordinadora Estatal de Productores de Café de Oaxaca (Statewide Coordinating Network of Coffee Producers of Oaxaca, CEPCO) gave its support to neoliberal reformer Carlos Salinas de Gortari in the lead-up to the Mexican presidential election in exchange for a 2 million peso loan (Synder 1999: 68). Once in power, Salinas ended the government's constitutional commitment to land reform, eliminated agricultural subsidies, allowed the privatization of communally held *ejidos*, drastically curtailed rural credit to poor farmers, and signed on to NAFTA, all of which have led to a crisis in smallholder agriculture in Mexico (Cornelius and Myhre 1998).

None of this is to suggest that fair trade coffee is incompatible with a national or even an international development strategy based on state intervention and market regulation. In fact, the opposite is true as state-provided infrastructure, extension services, market protection, and social welfare policies would be extremely valuable, and even necessary, for the long-term viability and broadening of fair trade (Oxfam International 2002a: 49–51). Certainly in Costa Rica, the joint efforts of the state and the cooperative sector were important to its developmental success. In addition, fair trade coffee cannot be criticized solely on the basis of its not being the sort of state-led project required in the long term. As fair trade activist Laure Waridel (2002: 115) reminds us, 'the ethical consumer's choice movement is only one strategy among many.' Nonetheless, as discussed in the previous chapters, under the current context of neoliberal reform, international financial institutions, national states, and NGOs have been increasingly opting for non-governmental, non-interventionist development strategies like fair trade *at the expense of* state-led development projects and international market regulation. As James Petras (1997: 14) notes in his broader critique of NGO-led development, this situation has resulted in the imposition of 'a double burden on the poor who continue to pay taxes to finance the neoliberal state to serve the rich, but are left with private self-exploitation to take care of their own needs.'

All of this is not to say that state-led development projects have managed to avoid the eroding imperatives of the international capitalist market. In fact, as discussed in earlier chapters, the statist initiatives promoted by UDT theorists have frequently been criticized for attempting to readjust unequal trading relations while neglecting the capitalist social relations that give way to them. They have sought to promote development through the capitalist world system, with projects based on elite-dominated states and private corporations, resulting in a situation in which, states Colin Leys (1996: 52), 'The solution always turns out to be part of the problem.' Thus the ICA eventually collapsed due to the aims of Northern TNCs and competitive pressures between capitalist states. The benefits of higher ICA prices and forward integration strategies were distributed highly unequally in the interest of national elites, depending on the social relations within a given state. The gains of the FNC, while significant, have been limited by civil war and the imperatives of Northern consumer markets. Finally, the Costa Rican welfare state, despite its many developmental achievements, is currently under threat of being dismantled due to a process of 'competitive austerity' set in motion by neoliberal reforms internationally and nationally.

Nonetheless, despite their weaknesses, these projects did represent a movement towards a model for a new international economic order in which fairer prices, labour rights, and a more just distribution of global wealth would be state-enforced and universally applied. The difficulties these projects ultimately faced under the pressures of market imperatives cannot be addressed by turning towards the market itself, but by building on the general direction of state enforcement and universal applicability, with a new and greater emphasis placed on democratic participation and the redistribution of wealth and resources at both national and international levels. In contrast to this, the fair trade network points in a different direction, towards a model that is voluntarist, market-dependent, and member-specific.

Within the international coffee industry, the market-driven approach of fair trade coffee has resulted in important developmental gains but has also left fair traders in a somewhat precarious position in the wake of the decline of market interventionist policies. Fair traders seek to promote stable and relatively higher green bean prices at a time when international commodity agreements have been abandoned and when extreme overproduction has dragged the coffee industry in the South into crisis. They seek to promote the provision of social welfare programs, infrastructure, and extension services at a time when the state is increasingly abandoning its responsibility for these provisions under the weight of neoliberal reforms. They seek to promote democratization, basic labour standards, and human rights at a time when the most important political decisions are being lifted out of national democratic control and placed into the hands of international financial organizations such as the World Bank and the WTO (Stiglitz 2003, 2002; Vilas 1997). How fair trade coffee cooperatives and roasters have manoeuvred within this precarious position and expanded the fair trade market is the subject of the next two chapters, which examine case studies of fair trade organizations in Mexico and Canada.

5 Fair Trade in Mexico: The Case of UCIRI

The objectives of UCIRI ... [are] not solely concerned with coffee, but with the fight for life, including health, housing, organic production, schools, families and communities.

UCIRI members[1]

The current structure of the Fair Trade system lends itself to the formation of elites and political bosses (*caciques*) among the producers ... For me Fair Trade should promote not only the participation of well-established cooperatives but also of the less fortunate and less privileged.

José E. Juárez Valera[2]

The previous chapters have analysed the broader historical and political-economic context in which fair trade and fair trade coffee emerged. The following two chapters move the level of analysis from the global to the national and local, and explore how specific fair trade groups in Mexico and Canada have survived and evolved within the broader context. In particular, they assess the extent to which fair trade groups have been able to meet the democratic, egalitarian, and social justice goals of fair trade through their mediated involvement in the international capitalist market within the context of neoliberal reforms. This chapter focuses on the Unión de Comunidades Indígenas del Región del Istmo (Union of Indigenous Communities of the Isthmus Region, UCIRI), a fair trade coffee-processing and marketing cooperative located in the Isthmus of Tehuantepec in the southern state of Oaxaca, Mexico. UCIRI, which has a membership of over 2,500 families, was involved in the original formation of Max Havelaar Netherlands and is widely regarded as one of the most successful fair trade cooperatives in the world. As such, the history of UCIRI and its achievements are particularly indicative of the developmental prospects and potential limitations of fair trade at the local level. The first part of this chapter provides a brief history of the coffee industry in Mexico along with an overview of the history of UCIRI. The second part describes and analyses the central aspects of UCIRI's developmental project and assesses its ability to enhance the capabilities of its membership while operating within the limits imposed by the imperatives of global capitalism.

The analysis provided in this and the following chapter is based on the use of case studies which are analysed comparatively in order to provide a frame of reference to make statements about generalities and peculiarities, and, through these statements, to develop explanatory and theoretical arguments.[3] The notion of comparison, however, is taken to include not just direct comparisons between agents, such as the comparison in chapter 6 between Starbucks and Planet Bean, but also to entail broad, historical comparisons between agents that might appear to be empirically distinct yet can be organized theoretically around 'a conjuncture of generative casual mechanisms' – in this case, those of the international capitalist system (Steinmetz 2004: 373, 392). Thus, UCIRI's cooperative fair trade project is assessed on the basis of information provided in previous chapters, in comparison to the living and working conditions of conventional coffee farmers and workers, the exploitative structures of the global coffee industry, and the various development projects within the industry. It is also compared to other fair trade cooperatives on the basis of secondary materials. Moreover, in its broadest sense, all cases explored in the following chapters – UCIRI, Planet Bean, Starbucks – are compared with reference to their impact on, and how they are impacted by, the capitalist system at local and international levels.

Historical Background

The Mexican Coffee Industry

Although not historically a major coffee-producing nation, Mexico developed its coffee industry substantially in the 1950s, which has made it currently the world's fifth largest coffee producer and its sixth largest coffee exporter (UNCTAD 2004). Between 1970 and 1989, the value of coffee exports in Mexico averaged around 5 per cent of the total value of all national exports, and 34 per cent of the value of all agricultural exports, making coffee a key source of foreign exchange (Synder 1999: 51n1). There are over 280,000 coffee producers in Mexico, around 200,000 of whom are smallholders with plots of less than two hectares, and over 60 per cent of whom are indigenous. The vast majority of Mexico's coffee producers come from communities that lack adequate access to basic social infrastructure, such as hospitals, schools, paved roads, running water, and electricity – over 84 per cent of communities in which coffee is a primary agricultural activity have high or very high poverty indicators. In addition to being a major conventional coffee producer, Mexico is the world's largest organic coffee producer, with over 12,000 Mexican organic coffee farmers accounting for nearly 60 per cent of the world's organic coffee (Hernández Navarro 2001; Pérez-Grovas, Trejo, and Burstein 2001: 26–7).

Prior to the Mexican civil war (1910–17), coffee was a relatively minor export crop that was grown only on large-scale haciendas (estates). This situation changed during the massive post–civil war land redistribution carried out by the newly formed, one-party state headed by the Partido Revolucionario Institutional (Institutional Revolutionary Party, PRI), which laid the basis for the formation of hundreds of thousands of small scale farmers.[4] The most significant period of agrarian reform occurred under the presidency of Lázaro Cárdenas (1934–40), during which time over 44 million acres (17.8 million hectares) of land were redistributed to over 800,000 people. Most of this land was redistributed to collective *ejidos*: a system wherein peasants were assigned individual plots but were organized by the state into farming collectives for the ownership of machinery, wells, fertilizers, insecticides, and other inputs (Hernández Navarro 2001; Hellman 1988: 84–90). Some land was also redistributed to small individual farmers and to communally owned indigenous reservations (*comunidades indígenas*).

Despite the massive land redistribution, the agrarian sector in Mexico remained dominated by large-scale landowners. In some states or regions where landed elites were particularly powerful, such as the state of Chiapas, land redistribution was slow and relatively minor (Hernández Castillo 2003: 66; Hernández Castillo and Nigh 1998: 138). In many cases throughout the country, the redistributed land was of poor quality or parcels were inadequate in size. In addition, state-provided access to rural infrastructure and credit disproportionately favoured large-scale farmers who already monopolized private processing, credit, transportation, and commercial facilities (Cockcroft 1998: 132–3; Hellman 1988: 88–98). In consequence, in the 1930s and 1940s a pattern emerged whereby small peasants were compelled to work seasonally on large-scale haciendas as wage labourers in order to survive. For the rest of the year, they worked on their own plots where they primarily grew subsistence crops such as beans and corn for local consumption. The resultant situation was one which Alain de Janvry and Carmen Diana Deere have characterized as 'functional dualism,' whereby semi-proletarianized labour can be paid highly exploitative, below-subsistence wages because part of their subsistence is provided by their own, non-waged labour on their family plots (Deere and de Janvry 1979: 608).

It was not until the 1950s and 1960s that significant numbers of small holders – particularly those in the southern states of Puebla, Oaxaca, Chiapas, and Veracruz – began increasingly to devote their subsistence plots to the production of coffee beans for sale on the market. This occurred in response to growing international demand for coffee, which sparked higher prices as well as increasing intervention by a federal government that sought to increase Mexico's foreign exchange earnings by promoting coffee exports. In 1946 the federal government created the National Coffee Council, which was replaced in 1958 by the Instituto Mexicano del Café (Mexican Coffee Institute, INMECAFÉ). INMECAFÉ was assigned the mission of regulating coffee prices, providing technical assistance, and conducting research on improving coffee production and controlling pest infestation (Hernández Díaz 1999: 83–8).

In the 1970s, Mexican coffee production expanded significantly and it was then that the nation became one of the largest coffee producers in the world (see figures 5.1 and 5.2, and table 5.1). This occurred in response to efforts by the federal government to intensify coffee production by offering greater support to small producers and promoting new technified coffee production. Driven by concerns about increasingly militant social unrest in poor rural areas, the federal government viewed coffee production, which required relatively little start-up capital and was ideal for the mountainous zones inhabited by many indigenous groups, as a potential solution to rural poverty and disorder (Pérez-Grovas, Trejo, and Burstein 2001: 2). Under the presidency of Luis Echeverría (1970–1976), INMECAFÉ and the corporatist Confederación Nacional Campesina (National Peasants' Confederation, CNC) organized small coffee producers into small cells called Unidades Económicas de Producción y Comercialización (Economic Units for

Figure 5.1 Largest coffee-exporting nations, 1970

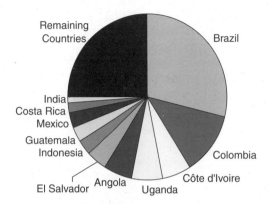

Source: UNCTAD (2004), *UNCTAD Handbook of Statistics On-Line*, http://stats.unctad.org.

Figure 5.2 Largest coffee-exporting nations, 2000

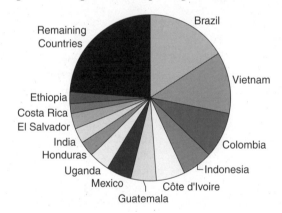

Source: UNCTAD (2004), *UNCTAD Handbook of Statistics On-Line*, http://stats.unctad.org.

Production and Marketing, UEPC). UEPCs were designed to distribute state-provided credit, deliver technical assistance, and organize marketing and processing. By 1989, smallholder production devoted to coffee had grown substantially and 80 per cent of all small coffee producers in Mexico had been organized into UEPCs (Hernández Díaz 1999: 88).

Table 5.1 Largest coffee-exporting nations, 2000

	Amount exported (thousand metric tons)	Percentage of global market
Brazil	878	16
Colombia	462	9
Vietnam	437	8
Indonesia	320	6
Côte d'Ivoire	311	6
Guatemala	265	5
Mexico	257	5
Uganda	214	4
Honduras	154	3
India	150	3
El Salvador	136	3
Costa Rica	124	2
Ethiopia	108	2
Nicaragua	25	1
Remaining countries	1511	28
Global exports	5353	

Source: UNCTAD (2004), *UNCTAD Handbook of Statistics On-Line*, http://stats. unctad.org.

The technical assistance and farming inputs that INMECAFÉ provided throughout the 1970s and 1980s were premised on the Green Revolution and entailed densely planted monoculture production that required heavy use of chemical fertilizers, herbicides, and pesticides. Some of the coffee fields that were arranged for monoculture were full-sun and unshaded, while the majority were 'shaded monoculture,' which entailed replacing the existing forest canopy with a monoculture canopy (generally composed of the Inga species of trees). The latter method, as is the case with full-sun, still requires the extensive use of pesticides and herbicides as the monoculture shade canopy lacks diversity and therefore has an insufficient variety of natural predators to eliminate coffee pests. By the 1990s, INMECAFÉ's efforts had resulted in 30 to 40 per cent of the nation's total coffee fields being planted under heavily chemical-dependent, monoculture conditions (6 to 8 per cent of which was unshaded monoculture, and 24 to 32 per cent shaded monoculture). The remaining two-thirds of the country's coffee lands remained under traditional, polyculture, shade-grown methods (Moguel and Toledo 1999).

Also during this period, INMECAFÉ emerged as the largest national buyer and exporter of coffee beans. INMECAFÉ developed a system whereby it advanced costly chemical inputs and credit to small producers, who in turn offered their harvest as collateral and agreed to sell their coffee beans to INMECAFÉ at guaranteed prices. In this way, INMECAFÉ provided small producers with a much-needed alternative to the local coffee oligarchy, who traditionally monopolized the processing, transportation, and marketing of coffee and used their advantageous position to purchase beans at very low prices. However, INMECAFÉ also sought to use its position to buy beans at low prices and extract surplus wealth from small producers to fund federal programs. Some of these funds were channelled back into programs that provided infrastructure, technology, and inputs to small producers, but a significant proportion was also channelled to the cities and squandered to meet the demands of the PRI's corrupt clientelist networks. In the 1980s, this situation sparked escalating protests by small coffee producers against INMECAFÉ's control of prices, credit, and technology (Simpson and Rapone 2000: 49).

INMECAFÉ was eventually disbanded in the late 1980s and early 1990s, not due to the protests of smallholders but due to the spread of neoliberal reforms at international and national levels. Under the presidency of neoliberal reformer Carlos Salinas de Gortari (1988–94), INMECAFÉ announced that it would begin to purchase only a minority of beans produced in major coffee states in 1989, the same year that the International Coffee Agreement (ICA) was suspended (Synder 1999: 67). By 1993, the year that the United States officially withdrew from the ICA, INMECAFÉ had been completely dismantled and its holdings, including most significantly its industrial processing plants, sold off (Pérez-Grovas, Trejo, and Burstein 2001: 3; Hernández Díaz 1999: 90). These reforms were accompanied by broader neoliberal reforms to the Mexican agricultural sector, which included an end to the government's constitutional commitment to land reform, allowance for the privatization of individual *ejido* plots (which previously had been banned to prevent the concentration of land), significant curtailment of credit to small farmers, elimination of agricultural subsidies, and implementation of the North American Free Trade Agreement (NAFTA) (Cornelius and Myhre 1998; Appendini 1998; Myhre 1998).[5]

The rapid decline of the Mexican state's interventionist policies in the coffee sector had a dual impact on small producers. On the one hand, the end of price regulations and declining provision of credit and technical assistance left small producers more vulnerable to the sway of local intermediaries (referred to disparagingly as *coyotes*) and the unpredictable swings of the international market. As the state withdrew, small producers – who generally lacked their own transportation, processing facilities, sufficient capital, and knowledge of markets – were left in a weak negotiating position relative to private intermediaries and were thus compelled to sell their beans at low prices, often to whomever 'had a vehicle and could pay cash' (Pérez-Grovas, Trejo, and Burstein 2001: 3). These matters were made worse by declining productivity, a result of insufficient access to agricultural inputs, which further reduced the incomes of small producer families.

On the other hand, the decline of the PRI's authoritarian, corrupt, clientelist, one-party state opened up new space for small producers to organize free from direct corporatist rule. According to Jonathon Fox, this provided local communities more space to enhance their 'associational autonomy,' whereby citizens can organize to defend their own interests and identities without fear of external intervention or punishment (Fox 1997). One of the best examples of the new organizational space that emerged within the context of neoliberal reforms was the formation in 1989 of the Coordinadora Estatal de Productores de Café de Oaxaca (Statewide Coordinating Network of Coffee Producers of Oaxaca, CEPCO), composed of 20,000 of Oaxaca's 55,000 small coffee producers. CEPCO was formed by dozens of local producer groups in response to moves by the state government of Oaxaca to create a top-down State Coffee Council which would take control of export quotas and financing in the wake of the decline of INMECAFÉ and the CNC – essentially recreating the federal corporatist system at the regional level. Some of the producer groups were disbanded state UEPCs while others were independent organizations, such as UCIRI, which had been formed in the 1970s and 1980s to struggle for specific local reforms (Calo and Wise 2005: 21–3; Synder 1999).

CEPCO mobilized members to protest the formation of the new coffee council, drew up a petition with over 20,000 signatures, and attended government meetings to force their views onto the agenda. As a result, although the new State Coffee Council was formed, it was not granted exclusive control of export quotas and financing, and CEPCO and three other NGOs were given a seat on its Executive Committee. Moreover, as CEPCO gained strength, it expanded and replaced the role once played by INMECAFÉ: purchasing coffee (often at higher prices than INMECAFÉ), offering credit and technical assistance, and processing and marketing coffee beans. CEPCO also played a key role in channelling state resources towards projects that benefited small producers, including the construction of local *micro-bodegas* (small storage houses) and the development of close to 3,000 small-scale wet-processing plants to serve 165 coffee communities (Synder 1999).

While the decline of the PRI's corporatist state may have opened up new spaces for local organization, there are two important caveats to this assertion. First, while the relative decline of the state has been paralleled by the expansion of NGOs, this situation does not represent a simple displacement of the former by the latter. While independent NGOs have largely welcomed the prospect of dampening some of the state's more corrupt practices, and in some instances (such as with CEPCO) have moved in to replace the activities of the state, in general a great many NGOs have also struggled to *maintain* the interventionist practices of the state. In the coffee sector, active lobbying efforts and mass protests spearheaded by various local, regional, and national NGOs have compelled the government to continue with some of its support policies despite neoliberal reforms. Thus, while the state has withdrawn from purchasing, processing, and marketing coffee beans, it has been compelled to continue to provide a degree of preferential credit and technical support to small producers through a variety of state bodies, including the Instituto Nacional Indígenista (National Indigenous Institute, INI), the Programa de Apoyo Directo al Campo (Direct Rural Support Program, PROCAMPO), the Programa Nacional de Solidaridad (National Solidarity Program, PRONASOL), and state and national coffee councils. While these agencies do not provide a level of support comparable to before neoliberal reforms, the support they do provide represents a victory for independent producer groups that continue to pressure the government to increase their funding for coffee programs – resulting in a situation in which NGOs pressure the state not to withdraw, but to get more involved in the coffee sector (Pérez-Grovas, Trejo, and Burstein 2001: 33–5).

Second, while the decline of the state has allowed small producers greater space to organize free from direct corporatist rule, it has also further exposed them to the imperatives of the market, which has not resulted in the defeat of clientelism or ensured the triumph of associational autonomy. Instead, as Fox has argued, what has emerged in Mexico is the replacement in the local political arena of 'authoritarian clientelism' – based on coercive threats by the state combined with a degree of material inducements – with 'semi-clientelism,' where material inducements and the threat of their withdrawal is the major form of state coercion. Within the context of neoliberal reforms, local groups are desperate to gain access to scarce resources and are thus increasingly vulnerable to material inducements by the state. Thus, external intervention, however altered, still poses a significant threat to associational autonomy (Fox 1997). For example, in 1988 CEPCO was compelled to give its official support to neoliberal candidate Carlos Salinas in the presidential election in order to attain a two-million-peso loan from the federal government which it needed to purchase coffee at competitive prices (Synder 1999: 68). In another instance, in 1996 the indigenous fair trade cooperative Los Indígenas de la Sierra Madre de Motozintla (Indigenous Peoples of the Sierra Madre de Motozintla, ISMAM) withdrew its passive support for and launched a series of critical newspaper advertisements against the actions of the Ejército Zapatista de Liberación Nacional (Zapatista National Liberation Army, EZLN), which emerged as a recognized leader in the defence of indigenous rights after initiating an uprising in the state of Chiapas in 1994. This decision by ISMAM came within a year after the cooperative was awarded the National Export Prize by neoliberal reformer President Ernesto Zedillo, and was granted the largest line of credit ever given to an organization of peasant producers. Since then, according to Rosalva Aída Hernández Castillo (2003: 81), 'Within the peasant movement in Chiapas, ISMAM is now seen as more closely aligned with the government than with the indigenous and peasant struggle.'

Nonetheless, despite the persistence of semi-clientelist politics in Mexico, neoliberal reforms have led to the opening of some additional spaces for the development of independent producer groups, such as those of fair trade partners. It is important to note, however, that the basis for the formation of many of these groups emerged out of Mexico's statist legacy, revealing the historical connections between the fair trade network and the other, statist projects traditionally promoted by the fair trade movement. Mexico's long history of state intervention in the rural areas has been a primary factor in the development of independent producer groups and has likely played an important role in making Mexico one of the world's leaders in fair trade and organic farming. The Mexican state's massive agrarian reform programs led to the formation of a significant smallholder class, while state-created infrastructure and state-trained technical cadres provided the basis upon which the coffee industry was developed and expanded. Since the dismantling of INMECAFÉ, much of the infrastructure, such as warehouses and processing plants, have been divested to small producer organizations at reduced prices (Pérez-Grovas, Trejo, and Burstein 2001: 34) and many technical cadres continue to provide their services to independent smallholder groups. Moreover, government initiatives have organized small producers into a variety of state-affiliated groups which have laid the basis for independent fair trade cooperatives. For example, former UEPCs were key to the foundation of CEPCO, which has since become an important fair trade producer group (Aranda and Morales 2002). In the case of UCIRI, discussed below, although it was originally formed out of a independent initiative, it relied heavily on CNC-developed collective marketing boards during its formative years.

The Mexican case reveals the complex manner in which the development of the fair trade network is owed both to the statist projects of the fair trade movement and to neoliberal reforms. Statist initiatives have laid the basis for the existence of an organized smallholder class, while neoliberal reforms have helped to somewhat curb the 'authoritarian clientalist' abuses of the corrupt and authoritarian PRI state, allowing for independent groups to emerge in a new 'semi-clientalist' environment. The latter occurrence, however, has been attained only at the expense of institutionalizing a broader agenda which has entailed transferring the most important political-economic decisions out of national control, democratic or otherwise, and into the hands of distinctly non-democratic international institutions like the World Bank, the IMF, and the WTO (Stiglitz 2003, 2002; Vilas 1997). It was within the context of this transformation that UCIRI emerged and developed alongside the further entrenchment of neoliberal reforms.

The History of UCIRI

UCIRI is a coffee-processing and marketing cooperative composed of members from fifty-four communities in twenty municipalities located in Oaxaca in the Isthmus of Tehuantepec (see figure 5.3). There are currently over 2,500 active member families in UCIRI, representing around 25,000 people. The dominant ethnic groups in UCIRI are the Zapotec, Mixe, and Chontales, and to a lesser extent Mixtecos and Chatinos. The communities involved in UCIRI are all *comunidades indígenas*, where land is owned communally and cannot easily be privatized or mortgaged. Each community grants land to its members based on a

Figure 5.3 Map of UCIRI region

Source: Waridel (2002).
Special thanks to Laure Waridel for permission to reproduce this map.

determination of how much land each family can manage. On average, each family unit has two to five hectares devoted to coffee cultivation, and five to eight hectares devoted to subsistence crops (UCIRI 2004m, 2004j; VanderHoff Boersma, interview 2002). The political system employed in the majority of the *comunidades indígenas* is a system of *usos y costumbres* (usages and customs) wherein municipal delegates and village representatives are elected by local assemblies composed of one member (invariably male) from each family. There are no political parties and the emphasis is placed on personal responsibility to the community and its general welfare (Waridel 2002: 68).

UCIRI originated at a meeting held in March 1981 between indigenous small coffee farmers from the municipalities of Guevea De Humboldt and Santa María Guienagatí and a Jesuit mission team from the Diocese of Tehuantepec to discuss solutions to the problem of poverty in their communities. There it was determined that a key source of poverty arose from low, unfair coffee prices and that a solution would be to seek out higher prices by avoiding intermediaries like INME-CAFÉ and local coyotes, and trading more directly with national and international market agents. That year, the farmers organized themselves and collectively sold more than 35 tons of coffee beans for slightly higher prices to the Asociación Rural de Interés Colectivo (Rural Collective Interest Association, ARIC), a state-developed collective marketing board in the state of Veracruz (UCIRI 2004i; Ramírez Guerrero, interview 2002; VanderHoff Boersma 2002: 1; Simpson and Rapone 2000: 49).

Spurred on by their success, the original two groups met with farmers from five other municipalities at the Assembly of Guevea de Humbolt in March 1982 to expand their efforts. They decided to organize themselves into UCIRI in order to address collectively the major problems affecting their communities: low coffee prices, inadequate access to credit, insufficient income, and a lack of access to basic necessities such as health care, education, transportation, potable water, electricity, and communication infrastructure. UCIRI aspired to address these concerns by dealing directly with coffee buyers and by undertaking community projects to construct social and economic infrastructure (Waridel 2002: 70; Ramírez Guerrero, interview 2002; VanderHoff Boersma 2002: 6–7). In 1983, after a protracted struggle with local and federal officials, which included several delegations visiting state offices in Oaxaca and Mexico City, UCIRI was granted legal status and was registered with the secretary of agrarian reform (Simpson and Rapone 2000: 50).

The following year, UCIRI broadened its forward integration strategy and moved into the value-added processing stage. Its members completed the construction of a warehouse in Lachiviza, a former logging compound, and installed a processing plant where coffee beans, after being depulped locally through the wet method, were sorted by quality, mechanically cleaned and bagged, and prepared for export (Guzman Díaz, interview 2002). Eventually UCIRI acquired a second processing plant in the town of Ixtepec, a small regional centre. In 1985, UCIRI became the first independent organization in the region to attain an export licence from the federal government, which permitted it to export directly. At this time, export licences were granted almost exclusively to large coffee producers, whose representative bodies participated directly in the directive council of INMECAFÉ and worked to ensure that the situation remained that way. However, due to the corporatist and populist nature of the PRI, there were some concessions granted to the best organized small producer groups, and UCIRI was among them (VanderHoff Boersma 2002; Simpson and Rapone 2000: 50–1).

In addition to seeking out higher coffee prices, in 1984–85 UCIRI initiated its community projects. They were premised on Trabajo Común Organizado (Organized Communal Work, TCO) and designed to foster social consciousness and meet the urgent material needs of local communities. UCIRI members organized themselves into committees to implement needed projects (such as building collective corn mills, dry toilets, and wood stoves), promote indigenous cultural values, and develop organic coffee production (UCIRI 2004b).

It was during the middle and late 1980s that UCIRI established its first linkages with organic and fair trade partners in the North. In 1985, a Dutch agricultural engineer working with a German NGO promoting organic agriculture visited UCIRI and convinced it of the benefits of obtaining organic certification for its coffee beans. In 1986, UCIRI began an organic coffee-production program, which included the foundation of the Centro de educación campesina (Farmer Education Centre, CEC), to teach organic farming techniques to UCIRI children, and it obtained its first inspection and certification with the German agency Naturland. That year, UCIRI was able to export 5,000 bags of certified organic coffee, out of a total production of 10,000 bags, through the state-organized collective marketing board, the national ARIC. It was also during this time that UCIRI signed its first coffee contracts with fair trade NGOs. When representatives from GEPA, a German NGO, and Simón Levelt, a small, family-owned Dutch roaster, visited the cooperative in 1985, UCIRI agreed to directly export 400 bags of coffee to them in 1987. UCIRI also began to export small amounts of coffee to Fair Trade Organisatie in the Netherlands, which had previously imported handicrafts from UCIRI communities. After 1986, UCIRI was consistently able to sell most of its coffee beans on the organic market, and, by the early 1990s, most of its organic coffee was sold on the fair trade market (UCIRI 2004i; VanderHoff Boersma 2002).

In 1987, four members of UCIRI were invited by the Dutch NGO Solidaridad to visit the Netherlands and promote their organic coffee at ATOs. During their visit, UCIRI members expressed their concern that the alternative market was too small to meet the needs of Southern producers and that its stores were not easily accessible to the general public. In response, a small team was formed consisting of Niko Roozen, the director of Solidaridad, and Francisco VanderHoff Boersma, a Jesuit priest who worked with UCIRI, to find new ways to expand the market available for fair trade coffee. Several different approaches were considered. First, VanderHoff and Roozen toyed with the idea of developing a producer-owned coffee company to import, process, and distribute their own coffee. However, they lacked the necessary capital. Second, they considered trying to convince mainstream coffee roasters to purchase a minimum of 12 per cent of their coffee under fair trade conditions. After long and heated discussions with large roasters in Amsterdam, nothing was gained. Finally, as described in chapter 2, it was decided to create the first fair trade seal, Max Havelaar, and offer certification to those companies willing to meet the fair trade criteria (VanderHoff Boersma 2002: 30).

The founding of Max Havelaar in 1988 gave further impetus to the development of UCIRI, which found it could rely increasingly on greater and more reliable access to fair trade markets. From 1989 to 1992, UCIRI was a producer representative on the administrative council of Max Havelaar Netherlands and contributed much to its development. During this time, UCIRI established a hardware store, enhanced its radio-communication capabilities, and developed a credit and savings fund for members (VanderHoff Boersma 2002: 30). In 1989, UCIRI played a key role in forming the Coordinadora Nacional de Organizaciones Cafetaleras (National Coordinator of Coffee Organizations, CNOC), a group of independent coffee organizations in Mexico that represent over 80,000 small coffee farmers. CNOC lobbies the federal government for favourable coffee sector policies, assists its members in marketing coffee internationally, and has been at the forefront of promoting fair trade participation for its members (Taylor 2002: 8).

UCIRI's success in promoting local development in the Isthmus and organizing small coffee farmers nationally did not go unnoticed by the coffee elite and the state, who employed violent forms of intimidation in an attempt to halt this threat to their economic and political interests. From 1985 to 1992, thirty-two men, women, and children from UCIRI were murdered by local elites who feared a loss of their monopoly control of processing, transportation, marketing, and input provision. In 1994, after the eruption of the Chiapas Rebellion led by the EZLN, the Mexican army invaded and temporarily occupied UCIRI's farming school, falsely accusing it of running a paramilitary training centre for the Zapatistas (Waridel 2002: 71). This sort of antagonistic relationship between the state and UCIRI stands in sharp contrast to Costa Rica, where the state has historically worked in close collaboration with independent local cooperatives – a fact which has been key to its broad developmental successes.

Such forms of intimidation and repression by the state, however, did not stop the development of UCIRI, which continued to grow and expand its efforts. In 1994, UCIRI constructed a much-needed health clinic at Lachiviza, and in 1997 it initiated two new projects to assist its members: the promotion of alternative crops to be used in the production of organic fruit preserves, and the development of a small clothing factory to provide extra income for UCIRI members (Nuñez Hernandez, interview 2002; Cowling, interview 2002). In addition to continuing to develop local social and economic infrastructure, UCIRI also expanded its efforts to organize small farmers and promote organic and fair trade coffee. UCIRI worked with other independent organizations and played a key role in the formation of CERTIMEX (1997), a Mexican ecological product-certifying agency; Comercio Justo México (1999), a Mexican fair trade regulating body; and Integradora Agromercados (2000), a marketing company based in the city of Querétaro and owned by small-scale and indigenous coffee farmers that markets fair trade coffee, along with other products such as amaranth, maguey, corn, and beans (Jaffee, Kloppenburg, Jr., and Monroy 2004: 184–6; VanderHoff Boersma 2002; Taylor 2002: 8).

While expanding its political involvement in local and national projects throughout the 1990s, UCIRI also took care to ensure that its coffee sales did not drop off. From 1993 to 2002, the quantity of export-quality green beans processed and sold by UCIRI on international markets remained fairly consistent and ranged between around 500,000 kg to 700,000 kg. (In addition, UCIRI also sold between 180,000 kg to 290,000 kg annually of non-export-quality coffee on domestic markets.) All of its international export-quality coffee was sold as certified organic, and nearly all of it was sold as fair trade, except for two years when UCIRI sold a small proportion (less than 10 per cent) of its export-quality coffee on conventional organic markets without fair trade certification (UCIRI 2004m; VanderHoff Boersma 2002: 8). The ability of UCIRI consistently to sell close to 100 per cent of its export-quality coffee on the fair trade market is unique, as the majority of fair trade coffee cooperatives can usually export only between 10 and 30 per cent of their beans to fair trade partners (VanderHoff Boersma, interview 2002; Raynolds 2002b: 11). A key reason for this distinction is that UCIRI has been involved with Max Havelaar since its formation and has developed strong ties with major fair trade ATOs who view UCIRI as a reliable and efficient partner.

Until 1990, UCIRI's largest fair trade partner was GEPA, which generally purchased around 70 per cent of the cooperative's annual production. Since then, UCIRI has sought to diversify its trading partners and has established strong ties with several other fair trade ATOs. In 2002, UCIRI's largest trading partners were Comercio Terzo Mondo of Italy (which purchased around 5,000 132-lb bags of coffee annually), Sacheus of Sweden (1,500 bags), Equal Exchange of the United States (1,300 bags), GEPA (1,000 bags), Urtekram of Denmark (over 500 bags); Café Campesino of the United States (500 bags), EZA of Austria (500 bags), and Just Us! of Canada (350 bags). While UCIRI exports most of its coffee to fair trade ATOs, it also exports FLO-certified coffee through the firm Van Weely to conventional roasters, including Malongo and Carrefour in France, Migros and Treubles in Switzerland, COIND in Italy, Neuteboom in the Netherlands, Viking in Finland, and Schimmer in Germany. UCIRI's domestic non-export-quality coffee is sold primarily through Royal Café in Monterrey; Integradora Agromercados, UCIRI's own café in Ixtepec; and some fair trade cafés in Mexico City (VanderHoff Boersma 2002: 9–10).

In recent years, UCIRI has placed growing emphasis on expanding trade with large conventional corporations. As described in previous chapters, this is part of a growing trend within the network that stems from the necessity to expand the market to meet the needs of Southern producers (Taylor 2002: 9–10). While UCIRI itself does not have difficulty selling its coffee on the fair trade market, many of the fair trade groups with which UCIRI works in solidarity are in a more precarious position. As UCIRI is well-established and well-connected, it has taken it upon itself to assist other, smaller fair trade cooperatives in exporting their coffee. In general, according to VanderHoff, an organization requires around twenty to thirty 17-ton containers to make exporting its own coffee financially viable. Most small cooperatives, however, can only fill two or three containers. UCIRI assists these organizations by exporting their containers along with UCIRI's. Each year, UCIRI exports around a hundred containers of coffee, of which sixty belong to UCIRI and the remaining forty belong to smaller groups (VanderHoff Boersma, interview 2002).

The most significant step that UCIRI has recently taken to expand the market is a ten-year deal that it signed with Carrefour, the world's second largest food chain, in February 2002, for an unspecified quantity of coffee. The coffee will be roasted by Malongo, a conventional roaster in southern France, and then sold in supermarkets owned by Carrefour. In the past, Carrefour has sold various quantities of coffee certified by FLO in its supermarkets, but this deal represents a new, direct trade relationship between Carrefour and a fair trade partner. To attain this agreement, UCIRI has had to make a significant compromise: although Carrefour will pay fair trade prices and adhere to fair trade rules, the coffee will not be independently certified by FLO. Instead, the coffee will be independently certified as organic and will be stamped with Carrefour's own quality seal (Renard 2005: 427–8; Ramírez Guerrero, interview 2002; VanderHoff Boersma 2002).

UCIRI's decision to enter into such an agreement with Carrefour has raised criticism from FLO representatives, who fear that it compromises the integrity of independent fair trade certification. Independent certification is essential to gaining credibility in the market as it demonstrates to ethical consumers, in an accountable and transparent manner, that fair trade standards are adhered to and are sufficiently different from conventional standards to warrant a higher price (Tallontire 2002; Renner and Adamowicz 1998: 5–7). UCIRI's deal with Carrefour is part of the growing trend of TNCs adopting their own 'fair' trade seals that lack independent certification (Giovannucci 2003: 21–71). These private initiatives threaten to swamp the ethical market, causing confusion among consumers and disrupting the uniqueness upon which fair trade's 'ethical premium' is premised. From UCIRI's perspective, the need to expand the fair trade market and meet the immediate needs of Southern producers takes precedence over the broader vision of FLO, which some UCIRI members see as overly idealistic (VanderHoff Boersma, interview 2002; Ramírez Guerrero, interview 2002). UCIRI plans to continue to explore new trading relationships with conventional TNCs, and is in the process of considering unspecified deals with Starbucks, Sara Lee, Philip Morris, and Grupo Neumann (VanderHoff Boersma 2002: 12; Taylor 2002: 9–10).

The controversy over UCIRI's deal with Carrefour draws attention to the unresolved conflict between the fair trade network's immediate, producerist goals, and its broader, long-term aspirations. The hinge upon which this conflict turns is the capitalist market. In the long term, fair traders aspire to develop an alternative form of trade which is driven by different motives than the capitalist imperatives of profit-maximization, labor productivity, and accumulation. In the short and medium term, however, fair traders seek to meet their democratic and developmental objectives through the capitalist market and are thus fundamentally still subordinate to capitalist imperatives. The result has been a process of negotiation as UCIRI has sought to enhance the capabilities of its membership while operating within the limits imposed by the imperatives of the international capitalist market. This process of negotiation has impacted not just on UCIRI's trade relations with TNCs like Carrefour but on its entire fair trade project, which is assessed in the following section.

Assessing UCIRI's Development Project

Guaranteed Prices

A guaranteed price that is above conventional market prices is a central aspect of the fair trade criteria. Currently, FLO standards peg the basic minimum guaranteed price for coffee beans at $1.21 per pound of green arabica beans (if conventional prices rise above this price, the fair trade price will readjust to remain at least $0.05 above conventional prices). This is the 'free on board' (FOB) price, which includes the cost of transporting the beans to port for export. In addition there is a social premium of $0.05 per pound and an organic premium of $0.15 per pound. In general, fair trade cooperatives garner around 80 per cent of the FOB price, compared to conventional farmers who generally received around 60 to 70 per cent (Talbot 2004: 207–9; Scholer 2004). UCIRI distributes the revenue gained from the basic minimum guaranteed price (minus operating costs) to member households on the basis of the quantity of beans each brings to be processed and sold by the cooperative. The revenue from the social premium is used to help pay for UCIRI's various social and economic projects, and the revenue from the organic premium is partly distributed to members and partly used to fund UCIRI's organic production programs (VanderHoff Boersma 2002: 14).

According to Niko Roozen and VanderHoff, the fair trade price is premised on the assumption that the capitalist market is the dominant mechanism of exchange and that fair traders must, to a certain extent, play within its rules. Thus, fair traders must focus significant energy on meeting market demands for quality and efficiency. However, they assert that along with the demands of the market, a 'process of incorporation of costs' is required in which the 'real' costs of production, including the social and environmental costs, are reflected in the final price. This is the case with the fair trade price, they argue, which integrates the cost of producing coffee in a socially just and environmentally sustainable manner and thus 'introduces an important correction in the market reality' (Calo and Wise 2005: 8; VanderHoff Boersma 2002: 26–8; Roozen and VanderHoff Boersma 2002: 23–6).

The extent to which the fair trade price makes the corrections to market reality that Roozen and VanderHoff maintain is highly questionable. Recently, some commentators have raised the concern that fair trade prices, rather than correcting conventional prices, can serve as a partial subsidy to offset the negative impact of low conventional prices. This is less so the case for UCIRI, which sells most of its coffee on the fair trade market, than it is for most fair trade cooperatives which sell most of their coffee beans in conventional markets (Vander-Hoff Boersma 2002: 12, 31; Taylor 2002: 18). Of greater concern, however, is that fair trade prices remain tightly constrained by conventional market prices against which they must, to some extent, compete.

Although ideologically premised on the need to incorporate the social and environmental costs of production, fair trade prices must remain close enough to conventional prices so as to not discourage ethical consumers in the North (Renard 1999: 497). The result is that fair trade prices, while higher than conventional ones, are ultimately limited by market imperatives, not an objective assessment of the 'real' costs of production. The basic minimum of $1.26 per pound has not changed in over ten years, and, according to one calculation, has lost 75 per cent of its value to inflation in Mexico during that time (Calo and Wise 2005: 40). Moreover, while the fair trade price is over twice the current conventional price, it is in fact very low in historical terms. In the past, UCIRI has typically been able to sell its coffee beans for between $1.40 and $1.70 per pound, but under current conditions it has been forced to accept the minimum price, which it considers to be inadequate to meet the basic needs of its members (VanderHoff Boersma, interview 2002). When examined through a broader historical lens, today's fair trade price appears to be relatively consistent with conventional prices. From 1976 to 1989 and from 1995 to 1998, a total of sixteen years, the international price for Brazilian arabica beans was generally close to or well above $1.26 per pound. Even taking into consideration that fair traders receive a greater percentage of the FOB price than conventional farmers, for most of these years conventional farmers received a final price that was higher or equivalent to the fair trade price. In some years, international prices were nearly twice as high as today's fair trade price, with Brazilian arabicas selling for upwards of $3.20 in 1977, $2.17 in 1977, $2.13 in 1980, $2.21 in 1981, and $3.03 in 1986 (see table 2.12) (UNCTAD 2004). It would be untenable, given the highly exploitative and environmentally destructive conditions under which coffee has been produced, to make the claim that during these years the conventional prices for coffee beans (equal to or higher than the current fair trade price) reflected the social and environmental costs of production.

The inadequacy of the fair trade basic minimum price for meeting the real costs of production and the basic needs of producer families is apparent in fair trade communities throughout the region (Calo and Wise 2005), and can be seen in a recent UCIRI report. According to the report, the higher income provided by the sale of fair trade coffee has increased the standard of living and eliminated extreme misery among UCIRI members. However, 'in spite of the increased incomes achieved through the sale of Fair Trade coffee, it can not be said that these incomes are adequate to secure the survival of the families of producers' (VanderHoff Boersma 2002: 20). Poverty still persists among UCIRI members, and matters have gotten worse with the rapid decline in prices over the past two years. In 2002, UCIRI members received a family income of only 15 pesos ($1.50) a day, which has led many young people to leave their communities in search of employment in the cities or as illegal workers in the United States. In 2002, around 150 of UCIRI's members were forced to leave their farms in search of temporary work to make ends meet (VanderHoff Boersma, interview 2002).

Direct Exchanges

Direct exchanges between producers and consumers are another key aspect of the fair trade criteria. Through its participation in the fair trade network, UCIRI has been able to avoid local coyotes and state coffee agencies and trade directly with Northern partners. In doing this, UCIRI has gained greater access to coffee revenues. First, UCIRI has been able to avoid unfair trading practices by middle agents who have often used their monopoly control of local markets to buy coffee beans at low prices that are well below the international prices on the New York commodity market. Second, UCIRI has been able to move into the value-added processing, transportation, and marketing stage of the coffee trade that these middle agents have traditionally monopo-lized. Third, UCIRI has forged solidarity-based trade relations with fair trade ATOs, which, unlike conventional market agents, seek to pay the highest price that is economically feasible for their beans (Vander-Hoff Boersma 2002: 7–8, 18–19).

While a policy of direct exchanges has brought much-needed reve-nue to UCIRI, one must be careful not to exaggerate the extent to which producers and consumers are brought together under the fair trade system. While fair trade is premised on the notion of bringing Southern producers and Northern consumers into direct relations with each other, in reality the direct relations that are formed in the fair trade network are primarily between Southern producers and North-ern ATOs, with the links to actual consumers still mediated by the market. Moreover, since the reorientation of the fair trade network in 1988, face-to-face visits from Northern consumer groups to Southern cooperatives have declined. According to Peter Taylor (2002: 10), in his synthesis of research conducted on seven fair trade cooperatives, 'This de-emphasis of such direct exchanges is widely viewed among the producer organizations studied as part of a wider shift away from viewing Fair Trade as a movement and toward seeing it as an imper-sonal market niche instead.'

In their relations with Northern consumers, UCIRI members have generally adopted a market-oriented approach and have viewed consumers abstractly as a source of higher coffee prices and better incomes. When a group of UCIRI members were asked at a Peasant Festival in October 2001 to explain the differences between fair trade and conventional markets, most responded by emphasizing that fair trade markets bring higher prices to producers and better-quality cof-fee to consumers. Little was said about building ties of solidarity and familiarity with groups in the North. When asked to explain the differ-ences between fair trade and organic markets, one farmer responded, 'There is no difference, because the products sold in the Fair Trade market also have to be organic, they both mean a higher price for the product' (VanderHoff Boersma 2002: 18–19).

In viewing direct exchanges primarily as a source of higher prices, UCIRI is similar to many other fair trade cooperatives who are pri-marily concerned with their survival needs (Taylor 2002: 16; Méndez 2002: iii; Lyon 2002: 5; Gonzalez Cabanas 2002: 25; Martinez 2002: 15; Fisher 1997). Reflecting on this, Sara Lyon (2003) has argued that the producer-consumer relationship promoted by the fair trade network is, in reality, more akin to Benedict Anderson's concept of an 'imagined community' than it is to an actual relationship based on mutual trust, understanding, and familiarity. The fair trade notion of producer-consumer links is one that is not generally held by Southern producers, but is instead 'maintained largely by print media and coffee experts such as Fair Trade institutional representatives, exporters, importers, and roasters.' This issue is explored in further detail in chapter 6.

Credit and Financing

Small-scale farmers throughout the South face a lack of adequate access to short- and long-term credit and financing. This access is generally either not available or is tied to semi-clientelist, highly exploitative arrangements with middle agents and the state. Such has traditionally been the case in the Mexican coffee industry where funding provided by local coyotes and INMECAFÉ has been tied to agreements on the part of the borrowers to sell their coffee beans to the lender at prices significantly below those on the international market. In FLO contracts, this situation is addressed by Northern partners offering Southern partners an up-front payment of 60 per cent of the value of their contract at the start of the harvest season when funds are needed the most. The loan can then be repaid by crediting it to the final price of the contract at the end of the season. In addition to this, the social premium and organic premium can also be regarded as sources of financing which are used to fund various social programs.

When UCIRI first started up, it relied on fair trade financing, along with a ten-year loan for $500,000 from the Ecumenical Development Cooperative Society (EDCS) (now know as Oikocredit), a church-run, alternative-development investment organization in the Netherlands. Over time, as is frequently the case among the more successful and stable fair trade cooperatives, UCIRI has turned towards private and government sources of financing (Taylor 2002: 22). Currently, UCIRI relies on credit from the Mexican bank, Banamex, which offers loans at an interest rate lower than the one offered by fair trade partners. UCIRI receives the loan from Banamex at the start of every harvest and then pays it back every July to avoid increased financing costs. The contract is renewed annually. In addition to this, UCIRI also obtains credit from a variety of government agencies to help cover the cost of its proposed programs, as the funding acquired from the social and organic premiums is never sufficient by itself (VanderHoff Boersma 2002: 14–15).

Although UCIRI relies more on outside funding than on funding provided by fair trade partners, the fair trade network still plays an important role in the cooperative's financial situation. First, UCIRI's participation in the fair trade network has enhanced its credibility among government agencies, development organizations, and private banks who view UCIRI as a stable organization with a degree of market security (Raynolds, Murray, and Taylor 2004: 1116–17). This has led to easier access to funding and other types of improvements, such as Banamex's recent decision to donate money from its social action fund for the construction of a computer room at UCIRI's farmer education school (Ramírez Guerrero, interview 2002). Second, knowing that pre-financing from fair trade partners is available if needed is an important source of stability for the organization (Taylor 2002: 6, 19–22). It allows UCIRI some room to manoeuvre and maintain some independence from domestic lenders and the semi-clientelist relations that inevitably emerge with such connections.

In addition to the credit and financing that UCIRI receives from external sources, the cooperative also offers local pre-financing to its members and has its own Fondo de Ahorro y Crédito (Savings and Credit Fund, FAC). The FAC is composed of two types of funds: a savings fund where members can save their money (each new member must contribute 2,800 pesos to the fund within five years); and a credit fund where credit is distributed to members on the basis of decisions made by FAC committees (VanderHoff Boersma 2002: 11, 16). According to UCIRI policy, credit can be given to members for health reasons (to pay for doctors or medicine), education (to buy books), family reasons (weddings or birthdays), necessary trips to the city, community work, or for other necessities. Credit will only be granted to UCIRI members, or to groups involved in local farming (growing vegetables or raising livestock) or services (transportation, clothing factories) (UCIRI 1991). Members can apply for loans of up to 100 pesos, which is currently the equivalent of around six or seven days of income, from local FAC committees (FAC-LOCALES). For extraordinary loans over 100 pesos, in situations such as a medical emergency, members need to apply to the central FAC committee (FAC-CENTRAL). UCIRI strives to give its loans at the lowest rate possible (UCIRI 1994). These loans provide a much-needed source of short-term credit to members, who as individuals would find it very difficult to get funds from government and private sources.

Social and Economic Infrastructure

The construction of social and economic infrastructure has been central to UCIRI since its formation and is one of the most successful aspects of its development project. Prior to UCIRI, the communities of the isthmus lacked adequate access to food, clothing, education, and medical and sanitation services. Communication infrastructure was extremely poor and there was no transportation system – coffee beans were transported to regional centres on the backs of the farmers or their mules through the difficult mountain terrain (VanderHoff Boersma 2002: 6–8; UCIRI 1987a). Local coyotes and the state monopolized the infrastructure and technology required to efficiently process, produce, transport, and market coffee beans.

Over the years, UCIRI has made significant strides in developing the infrastructure required to gain greater control over the production and sale of coffee and improve the lives of its members. UCIRI currently owns two of its own coffee bean-processing plants, one in Lachiviza and one in the regional centre of Ixtepec, where it stores, mechanically cleans, sorts by quality, and bags its own beans ready for international export. Its beans are transported by two large long-haul trucks and five smaller pickup trucks that are owned by the cooperative (Guzman Díaz, interview 2002). To gain greater control of the local production process, UCIRI has assisted its members through its organic agriculture program, which eliminates the need for costly chemical inputs, and through the construction of small supply stores and its own hardware store in Ixtepec. At these stores, all farmers can buy tools at a reasonable price (UCIRI members get an additional 20 per cent discount), free from the coffee oligarchy's monopoly of local supply stores (UCIRI 2004e; Simpson and Rapone 2000: 51). In addition, UCIRI has even made some moves into the roasting and retailing of coffee with the construction of its own coffee shop in Ixtepec and the purchase of a 25 per cent share in the Swedish roaster, Sacheus (VanderHoff Boersma, interview 2002).

Not all of UCIRI's economic infrastructure is devoted to coffee. In 1997 UCIRI initiated two new non-coffee projects designed to provide its members with alternative sources of income: the production of organic fruit preserves and the manufacture of clothing. These projects have emerged out of a growing recognition that 'we are all aware that only coffee, even high quality organic coffee, is not going to be the solution for us. The price of coffee fluctuates greatly and in the last few years the prices have been very low' (UCIRI 2004f). Through its organic fruit preserves project, UCIRI has encouraged its members to grow organic passion fruit, blackberries, and raspberries on non-coffee land. The fruit is processed into marmalade and juice in the compound at Lachiviza and in small facilities run by women in local villages. The final product is sold throughout the region and certification for international export is pending. In 2002, fifty-seven members had begun growing blackberries and raspberries and five members had begun growing passion fruit, resulting in a total production of around 30 tons of fruit (UCIRI 2004l; Guzman Díaz, interview 2002; Nuñez Hernandez, interview 2002).

Through its clothing manufacturing project, UCIRI constructed a small factory in Ixtepec where it employed around 90 people under the fair trade principles of fair pay and basic labour rights. The primary aim of this project was to provide employment for young adults from UCIRI families who would otherwise have to leave their communities in search of work, although employees were not exclusively UCIRI members. Beginning in 1997, the factory produced clothing for coffee farmers as well as uniforms for local schools and the municipal police department and international customers (UCIRI 2004l; Cowling, interview 2002). In 2004, the factory was closed down after conflict with a raw-material provider resulted in UCIRI losing an important European customer. According to Normand Roy, a member of the Montreal-based NGO, Équiterre, UCIRI members attributed the failure of the factory not just to the specific loss of the European customer, but also to the high costs of social security provisions that were commensurate with relatively higher wages, and fierce competition from low-wage clothing factories in China which has affected the entire global textile industry (Roy, personal communication 2004). This reveals the significant barriers that the international market places on UCIRI's ability to expand its fair trade principles outside its established commodity networks.

Along with economic infrastructure, UCIRI has made significant progress in the construction of much-needed social infrastructure for its communities. This includes such projects as the farmer education center, CEC, which will be discussed in the following section, and the Unión de Pueblos Zapotecas del Istmo (Union of Zapoteco and Mixe Towns of the Isthmus, UPZMI) bus service. UPZMI's five buses make daily trips through the mountainous and largely unpaved roads of the region, from Ixtepec to CEC with several stops along the way, for the cost of around 25 to 30 pesos. It is an unprecedented service in a region without any public transportation (Guzman Díaz, interview 2002).

Perhaps UCIRI's greatest success in social infrastructure is the health clinic in Lachiviza, which was first constructed in 1994. In a region where there is only one doctor for every 2,780 inhabitants, the health clinic addresses a major need for UCIRI's communities (Waridel 2002: 42). The clinic is premised on the concept of merging modern medicine with the revival and use of natural herbs and plants that draw on local understandings of the connection between nature, community, and spirituality (UCIRI 2004c). On-site medical and dental care is offered at relatively affordable rates for the entire community. The medical care is provided by doctors who pay weekly visits to the health clinic, although over the past two years UCIRI has been unable to find a doctor willing to make regular visits. The dental care is provided by dentists who spend fifteen days living at Lachiviza, and fifteen days visiting local communities. In 2002, there were four dentists working for UCIRI. They charged patients between 50 to 150 pesos ($5 to $15) for dental assistance (Vázquez Lucas, interview 2002; Martínez Tapia, interview 2002).

Along with the medical care provided by visiting practitioners, the health clinic also runs an apprenticeship program that focuses on teaching preventative health. Through the program, dozens of volunteer 'health promoters' have been trained to teach their communities about such things as proper diet and hygiene, the medical use of local herbs, and the importance of dry latrines (UCIRI 2004c; Vázquez Lucas, interview 2002). This health program is one of several projects organized by UCIRI under the principle of its organized communal work program, TCO. TCO projects have also been organized to assist members in a variety of home improvements, including the development of vegetable gardens, better roofs, cement floors, dry latrines, and fuel-efficient Lorena stoves, as well as community improvements such as the construction of collective corn mills in every community for the preparation of tortilla dough to ease women's work (UCIRI 2004l, 2004b; Waridel 2002: 78–9; Simpson and Rapone 2000: 51). These local projects have assisted UCIRI members in attaining one of their main goals, which is 'to live in a dignified and humane house.' Now they aspire to get proper electricity, potable water, and communications services in their communities (UCIRI 2004d; VanderHoff Boersma 2002: 4).

Education and Training

The education and training that members receive from UCIRI come primarily from two sources: the fair trade network and CEC. Through the fair trade network, participants are able 'to learn how the market works and to become involved professionally in it' (VanderHoff Boersma 2002: 7). This is one of the main goals of fair trade, which seeks to offer Southern partners greater access to marketing and technical skills to assist them in increasing their revenues. Through 'mutual apprenticeship' with fair trade and organic licencers, roasters, and affiliated NGOs, UCIRI members have been able to acquire a better understanding of how the coffee market operates. This includes information on such things as permits, paperwork, import and export licences, organic certification, and the determination of prices on the New York commodities market. It also involves knowledge of organic production methods and new technological advances, such as the latest tools, solar driers, and electronic graders for producers. In addition, through the fair trade network UCIRI has gained access to constant market information, including data on consumer trends and a list of buyers, importers, and producers (Raynolds, Murray, and Taylor 2004: 1117; VanderHoff Boersma 2002: 10; Taylor 2002: 21).

UCIRI has used the marketing skills it has acquired through the fair trade network to enhance its competitiveness and efficiency. In recent years, UCIRI has placed growing emphasis on improving the quality of its coffee beans to meet the perceived demands of Northern consumers. Producers are given technical information on how to improve the quality of their beans, and a system has been established where members' beans are graded by quality upon arrival at UCIRI's processing facilities, with a higher price paid for higher-quality beans. In this way, UCIRI attempts to buy, process, and sell the highest-quality beans, *café oro* (gold coffee) (Guzman Díaz, interview 2002).

The most innovative aspect of UCIRI's education and training program is CEC, founded in 1986, which serves as a secondary school and a training school for organic production promoters in the region. Located within the mountainous coffee region near the small town of San José el Paraíso, several hours by bus from Ixtepec, CEC is the only secondary school in the region outside of the cities. Consistent with the pedagogy of Paulo Freire, CEC seeks to teach young students from UCIRI communities not just the skills typically required in secondary schools in urban centres but skills that are required to serve the needs of the community (UCIRI 2004a; Ramírez Guerrero, interview 2002; Simpson and Rapone 2000: 51–2). According to a UCIRI pamphlet, CEC does not seek to teach its students the version of the world adopted by the dominant and powerful classes, but gives them 'an education of the people and for the people, born from our own organizations like UCIRI and for our own children' (UCIRI 1985). The main focus at CEC is not education for a student's own self-advancement, but for the advancement of the entire community (UCIRI 1986).

In 2002, there were twenty-six students in attendance at CEC. According to CEC policy, all students must be children of poor farmers between the ages of 15 and 18 years, want to work the land and serve the community, and have completed primary school. Enrolment is based on a letter of recommendation from a UCIRI community. Originally, CEC started with a three-year program, but participating families decided this was too long for the children to be away from home and the program was shortened to two years and then to one (Ramírez Guerrero, interview 2002; UCIRI 1989). At the school, the students are taught basic areas (Spanish, math, social studies, geography, history), agriculture (organic coffee production), livestock farming, technical skills (computers, sewing), and other support skills (commerce, accounting, issues of fair trade and human rights) (Cabrera Vázquez, interview 2002).

CEC is the centrepiece of UCIRI's organic farming program and its other community projects. After completing their schooling, many alumni (of which there are over 280) have gone on to work for UCIRI communities as technical or social service advisers, although a small minority have also gone on to pursue further studies outside of the region (UCIRI 2004a; Cabrera Vázquez, interview 2002). CEC is also an important centre of cultural and information exchange between the various UCIRI communities, and between these communities and visiting experts and NGO personnel from Mexico and abroad. Jesús Antonio Ramírez Guerrero, the general coordinator of CEC, aspires to enhance the school's role in facilitating exchanges between various groups through the use of the Internet and CEC's new computer room, donated by Banamex. Although sceptical that the new computer room can serve as a 'trampoline out of poverty,' as Banamex believes, Ramírez does hope to use the new technology to connect UCIRI communities through audio/visual communications and bring them closer together (Ramírez Guerrero, interview 2002).

Environmental Sustainability

All FLO-certified partners must adhere to a broad understanding of environmental sustainability. In meeting this criteria, UCIRI members have promoted a vision of living and working in a manner that utilizes natural resources while at the same time respecting the need to manage and protect a healthy ecosystem. This includes projects to confront an over-reliance on monocrop production by promoting greater diversification of food crops (corn, beans, vegetables, fruit), as well as UCIRI's recent investigation into the possibility of reforesting certain areas to create 'analogue forestry nurseries' that mimic the natural forest structure but include plants and animals that can provide a source of income and food (UCIRI 2004l; Nuñez Hernandez, interview 2002; Cowling, interview 2002). The main focus of UCIRI's vision to promote sustainability, however, as is the case of many fair trade coffee cooperatives, is its organic coffee program.

The origin of UCIRI's organic coffee program began with a 1985 visit from a Dutch agricultural engineer who pointed out that UCIRI members were already growing much of their coffee in line with organic principles and could easily meet organic certification with a few alterations. Although UCIRI members did use some chemical inputs, the high cost of such products generally kept their use to a minimum and farmers continued to grow their beans in shade-grown conditions, rather than the highly technical and chemical-dependent sun-grown method promoted by the Green Revolution. After UCIRI representatives visited La Finca Irlanda, an organic coffee farm in Chiapas, it was decided that UCIRI would promote organic farming among its members in a manner which combined traditional peasant practices with new organic farming methods. According to a pamphlet produced by UCIRI in 1987, organic farming methods were desired because they would put an end to the use of chemical fertilizers and other inputs which were bad for the health of farmers and the environment; killed microorganisms in the soil and made it sterile; led to salination and acidic, nutrient-poor soil; did not improve soil quality; and were very expensive (UCIRI 2004g, 1987b). In contrast, the adoption of organic farming techniques promised to ensure the health of farmers and the environment by protecting the biodiversity of local flora and fauna and by improving soil structure and fertility along with the soil's capacity to retain humidity and nutrients. Moreover, it was considered by

UCIRI to be a relatively inexpensive venture (Waridel 2002: 75–7; Rice 1998; UCIRI 1987b).

In 1986, UCIRI established its organic coffee program, founded CEC, and obtained its first organic inspection and certification with the German agency Naturland. At that time, attaining organic certification was relatively simple and required meeting a few general guidelines. Today, certification requirements are more strict and coffee beans must be grown under 'natural' conditions for three years before they can be considered officially organic. In 2002, 84 per cent of UCIRI's total production was certified as organic, with the remaining 16 per cent considered 'natural' (UCIRI 2004g; Guzman Díaz, interview 2002; VanderHoff Boersma, presentation 2002). UCIRI's organic production program involves the use of organic compost as a non-chemical fertilizer. This compost is derived from local plants and from coffee pulp produced during wet processing, which helps to avoid the pollution problems typically associated with the careless dispersal of pulp (Talbot 2004: 46–7; Topik 1998: 66). Organic production also entails the careful pruning, thinning, and clearing of coffee plants to ensure good yield and healthy growth; the maintenance of the forest canopy (with the branches trimmed to allow in sunlight) to protect the soil from nutrient loss and erosion; and the construction of terraces and living barriers (dense hedges of plants) on slopes to retain soil and prevent erosion (UCIRI 2004g, 1987b; VanderHoff Boersma 2002).

The organic program has allowed UCIRI to produce coffee in an environmentally sustainable manner and attain a price premium on markets in the North. In addition, the organizational and administration requirements of monitoring production to attain organic certification have strengthened UCIRI's organizational capabilities. Nonetheless, the demands of organic certification require a significant investment in time and resources, especially considering that the cost of organic certification is paid for by the producers (in contrast to fair trade certification which is paid for by the buyers). For this reason, producers have placed increasing pressure on Northern partners to merge the organic and fair trade certification processes and thus save on the physical and monetary costs of each (Ramírez Guerrero, interview 2002). At the same time, FLO has increasingly encouraged its Southern partners to turn towards organic production, and many lenders are reluctant to fund any non-organic cooperatives (Taylor 2002: 4, 15). The result has been the gradual merging of fair trade and organic coffee production, which is likely to become more pronounced in the future. Internationally, in 2000, 40 per cent of the total of certified fair trade coffee exports was also certified organic. In Latin America the average was even higher, with around 50 per cent of all fair trade coffee exports certified organic. In Bolivia and Mexico, 70 per cent of all fair trade coffee exports was certified organic (Raynolds 2002b: 6, 9).

Democratic Organization

UCIRI is organized at the level of local communities and the central administrative body through a system of direct and representative democracy that adheres to FLO's generic standards. At the local level, each UCIRI community has a board of directors, a monitoring committee, a representative delegate for the central Delegate Assembly, and committees for local work projects. The members of these bodies serve for one or two years – except for the delegates, who serve for three years – and are elected by direct vote in community meetings on the premise of one vote per family (the implications of this for gender inequality will be discussed in the following section on 'gender discrimination'). On the twenty-ninth and thirtieth of each month, the local delegate and one board member attend the meetings of the Delegate Assembly in Lachivizá. At the Delegate Assembly, decisions are made about the overall direction of the cooperative and Central Committee members are elected to run UCIRI's various projects. A written report of the issues discussed at the assembly is then taken back to the communities by their delegate to be discussed at local meetings (UCIRI 2004h; Waridel 2002: 72–3; VanderHoff Boersma 2002: 2).

At the centre of UCIRI's political apparatus is an administrative council (composed of a president, a secretary, and a treasurer), which is in charge of the cooperative's daily operations, and a security council, which supervises the implementation of agreements. These councils, along with the delegate assembly, determine UCIRI's general direction. Council members are elected every three years at a general assembly in a direct vote involving all of UCIRI's members, again on the premise of one vote per family. The general assembly is held annually, regardless of whether or not it is an election year, before the harvest in October and entails several days of celebration involving singing, dancing, basketball tournaments, traditional art displays, and a Catholic mass. UCIRI members who occupy important positions do not receive any extra income but are seen as volunteering their time for the sake of the community. Participation in all relevant local and central meetings is obligatory for all members, and unexcused absences can result in a fine determined by the appropriate committee (UCIRI 2004h; Waridel 2002: 72–3; VanderHoff Boersma 2002: 2; Simpson and Rapone 2000: 52).

Membership in UCIRI is open to all small coffee farmers, and petitions for new members – either individuals or entire communities – are received on the first of April and the end of May to give farmers time to meet UCIRI's organic requirements before the next harvest. Each new member must agree to receive technical assistance to initiate organic production and to pay 2,800 pesos over a period of five years to establish an account in UCIRI's savings and credit program, the FAC. The general assembly is responsible for assessing all new membership petitions (VanderHoff Boersma 2002: 15–16). As is the case with most fair trade cooperatives, while membership consideration is open to all, UCIRI is highly selective in admitting new members. This is due to the fear that potential new members may be seeking the short-term gain of higher prices without being devoted to UCIRI's long-term goals. Many fair trade cooperatives have had to confront a scenario where members have abandoned the cooperative when conventional market prices have risen and thus left it unable to fulfil its contracts (Taylor 2002: 12–13). Consequently, loyalty is very important and UCIRI has developed a strict list of rights and obligations to which all members must adhere. According to UCIRI's basic rules of operation, all members must:

1 Agree to be an active member.
2 Attend monthly assemblies and training courses given occasionally in the community of Lachiviza and the CEC.
3 Refrain from consuming alcohol during official meetings at Lachiviza or Ixtepec.
4 Be completely honest.
5 Do not behave like a coyote or even a small coyote (do not buy or resell the coffee of other producers).
6 Only sell your own coffee; do not even sell your brother's, uncle's, or friend's coffee.
7 Do not become involved in any potentially compromising organizations.
8 Be an authentic peasant.
9 Do not be an opportunist for personal gain.
10 Do not behave badly, or you will face expulsion from the Union.

The assembly will decide if a member can re-enter the Union, on a case by case basis.

11 Do not grow marijuana or any crops related to the illegal drug trade.
12 Do not possess military equipment.
13 Do not use chemical fertilizers or pesticides.
14 Make and use organic fertilizers (compost).
15 Undertake to fulfil one's cultural obligations.
16 Be prepared to give a helping hand when it is required.
17 Be prepared to support UCIRI's objectives including growing coffee, improving the quality of life, health, home, as well as encouraging Communally Organized Work (TCO), organic agriculture, local schools, etc. (UCIRI 2004k)

While there are strict standards regulating democratic participation at the cooperative level, at the level of the international fair trade network, producer organizations such as UCIRI have little formal democratic participation in how FLO and its various National Initiatives (NIs) operate. Informally, there is significant information exchange, dialogue, and discussion throughout the network, but formally the democratic participation of southern partners in FLO is confined primarily to the position of producer representatives on FLO's board of directors (VanderHoff Boersma 2002: 12–13). (As described in chapter 2, six of FLO's twelve board members are elected every three years by fair trade producers and traders (FLO 2003b).) This situation has led UCIRI and other cooperatives to charge that producers have no real voice in how FLO is run and how it formulates criteria and inspects southern partners (Ramírez Guerrero, interview 2002; Taylor 2002: 26). According to one UCIRI report: 'Because the standards of FLO lack transparency and credibility, the inspection often depends much on the inspector and how he or she goes about the inspection. We have never received any feedback from the inspection that would allow us to make improvements or changes to facilitate the inspection process' (VanderHoff Boersma 2002: 16).

The fact that producer organizations such as UCIRI do not have as much democratic say in the operation of FLO as they would like does not stem merely from weaknesses in FLO's organizational structure, but is a result of the demands of the fair trade market niche. To gain credibility in the eyes of ethical consumers in the North and meet international standards as an independent certification body, FLO must act with a degree of autonomy from Southern producers to demonstrate its legitimacy as a certification body (Renard 2005: 425–6). Nonetheless, from UCIRI's perspective, more needs to be done to increase producer input in how FLO is run, and it believes that the building of larger coalitions of fair trade producers, such as Integradora Agromercados, has helped give it a greater, unified voice and a broader say in the orientation of the fair trade network (Taylor 2002: 13, 21).

Gender Discrimination

Perhaps no issue better exemplifies FLO's use of 'minimum criteria' and 'process criteria' than the approach to dealing with gender discrimination on fair trade cooperatives. FLO's minimum criterion, which must be met to attain certification, demands no official policies based on gender discrimination. Its process criterion requires evidence of some progress towards greater gender equity over time (FLO 2001: 4). According to Hans Bolscher, the former director of Max Havelaar Netherlands, in this way FLO aspires to open the door to increasing dialogue over practices which Southern groups would otherwise resist if they viewed them as a paternalistic imposition from abroad (Bolscher, interview 2002).

As discussed in chapter 3, patriarchal social relations are prevalent throughout the coffee industry, with males frequently getting privileged access to property and income, and females generally confronted with a 'double burden' that requires them to take on heavy workloads in both the field and the home. The communities that belong to UCIRI are no exception. Although the Zapotec culture, which represents the largest ethnic group in UCIRI, is historically a matriarchal culture in which women controlled most of the family's social and economic affairs, much of this tradition has disappeared with the imposition of a Western patriarchal system that has assigned such things a property rights and work in the public sphere to men (Waridel 2002: 73–5). As a result, work and reproduction in UCIRI communities are, in general, strictly divided along patriarchal lines.

In line with FLO's process criterion, over the years UCIRI has taken measures to gradually improve the position of women within the cooperative. This includes a variety of projects designed to ease the burden of women's work and improve the well-being of the family, such as small animal projects to enhance family diets; housing improvement projects like improved latrines and wood-burning stoves; income-generating projects such as the employment of women in processing organic fruit; and projects to ease women's daily chores such as the construction of corn mills in many communities to assist in making tortillas (Nuñez Hernandez, interview 2002; Cabrera Vázquez, interview 2002). UCIRI has also taken various measures to raise awareness of women's issues and promote greater gender equality within the cooperative, such as the celebration of a 'Farmers Festival' dedicated to women, the formation of a women's board of directors at the general assembly to raise women's concerns, and the enrolment of CEC's first female students in 1995 (VanderHoff Boersma 2002: 3). The latter achievement took nine years to attain, as local communities were reluctant to break with patriarchal norms and send girls off to school and away from home. In 2002, there were twenty teenage boys and six girls enrolled at CEC (Ramírez Guerrero, interview 2002).

Despite the gains that UCIRI has made over the years, much more remains to be done, and families and communities remain divided along unequal gender lines. Within the family, the double burden imposed on women farmers remains intact. Some of UCIRI's projects, such as the creation of corn mills, have eased this burden but have done little to effect a more equal redistribution of duties within the family. Other projects, such as small-animal raising and employment in organic fruit processing, may have enhanced the well-being of the family but have not limited, and may even have *increased*, the amount of work that women must perform. In addition, within the cooperative facilities work also remains largely divided along gendered lines. In general, men occupy all upper level positions at the cooperative and perform the 'masculine' jobs such as operating technical equipment, running the processing facilities, working in the supply stores, and driving the trucks and buses. Women tend to occupy positions more in line with socially constructed 'feminine' tasks, such as operating the health clinic and working in the canteen.[6]

Perhaps the single greatest example of the persistence of gender inequality within the cooperative is UCIRI's membership and voting structure. As is typically the case with fair trade cooperatives, membership and voting rights are premised on one vote per property-owning family (or de facto property-owning family in the case of UCIRI, since land is officially owned communally) (UCIRI 2004j). Due to patriarchal customs, the family representative is invariably the male 'head of household,' and females generally do not vote. Reflecting on this situation, Vanderhoff and others argue that this unequal scenario is somewhat mitigated by the continued existence of matriarchal customs among the Zapotec members of UCIRI, which has frequently resulted in males returning home to consult with their wives before casting their votes the next day. (The same cannot be said for the Mixtec members of UCIRI, whose customs are highly patriarchal.) (Waridel 2002: 73–5; VanderHoff Boersma, interview 2002; Raynolds 2002b: 17). Nonetheless, however strong Zapotec customs may still be, such assertions cannot detract from the fact that female fair traders are structurally barred from equal access to membership meetings and are essentially *disenfranchised* on their own cooperatives. This casts a large shadow over UCIRI's claims of democratic participation.

While acknowledging that patriarchal structures remain strong at UCIRI, Vanderhoff asserts that many gains have been made and that the process of combating gender inequality is necessarily a long one as such structures are rooted in local understandings of the family and community. In the early 1980s, when UCIRI communities were on the brink of extreme poverty, it was impossible to envision addressing these inequalities. At least now, he asserts, the problems associated with gender discrimination are being articulated (VanderHoff Boersma, interview 2002). While there is validity to these claims, it is clear that more needs to be done at a more rapid pace if UCIRI wishes to truly promote a democratic environment for all of its members. This is particularly the case with UCIRI's membership and voting structure, which is not only a product of patriarchal customs but also actually serves to reinforce these customs by granting suffrage to families as opposed to individual adults.[7] UCIRI's weaknesses in combating gender discrimination are a reflection of broader problems throughout the FLO system that need to be addressed more seriously than they have been to date. In his comparative assessment of seven fair trade coffee cooperatives, including UCIRI, Taylor (2002: 4) states that: 'All of the organizations explicitly address gender issues, though as one interviewee in Majomut put it, the commitment to gender issues emerged largely because of the explicit interest expressed by international donors and certifiers ... In no case was there a clear indication that gender was currently an important internal issue. In no case do women play an important role in governance of the organization. Men appear to dominate in decision making around coffee production.'

Combating Ethno-Racism

The goal of combating ethno-racist discrimination is thoroughly integrated into UCIRI's mission and its many projects. UCIRI members belong to rural indigenous communities that have historically been highly marginalized and discriminated against by the state and civil society in general. From colonial times through independence in the nineteenth century and up to the present day, indigenous communities throughout southern Mexico have frequently been targeted for a variety of oppressive measures, including forcible displacement from their traditional landholdings, compulsory labour under the barrel of a gun, and state homogenization policies designed to strip indigenous groups of their local customs and language and impose a national, 'mestizo' identity. Against this onslaught, indigenous groups have frequently struggled to defend the autonomy and solidarity of local communities and limit the power exercised over them by the state and the landed elite (Rus, Hernández Castillo, and Mattiace 2003; Rus and Collier 2003; Hernández Castillo 2003). Often this has entailed day-to-day forms of resistance, such as local community members choosing to direct their social and political energies inward, towards upholding indigenous customs and becoming 'upright, correct community citizens,' even while they have become increasingly dependent on 'outside' jobs and markets (Rus and Collier 2003: 38–9).

Since the 1970s, many indigenous groups in Mexico have developed a new political consciousness based on a renewed sense of their ethnic identity. The economic downturn beginning in the 1970s, combined with the decline of state corporatism – which meant reduced access for poor producers to state-subsidized fertilizers, fuel, credit, and technology – compelled rural indigenous groups to begin to organize independent associations at local, state, and regional levels to respond to the crisis in the agriculture sector (Rus, Hernández Castillo, and Mattiace 2003; Rus and Collier 2003). Combined with this were growing efforts by Christian missionaries to mobilize grassroots, indigenous groups in a manner that respected indigenous culture, as well as moves by the national government to abandon its homogenization policies in favour of a new discourse that recognized the 'pluricultural' character of Mexico. While this reorientation by the state represented a new approach towards assimilating indigenous groups into the Mexican nationalist project, in many cases the discourse of 'indigenism' and 'pluriculturalism' were merely appropriated by indigenous groups and used to advance their own demands for such things as land rights, access to credit, municipal autonomy, and state recognition of indigenous laws and customs (Hernández Castillo 2003). Consequently,

throughout the 1980s and 1990s a vast array of independent indigenous organizations emerged, ranging from explicitly political groups
that have conducted militant and peaceful civil disobedience (most
famously, the Zapatistas in Chiapas), to isolationist movements that
have sought to colonize uninhabited land in the jungles, to producer
cooperatives that have directed their attention towards meeting the
income and resource needs of their members through participation in
fair trade or organic markets.

It is within this context that UCIRI emerged and developed, and
indigenous identity and customs are deeply rooted in virtually every
aspect of its development project. Its formal political structure is
derived from an integration of outside cultural values with UCIRI
members' own understanding of their traditional indigenous political
system of *usos y costumbres*, wherein local representatives are elected to
serve the general welfare of the community (Waridel 2002: 68). The
cooperative has an informal 'Council of Elders,' based on indigenous
customs and composed of around ten founders and older activists (all
of whom are male) who act as the ultimate arbiters in cases of internal
conflict (UCIRI 2004h). The persistence of the system of usos y costumbres is something that is particularly pronounced, not just among
UCIRI communities but in the state of Oaxaca in general, which is the
only state in Mexico where indigenous people comprise the majority of
the population. While indigenous groups in Oaxaca have historically
faced the same oppressive measures experienced by indigenous people throughout the country, the sheer strength of their numbers has
allowed them somewhat greater success in their struggles for municipal autonomy. The Oaxacan state government has typically tolerated
indigenous political practices at the municipal level, and, after much
pressure from indigenous organizations, has even recognized this officially with reforms to the state electoral code and constitution, in 1995
and 1998 (Esteva 2003: 258–62).

In addition to its formal political structure, UCIRI has sought to
combat ethno-racist stereotypes and the denigration of indigenous culture through a variety of practices designed to preserve local traditions
and knowledge and build a sense of pride in being indigenous, 'not in
a romantic form but as ancestral inhabitants of their land and their
country' (cited in Taylor 2002: 20). The annual General Assembly, held
in October before the harvest, involves indigenous songs and dances
and traditional art displays. The health clinic in Lachiviza supports the
revival and use of natural herbs and plants based on local indigenous

values of connecting nature, community, and the spiritual world (Vázquez Lucas, interview 2002; Simpson and Rapone 2000: 51). The same can be said about UCIRI's organic coffee program, which, although vastly different from traditional agriculture in the region (which involved growing food crops through slash and burn methods), is conceived by members as being in line with local values of living in harmony with nature (UCIRI 2004g; Waridel 2002: 75–7). In addition, at CEC children are taught not only organic farming but to respect and protect indigenous culture and traditions (Cabrera Vázquez, interview 2002; UCIRI 1985). By making these manifold links between its development projects and the preservation of local customs, UCIRI has been able to strengthen indigenous culture, which has become a central pillar of its collective identity and dignity.

Collective Identity

The collective identity through which UCIRI members have developed a sense of unity and common purpose is premised on a mixture of ethnic, religious, and class identities that have emerged both out of local conditions and as a result of external influence. It is important to note that the collective identity of UCIRI members is not composed of static traditions that have survived the past 500 years more or less unchanged by historical processes and external intervention. Instead, their identity, as is the case with all ethnic identities, is changing and situational and composed of an integration of a variety of cultural elements merged into a common discourse of identity. This merger has been composed of local traditions, some of which have survived from the past and some of which represent 'reinventions' of tradition derived from common myths; new, local values inspired by cooperative members' understanding of their current situation; and the appropriation of outside cultural elements into their own local discourse (Hernández Castillo and Nigh 1998).

Perhaps the best symbol of how UCIRI members have recreated their collective identity is their depiction of their organizational structure, which they represent through the metaphor of a large tree (see figure 5.4). The *branches* of the tree represent the various projects that UCIRI is involved in: Health (*Salud*), Solidarity (*Solidaridad*), TCO and FAC, Hardware Store (*Ferretería*), Youth Projects (*Jóvenes*), Organic Fruit/ Marmalade (*Mermeladas*), Manufacturing (*Manufacturera*), Women's Projects (*Mujeres*), Transportation (UPZMI), CEC and the Organic

Figure 5.4 The UCIRI tree

Source: UCIRI web site (2004), http://www/uciri.org.

Project (*Proyecto orgánico*), Communication (*Comunicación*), and Education (*Formación*). The *trunk* of the tree represents the Delegate Assembly, the Administrative Council, and the Surveillance Council, which coordinate the actions of committees, communities, and members, and makes possible the commercialization (*comercialización*) of coffee beans upon which the cooperative depends. The role of *gardener* is assumed by UCIRI's advisers and assessors who gather ideas and suggestions from cooperative members to use, 'like organic compost for the tree.' At the *roots* of the tree are representatives of the families of the fifty-four communities that belong to UCIRI. The three main roots absorb the 'Word of God' (*Palabra de Díos*), indigenous and community cultural values (*cultura*), and consciousness (*conciencia*) to nurture the tree so that it is healthy and bears fruit (UCIRI 2004h).

The three main roots of the UCIRI tree are the central aspects of the cooperative's collective identity. The first root, the Word of God, stems from the UCIRI communities' connection to Catholicism and to the Jesuit mission team from the Diocese of Tehuantepec, especially the Jesuit priest and UCIRI adviser Francisco VanderHoff Boersma. Influenced by liberation theology, VanderHoff and the Jesuit mission have aspired 'to give food to those that are hungry and drink to those who are thirsty,' which they see as central to the service of God (UCIRI 2004i; VanderHoff Boersma 2001). The Jesuits have been key to the formation and development of UCIRI, and, as stated by Richard Synder (1999: 62), have 'instilled its Zapotec and Mixe rank and file with what might be called a "Jesuit work ethic," emphasizing producers' moral obligations to grow high-quality, organic coffee.'

The central role played by Jesuits in the formation and development of UCIRI is part of a long history of Jesuit missionaries combining evangelization with local economic development among indigenous groups in Mexico and Latin America. During the colonial era, while Christian doctrine was frequently evoked to justify the enslavement of non-Christian 'savages,' the Jesuits sought instead to 'civilize' indigenous groups and make them into tribute-paying subjects of Europe. One of their greatest successes in this regard was the emergence of the Guaraní Republic in the sixteenth and seventeenth centuries in what is now Paraguay. Under Jesuit direction, Guaraní indigenous groups constructed a relatively wealthy, agriculturally productive, and relatively egalitarian mini-republic which was then violently quashed in the 1750s by Portuguese slavers and Spanish colonizers angry over the success of indigenous competitors (Lacouture 1995: 227–54).[8] In modern times, Jesuits have played a key role in the propagation of liberation theology in the 1970s and 1980s, and have sought to reinterpret the Christian notion of 'liberation' to entail not just spiritual deliverance but emancipation from material oppression and injustice. In this vein, Jesuit missionaries have frequently played important roles in mobilizing poor indigenous groups for collective development projects and to fight for social justice in Latin America (Rus, Hernández Castillo, and Mattiace 2003; Harvey 1998: 69–76; Lacouture 1995: 459–72). This includes active involvement in the fair trade network, which, as described in chapter 1, has also relied heavily on the participation of a variety of missionary groups with social justice orientations, including Mennonites, Quakers, and various Protestant and Catholic groups.

Among UCIRI members, Jesuit values have developed in syncretism with the second root of the UCIRI tree, indigenous and community culture – also common to Jesuit-indigenous interactions in Latin America. At the annual general assembly, the celebration of indigenous traditions is intertwined with the Catholic Mass and various other Catholic traditions. Through the protection, promotion, and reinvention of local indigenous customs, UCIRI members have instilled their collective identity with the values of communal responsibility, pride in their traditions and history, and the connection between nature, community, and the spiritual world (VanderHoff Boersma, interview 2002; Cabrera Vázquez, interview 2002; UCIRI 1987a). The result has been a mixture of their particular interpretations of Catholicism and indigenous culture which is apparent in the following statement by UCIRI members to a Peasant Festival in 2001: 'The members of UCIRI do not consider themselves to be miserable, but they are poor. They are human beings who defend their dignity and have hope and faith in themselves because they believe in the God of Jesus Christ who gives them strength, the light, the heat, the water, the fruit and everything from the earth which they need. The solidarity and care for each other that they are planting in the mountains is the same solidarity and care that Father God has for them' (VanderHoff Boersma 2002: 4).

The third root of the UCIRI tree, consciousness, derives from the understanding that 'UCIRI's members are self-consciously a union of *small* (poor) coffee producers,' with strict rules forbidding participation of larger producers and exploitative intermediaries (emphasis in original, UCIRI 2004h). Their class identity as small producers is intertwined with their liberation theology-influenced Catholicism, which views the poor as having a privileged and dignified place in the eyes of

God, and their indigenous cultural values, which are derived in part from UCIRI members' understanding of themselves as having been exploited and oppressed by the rich and powerful (UCIRI 1987a). Thus, all three roots converge on the basis of a collective sense of shared poverty, exploitation, and suffering (Rus and Collier 2003: 45).

UCIRI members' sense of their class identity has also been influenced by their evolving understanding of themselves as organic, fair trade coffee farmers. As is the case with most other fair trade coffee cooperatives in Latin America, UCIRI members' identity as organic farmers tends to be stronger than their identity as fair trade farmers (Raynolds 2002b: 14; Taylor 2002: 16–17, 28). According to Taylor (2002: 16), this stems from the fact that, in general, fair trade coffee represents only a proportion of a cooperatives' sales and is 'more distant from producers' everyday work lives than organic certification because Fair Trade is more abstract and handled at the organizational level.' Nonetheless, fair trade is still an important aspect of the collective identity of UCIRI members, and social justice issues around health, housing, schooling, and community need are as central to the daily work and monthly meetings of UCIRI committees as organic farming. UCIRI's involvement in founding the FLO system, its consistent ability to sell 100 per cent of its export beans on fair trade markets, and its success as a fair trade cooperative has ensured that fair trade has remained an important aspect of cooperative life, which is not always the case among fair trade cooperatives (Lyon 2002; Aranda and Morales 2002: 14; Pérez-Grovas and Cervantes Trejo 2002: 15; Martinez 2002).

Another important aspect of UCIRI members' class consciousness as small producers is their understanding of themselves vis-à-vis the capitalist system. During their formative years in the 1980s, UCIRI members very clearly viewed the exploitation and marginalization that they faced as being a direct result of the capitalist system, and they were explicitly anti-capitalist. At the 'First Encounter' of UCIRI committees in 1987, UCIRI members produced a pamphlet that represented the cause of their social problems through the drawing of a metaphorical 'social tree' (*Arbol social*). In the drawing, the main trunk of the tree is the 'capitalist system,' and its roots are 'oppression,' 'exploitation,' and 'alienation.' The branches of the tree contain the various 'illnesses' caused by the tree, which includes lack of food, clothing, housing, and medicine. Beside the tree is a dead skull representing 'the poorly organized people' who have been victimized by the capitalist system (UCIRI 1987a).

Over time, UCIRI's strongly anti-capitalist ideology has dissolved in response to a variety of changing conditions. Broadly speaking, the collapse of Soviet-style communism, the decline of state-led development in the South, and the rise of neoliberal hegemony have eroded much of the ideological and political support that would have been required to assist UCIRI in maintaining an anti-capitalist stance. On a more specific level, fair trade's market-oriented approach has compelled UCIRI to abandon anti-capitalist discourse and place increasing emphasis on marketing strategies, productivity, and efficiency as it has sought to gain the support of conventional corporations and neoliberal public institutions. For example, during our interview, Ramírez Guerrero, the general coordinator of CEC, charged FLO with placing a disproportionate amount of emphasis on promoting the ideals of fair trade as opposed to the high quality of the coffee, the latter of which he asserted was key to gaining further consumer and corporate support (Ramírez Guerrero, interview 2002).

According to VanderHoff, in recent years UCIRI members have developed an interpretation of the international political economy that purports to be neither for nor against capitalism. What they seek is 'sustainability,' which is premised on the notion that everyone should have the right to basic survival (VanderHoff Boersma, interview 2002, 2001). This represents a move away from an anti-capitalist conception of class identity and towards one which is more reflective of pre-capitalist notions of what E.P. Thompson has referred to as a 'moral economy of provision.' While not necessarily at odds with a critique of underlying political-economic structures, the notion of a moral economy is premised primarily on asserting the right of local communities to gain access to the basic necessities of life regardless of the imperatives of these structures (Thompson 1971).

Solidarity and Social Networks

Although not a quantifiable aspect of FLO's criteria, the fair trade network is premised on a culture of solidarity which promotes ties of cooperation between groups at local, national, and international levels. The sum of these ties forms the basis of the network's international moral economy that seeks to reassert the notion of people's right to live taking precedence over the flows of supply and demand. Due to its relatively long history of involvement in fair trade, UCIRI has established many social networks and has done much to promote solidarity and cooperation with a variety of groups both within and outside the fair trade network. In addition to its ties with Northern trading partners and certification organizations, UCIRI has established networks with NGOs that have provided technical and marketing assistance, with national organizations representing small producers and with other fair trade cooperatives in Latin America.

Since its formation, UCIRI has received assistance from outside groups interested in promoting fair trade, organic farming, and rural development. While linkages with these groups cannot be attributed entirely to the fair trade network – ties to organic organizations have also been particularly important – it is clear that the fair trade network has served as an important source of information exchange and dialogue with a variety of NGOs. The result has been a steady flow of technical and marketing assistance which continues to this day. During my own visit to UCIRI in the fall of 2002, two outside advisors were present at CEC: Silvia Nuria Jurado Celis, an agricultural engineering student from the Universidad Nacional Autónoma de México (National Autonomous University of Mexico, UNAM) who was conducting tests to assist members in the production and processing of organic fruit; and Adam Cowling, a Canadian International Development Agency (CIDA) intern from the Falls Brook Centre in Knowlesville, New Brunswick, who was constructing UCIRI's website, exploring new marketing strategies, and helping to develop an analogue forestry nursery (Jurado Celis, interview 2002; Cowling, interview 2002).

In addition to receiving assistance from NGOs, UCIRI has also played a central role in the *creation* of many NGOs, including labelling organizations like Max Havelaar, CERTIMEX, and Comercio Justo México, as well as organizations that support small producers, such as Integradora Agromercados, CEPCO, and CNOC. The requirements of forming and maintaining a fair trade cooperative have enhanced UCIRI's organizational and political capacity and prepared it better to defend the interests of its communities as well as those of small farmers throughout Mexico. This is particularly evident in its involvement in organizations like CEPCO and CNOC, which represent tens of thousands of conventional small producers and have mandates that are broader than supporting fair trade. But, while UCIRI's involvement in national organizations extends beyond promoting fair trade, it remains limited to lobbying the federal government for favourable small-farming policies and does not involve official connections with explicitly political organizations. To do the latter would lead to confrontation with the state and local elite, and it would violate FLO's policy of political neutrality (FLO 2003a; Bolscher, interview 2002).

Perhaps one of the greatest indications of the strength of solidarity within the fair trade network has been UCIRI's role in assisting other Southern fair trade coffee cooperatives. UCIRI has sent technical teams to assist farmers who wanted to set up fair trade cooperatives in central and southern Mexico, Guatemala, and Nicaragua. It has made its facilities available to other cooperatives for coffee processing and marketing and has hosted children from other cooperatives at CEC. In addition, it has shared contracts with other cooperatives out of solidarity and to meet the demands of buyers who frequently request more coffee than a single cooperative can provide. In fact, most of the fair trade cooperatives in Mexico first participated in fair trade through shared contracts with other cooperatives, and UCIRI has been particularly important in this regard. In 1985, UCIRI agreed to assist the newly formed ISMAM cooperative by selling its coffee. Then, when ISMAM was established, it offered its support to other smaller cooperatives in the region (Simpson and Rapone 2000: 52). Similarly, in 1990 UCIRI shared its contract with La Selva cooperative to allow it to sell its first coffee on the fair trade market. After that, La Selva introduced the Majomut cooperative to the fair trade market with a shared contract in 1993–4, and then Majomut shared its contract with the Tzotsilotic cooperative in 2001 (Taylor 2002: 7; Pérez-Grovas and Cervantes Trejo 2002; Gonzalez Cabanas 2002).

Despite the strong culture of solidarity within the fair trade network, some commentators and fair traders believe that competition between cooperatives is increasing and threatens to erode the network's cooperative values. With the fair trade coffee market saturated, it is becoming increasingly difficult for newer, less developed cooperatives to find a market share, and extremely difficult for new groups to gain a place on the FLO register (Méndez 2002: 9; Pérez-Grovas and Cervantes Trejo 2002: 21; Gonzalez Cabanas 2002; Martinez 2002). Under these conditions, it is the strongest and most well established cooperatives, such as UCIRI, that obtain the greatest benefits from fair trade, while weaker groups are increasingly crowded out. For example, it took the FLO-certified Tzotzilotic Tzobolotic Coffee Cooperative in Chiapas, Mexico, eight years to find a buyer for their first shipment of fair trade coffee in 2001 (Martinez 2002). Moreover, donors and lenders tend to favour well-established cooperatives with a solid presence in fair trade and organic markets, which serves only to give further advantage to groups that are already relatively stable and strong (Raynolds, Murray, and Taylor 2004; Taylor 2002: 7, 25–6). Thus, unless fair traders can ignite a rapid expansion of fair trade coffee sales, it is likely that market pressures will impose increasing competition among fair trade cooperatives seeking to expand their market shares and among uncertified cooperatives seeking entrance into the network.

Conclusion: Assessing UCIRI's Capabilities and Concessions

Before proceeding with an assessment of UCIRI's developmental project, it is necessary to note that the cooperative's successes can be partially attributed to various specific factors that have proven advantageous throughout its history. Two of these factors are similar to those of other fair trade cooperatives and help explain their relative success in relation to other, non-fair trade producer groups and communities. First, most successful fair trade cooperatives had developed into committed, well-organized, socially coherent organizations prior to their entrance into the fair trade network. These efforts were frequently initiated by Catholic missionaries or regional small-farmer associations. The fair trade network then served to strengthen pre-existing organizations (Méndez 2002; Lyon 2002; Aranda and Morales 2002; Pérez-Grovas and Cervantes Trejo 2002). This is the case with UCIRI, which developed into a solid organization out of its struggles with the state and due to the efforts of Jesuit missionaries prior to its involvement in fair trade. Its members have generally been better organized and more highly politicized than small farmers in other communities in the region (Jurado Celis, interview 2002).

Second, most successful cooperatives have had the long-term presence of an 'international interlocutor' who has been essential for gaining access to the fair trade network and developing ties with Northern partners. These interlocutors have been Christian missionaries, agricultural technicians, or representatives from Northern fair trade partners that have formed personal bonds with Southern cooperatives (Lyon 2002; Aranda and Morales 2002; Pérez-Grovas and Cervantes Trejo 2002; Gonzalez Cabanas 2002). Throughout its history, UCIRI has relied a great deal on VanderHoff, a Jesuit missionary who is highly educated, speaks several languages, and has been essential to establishing contracts with Northern partners and promoting UCIRI (Raynolds 2002b: 12; VanderHoff Boersma 2002: 7–8; Taylor 2002: 3).

In addition to sharing specific characteristics with other fair trade cooperatives, UCIRI also has enjoyed one advantage that is unique to it and accounts for its relative success within the network, namely its particular history as a co-founder of Max Havelaar and the entire FLO system. This has allowed UCIRI a solid and stable place within the network and has been at least partially responsible for its ability to sell close to 100 per cent of its export-quality beans on the fair trade market. The result of such a unique history is that UCIRI can hardly be taken as an example of the average fair trade coffee cooperative. Rather, it represents what is likely the most successful fair trade cooperative in the world. As a result, an assessment of UCIRI is in many ways an assessment of the greatest achievements that the fair trade network has thus far been able to attain, as well as an appraisal of the most significant limitations that the network faces.

There is little doubt that UCIRI has brought significant benefits to its members over the years. UCIRI has made important gains in enhancing the capabilities of its members. Through their relatively higher incomes and varied social programs, members have improved their basic capabilities to combat such things as extreme poverty, hunger, malnutrition, environmental degradation, and inadequate housing. They have significantly increased their access to proper health and dental care, education and training through CEC, and a variety of home and community improvements. As an organization, UCIRI's involvement in fair trade has enhanced its capacity to survive and compete in the international market through the construction of processing and transportation infrastructure; improved access to credit and financing; 'mutual apprenticeship' in technical and marketing skills; and the benefits that accrue through social networks and bonds of solidarity. In addition, over the years UCIRI members have developed their sense of unity, collective identity, and self-respect, which have enhanced their ability to protect and reaffirm community and indigenous traditions as well as their capacity to organize and lobby the government in defence of their interests. The result has been improved capabilities to attain valued activities that have enhanced the quality of life in UCIRI communities.

While the capability approach is useful for assessing how UCIRI members have improved their abilities to operate *within* the existing social structures of international capitalism, its tells us very little about UCIRI's ability to confront and change these structures. This is inherent in the capability approach and all of the shaped advantage approaches, which limit their vision of development to working within the limits imposed by neoliberal globalization. Yet, the ultimate goal of fair trade organizations is not just to enhance the capabilities of Southern producers to survive within the existing order, but to enhance their abilities to confront and change it. In this vein, as described in previous chapters, some authors have argued that fair trade confronts the commodification of goods, where, as Marx phrased it, social relations among people appear as relations among things (Waridel 2002; Lappé and Lappé 2002: 93–6, 199–203; Elson 2002, 1988; Raynolds 2002a; Simpson and Rapone 2000). As Marx (1978: 326) argued, such a situation can only be challenged by a democratic and participatory form of production that entails 'an association of free people, working with the means of production in common, in which the labour-power of all the different individuals is consciously applied as the combined labour-power of the community.'

UCIRI's development project certainly contains much within it that challenges the principles of commodity fetishism. Production, processing, transportation, and marketing are organized along the lines of 'an association of free people, working with the means of production in common.' UCIRI has made important strides towards developing a system of workers' self-management that involves regular assemblies, elections, information exchange, debate, and discussion. Economic and social infrastructure are owned cooperatively and land is communally held (although this last characteristic is specific to UCIRI and not a result of fair trade criteria). Among UCIRI members, the goal of work is not to accrue private profits for individual members but to meet the needs and priorities of the community, and a great deal of unpaid labour and socially produced wealth is expended with these goals in mind. One area, however, that remains far too neglected is the persistence of significant gender inequalities within the cooperative. Much more needs to be done to confront this if UCIRI wishes to progress in meeting its democratic aims. Nonetheless, given the historical, political-economic, and cultural context within which the cooperative emerged, UCIRI's project still represents a significant movement towards the development of a participatory production model.

Yet, while UCIRI is organized around the principles of worker control and ownership of the means of production, it falls short of having its economic life 'consciously applied as the combined labour-power of the community.' This would entail having decisions about production determined democratically through a process that involves *both* producers and consumers. In the fair trade network, while producer groups such as UCIRI have developed direct linkages with Northern roasters, the consumer remains an atomized individual who may freely choose whether or not to buy fair trade coffee on the basis of a variety of factors, including cost, convenience, and image. Northern consumers are not held responsible for the outcome of their decisions and are not engaged in a democratic process with Southern producers whose only influence over the latter is moral persuasion and marketing strategies. Thus, however much UCIRI strives to create democracy at the local level, it remains dependent on the whims of the international capitalist market for its survival and growth.

The pressures imposed on the fair trade network by the imperatives of the international capitalist market have had both a limiting and an eroding effect on the network, which can be seen in the case of UCIRI. The market has imposed strict limitations on the fair trade price, which is relatively low by historical standards and has not saved UCIRI members from experiencing general poverty and the necessity to migrate in search of work. Attempts to broaden UCIRI's project into local textile manufacturing have failed due to fierce market imperatives. The pressures of the market have eroded UCIRI's anti-capitalist stance, forcing it to place greater attention on efficiency, productivity, and meeting market trends. In recent years, the saturation of both fair trade and conventional coffee markets have compelled UCIRI to seek out greater ties with conventional TNCs, who do not participate in fair trade out of solidarity but out of the need to protect their public image for the sake of profitability.

These escalating market pressures raise two serious questions about UCIRI's development project, which are, as of yet, impossible to answer. First, will UCIRI be able to maintain and expand its gains in the future? Due to its privileged position within the fair trade network, UCIRI is better prepared than most cooperatives to fend off the pressures of a stagnating coffee market and maintain its gains. However, as can be seen in its recent decision to sign a deal with Carrefour without FLO certification, UCIRI is eager to expand its market share and willing to make concessions to do it. Second, do the conditions exist that would allow UCIRI's project to be replicated on a larger scale? This question is central to development theory, which aims to construct strategies that have the potential to benefit not just small segments but broad sectors of the socially and economically disadvantaged (North and Cameron 2000). It is unlikely that UCIRI's project could satisfy this criterion. This is because UCIRI's success has relied in part on a set of specific historical advantages that cannot be easily replicated, and because there currently is no more space on the fair trade coffee market for new cooperatives (Oxfam International 2002a: 42–3). The fair trade market niche appears to have limited growth potential, and the strongest cooperatives, like UCIRI, have firmly established their market shares, leaving little room for new entrants. Thus, while UCIRI has been able to make significant gains despite the eroding pressures of global capitalism, the imperatives of the international capitalist market have imposed strict limits on the extent to which UCIRI's developmental project can be broadly replicated.

6 Fair Trade Coffee in Canada

More investors and consumers today are demanding that companies be accountable for the environmental and social impacts of their operations. There is a growing body of empirical studies demonstrating the positive impact [Corporate Social Responsibility] has on business economic performance and shareholder value.

Starbucks Coffee Company (2003)

Trade isn't about global control and profit maximization. Trade, economics, and business should be about all people – our relationship with each other, with the earth, and with future generations. Within Planet Bean, fair trade and co-operation are our main focus.

Planet Bean (2004c)

As is the case in all market exchanges under capitalism, fair trade producers are entirely dependent on the voluntary purchasing decisions of consumers to provide a market for their goods and through it the income required to survive. Moreover, within the fair trade network the relations between producer and consumer mirror those of the conventional international trade in commodities: fair trade producers are located in poorer, Southern nations while the vast majority of their consumers are located in rich, Northern nations for a variety of historical reasons, described in chapter 3. This means that in the final analysis the fair trade network is dependent on Northern consumers and Northern fair trade partners – importers, roasters, and distributors – for its survival and growth. Yet, despite this fact, fair traders and fair trade analysts have paid little attention to Northern partners, beyond encouraging them to buy and sell fair trade goods. Fairtrade Labelling Organizations International (FLO) does not have any social or environmental standards for Northern partners except for those that regulate their exchange relations with Southern partners (a guaranteed price and social premiums, long-term commitments, advanced partial payments, licensing fees). Moreover, fair trade analysts have done little to develop a critical analysis of Northern fair traders, the obstacles they face, and their role in influencing the evolution of the fair trade network.[1]

While there are no doubt many reasons for the lack of analysis on Northern fair trade partners, two broad assumptions that are generally apparent among fair traders and analysts are particularly important in explaining this. First, among fair traders it is generally *assumed* that the fair trade network has a beneficial impact on the North in terms of promoting international solidarity and social justice. As a result, little work has been carried out to assess if this is indeed the case. Second, many fair traders take as a given that the North has already attained 'development' and that the goal of the fair trade network is primarily to assist Southern partners in catching up. Consequently, the North is generally not viewed as a target for development, beyond changing the views of consumers regarding international trade and North-South inequalities.

Both of these assumptions neglect the complexity of fair trade in the North and leave important questions about its possible impact, both negative and positive, unanswered. This impact should not just be assumed; it should be assessed and critically analysed. Moreover, while the rich nations in the North have certainly attained a higher standard of living than all but a few Southern nations when measured in terms of labour rights, social welfare, and basic social indicators such as life expectancy at birth, literacy rates, and income per capita, widespread inequality, poverty, alienation, and social conflict still persist in the North. Economist Amartya Sen has criticized the view, held by many in development circles, of 'development' as the process of combating poverty, deprivation, and injustice in the South alone. Instead, he argues for the need to approach development as a process required for all nations, rich or poor, because 'richer countries too often have deeply disadvantaged people, who lack basic opportunities of health care, or functional education, or gainful employment, or economic and social security. Even within very rich countries, sometimes the longevity of substantial groups is no higher than that in much poorer economies of the so-called third world' (Sen 1999: 15, 13–34).

This is increasingly the case for rich nations in the North, especially as neoliberal reforms have eroded public spending on health care, education, and social welfare and initiated a process of 'downward harmonization' that has reduced working-class wages and unionization rates, along with corporate taxes. In Canada, since the signing of the Free Trade Agreement with the United States in 1989, inequality between the richest and poorest Canadians has increased significantly. In terms of income, for example, the inflation-adjusted market incomes of the wealthiest 20 per cent of Canadians rose by 16 per cent from 1989 to 2001 compared to a loss of nearly 7 per cent for the poorest 20 per cent (Jackson 2003a). These trends are a reflection of the growing polarization of the workforce between workers with high-income 'core jobs' and those with low income 'precarious jobs' with little or no employment security. The latter tend to be primarily concentrated among youths and 'high-risk' groups such as single mothers, recent immigrants, Aboriginal Canadians, persons with disabilities, and adults with limited education (Jackson 2003b; Burke and Shields 2000). In recent years, growing concern among unions and non-governmental organizations (NGOs) in Canada has emerged over the need to counter these trends through the promotion of 'human capital' and 'community economic development' to assist disadvantaged workers (Jackson 2003b; Human Capital Development Sub-committee 2003). Reflecting on this, Andrew Jackson, the senior economist at the Canadian Labour Congress (CLC), states: 'The key point is that most low-pay jobs held by adults are not just insecure, they also tend to be 'dead-end' jobs which offer little or no opportunity to develop skills, capacities and capabilities which are important from the perspective of social inclusion' (Jackson 2003b: 9).

Precarious employment tends to be predominant among the service-sector in Canada. This includes the Canadian coffee industry, whose service sector jobs are generally low-paid, insecure, and non-unionized, and whose employees by and large lack sufficient capabilities to attain more meaningful and secure work. Although the lives of coffee industry employees in the North are significantly different than those of rural coffee workers and small-scale farmers in the South, they too have been negatively impacted by neoliberal reforms and the exploitative practices of giant coffee transnational corporations (TNCs). Like fair trade partners, Canadian coffee workers have also mobilized to demand fairer wages and working conditions. Moreover, an important minority of fair trade alternative trade organizations (ATOs) in Canada, driven by the desire to promote community economic development, have explicitly devoted themselves towards adhering to the values of fair trade in their Northern operations.

Thus, the fair trade network must be assessed as much for its impact on the North as its impact on the South. Just as is the case in the South, the fair trade network in the North has aspired to meet its democratic, egalitarian, and social justice goals through its mediated involvement in the international capitalist market within the context of neoliberal reforms. Through this mediation, fair trade in the North has evolved in a manner which has entailed both gains and concessions, which raises important questions about fair trade and its future development: What is the impact of the fair trade network's relationship with giant TNCs, international financial institutions, and public institutions, which, as discussed in chapter 2, have turned increasingly towards supporting fair trade to mask their devotion to a broader neoliberal agenda? What is the role played in the network by small-scale fair trade ATOs and how does this differ from that played by conventional TNCs? What does it mean to be an 'ethical consumer' and how does fair trade's reliance on social justice shopping affect the nature of the sort of international solidarity that it promotes? The purpose of this chapter is to explore these questions through an examination of fair trade coffee in Canada, a country which has historically been a relatively insignificant participant in fair trade but has emerged over the past few years as an important growing market.

The History of Fair Trade Coffee in Canada

Following the general trend in coffee sales in advanced capitalist countries in the North, Canada emerged in the post–Second World War era as a major coffee-consuming nation. In the 1970s and 1980s, Canada imported around 2 per cent of the world's coffee (around 78,000 tons) and was tied with smaller European nations such as Switzerland, Finland, Denmark, and Belgium for tenth place among coffee-importing nations globally. The growth of the Canadian coffee industry increased from the late 1980s, so that by 2000 Canada had emerged as the seventh largest coffee importer in the world, accounting for around 3 per cent of world coffee imports (around 171,000 tons), just above the imports of the United Kingdom, the Netherlands, and Belgium. Canada's rapid growth in coffee imports was part of a broader trend among rich countries, following consumption trends that were already

Figure 6.1 Largest coffee-importing nations, 1970

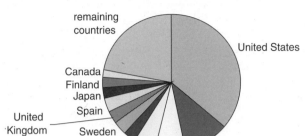

Source: UNCTAD (2004), *UNCTAD Handbook of Statistics On-Line*, http://stats.unctad.org.

Figure 6.2 Largest coffee-importing nations, 2000

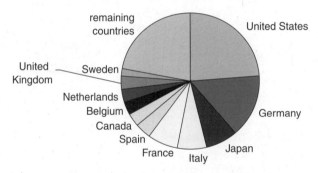

Source: UNCTAD (2004), *UNCTAD Handbook of Statistics On-Line*, http://stats.unctad.org.

established in the United States, the largest coffee-consuming country in the world. This led to a decline in the U.S. share of total world coffee imports, which, from 1970 to 2000, dropped from 36 per cent to 24 per cent (despite an increase in the quantity of total coffee imports). Meanwhile the share of world coffee exports to western Europe increased from 46 per cent to 49 per cent, to Japan from 3 per cent to 7 per cent, and to Canada from 2 per cent to 3 per cent (see figures 6.1 and 6.2 and table 6.1) (UNCTAD 2004).

Canada's boom in coffee sales can be largely attributed to advertising campaigns initiated by large-scale coffee corporations (many of

Table 6.1 Largest coffee-importing nations, 2000

	Amount imported (thousand metric tons)	Percentage of global market
United States	1215	24
Germany	752	14
Japan	349	7
Italy	336	6
France	328	6
Spain	199	4
Canada	155	3
Belgium	144	3
Netherlands	135	3
United Kingdom	122	2
Sweden	87	2
Switzerland	64	1
Finland	59	1
Austria	54	1
Denmark	54	1
Portugal	41	1
Norway	33	1
Greece	25	1
Remaining countries	1200	22
Global exports	5353	

Source: UNCTAD (2004), *UNCTAD Handbook of Statistics On-Line*, http://stats.unctad.org.

which were U.S.-based) seeking to expand their market, the growing popularity of local speciality coffee shops, and a rapid decline of coffee bean prices in the wake of the collapse of the International Coffee Agreement (ICA) in 1989.[2] The decline in coffee prices over the past decade and a half, which has culminated in the current coffee crisis, has likely played a significant role in sparking consumer demand in Canada. From 1986 to 2001, total coffee imports to Canada increased by over 75 per cent (UNCTAD 2004). During this same period, the percentage of total food expenditure that Canadians spent on coffee and tea declined by 48 per cent (Statistics Canada 2003). Thus, Canadians have been spending much less on coffee while at the same time consuming much more. This means that, as an outcome of the grossly unequal world system, the Canadian coffee industry and Canadian consumers have benefited significantly from the current coffee crisis that has had such devasting consequences on producers in the South (Ross 2002; Oxfam International 2002a; Global Exchange 2001).

Figure 6.3 Share of fair trade coffee sales compared to conventional coffee imports, 2001

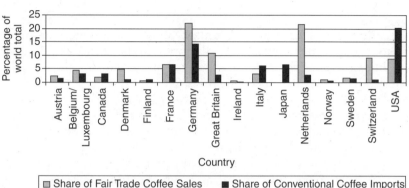

Sources: International Coffee Organization (2005), *Historical Data*, http://www.ico.org/asp/display3.asp.
FLO (2005), web page, http://www.fairtradenet/sites/products/coffee/markets.html

Yet, while Canada's position as a major coffee-consuming country has grown significantly in the post–Second World War era, it has historically been a relatively insignificant consuming country for fair trade coffee compared to the major markets in Europe, and has, with some variation, remained so to this day (see figure 6.3). The history of the fair trade network in Canada, as was the case throughout the North, can be traced back to the 1940s and 1950s when Christian missionaries began selling crafts produced by disadvantaged Southern artisans in direct-purchase projects. This effort was led by the Mennonite Central Committee (MCC), which, as described in chapter 1, began selling embroidered textiles from the South in the 1940s and opened its first SELFHELP Crafts retail store in 1972 (Ten Thousand Villages Canada 2004; Littrell and Dickson 1999: 61–88). SELFHELP Crafts was primarily devoted to the sale of handicrafts, although it did begin offering commodities for sale that were imported and processed by other fair trade ATOs.

The first ATO to import fair trade commodities in Canada was Bridgehead Trading, which introduced fair trade coffee into Canada in 1981, nearly eight years after it had been introduced into European markets by Fair Trade Organisatie in the Netherlands (EFTA 1995: 3). Bridgehead was formed by two United Church ministers and two social justice activists to buy and sell coffee from Nicaraguan coffee farmers to battle against the effects of the U.S. trade embargo and the U.S.-sponsored civil war against the then ruling socialist government of the Sandinistas. At first, Bridgehead was run by volunteers and sold fair trade coffee from Toronto church basements. By 1984, support for Bridgehead had grown so that it was incorporated as a federal, for-profit company and was purchased by Oxfam Canada (Bridgehead 2004).

As was the case globally, Oxfam played a key role in the organization and promotion of fair trade in Canada, and it continues to play a significant role in fair trade today. Oxfam publishes policy papers and raises consumer awareness about the inequalities of global trade and participates directly in the import, processing, and distribution of fair trade goods (Conlon, presentation 2004a). Its greatest impact has been in the United Kingdom, where it has developed into the largest fair trade ATO in the country (Bird and Hughes 1997). In Canada, Oxfam has been a major promoter of fair trade, and, in terms of direct involvement, played an important role in the formative years of Bridgehead. The capital and other support that Oxfam provided Bridgehead allowed it to expand, so that by the start of the 1990s it had extended its product line from coffee to include handicrafts; operated retail stores in Ottawa, Toronto, and Vancouver; and had annual sales figures of around $5 million with a mailing list of 200,000 active names (Bridgehead 2004).[3]

Despite the relative success of their formative years, the 1990s initiated a period of readjustment for fair trade ATOs in Canada as they found it increasingly difficult to remain profitable due to lack of capital, inefficient management strategies, and competition from conventional retailers. As described in earlier chapters, this has led to attempts to 'professionalize' fair trade ATOs by adopting marketing and managerial strategies common to conventional businesses so that they are better able to compete against conventional corporations. Specifically, this has meant that a greater emphasis has been placed on efficiency through staff training and computerization; the development of new, stylish magazines and catalogues; consultation with Northern fashion designers on how to develop goods that reflect market trends; and better promotional strategies for radio and television (EFTA 2001a: 35). These efforts have been led by the International Federation for Alternative Trade (IFAT), formed in 1989, whose founding members included SELFHELP Crafts, Bridgehead, and Oxfam International (IFAT 2001).

The professionalization of SELFHELP Crafts emerged in response to fierce competition from a growing number of mail-order catalogues specializing in 'ethnic products,' as well as major specialty retailers such as Pier 1 Imports (Littrell and Dickson 1999: 17). In Canada, SELF-HELP Crafts' sales growth stagnated in the 1990s and hovered between $1.4 million and $1.7 million per year from 1994 to 1998 (Ten Thousand Villages Canada 2003). In response, MCC officials decided that it was time to shift SELFHELP Crafts from a largely mission-driven focus to one which placed greater emphasis on business strategy and consumer demands. In 1996, its named was changed to Ten Thousand Villages (TTV) (deemed more appealing to consumers) and its first board of directors, composed of members with extensive business and retail experience, was established to advise the director and staff on its new business-oriented strategy (Ten Thousand Villages Canada 2004; Littrell and Dickson 1999: 61–88).

The new strategy adopted by TTV entailed two major changes in its purchasing and product development policies. First, TTV abandoned it tradition of honouring artisans' indigenous knowledge and artistic skills through limited product intervention in favour of purchasing products based on saleability and suggesting changes to meet market trends. Second, TTV redirected the majority of its purchases towards larger, more sophisticated Southern partners who were willing and able to invest over a three-year period in becoming more technically efficient, increasing volume, producing more quickly, and expanding its product line (Littrell and Dickson 1999: 61–88). These changes have led to a revival of sales growth: in 1999, TTV Canada's annual sales leapt up to $2.37 million and grew steadily up to $4.67 million in 2003 (Ten Thousand Villages Canada 2003). However, they have also involved major concessions to TTV's mission-driven goals. The imperatives of the market have compelled TTV to weaken its commitment to preserving indigenous craft traditions and to helping those groups that are most in need, as opposed to those groups that are relatively larger and better organized.

Bridgehead Trading also undertook a similar process of professionalization in the 1990s. Although sales revenue grew steadily throughout the decade, profits declined and eventually turned to losses as it became apparent that the ATO was holding too much inventory and had too little working capital. In 1998, the stumbling enterprise was sold to Shared Interest, a cooperative lending society in the United Kingdom that specializes in financing for fair trade organizations.

Shared Interest formed a new company, Bridgehead Inc., and determined that the ATO must abandon its craft sales, which were responsible for its large inventory, and refocus its energies entirely on coffee. In 2000, Bridgehead declared bankruptcy, closed its retail stores in Toronto, Vancouver, and Ottawa (except for its Ottawa flagship store), and was bought by a group of investors led by former members of the Bridgehead management team.

Under the new directors, conventional business practices were put into effect, greater efforts were directed towards pleasing consumers with trendy marketing strategies, and coffee became the ATO's primary focus. In addition, Bridgehead returned to importing and roasting its own coffee, as opposed to purchasing it from the U.S. ATO Equal Exchange (which it had done since 1997), a process which had bumped up the final price to the consumer. By 2002, Bridgehead's profitability was restored and it began opening new stores, so that in 2004 it consisted of five stores in Ottawa (Bridgehead 2004; Chianello 2002). Bridgehead's sustainability has been revived, albeit with a limited product line and a new marketing strategy which places as much emphasis on pleasing consumers as in promoting fair trade and educating consumers about global injustices. Reflecting on the need to win consumers with marketing strategies, manager Tracey Clark asserts that Bridgehead cafés offer 'a comfortable environment, a great product, and the *fair trade makes it that much better*. But we realize that not every customer is going to be as passionate about fair trade as we are' (cited in Chianello 2002; emphasis added).

Reforming the Conventional Coffee Market in Canada (1997 to the present)

As has been the case internationally, the major reorientation in the fair trade network in Canada has been initiated by the fair trade labelling system and the founding of TransFair Canada, the national member of FLO International. TransFair Canada emerged out of the growing belief expressed by one of its board members, John Wong (2004), that 'in order for this movement to really move forward, we need to engage the multinationals.' TransFair Canada was founded in 1994 but was not fully operational and did not give out its first certification seal until 1997, nearly nine years after Max Havelaar had been established in the Netherlands. Similarly, TransFair USA was founded in 1995 and did not give out its first certification seal until 1998. Since then, sales of fair trade certified coffee have grown rapidly, quadrupling in Canada and multiplying by thirty-seven in the United States from 1998 to 2000 (Waridel 2002: 99–100). This rapid growth has been typical of previously untapped fair trade markets and has generally tended to level off (EFTA 2001a: 33–6). In 2001, TransFair Canada estimates that around 600,000 pounds of roasted fair trade coffee were sold in Canada, a figure which represents less than 0.2 per cent of Canada's coffee imports for that year (UNCTAD 2004; TransFair Canada 2004).

TransFair Canada is an independent, third-party certification body that adheres to monitoring criteria and standards that are set out by FLO. Its primary mission is twofold: to promote fair trade among consumers and businesses, and to protect the integrity of fair trade certification by providing independent and open monitoring (Whitby, presentation 2004). For corporations to attain certification from Trans-Fair Canada, they must agree to adhere to fair trade standards; to report their purchases, processing, and sales of certified products; to open their financial accounts up for periodic verification; and to pay the bulk of the licence fees. TransFair Canada aspires to be self-sufficient and attain the majority of its income from licensing fees, but in practice this has not yet been possible in Canada where the fair trade market niche is still too small. In 2000, around 30 per cent of TransFair Canada's income came from licence fees, with the remainder coming from funding from the Canadian International Development Agency (CIDA) and various churches, unions, and NGOs (TransFair Canada 2004, 2003).

In addition to standards set for Canadian licensees, TransFair Canada must also adhere to a set of minimum standards to maintain its status as a National Initiative (NI) with FLO. According to FLO's Flow of Goods Policy, finalized in 2000, TransFair Canada must ensure:

- That companies representing 95% of the volume of commodities labelled by TransFair Canada be audited every year.
- That site visits be made to at least 5% of licensed companies each year.
- That all data about imports to Canada are channelled to FLO.
- That companies provide information quarterly as set out in standard forms developed by FLO and adapted by National Initiatives. (TransFair Canada 2004)

As of 2004, the products certified by TransFair Canada were coffee, tea and tea products, chocolate, cocoa powder, sugar, soap, bananas, frozen desserts, mangoes, and soccer balls (TransFair Canada 2004;

Whitby, presentation 2004). Of these goods, coffee was by far the most popular product. In 2004, TransFair Canada had 115 fair trade licensees for all products on its register, of which 99 were coffee licensees (including importers, office providers, wholesalers, and restaurants/ cafés). With regard to retail outlets, where fair trade coffee was available for purchase, TransFair Canada reported that there were 600 such outlets nationally, of which 284 (nearly 47 per cent of the total) were in the province of Quebec, followed by Ontario (21 percent), British Columbia (17 per cent), Alberta (7 per cent), and the rest of Canada (7 per cent) (TransFair Canada 2004).

These figures demonstrate a disproportionate amount of support for fair trade in Quebec, which has nearly half of all fair trade retail outlets in Canada yet possesses only 25 per cent of Canadian households and is responsible for around 29 per cent of national coffee expenditure (Statistics Canada 2003). The relatively strong support for fair trade in Quebec can be explained in part by the determined promotional efforts of the Montreal-based NGO Équiterre, whose activities will be discussed below, as well as the different consumption habits in Quebec that are better suited to fair trade consumerism. Fair trade coffee is sold as a gourmet product that sells for higher prices than conventional coffee (in 2004, fair trade coffee, in line with the high-end of specialty coffee prices, retailed for around 250 to 300 per cent more than regular coffee prices)[4] and is more readily available in local specialty stores than in large chain stores. Quebec's consumption habits are well suited to this sort of product. In 2001, the average Quebec household spent 12 per cent more of its weekly expenditure on coffee and 28 per cent more of its weekly expenditure at food specialty stores than the national average, indicating a greater preference for more costly coffee and specialty products (Statistics Canada 2003).

While sales of fair trade coffee have grown significantly since the formation of TransFair Canada, there is a clear need to expand the fair trade market to meet the needs of Southern producers, and Canada remains a minor supporter of fair trade compared to other countries in Europe, some of which have smaller consumer markets and a disproportionately high support for fair trade. The Netherlands, the world's largest importer of fair trade coffee, was responsible for 24 per cent of all FLO-certified coffee imports in 2000, yet accounted for only 3 per cent of all international conventional coffee imports for that year. That same year, Germany was responsible for around 24 per cent of fair trade coffee imports but only 15 per cent of conventional coffee imports, Switzerland accounted for 11 per cent of fair trade coffee imports compared to 1 per cent of conventional imports, and Great Britain accounted for 10 per cent of fair trade coffee imports compared to 3 per cent of conventional imports. In sharp contrast to this, in 2000 Canada accounted for only 1.2 per cent of the total of fair trade coffee imports even though it was responsible for 3 per cent of the world's coffee imports. The figures for the United States reveal an even greater imbalance, with the country accounting for 5.5 per cent of fair trade coffee imports compared to a 24 per cent share of world coffee imports (see figure 6.3) (UNCTAD 2004; Raynolds 2002b: 27). In response to these realities, in recent years activists in North America have stepped up their efforts to promote fair trade, and aspire, at the least, to bring Canada and the United States up to a level commensurate with the major fair trade countries in Europe. The two major strategies they have pursued, as has been the case internationally, have been 'buycotting' campaigns and attempts to gain the support of public institutions through their procurement policies.

As explained in chapter 2, buycotting campaigns have been a prime strategy for fair trade activists to gain the support of conventional TNCs. Such a campaign in the United States successfully pressured Starbucks to begin selling limited quantities of fair trade coffee at its stores in the United States in 2000, followed by Canada in 2002 (Waridel 2002: 108–9; Global Exchange 2000). Unlike in the United States, where Starbucks sells fair trade coffee only in whole bean bags, in Canada the TNC agreed to sell fair trade coffee whole bean and as a brewed 'cup of the day' once a month (CBC 2002). While this initiative was primarily a result of pressure in the United States, Canadian social justice activists have also mounted their own successful buycott campaign. In the 1990s, Équiterre initiated a campaign targeting one of the largest Canadian coffee corporations, Van Houtte. Over a period of three years, Équiterre supporters sent thousands of postcards demanding fair trade to Paul-André Guillotte, the head of Van Houtte. Eventually, the company ceded to the pressure and agreed in 2002 to offer one type of fair trade coffee through its organic line (Bernier-Genest, presentation 2004; Waridel 2002: 106–7). Combined with the decision by Starbucks Canada, this move has compelled other Canadian roasters to get involved in fair trade, and in 2004 Timothy's World Coffee, one of the largest Canadian specialty coffee companies, began offering limited quantities of fair trade coffee in its 140 stores (TransFair Canada and Timothy's World Coffee 2004).

While fair trade activists generally depict buycotting as a innovative new strategy, in that it involves mobilizing consumers not only *against* a particular product but *for* a positive alternative, it in fact has many similarities with the boycotting campaigns of the 1970s and 1980s. This can be seen in a comparison with the well-known Nestlé boycott, which was initiated by activists in the late 1970s in response to that TNC's strategy for marketing and selling infant formula to poor communities in the South. Due to contaminated water in many of these communities, and lack of family income leading to excessive dilution of the formula, its use frequently led to malnutrition and death among babies. Moreover, Nestlé employed a marketing strategy that involved giving out free samples, to get poor mothers to give the formula to their newborns, and deploying 'mothercraft nurses,' who were in reality Nestlé salespeople dressed as nurses. In response, activists initiated a boycott in the North and asked consumers to cease purchasing Nestlé goods until the food giant agreed to change its advertising strategies. The boycott was called off in 1984 after Nestlé agreed to adhere to the World Health Organization's (WHO) International Code of Marketing Breast Milk Substitutes, which entailed appropriate advertising methods and provisions for adequate information to consumers. It was then re-initiated in 1988 after it was discovered that Nestlé was continuing to give out free samples. The boycott is active to this day in over twenty countries in Europe and North America (Baby Milk Action 2002; Gerber 1990).

Comparing the two strategies, both the Nestlé boycott and fair trade buycotting campaigns represent attempts to regulate the behaviour of TNCs in the absence of an international governmental agency with the will and the power to impose regulations on the private sector (Follesdal 2004; Micheletti, Follesdal, and Stolle 2004). In both cases, the tool of 'enforcement' is the threat of adverse publicity, and consumers are asked to support the campaign by making relatively minor sacrifices in their purchasing strategies (Gerber 1990). Thus, at their core both strategies are attempts to impose self-regulation on TNCs. Nonetheless, there are two important differences between them.

First, buycotting campaigns present not just the threat of negative publicity but offer the attraction of positive publicity and increased profits to corporations who agree to play ball. Second, buycotting campaigns make more mild and incremental demands than boycott campaigns: whereas the Nestlé boycott demands that the TNC change its entire marketing strategy, fair trade buycotts demand that corporations show a basic commitment to fair trade, which can entail only a small percentage of their total business operations. As a result of these differences, fair trade buycotting has been more warmly embraced by TNCs than traditional boycotts, as can be seen by the growing corporate involvement. However, fair trade's strategy has also made it more vulnerable to moves by TNCs to devote minor attention to fair trade in order to gain positive publicity while at the same time continuing with business-as-usual in the vast majority of their corporate operations. The full implication of this is explored in the second part of this chapter.

Another way that fair trade activists in Canada have sought to expand the market for fair trade goods has been through attempts to gain the support of public institutions – high schools, universities, places of worship, unions, city councils – whose public procurement policies can be a significant avenue for increasing sales. Through actions such as this, what journalist Naomi Klein refers to as 'local foreign policy,' fair traders seek not only to expand sales but to exert extra pressure on TNCs which view bulk institutional purchases as among the most lucrative and coveted in the market (Klein 2000: 400–1). Public support for fair trade has been key to the popularity of fair trade in Europe, where fair trade tea and coffee is served at hundreds of local, national, and regional bodies (EFTA 2001a: 34, 2001b).

In North America, the support of public institutions for fair trade has been relatively insignificant, and procurement policies have only recently become a focus for fair trade activists. In Canada, city councils in Toronto, Winnipeg, and Saskatoon began to offer fair trade coffee to their members at the start of the millennium. Perhaps the broadest public procurement campaign has been the one directed at university campuses, where student groups have organized information tables, teach-ins, fair trade coffee tastings, petitions, and letter-writing campaigns to gain the support of campus food services. The growing campus-based fair trade movement has received significant impetus from the success of campus 'no-sweat' campaigns in the United States. Following an explosion of media coverage in 1996 about the highly exploitative working conditions found in sweatshops in the South, student groups formed to demand that products sold with their college logos – an industry worth billions of dollars a year – be produced 'sweat free.' In 1998, these groups formed the United Students Against Sweatshops (USAS) which initiated a campaign to compel universities to force companies licensed to sell university products to adhere to a strict code of conduct, which included workers' rights to freedom of association and collective bargaining, public disclosure of factory locations, periodic independent monitoring, and a living wage. Through a series of activist campaigns, which included protests, sit-ins, and hunger strikes, the USAS has thus far succeeded in compelling over 100 academic bodies in the United States and Canada to adopt a code of labour practices and affiliate themselves with the Worker Rights Consortium (WRC), an independent organization which assists the universities with monitoring and compliance issues (Klein 2000: 400–36; Benjamin 2000).

Thus far, campus fair trade campaigns have not achieved the level of institutional support, in terms of official university codes and policies, that the no-sweat campaign has attained. However, university activism has been of key importance to the fair trade network in North America. Various student campaigns in English-speaking Canada have succeeded in pressuring some campus retailers, student organizations, and university service providers to begin offering fair trade coffee at the following universities: British Columbia, Calgary, Carlton, Trent, Montreal, McGill, and Guelph. In Quebec, the efforts of Équiterre succeeded in compelling retailers in nine universities to offer fair trade coffee (French 2001). Similar successes are apparent in the United States, where retailers and university service providers have been persuaded to offer fair trade coffee at over 300 campuses, including Georgetown, Yale, Harvard, UCLA, and the state universities of New York (Oxfam America 2003; FLO 2003b; Kniffin 2000: 47).

The strongest institutional statement in support of fair trade on campuses, and one which is an important precedent for the fair trade network in North America, was the decision by McMaster University in Hamilton, Ontario, in June 2002, to become the first university in North America to adopt a no-sweat code of conduct *and* an official fair trade purchasing policy that forces campus coffee retailers to offer the choice of FLO-certified coffee to their customers. This outcome resulted from two years of negotiations, initiated by the president of the university, between representatives of campus groups, students, the administration, faculty, staff, the bookstore, and the athletics and recreation departments. In addition, the university pledged to look into the possibility of expanding its policy to include other fair trade products like tea and cocoa in the future. Unfortunately, the code excludes retailers that signed contracts prior to its adoption, including the campus Tim Hortons, whose head office refuses to offer fair trade coffee at any of its stores in Canada (Grigg, Puchalski, and Wells 2003; Curwin 2002; McMaster Ad Hoc Code of Labour Practices Development Committee 2002). Nonetheless, fair trade activists hope to use this precedent as leverage to compel other universities in Canada and the United States to adopt similar policies. Already, in early 2004, Trent University in Peterborough, Ontario, followed suit and adopted its own official fair trade coffee code.

The growth of the public procurement of fair trade coffee in Canada is certainly a positive step for fair trade producers in the South. Not only does expanded public procurement directly result in increased sales, but it also serves to promote fair trade and put further pressure on corporations and public institutions at national and international levels to support fair trade. Its overall impact on the North, however, must be assessed more cautiously. While the expansion of fair trade in Canada certainly has a positive impact on raising awareness and promoting North–South solidarity, it also has the potential to be used by public and private institutions to mask their devotion to a broader neoliberal agenda, which, as described in previous chapters, appears to have increasingly become the case internationally.

The potential for university administrations in Canada to employ fair trade as an ethical fig leaf to mask the negative impact of their own neoliberal restructuring is indeed strong (Fridell 2004b). Due to public spending cuts imposed by neoliberal reformers, university administrators have had to make major adjustments in recent years in order to raise sufficient funds to cover their full operating costs. This adjustment has entailed the growing corporatization of the university. Desperate to raise funds, universities have turned increasingly towards relying on corporations to provide donations, directly fund courses, finance endowed chairs, and sponsor research centres. At the same time, corporations have placed growing emphasis on contracting university research projects and hiring professors as private consultants. As a result, educational priorities have been reoriented towards activities and research which support corporate profitability and away from non-profit-making programs such as those in the liberal arts. Along with an increasing reliance on corporate funding has come the growing encroachment of corporations on campus life through campus advertising campaigns, corporate sponsorship of sports teams, exclusive-rights contracts for TNCs like Coke and Pepsi, and joint university/private-sector-provided services and products. Moreover, there is a growing trend towards the 'university-as-real-estate-broker,' with universities renting out campus space and services to giant corpo-rations, some of which have developed near-monopoly control of their sectors (Dugger 2000; Soley 2000; Kniffin 2000; Newton 2000). These alarming trends reflect the growing corporate influence over research, teaching, and all aspects of campus life in general.

Within the context of the corporatization of the university, the poten-tial is strong that support for fair trade could be adopted as a strategy by university administrators to promote the university's reputation as a moral leader at a time when, in a broader sense, moral concerns and the very mission of the university to act as a forum for independent thought are increasingly being ceded to the imperatives of corpora-tions and the logic of competition and profitability (Fridell 2004b). Thus McMaster University, while taking progressive steps in its sup-port for fair trade, continues to pander to the needs of corporations to gain much-needed revenue. This includes growing ties with Coca-Cola Company through a multi-year, multi-million-dollar contract for exclusive rights over campus beverages, along with a 'Coke Represen-tative' in the McMaster Student Union to deal directly with campus sponsorship. McMaster student activists and unions have recently questioned these ties and protested the corporation's involvement in the murder of union representatives from Coca-Cola factories in Colombia (Killing for Coca-Cola in Columbia 2001). The university's decision to obtain millions of dollars by assisting the giant TNC in gaining brand loyalty from young students and expanding its monop-oly control over the North American beverage market casts a shadow over McMaster's attempt to present itself as a socially responsible institution.

Despite its potential to be used to mask neoliberal restructuring, fair trade in Canada nevertheless represents more than this. To many social justice activists and organizations, fair trade is a focal point for a broader struggle against neoliberal globalization and the current struc-tures of international trade. It cannot be denied, however, that as fair trade becomes increasingly more mainstream, so does its potential to be used by mainstream institutions to mask their unwavering support for the current, highly unequal global system. Thus, in the long run, fair trade could end up concealing as much as it reveals. To explore this potential in further detail, the following section compares two dis-tinctly different uses for fair trade coffee in Canada: as a tool of social justice by the worker-owned coffee cooperative Planet Bean; and as an ethical fig leaf by the giant TNC, Starbucks.

Comparing the Impact of Fair Trade Partners in the North

As mentioned in the beginning of this chapter, the FLO system does not provide any standards for Northern licensees beyond those that deal with the trading relations between them and their Southern partners. This fact does not represent merely an oversight on the part of FLO's founders. It is also a necessary aspect of fair trade licensing that is required to gain the support of conventional corporations, the majority of which do not and would not adhere to the strict social and environmental standards in their Northern operations that fair trade demands of its Southern partners. While fair trade standards for Northern partners were never clear within the network, prior to the introduction of the FLO system the primary agents of fair trade were ATOs, which, while still concerned primarily with standards in the South, were generally small-scale, non-profit, or not-for-profit organizations with an employee structure that was either voluntary, cooperative, or based on wage labour with a modest pay scale. The reorientation of the fair trade network, however, has ushered in the growing involvement of giant, hierarchically organized corporations whose main concern is with employing sophisticated marketing strategies to increase consumer demand for their products and bolster corporate profitability (Dawson 2003). As a result of the undefined standards of the past and the new orientation of the present, fair trade coffee partners in Canada represent a broad range of vastly different organizations: from large corporations like Starbucks and Timothy's World Coffee; to small-scale, for-profit roasters like Alternative Grounds in Toronto, which devotes significant energy to promoting fair trade and community social justice initiatives; to TTV stores, which are driven primarily by volunteer labour and focus on handicrafts; to small worker-owned cooperatives like Planet Bean and La Siembra in Ontario, and Just Us! in Nova Scotia (Alternative Grounds 2004; Frey, presentation 2004; La Siembra 2004; Just US! 2004; de Jong, interview 2004; Ten Thousand Villages Canada 2003). These organizations offer vastly different and competing visions of what fair trade represents in Canada, which is analysed below in a comparison between two starkly dissimilar fair trade partners.

Planet Bean

Fresh Roasted means we can boast to have the most flavourful coffee in town. Fair Trade means we have negotiated a fair price with our co-op growers and paid an extra premium for investments in their communities like education and health care.

Ecologically Grown means that out coffee is grown in the shade of tropical forests, which protects habitat for creatures including many of our migratory songbirds. It also means the farmers and drinkers of our coffee are not exposed to harmful chemicals.

Co-operatively Produced means we put *job creation and democracy into our bottom line* (emphasis added).

Mission statement, Planet Bean (2004d)

Planet Bean Inc. is a worker-owned coffee importer/roaster cooperative in downtown Guelph, Ontario, that sells around 15 different blends of 100 per cent fair trade, organic, arabica coffee. It was originally founded in the 1990s as a cooperative coffee roaster, restaurant, catering business, and bakery owned by the Speed River Co-operative. It added fair trade coffee to its overall project in 1998. The cooperative grew rapidly and was successful, although it suffered from a lack of investment capital that became more apparent as it grew. The under-capitalization of Planet Bean, along with a sense among its workers that they were becoming 'consumed by business' and were neglecting their cooperative and social justice goals, led to Planet Bean being closed and then reopened in 2002. The new Planet Bean has abandoned its other operations to focus on roasting, retailing, and wholesaling fair trade coffee, and it is owned by the Ontario Worker Co-operative Federation (OWCF). Planet Bean coffee retailed for around U.S.$12.97 (CAD$17.20) per pound in 2004, which is the high end of specialty coffee prices and around three times the cost of regular coffee prices.[5] In addition to coffee, Planet Bean also retails fair trade products processed and distributed by other ATOs, including teas and chocolate bars from GEPA in Germany, organic chocolate from Just Us!, and organic cocoa from La Siembra (Planet Bean 2004b; Barrett, interview 2004).

Planet Bean is a small-scale coffee roaster whose gross sales figures for fiscal year 2004–5 were predicted to be a fairly modest $220,000, followed by gross sales in 2005–6 of around $370,000 (Barrett, interview 2004). According to Bill Barrett, the director and marketing manager of Planet Bean and the sole continuing member from its pre-2002 days, Planet Bean's small-scale, cooperative fair trade project represents a conscious attempt to provide an alternative to a vision of fair trade dominated by giant TNCs. Barrett asserts that TNCs commitment to fair trade is marginal and driven solely by the need to respond to consumer pressure, and the involvement of TNCs within the fair trade network does not represent the sort of structural changes that are required to build a truly socially just global economy. To Planet Bean, fair trade is a movement that aims to attain social justice in the South *and* the North, which means that Northern fair traders should be oriented towards 'the community ownership of the means of production and economic democracy.' As giant TNCs are profit driven and are not interested in local job creation and a more equitable distribution of wealth, Barrett asserts that they do not share the values of 'true' fair trade (Barrett, interview 2004).

The vision of fair trade expounded by Barrett and Planet Bean is very much in line with the older vision of fair trade prior to its reorientation. Planet Bean sees fair trade not just as an attempt to reform the existing trading system, but also as an attempt to lay the basis for an alternative trading system that operates independently of the conventional international market and is composed of democratically run organizations in the North and the South. This radical vision of fair trade is apparent on Planet Bean's web site, which states that in order for fair trade to truly work: 'We need changes in the structure of business itself. Under public pressure a global company may finally agree to carry a line of fair trade coffee. But this window-dressing doesn't address the core issues of control and profit maximization that are at the heart of the inequities in global trade. Which is why you don't see such companies putting their fair trade products at the center of their marketing and promotion efforts. The dominant global corporations will never create a more just world for all' (Planet Bean 2004c).

At the core of Planet Bean's alternative project is its strategy for developing cooperative ownership and control, which its members view as an equivalent to fair trade standards in the North (Barrett, presentation 2004). Planet Bean is still in its infancy and as such is still developing its cooperative project. Currently, its labour force is composed of four board members and three employees. The board members run Planet Bean as a team but have a fairly traditional management style towards their employees, except that they are consulted on setting longer-term objectives. However, Planet Bean is in the process of constructing a full worker-owned cooperative that will be connected to other cooperatives in a new model designed to address the undercapitalization experienced by cooperatives in general. According to Barrett (interview, 2004), the new model will consist of various cooperatives participating in different activities that will be owned by a larger, 'mother' cooperative; through the mother cooperative, smaller cooperatives will be able to coordinate their activities and take advantage of economies of scale by sharing such things as a single accountant or graphic designer, rather than each having to employ its own.

The cooperative model that Planet Bean is constructing has two central dimensions: ownership/control and equity. First, in terms of ownership and control, Planet Bean is in transition to being run at the micro level by its members. At the macro level, Planet Bean will be owned and its operations overseen by the mother cooperative. Cooperative workers will be members of both the Planet Bean board and the board of the mother cooperative. Employees will attain membership status after a one-year probationary period designed to determine if they fit well into the cooperative and if the cooperative can support the new job. After this is determined, new members will be invited to buy a share of the cooperative (a symbolic $1) and make an equity investment of around U.S.$3,700 (CAD$5000), which can come through payroll deductions (Barrett, interview 2004).

The second dimension of Planet Bean's model concerns equity, which will be distributed both through the local cooperative and the mother cooperative to all of the worker-owners. According to Barrett, members of Planet Bean will not have to invest in mutual funds or registered retirement savings plans (RRSPs) to save for the future, but will build equity in their own cooperatives and can be bought out when they wish to move on or retire. This way, local capital remains in local hands and can be used to provide jobs for the community rather than being invested outside of Guelph on the basis of maximum return on investment. As Barrett (interview, 2004) states: 'Why invest in California when we need jobs here?' This is central to Planet Bean's mission, which places as much emphasis on its role in the Canadian cooperative movement as it does in its role in the international fair trade network (Planet Bean 2004c; Barrett, presentation 2004). As a Canadian cooperative, Planet Bean seeks to provide local employment and a democratic work environment, and, ultimately, to act as a 'regional engine for community development' (Barrett, interview 2004).

Planet Bean distinguishes itself from conventional corporations that participate in fair trade not just through its cooperative project, but through its commitment to selling 100 per cent fair trade coffee beans, and through the centrality it places on raising awareness about fair trade and the injustices of the current global system. Planet Bean's marketing strategy focuses on relaying the basic goals of fair trade to consumers (in addition to roasting high-quality coffee) (Planet Bean 2004c). Thus, members of Planet Bean have given talks in local forums on the benefits of fair trade, and throughout the years Planet Bean has helped to host Southern fair trade partners for community tours.[6] According to Barrett, these initiatives have the potential to raise awareness about the lives of Southern producers, as can be seen by a recent visit by a Southern partner to a local grocery store in Toronto that retailed Planet Bean coffee. The manager of the store, upon meeting the coffee farmer, said that it was the first time he had *ever* met someone who had produced *any* of the goods sold in his store (Barrett, interview 2004). This anecdote is a useful metaphor for revealing the power of Marx's concept of the fetishism of commodities: alienated producers and consumers having no actual contact other than that which is mediated by the market and through an abstract commodity (McNally 1993: 233–4; Marx 1978: 319–29). Through their different vantage points, each has a certain understanding of the commodity – coffee – but no real knowledge about the life of the person who produces it or consumes it. It also reveals the potential of fair trade to subvert this relationship, although the extent to which this is a systemic or merely a symbolic subversion will be discussed in the third part of this chapter.

Although still in its infancy, Planet Bean has achieved a degree of financial success over the past few years, and it is predicted that sales figures will increase by over 65 per cent from fiscal year 2004–5 to fiscal year 2005–6 (Barrett, interview 2004). However, there are also some signs of difficulties ahead, which are common to cooperative projects that have sought to accomplish the very difficult task of constructing 'cooperative islands in a sea of capitalism' (McNally 1993: 126). While Planet Bean continues to construct an equitable and democratic work environment, it must engage in the capitalist market in order to survive, and is therefore subject to the market imperatives which lead to exploitation under capitalism. These imperatives impose limits on Planet Bean's cooperative model and threaten its ability to survive and thrive in the long term. This can be seen in three examples. First, like all small-scale cooperatives, Planet Bean lacks sufficient investment capital, which was a major factor in its first closure before it was reopened in 2002. To combat this, Planet Bean has developed a new model based on interconnected local cooperatives and a mother cooperative that can take advantage of economies of scale. It remains to be seen if this model will provide it with the investment it requires, but in all likelihood undercapitalization will remain a major concern to Planet Bean in the foreseeable future.

Second, in order to keep Planet Bean afloat, members of the board frequently have to work beyond their paid hours, essentially participating in self-exploitation. All unpaid hours are recorded, and it is hoped that they will be able to withdraw the wages owed to them in the future (Barrett, interview 2004). This, of course, depends on Planet Bean's long-term growth and stability, which is by no means certain.

Third, Planet Bean has been impacted by competition from other fair trade licensees which will likely become more intense in the future. In some instances, grocery stores have refused to stock Planet Bean coffee because they are already stocking a single brand of fair trade coffee distributed by large corporate competitors like Van Houtte. In other instances, Planet Bean has lost customers to (as well as stolen customers from) competing fair trade ATOs. Yet, Barrett asserts that these instances are minor so far, and will not be a problem as long as the fair trade market in Canada continues to expand (Barrett, interview 2004). However, there are likely significant limits to the size of the fair trade market, which cannot expand indefinitely, and competitive pressures are bound to increase due to the growing participation of TNCs with massive marketing and financial resources. In consequence, it is likely that Northern ATOs will begin to feel intensive competitive pressures in the near future, as has been the case with their Southern counterparts.

The members of Planet Bean are not unaware of the limits imposed on them by the capitalist market. For this reason they have a short-term vision, which is to try to work and trade in as just a way as possible; and a long-term vision which, in line with the original vision of fair trade, entails laying the groundwork for an alternative trading system that is distinct from the international capitalist system (Barrett, interview 2004). For them, fair trade ultimately involves using 'coffee as an agent of change' (Planet Bean 2004a). This vision of fair trade is by no means representative of the fair trade network in general, and instead represents the most radical position. Along with Planet Bean, there are only two other fair trade cooperatives in Canada, Just Us! and La Siembra, all three of which have strong ties with each other (Barrett, interview 2004; de Jong, interview 2004). Together, they represent only 3 per cent of all fair trade coffee licensees in Canada. Throughout the network, fair trade is interpreted in a variety of ways: as a form of corporate social responsibility for conventional TNCs; as a reformist project seeking changes in international trade *within* the international capitalist system as generally promoted by FLO representatives (Smagge, presentation 2003; Bolscher, interview 2002; VanderHoff Boersma, interview 2002); or as a component of the Global Justice Movement that seeks to challenge corporate rule internationally, as promoted by Oxfam and Équiterre (Bernier-Genest, presentation 2004; Conlon, presentation 2004a; Waridel 2002; Oxfam International 2002a). To Barrett (interview 2004), 'There is a whole bunch of trains going in all sorts of directions,' and Planet Bean is part of all the movements that challenge the injustices of global trade: whether its incremental change to provide better daily lives for workers, the Canadian cooperative movement, the movement towards creating an alternative trading system through the fair trade network, or the Global Justice Movement. He states: 'Its hard to get on the right train. I'm taking them all.'

Starbucks

Establish Starbucks as the premier purveyor of the finest coffee in the world while maintaining our uncompromising principles while we grow.
The following six guiding principles will help us measure the appropriateness of our decisions:
Provide a great work environment and treat each other with respect and dignity.
Embrace diversity as an essential component in the way we do business.
Apply the highest standards of excellence to the purchasing, roasting and fresh delivery of our coffee.
Develop enthusiastically satisfied customers all of the time.
Contribute positively to our communities and our environment.
Recognize that *profitability is essential to our future success* (emphasis added).
Mission statement, Starbucks 2004f)

Comparing Starbucks Coffee Company, a fair trade licensee, to Planet Bean is a comparison between a lion and a mouse.[7] Starbucks is the world's (and Canada's) largest specialty coffee roaster and buys about 1 per cent of the world's green coffee beans and about 10 per cent of the specialty coffee market's green beans. Starbucks total net revenue in fiscal 2002 was $3.3 billion, which is well over 10,000 times the size of Planet Bean's. That year, there were 3,496 company-owned Starbucks stores and 1,078 franchises in North America, and 384 company-owned stores and 923 franchises internationally; Starbucks employed over 62,000 workers and served 20 million customers per week world-wide (Starbucks 2004c). Of this total, over 270 retail stores were in Canada (Starbucks 2004g). In April 2000, Starbucks became one of the largest fair trade roasters in North America when it signed its agreement with TransFair USA, which was followed by a similar agreement with TransFair Canada in 2002.

Starbucks opened its first store in Seattle's Pike Place Market in 1971 and underwent a massive expansion beginning in the late 1980s under the leadership of its famous owner and CEO, Howard Schultz (currently chief global strategist). In 1987, Starbucks opened stores in Chicago and Vancouver and by the end of the year had over seventeen stores. Despite annual losses at first, Starbucks expanded rapidly and in 1992 made its first initial public offering at $17 a share with a market capitalization (the value of all shares) of $273 million (Schultz had originally purchased the company in 1987 for $4 million). At this time, there were 165 stores in North America. In 1995, Starbucks went international, opening its first store in Japan. By the turn of the millennium, Starbucks was the undisputed largest speciality coffee roaster in the world and had over 3,500 stores worldwide, including a new outlet in Beijing's Forbidden City, which provoked protests from Chinese nationalists (Starbucks 2004g; Pendergrast 2002).

The reasons for Starbucks' rapid success are manifold. First, while relying relatively little on advertising (it spent less than $10 million on advertising during its first twenty-five years), Starbucks was able to tap into the growing interest in speciality coffee by maintaining strict control of quality and training by using primarily company-owned stores, as opposed to licensed franchises, during its initial expansion. Second, Starbucks has employed an aggressive strategy for beating out competitors, which has entailed a variety of actions such as opening up directly across the street from competitors; suing (unsuccessfully) the Second Cup, one of its biggest Canadian competitors, for allegedly copying the look and feel of its stores; pressuring landlords to refuse to renew competitors' leases and instead hand the lease to Starbucks; and in one case trying to buy an entire building to deny its competitor a renewal on its lease (Pendergrast 2002, 1999: 367–79). Third, Starbucks has made many strategic takeovers that have eliminated the competition and expanded its market share, such as the acquisition of the Seattle Coffee Company in the United Kingdom (1998), Pasqua in San

Francisco (1998), and the Seattle Coffee Company, Seattle's Best Coffee, and Torrerfazione in North America (2003). Fourth, Starbucks has forged key business partnerships which have broadened and solidified its consumer base, including partnerships with Barnes & Noble, Dreyer's Ice Cream, Pepsi-Cola (to sell bottled Frappuccino), Chapters bookstores in Canada, and Safeway grocery stores in western Canada, as well as a 1998 agreement signed with Kraft General Foods, the world's largest coffee company, to distribute Starbucks coffee to over 18,000 retail outlets throughout the United States (Starbucks 2004g).

Another major aspect of Starbucks' success has been its emphasis on providing a comfortable, trendy, café environment where customers are allowed to linger and read, creating a sense of local community. Constructing this sort of atmosphere has involved not just attention to interior design and customer service but also a focus on building Starbucks' brand image as a socially and environmentally responsible corporation. This image is actively promoted on store displays, pamphlets, and 'sustainable' coffee products that highlight the corporation's ethical claims. In this way, Starbucks has sought to make consumers feel *good* about drinking its coffee by presenting them with a comfortable atmosphere and 'ethical' products designed to make them feel as though they have connected with (rather than exploited) workers and farmers in the South.

In addition to its own specific marketing needs, Starbucks has been at the head of the corporate social responsibility (CSR) movement, which has grown over the past decade as corporations have sought to stave off bad publicity stemming from the negative impact of neoliberal reforms. The emergence of neoliberal globalization in the 1970s effectively brought a halt to the movement towards an increasingly regulated international economy in which, among other things, the actions of TNCs were more strictly overseen by state policies nationally and internationally. In the coffee sector, this has resulted in a crisis for Southern farmers due to unprecedented declines in green bean prices in the wake of the collapse of the International Coffee Agreement (ICA), but greater profit margins for giant TNCs in the North (Oxfam International 2002a). Outcomes such as this have given increased impetus to public perceptions that TNCs are purely profit-driven and concerned only with the interests of shareholders, and not with the interests of 'stakeholders' (farmers, workers, consumers, local communities).[8] To counter these perceptions, a growing number of TNCs have pursued CSR policies, following the lead of corporations like Starbucks, which believes that such efforts are essential to 'sustain the prominence of [the] Starbucks brand in the marketplace and build stakeholder trust' (Starbucks 2003: 2).

As a leader in CSR, Starbucks has been granted dozens of awards and honours since the mid-1990s, mostly from corporate magazines and institutions (some of which are heavily sponsored by Starbucks), but also from charities and NGOs.[9] The full list is proudly displayed on Starbucks' web site (Starbucks 2004a), which also includes a maze of links to various pages designed to demonstrate its commitment to CSR. From this maze, four main aspects can be discerned that are central to its CSR program. The first is charitable contributions, which are common to most major TNCs. In 2002, Starbucks donated a total of $8.3 million (0.3 per cent of its net revenues) internationally to various charities that participate in a variety of activities, including combating illiteracy, building low-income housing, and responding to emergencies and natural disasters (Starbucks 2004c, 2003). A second key aspect of Starbucks' CSR is its official commitment to environmental responsibility (Starbucks 2004d). This entails a variety of activities, including recycling programs at its stores and corporate operations; a program to donate used coffee grounds to customers, schools, parks, and nurseries to use as a soil amendment; a 10-cent beverage discount if you bring your own mug; a commitment to not purchase genetically modified coffee and tea and to not support research in this direction; and annual promotions for Earth Day (Starbucks 2004c, 2003: 13–17). The remaining two aspects of Starbucks' CSR program must be examined in greater detail, as they are essential to assessing the TNC's overall commitment to the principles of fair trade: Starbucks' employee relations and its 'Commitment to Origins' (which includes the sale of fair trade coffee).

Starbucks' Employee Relations

In sharp contrast to fair trade's Southern partners and to Planet Bean, Starbucks is a conventional corporation driven by the interests of its major shareholders, with a management system that is hierarchical and highly unequal, and an employee base consisting primarily of low-wage and non-unionized 'precarious' workers. The wages of Starbucks' thousands of retail workers, which are slightly above the minimum wage in their region, contrast sharply to the total pay (including bonus and exercised stock options) of Starbucks' CEO Orin Smith, the top-paid CEO in North America in 2003, of $38,772,712 (Million-Dollar Club 2003; Pendergrast 2002). Consequently, it would be impossible for Starbucks to participate in fair trade if certification required that it adhere to FLO labour standards in the North. Moreover, it is also important to note that fair trade standards do not apply to Starbucks' relationship with *Northern* partners. This means that Starbucks can maintain its certification as a fair trade partner even though it has its Christmas products packaged by Signature Packaging Solution, a company that employs inmate labour from the Washington State prison system. The use of prison labour in North America has been growing since the late 1980s as companies have sought to reduce costs by exploiting prison workers, who are paid very low wages, without health or retirement benefits, and can be instantly laid off without consequences when they are no longer needed after the holiday rush (Barnett 2002). Starbucks uses prison labour during major holidays to complement its own low-wage labour force and keep costs down as low as possible.

Putting Starbucks' outsourcing policies aside, it must be stated that while its employees are generally low-wage and non-unionized, within the retail sector they are relatively well paid and receive better benefits than most service-sector employees in North America. Starbucks has even won awards for having one of the lowest annual employee turnover rates of any restaurant or fast-food company, with a rate of 60 per cent (Workforce Management 2003). While this is extraordinarily high when compared to most other sectors of the economy, it is low compared to the industry average, which ranges from between 150 to 200 per cent (Pendergrast 2002; Gruner 1998). The reason for Starbucks turnover rate is its payment and benefits plan for full- and part-time employees (whom Starbucks calls 'partners'), which includes basic medical, dental, and vision coverage, as well as coverage for short-term counselling and basic mental health and dependency treatment. Special coverage for things such as sick time, long-term disability, and life insurance apply only to salaried and non-retail employees. Starbucks also has special plans to sell employees discounted stock or stock options, but as most employees are paid low wages and less than half of them last one year in employment, few employees can take advantage of this. In addition, Starbucks also offers its employees 'extra shots,' which include one free pound of whole bean coffee per week; free beverages at work; a 30 per cent employee discount on merchandise; and its Caring Unites Partners

(CUP) fund, based on voluntary payroll deductions, which provides financial assistance to employees facing emergency situations (Starbucks 2003: 22, 2002; Pendergrast 2002).

In line with Starbucks' entire CSR project, its employee payment and benefits plan represents an attempt to offer mild, top-down concessions in order to provide a stable and profitable working environment and avoid more radical demands from below, such as employee unionization, which Starbucks has fought at every turn. Yet, while Starbucks employees do receive relatively higher wages and get relatively better benefits than their competitors, this comparative assessment cannot take away the fact that the majority of Starbucks employees ultimately remain low-paid workers who lack effective, democratic representation – principles which are central to fair trade. Given few other positive alternatives, it is only logical that workers would opt for Starbucks, with its paternalistic, top-down benefits, over other companies that lack such benefits. A 60 per cent turnover rate, however, is hardly a strong vow of confidence, and despite Starbucks' efforts, its employees have resisted and demanded higher income and more effective employee representation.

Perhaps one of the greatest examples of employees battling against Starbucks for greater benefits and representation emerged in Vancouver, BC, in 2000, when retail employees from ten Starbucks outlets successfully unionized under one master agreement as a member of the Canadian Auto Workers, Local 3000 (CAW 3000), an amalgamated union of employees working in restaurants, hotels, and other service sectors. This marked an important precedent for Starbucks' retail employees worldwide. Since then, CAW 3000 has succeeded in negotiating two collective agreements with Starbucks that have led to wage improvements and guaranteed overtime provisions, made seniority a key factor in scheduling hours, and entitled employees to two consecutive days off rather than Starbucks' policy of split days off. Many of the gains made by CAW 3000, such as wage improvements, were extended afterwards throughout the country, leading union president Frank Sobczak to correctly conclude that they 'were bargaining for all of Canada' (Sobczak, interview 2005). Along with the benefits included in the collective agreement, the CAW 3000 also ensures 'that union stores have access to an effective grievance procedure with an effective union to successfully challenge Starbucks' unreasonable decisions or unfair performance reviews and more' (CAW Starbucks Unstrikers 2002).

Fearing the precedent of unionization among its retail workers, Starbucks has launched a determined effort to crush the new union and in the process has revealed itself, in the words of CAW 3000, 'to be a paternalistic, anti-union employer despite their veil of social responsibility' (CAW Starbucks Unstrikers 2002). In 2002, Starbucks refused to bargain with CAW 3000 on all aspects of a third collective agreement and insisted on eliminating previous gains on job security and seniority provisions. In response to these pressures, the union launched an 'UnStrike' campaign on 13 May 2002. This has entailed asking consumers in BC to show solidarity with CAW 3000 by ceasing purchases from all Starbucks stores except those that are unionized (CAW 2002). The UnStrike strategy is not without precedent, and was used effectively by CAW 3000 in the 1990s to unionize stores belonging to the food chains Whitespot and KFC. Through these initiatives, CAW 3000 has been at the head of attempts to unionize the traditionally low-wage, non-unionized service sector in Canada (Sobczak, interview 2005).

Along with calling on consumers to shop only at unionized Starbucks stores, the Starbucks UnStrike has also involved a request that customers stop using Starbucks charge cards instead of cash, which has led to less tipping and a decline in total income for employees of around 2 per cent. During the UnStrike, employees continue to go to work but engage in activities normally not tolerated at work, such as disregarding the corporate dress code (revealing tattoos, coloured hair, and piercings) and handing out flyers to customers explaining their demands (CAW Starbucks Unstrikers 2002).[10] As they are in a legal strike position, Starbucks cannot fire or discipline workers for UnStrike activities (Sobczak, interview 2005). According to CAW 3000, the goal of such a campaign has been to 'attack Starbucks' corporate image as well as exercise economic pressure on the world's largest coffee corporation' (CAW Starbucks Unstrikers 2002). This strategy is very similar to the buycotting strategy pursued by fair trade activists: it involves workers making appeals of solidarity to ethical consumers and threatening corporate heads with bad publicity if they do not meet their demands.

Starbucks' hard anti-union position in its dispute with CAW 3000, which continued unresolved as of the spring of 2005, reveals the hypocrisy of its purported commitment to social responsibility and fairness. Along with refusing to negotiate a new contract, CAW 3000 alleges that Starbucks has unfairly targeted pro-union employees with 'job performance reviews' and has inspired and promoted decertification efforts at unionized stores. The latter actions are illegal and the case is currently under litigation at the BC Labour Relations Board.[11] Under these conditions, it has at times been difficult for CAW 3000 to maintain its strength, especially given the high turnover rate for Starbucks' employees – none of the employees that were originally on the CAW 3000 bargaining committee prior to 2002 are still working at Starbucks. CAW representatives, however, have responded with continuous efforts to mobilize new members, expand union organizing, and force Starbucks back to the negotiating table (Sobczak, interview 2005).

The actions of CAW 3000 have a greater potential to promote real improvements in the working conditions of its members than Starbucks' proclamations regarding its purported commitment to social responsibility. In fact, Sobczak (interview 2005) asserts that Starbucks' CSR program is in many ways an attempt on the part of the corporation to claim responsibility for employee benefits that were actually a result of pressure from below and never would have occurred 'if it wasn't for the union arriving on the scene.' In the final analysis, Starbucks' CSR program is driven not by the desire to meet the demands of its workers for higher income and democratic representation, but precisely to avoid these demands by offering mild, paternalistic, top-down concessions while remaining devoted to employing low-wage, non-unionized retail workers in Canada and the world. CSR is designed to obscure this fact and protect Starbucks' brand image, which is essential to gaining consumer loyalty and ensuring its corporate profitability.

Starbucks' 'Commitment to Origins'

Starbucks and the Fair Trade movement share common goals – to ensure that coffee farmers receive a fair price for their beans, and to ensure they can sustain their farms in the future.

Starbucks Customer Relations, personal communication 2005

Starbucks' 'Commitment to Origins' entails a series of measures that it has adopted as part of its CSR program to officially promote 'sustainability' in the South. This has occurred in response to pressure from social justice NGOs, especially fair trade groups, and is due to Starbucks' own fears that continued low prices could lead to a depletion of a steady, long-term supply of high-quality coffee which the TNC depends on (Starbucks 2003: 6). The 'commitment' includes the import and sale of sustainable coffees (such as fair trade), a 'Preferred Supplier Program,' and changes to Starbucks' overall coffee purchasing policy.

The first main component of Starbucks' Commitment to Origins is the import and sale of sustainable coffees that focuses on three main types: Conservation International (CI) Shade Grown coffee, certified organic coffee, and FLO-certified fair trade coffee. In fiscal year 2002, Starbucks international imported 1.8 million pounds of CI shade-grown, 1.7 million pounds of organic, and 1.1 million pounds of fair trade coffee (Starbucks 2003: 8). With respect to fair trade beans, this represents a relatively mild commitment – around 1 or 2 per cent of Starbucks total coffee bean imports – even while it is an important precedent for corporate support in North America (Rogers 2004). Similarly, Starbucks' efforts to promote and sell fair trade are relatively mild. As stated earlier, in Canadian Starbucks stores, fair trade coffee is available primarily in whole bean bags and is offered as a brewed cup only once per month (CBC 2002). In June 2004, a pound of fair trade coffee at Starbucks retailed for U.S.$11.05 (CAD$14.95), around 87 per cent of the cost of a pound of Planet Bean coffee.[12]

Combined with its mild commitment to fair trade, a disturbing trend in Starbucks' sustainable coffee policy has been its growing tendency towards disproportionately emphasizing the sale of CI shade-grown and organic coffee at the expense of fair trade, which has much more rigorous social standards. From fiscal 2001 to 2002, Starbucks' imports of CI shade grown coffee increased by 163 per cent and its imports of organic coffee increased by 98 per cent, while its imports of fair trade coffee increased by only 68 per cent (Starbucks 2003: 8). The most alarming aspect of this has been Starbucks' partnership with CI. Beginning in 1998, the two have worked in partnership to provide assistance to small producers in developing shade-grown coffee techniques in areas with immense biodiversity that have been deemed in need of environmental protection, first in Chiapas, Mexico, and then in regions in Colombia and Peru. While ensuring biodiversity through shade-grown coffee is important (and is a key aspect of fair trade), CI's project is primarily focused on the environment, and its social standards are unclear: while higher prices are paid, it is not apparent what these prices are and how they are determined; and its labour standards are vague and much less strict than FLO's highly codified standards.[13]

Moreover, CI's credentials as an ethical partner are highly questionable. Its major sponsors consist of some of the largest and most environmentally destructive companies in the world – including Citigroup, Chiquita, Exxon Mobil Foundation, and McDonalds – and it has been accused of being a corporate front designed to greenwash its sponsors' images and act as 'the friendly face of biocolonialism.' CI's tarnished record includes actively assisting giant pharmaceutical companies in gathering indigenous knowledge on local plants and insects in order to patent them; assisting the Mexican government in forcibly evicting poor indigenous communities from the Lacandon Jungle in Chiapas for allegedly destroying the rainforest; conducting environmental 'fly-overs' in southern Mexico and providing the information to USAID, for commercial reasons, and to the Mexican military to use in their campaign against the Zapatistas; and purchasing biodiverse regions throughout the world to put them at the disposal of giant TNCs (Renard 2005: 429–30; Choudry 2003).

Starbucks' growing relationship with CI represents an attempt to respond to the pressure placed on it by activists with an alternative to fair trade that is more corporate-friendly and environmentally focused (as opposed to labour-focused). This is an option that is increasingly being favoured by giant TNCs (Lewin, Giovannucci, and Varangis 2004: 116–27; Giovannucci 2003). In October 2003, Kraft Foods, which has refused to support fair trade coffee, announced that it would begin importing and selling Rainforest Alliance–certified coffee starting with an initial purchase of over five million pounds (Rainforest Alliance 2003). The standards applied by Rainforest Alliance (RA) were developed in conjunction with CI and other environmental groups – no labour groups were involved – and devote only one of seven key principles to 'sustainable livelihoods.' Moreover, the standards for sustainable livelihoods are vaguely worded and significantly weaker than FLO standards: instead of coffee being produced by worker-owned cooperatives, RA standards refer to basic rights to freedom of association; instead of a guaranteed price determined by basic needs, RA offers an 'equitable price' that will vary according to market conditions (Kraft expects to pay around 20 per cent more than the market price) (Carpenter 2003; Tea & Coffee 2003; Conservation International et al. 2001). As discussed in chapter 2, the popularity of alternative options such as this is growing, and within months of Kraft's announcement Procter & Gamble (which does offer some fair trade coffee) announced it would also begin selling RA-certified coffee. While TNCs prefer FLO's voluntarist measures over state-enforced regulations, they also prefer the less rigorous and demanding third-party certification of RA and CI over that of FLO.

In addition to purchasing sustainable coffees, Starbucks has also developed a 'Preferred Supplier Program,' which was introduced in fiscal year 2002. This followed years of pressure from the U.S./Guatemalan Labor Education Project (US/LEAP), which compelled Starbucks to make a variety of commitments to a code of conduct for Southern producers, which it continually reneged on (US/LEAP 2004, 2001). It was not until Starbucks was compelled to begin offering FLO-certified coffee that it paid serious attention to new sourcing guidelines, which it likely sees as an alternative to fair trade. Developed in conjunction with CI, the Preferred Supplier Program is an incentive-based program that rewards farmers with higher prices (an extra 10 cents per pound) if they meet various quality, environmental, social, and economic criteria. Suppliers are assessed on the basis of a point system and must attain 100 points: 50 points for environmental standards; 20 points for 'economic transparency'; 10 points for health and safety; 10 points for living conditions; and 10 points for wages, benefits, and basic rights. By the end of 2002, only fifty suppliers had applied to be considered for preferred supplier status (Starbucks 2004c, 2004b; US/LEAP 2001).

Starbucks' Preferred Supplier Program has the same weaknesses as its commitment to CI shade-grown coffee. Its standards are disproportionately focused on environmental criteria at the expense of labour criteria, the social standards it does have are basic and general (and oriented towards large-scale plantations), and its price commitment remains tied to market fluctuations. Moreover, the third-party verification agents of the program are corporate-friendly and hand-picked by Starbucks. In Guatemala, one of the verification agents for the program is the National Association of Coffee Exporters (ANACAFE), which, according to US/LEAP, 'has generally denied that there are any labour problems in the Guatemalan coffee sector, and rejected out of hand the most comprehensive study ever done of working conditions in the sector, a study ... financed by Starbucks that found extensive labour violations' (US/LEAP 2001).

Along with its commitment to CI coffee and its Preferred Supplier Program, Starbucks has also made changes to its overall coffee-purchasing policies, beginning in 2001, in an attempt to adopt (or co-opt) several key aspects of fair trade. These changes include a new emphasis on purchasing coffee at 'outright prices, independent of the commodity market.' In 2002, Starbucks claims to have made 74 per cent of its green bean purchases at 'outright' prices, compared to 12 per cent in 2001. Moreover, Starbucks maintains that its average outright price in 2002 was $1.20 per pound for green bean coffee, only six cents below the fair trade minimum. The changes also include buying coffee directly from producers, with help from a 'third-party facilitator' (32 per cent of Starbucks' green bean purchases were direct in 2002, compared to 9 per cent in 2001) and a new emphasis on signing long-term contracts that last three to five years (36 per cent of Starbucks' green bean purchases were long-term in 2002, compared to 3 per cent in 2001) (Starbucks 2003: 5–7).

Starbucks has also sought to somewhat emulate fair trade's policies for credit access and its social premium. In 2002, Starbucks helped make $500,000 in credit available to small producers in Latin America through a loan guarantee in conjunction with CI and Ecologic Enterprise Ventures (EEV) (Starbucks 2003: 5–7). In addition, Starbucks gave $25,000 to Coffee Kids (an NGO that seeks to improve the lives of children in coffee regions through local micro-credit projects), and gave $85,000 in 'premiums' to local communities to set up such things as lavatories, health clinics, and schools. Unlike the fair trade premium, Starbucks' premium is a matching grant which means that local communities must match the funds given them to ensure that 'they have a vested interest in the project,' which places a greater burden on poor communities (Starbucks 2003: 10). Moreover, the sum total of $85,000, equivalent to 0.2 per cent of the total pay of Starbucks CEO Orin Smith in 2003, is very small for a huge TNC like Starbucks (Million-Dollar Club 2003).

The new purchasing policies adopted by Starbucks reveals the success of the fair trade campaign in North America. Under pressure from fair trade activists, Starbucks has been forced to protect its public image by adjusting its policies to meet many of the expectations of fair traders (higher prices, direct purchases, long-term contracts, access to credit and infrastructure). However, at the same time, the changes that Starbucks has made reveals its counter-strategy and the purpose of its CSR project. While giving minimal support to fair trade, Starbucks has buffered up its other projects in an attempt to make the argument that all Starbucks coffee is traded fairly, whether it is certified by FLO or not. Just as Starbucks' CSR program in the North represents an attempt to avoid more radical demands for higher wages and unionization, so its CSR program in the South represents an attempt to stymie the more radical demands of fair trade. Starbucks has placed increasing attention on purchasing CI coffee and on its Preferred Supplier Program because it lacks fair trade's rigorous social standards and price guarantees, and its verification agents are strongly pro-business. Starbucks has also altered its main purchasing policies in replication of fair trade, while completely neglecting the social standards and independent certification that fair trade entails. Thus, while Starbucks has made concessions that are important to its Southern partners, it has done only the minimum required to stave off public criticism, while at the same time developing its own strategy to ensure that it can continue to act independently without any genuine third-party involvement in its corporate affairs. In the final analysis, Starbucks is concerned about its brand image and its independence from regulation, be it the state or NGOs, not the values of fair trade.

Starbucks and Fair Trade Coffee: Why They Don't Mix

As is often pointed out by fair trade supporters, fair trade is not the same as corporate codes of conduct and CSR. Whereas fair trade is driven by the interests of Southern producers and based on organizing and empowering small farmers and workers, CSR is driven by the interests of corporate profitability, is top-down, and is often little more than window dressing designed to protect a corporation's brand image (Bolscher, interview 2002; FLO 2001: 3). The increasing participation in fair trade of giant TNCs, however, represents a growing congruence between the two. To Starbucks, fair trade, despite the intentions of its promoters, is part of its broader CSR strategy. This has proven to be a useful entry point for fair traders, who have been able to use Starbucks' image as an 'ethical' corporation to pressure it to sell fair trade coffee. Yet, just as CSR was conceived to avoid demands for international and national market regulation, so it can be used ultimately to avoid even the voluntarist demands of fair trade (Klein 2000: 334–7, 430–6).

This has been the goal of Starbucks, whose commitment to fair trade is at best weak and whose involvement in the network threatens to distort the principles of fair trade and its future direction. There are several aspects of Starbucks' overall policies, its CSR program, and its fair trade commitment that reveal this to be the case. First, Starbucks does not apply the fair trade principles of democratic organization and paying as high a price as possible for labour to its Northern workers nor to its Northern partners. This means that fair trade-certified coffee available at Starbucks can be packaged by prison labour and sold by low-wage, non-unionized labour, which from a social justice perspective hardly seems to be 'fair' at all.

Second, Starbucks' commitment to fair trade does not extend beyond coffee to other products such as cocoa and tea, where Starbucks has not been under pressure from activist groups. Responding to concerns that its chocolate suppliers exploit forced child labour in West Africa, Starbucks asserts that it has encouraged its suppliers to address these 'allegations' (which are well-documented by many organizations), but that it does not believe that fair trade is the answer because it only helps 'a select group of producers' (Starbucks 2004e).[14] Third, Starbucks' existing commitment to fair trade coffee is mild compared to fair trade ATOs like Planet Bean that import 100 per cent fair trade coffee. Yet, for a 1 or 2 per cent commitment, Starbucks gets 100 per cent publicity and a valuable addition to its CSR program that helps divert attention away from the working conditions of the remainder of its Southern partners and its Northern workers (Rogers 2004; Barrett, interview 2004; Conlon, presentation 2004a).

Fourth, Starbucks has devoted more energy to developing alternatives to fair trade, such as CI shade-grown coffee and its own internal policy changes, than it has spent promoting it. These alternatives threaten to swamp the 'sustainable' coffee market, adding confusion to ethical consumers over what products to buy (sustainable, shade-grown, organic, rainforest-certified) and competing with fair trade over its tiny market share (Conlon, presentation 2004a). Fifth, in the long term, Starbucks and other TNCs may pose a significant threat to small-scale fair trade ATOs that lack the latter's advertising and marketing resources. While Planet Bean does not yet see this as a major threat, their products have been kept off the shelves of various supermarkets due to competition from Van Houtte. Pressures such as this are likely to increase as TNCs become more involved and make greater efforts to monopolize the fair trade market niche.

Sixth, while Starbucks' fair trade imports are only a tiny proportion of its total sales, they represent a major gain for the fair trade network. Upon agreeing to sell fair trade coffee in 2000, Starbucks instantly became one of the largest fair trade licensees in North America and nearly doubled the number of fair trade sales outlets in the United States (Global Exchange 2000). As Starbucks and other major TNCs increase their imports of fair trade products they will also increase their power and influence on the network and its future orientation. As this power imbalance grows within the network, fair trade may become increasingly top-down as fair trade licensers and Southern partners are compelled to make adjustments to meet the demands of powerful TNCs on whom they have become increasingly dependent, somewhat mirroring international trade relations in the conventional coffee market (Renard 2005). Thus, in the long term, the potential exists that TNCs like Starbucks might have a greater influence on changing fair trade than the fair trade network will have on changing it.

The Ethical Consumer and Commodity Fetishism

Whether driven by the desire to develop an alternative trading system, as is the case with Planet Bean, or by the desire to protect their brand image and increase profitability, as is the case with Starbucks, all Northern partners' fair trade programs are ultimately dependent on the existence of 'ethical consumers' to purchase their products. From the perspective of fair traders and many fair trade analysts, ethical shopping is central to the network's goal of bridging the gap between producers and consumers, and 'decommodifying' goods. In purchasing fair trade goods, it is argued, ethical consumers are not merely buying a commodity for sale, but are relating directly with Southern producers through an alternative network based on ethical values. This represents an implicit challenge to the fetishism of commodities under capitalism.

Due to the high cost of carrying out marketing surveys, little systematic empirical work has been conducted by fair traders in Canada to assess the perspectives of consumers when it comes to fair trade and ethical shopping in general (Whitby, presentation 2004). Marketing research carried out in Europe, however, has guided the perspective on ethical consumers held by fair traders in North America. This perspective is generally based on two main assumptions. First, marketing research suggests that a significant proportion of consumers claim to be willing to make purchases on the basis of ethical decisions (Crawshaw 2006; Blowfield 1999: 760–1; Bird and Hughes 1997: 160). Second, marketing research reveals that the majority of ethical consumers are women who have managerial or administrative jobs and tend to be from the middle or upper class (Pendergrast 2002).

Women shoppers are likely more amenable to ethical marketing as a result of socially constructed gender distinctions between masculine and feminine roles. These roles assume that men are individual, competitive, rational, utility maximizing, and non-altruistic, that women are social, cooperative, emotional, and community-oriented, and that the values of the 'social woman' are more in line with ethical consum-

erism than those of 'economic man.'[15] Moreover, traditional socialization that has assigned women to the private sphere and men to the
public sphere has led many women to be more amenable to voluntary
community activism than system-oriented politics. Marginalized from
the sphere of traditional politics, women have at times found the market a convenient avenue for 'political consumerism,' whether in the
form of boycotts or various labelling schemes (Micheletti 2004).

In terms of socio-economic class, ethical consumers tend to be from
the middle and upper classes because they have the income required to
pay more for specialty food items like fair trade coffee. In 2001, the
wealthiest 16.2 per cent of Canadian households spent 56 per cent
more money on coffee per person and were 46 per cent more likely to
shop at food specialty stores than the poorest 43.2 per cent of Canadian
households (Statistics Canada 2003). Having more money, of course,
does not in and of itself explain why people in higher income groups
would be willing to spend more on specialty products. As Thorstein
Veblen, writing at the turn of the twentieth century, effectively argued,
these consumption patterns stem from complex social customs that
have developed alongside the emergence of modern industrial society.
These customs have increasingly assigned the possession of private
property as the single greatest symbol of honour and success. Under
these conditions, argued Veblen, the easiest way for one to demonstrate his or her 'pecuniary strength' in relation to others is through
'conspicuous consumption' – explicitly wasteful and indulgent consumption. While people from all classes generally struggle to demonstrate some level of conspicuous consumption to stave off feelings of
inadequacy, ultimately those who have the greatest wealth are in the
best situation to do so (Veblen 1953: 36–40, 60–80).[16] On this basis,
when middle- or upper-class consumers purchase specialty coffee in
greater quantities than poorer consumers, they are not doing so merely
as a result of taste preferences – few, one would think, would effectively argue that they are coffee 'experts' – but as a demonstration of
their 'pecuniary ability' and class status.

While the notion of conspicuous consumption can help to explain
why wealthier consumers are willing to spend more on specialty products in general, it tells us little about why some would choose to exercise
their 'pecuniary strength' on ethical products like fair trade coffee. To
understand this, an exploration of the social and psychological dimensions of specifically ethical consumerism is required, and is attempted
below. Nonetheless, it is important not to lose sight of the class dimen-

sions of consumerism that underpin the fair trade network. While fair trade within the South is based on class solidarity between poor workers and farmers, at an international level, in order to meet the demands of the market in the North, fair trade is premised on inter-class solidarity between poor producers and rich consumers. This solidarity is not based on class unity against a common oppressor (in this case, 'unfair' TNCs) but on moral appeals from Southern producers for assistance against *their* oppressor. Northern consumers do not have a direct stake in fair trade and its success other than their own ethical motivations.

Given the fact that ethical consumerism does not appeal directly to self-interested motivations, many popular commentators have suggested that the potential for the growth of ethical markets is very limited. For example, mainstream journalist Mark Pendergrast asserts that, while fair trade might appeal to a few 'good Samaritans,' in the end 'even they might squawk if all coffee provided a decent living for those who produce the crop' (Pendergrast 1999: 395). In her book *No Logo*, journalist and global justice activist Naomi Klein provides an excellent account of how massive corporate advertising campaigns have been able to induce consumers to pay exorbitant prices for brand name goods – such as paying $100 to $180 for a pair of Nike shoes that only cost $5 to produce (Klein 2000: 372). She does not believe, however, that ethical products possess the same potential, and states that, beyond appealing to a relatively tiny group of consumers, 'any movement that is primarily rooted in making people feel guilty about going to the mall is a backlash waiting to happen' (429).

Nonetheless, there is no reason to assume that marketing strategies aimed at selling 'ethics' could not appeal to a broad base of consumers, and the proliferation of countless social and ecological products and Corporate Social Responsibility programs over the past decades would suggest that significant potential for the growth of ethical markets may well exist (Seligman 2002). For the fair trade network, however, this assertion must be made with two important caveats. First, while there is potential for growth in ethical markets in general, this does not necessarily reflect the potential for growth in the fair trade network, which lacks the marketing, advertising, and distributional resources required to significantly expand its market niche. As discussed in chapter 2, the most likely beneficiaries of the future growth of ethical markets will be giant TNCs which have increasingly devoted attention to developing their own, watered-down, private 'ethical' initiatives and possess the required resources to dominate and expand emerging markets.

Second, even if the fair trade network is able to continue to expand on the basis of ethical consumerism, this still leaves open the question as to whether or not such consumerism has the potential to brings producers and consumers together in the way fair traders' suggest. Does fair trade consumerism truly offer an alternative avenue through which goods can be decommodified? Why do consumers in the North purchase fair trade goods, and, when they do, what does it mean for the sort of international solidarity that fair trade promotes? These issues are of central importance, especially within the current context of the growing corporatization of the network. While fair traders generally emphasize those aspects of fair trade that challenge conventional consumerism, such as the provision of information on how goods are produced, this is only one side of the ethical consumerist coin. The other side is, in fact, similar in many ways to conventional consumerism, and reproduces many of its negative effects.

As is the case with conventional consumerism, fair trade consumerism remains fundamentally premised on the notion of 'consumer sovereignty.' This concept suggests that industry only responds to consumer demand, and that the lack of or existence of socially and ecologically just production methods are, in the final analysis, an outcome of the ethical decisions of consumers who possess 'consumer power.' This perspective has been rightly criticized for neglecting the fact that consumers do not have near-perfect or even adequate information upon which to base their market decisions (Dawson 2003; Princen, Maniates, and Conca 2002a). Instead, they must engage the market under the coercion and manipulation of massive corporate advertising campaigns designed to engineer consumer choices – in the United States alone big business now spends over a trillion dollars a year on marketing (Dawson 2003).

While the fair trade network challenges the assumption that consumers have adequate information upon which to base market choices, it remains rooted in the belief that these same consumers should have the final say in how goods are produced and distributed on a global scale. As is the case with conventional consumerism, fair trade consumerism accepts that the needs of poor Southern producers are ultimately subservient to the demands of Northern consumers. Yet, from the perspective of promoting democracy and social justice, there is no valid reason to purport that consumers should be 'sovereign' and that one person's demands as a consumer should take precedence over another person's needs as a producer (Hudson and Hudson 2003: 426).

As Ernest Mandel (1986: 22) effectively argues in his critique of the limits of the capitalist market, 'by what principles of "fairness," "justice," "democracy" or "humanity" are the sovereign rights to decide what time and effort to devote to the satisfaction of consumer needs snatched from the hands of the producers themselves?'

Moreover, in accepting the core premise of consumer sovereignty, fair traders are taking as a given current highly unequal and environmentally destructive global consumption patterns. Within the North, the consumer base upon which fair trade relies is composed of relatively affluent consumers whose wealth is derived from a highly unequal distribution of income. Internationally, fair trade depends on existing consumption patterns which are characterized by 'over-consumption' in the North that threatens the depletion of natural resources and perpetuates the existing highly unequal distribution of global wealth (Hudson and Hudson 2003: 426; Dawson 2003; Princen, Maniates, and Conca 2002b, 2002a). Thus, fair traders are seeking greater global justice on the basis of highly unjust global consumption patterns. According to Michael Maniates, this is frequently the case with 'sustainable development' projects that all too often ignore the fact that 'if the 4 billion or more global underconsumers are to raise their consumption levels to some minimally rewarding and secure level, the 1 billion or so global overconsumers will first have to limit and then reduce their overall level of consumption to make ecological room' (Maniates 2002: 206).

Operating within the context of conventional consumption patterns, many ethical consumers likely purchase fair trade goods in part for the same reasons that they or others purchase 'unfair' commodities produced by conventional corporations: to buffer up their own sense of self-validation. Awareness of this psychological motivation lies at the heart of contemporary advertising strategies and is frequently depicted by corporate marketing experts as deriving from people's allegedly 'natural' inclination towards 'selfishness' (see Seligman 2002). Such a perspective, however, offers a flawed and superficial assessment of human behaviour and deflects attention away from the marketing experts themselves, who employ sophisticated marketing techniques to manipulate consumers' 'natural' desires in the interest of corporate profitability (Dawson 2003: 132–54).

Applying the psychoanalytic concept of 'narcissism' to the striving for self-validation provides a far richer means of exploring the possible psychological motivations behind fair trade consumerism. In psychoanalytic theory, narcissism is not driven by selfishness or self-love, but by deep anxiety and self-hate, which leads to a desperate desire to gain validation from others (Lasch 1979: 72–5).[17] As Christopher Lasch has argued in his work *The Culture of Narcissism*, capitalist society tends to promote narcissistic impulses by alienating workers from what they produce and from each other and pitting them against one another in a highly competitive environment in search of jobs and validation. To impress those higher up in the corporate hierarchy, workers must sell their personalities as if they were commodities on the market, resulting in intense anxiety, self-absorption, and narcissism. At the same time, people are freed from traditional bonds of family and institutions (such as the church), which leaves many feeling isolated and lonely (Lasch 1979).

According to Lasch, against the feelings of narcissistic anxiety, loneliness, and alienation, capitalism offers consumption as the cure. Consumption is offered both as an alternative to protest or rebellion (workers turn towards the immediate gratification of consuming new goods), and as a remedy to spiritual desolation and status anxiety. Convinced that they are too powerless to affect life in a meaningful way, people turn towards self-improvement and building a superficial identity based on 'material furnished by advertising and mass culture, themes of popular film and fictions, and fragments torn from a vast range of cultural traditions' (Lasch 1979: 166). In this, Lasch sees a retreat from politics and a turn towards 'psychic self-improvement: getting in touch with their feelings, eating health food, taking lessons in ballet or belly-dancing, immersing themselves in the wisdom of the East, jogging, learning how to "relate," overcoming the "fear of pleasure"' (29). To this list, one could potentially add fair trade products. Feeling powerless and anxiety-ridden, ethical consumers can turn towards purchasing fair trade goods on the market, both to somewhat appease their feelings of powerlessness and to construct their own self-identity as 'ethical' people. In essence, fair trade entails the commodification of social justice and allows consumers to channel their desire for a more just world into purchasing goods on the market to validate their own self-esteem.

Nonetheless, while narcissistic self-validation is likely a key factor in explaining what drives some consumers to purchase fair trade goods, there are still fundamental differences between fair trade and other forms of 'self-improving' consumption. The former requires a degree of personal sacrifice, even if only relatively marginal, for the sake of improving the lives of others. Moreover, many fair trade consumers are also, no doubt, active participants in various social justice moments who view fair trade not as a retreat from politics but as a component of their broader political activities. Fair trade consumerism represents an attempt to connect with others in cooperation and solidarity. The work of Eric Fromm is particularly instructive in exploring this aspect of ethical consumerism and fair trade.[18]

According to Fromm, capitalist society is the cause of great feelings of insecurity, powerlessness, aloneness, and anxiety due to a vast imbalance between 'negative freedom' ('freedom from') and 'positive freedom' ('freedom to'). Whereas capitalist social relations free people from the bondage of traditional political and economic ties – the church, the community, the tributary state – and give them a degree of negative freedom, such relations grant them little in the way of positive freedom and overwhelm them with a sense of individual nothingness and powerlessness in the face of giant monopolistic capitalist enterprises and modern bureaucratic states over which they can have little effect or control (Fromm 1941: 32–78). According to Fromm, to combat this powerlessness people must progress from negative freedom to positive freedom, which would entail individuals working in solidarity with one another for a common purpose, united in the pursuit of 'spontaneous activity, love and work' (36).

In order for people to work in solidarity and unity and attain positive freedom, Fromm asserts that society must overcome the fetishism of commodities under capitalism, where social relations are mediated by the market and people engage one another as alienated individuals in relationships based purely on 'instrumentality' (Fromm 1941: 119). Market relations under capitalism are fundamentally antagonistic and pit workers against workers, and consumers against producers in the pursuit of individual gain. According to Fromm, these market relations must ultimately be replaced by a democratically planned process in order to create a society in which individuals engage one another in solidarity and 'share responsibility' for society's development as a whole (273). Drawing on the work of Fromm, Frances Moore Lappé and Anna Lappé suggest that fair trade and other alternative projects represent attempts by consumers in the North to reach out for some positive freedom and connect in solidarity with others. Fair trade provides Northern consumers with an important symbolic tool to 'laugh at the caricature' of themselves as selfish, atomized, utility maximizers (Lappé and Lappé 2002: 291–3). In this sense, fair trade consumerism can serve as a popular form of 'symbolic inversion' that allows people to momentarily express their desire for a different world (Featherstone 1990: 14–15).

While fair trade consumerism does provide a symbolic tool to critique conventional trade – which has the potential to educate and raise political awareness – the extent to which it offers any substantial gains to ethical consumers in terms of positive freedom and solidarity are significantly limited. Ethical consumers remain isolated individuals whose primary responsibility to the fair trade network is to engage in the market (to buy fair trade coffee). Consumers are not connected with producers or other consumers in a democratic process and their influence on fair trade (and on the broader structures of global capitalism) is limited to their 'purchasing power' as isolated individuals. Their knowledge of fair trade and the lives of producer communities in the South is confined largely to advertising media, and it is not based on direct and personal ties but is mediated by the market (Lyon 2003). In this context, solidarity is premised on individual moral appeals and not on a *shared responsibility*. Wealthy ethical consumers are not engaged in a shared struggle with Southern producers (unlike Starbucks' employees who seek many of the same rights as fair traders), and, of greater significance, do not have a shared responsibility for the outcome of their purchasing decisions. Decisions that are a matter of grave significance for Southern producers are merely a matter of individual purchasing preferences for ethical consumers. As alienated, isolated individuals, ethical consumers remain disconnected and shielded from the direct outcome of their market decisions.

Yet, while relations between producers and consumers remain mediated by the market, some scenarios have greater potential than others for the development of a sense of unity and connectedness through ethical consumerism. A small ATO like Planet Bean, for example, provides much greater opportunities to build bonds of solidarity between producers and consumers than a giant TNC like Starbucks. Planet Bean views educating consumers as central to its mission, and, as a small ATO, provides an environment where consumers can develop personal ties with Planet Bean members who in turn have direct linkages to Southern partners. In consequence, Planet Bean is able to shorten the 'distance' between producer and consumer, which in conventional trade frequently results in a severing of feedback and accountability regarding social impacts of market decisions (Princen 2002). This is exemplified by the story described earlier in this chapter when Planet Bean introduced one of its retail customers to one of its Southern partners. In sharp contrast to this, Starbucks is concerned only with gaining the brand loyalty of millions of abstract customers and is a massive, hierarchical organization composed of thousands of alienated workers, the majority of whom do not have any connection to Southern producers. When consumers buy fair trade coffee from Starbucks, they are essentially as disconnected from the actual producers and their real lives as they are when they buy any conventional commodity on Northern markets (116). Thus, the growing participation of TNCs in fair trade represents a decline in the network's potential to shorten the distance between producers and consumers.

In the final analysis, the notion that fair trade builds international bonds of solidarity between producers and consumers must be taken with a grain of salt. While peoples' desire for positive freedom, solidarity, and connectedness are necessary to spark consumer demand, fair trade's ability to meet these desires is limited: positive freedom is confined to purchasing ethical goods; solidarity is based on moral appeals as opposed to a common cause; and connectedness between consumers and producers is mediated by the market, which shields consumers from shared responsibility for their actions. This is not to say that the fair trade network does not promote bonds of international solidarity, but that these bonds are largely confined to the relationships between Southern and Northern partners within the network. These relationships, in turn, vary significantly depending on the Northern partner – a small ATO or a giant TNC – which raises serious questions and concerns about the future direction of fair trade in the North.

Conclusion: The Future of Fair Trade in Canada

This assessment of fair trade in Canada reveals that fair trade in the North is significantly different from fair trade in the South. After being produced and processed by worker-owned cooperatives in the South, fair trade beans head North where they are then imported, roasted, and distributed by a variety of partners that are organized in significantly different ways and possess vastly different resources and motivations. The success of these partners is dependent on the demands of ethical consumers, who remain isolated and shielded from the outcome of their market decisions. The result is a complex mixture of market imperatives – the need to gain the loyalty of ethical consumers, the need to broaden distribution channels, the need of small ATOs to keep own and gain access to capital, the need of TNCs to protect profits and remain competitive against other large competitors – all of which drive and determine the limits of fair trade in the North, and, ultimately, of the fair trade network internationally. Moreover, fair traders have confronted these imperatives during the era of neoliberal globalization and in the wake of the decline of international market regulation which had sought to *impose* – through the mechanisms of the state – the cost of higher prices and labour standards in the South on all corporations and consumers. Without these impositions, fair trade in Canada has made important gains, but these have been limited by the need to win support from ethical consumers and prove that fair trade can be *profitable* for corporations in a highly competitive international economy.

Despite the many challenges that the market has imposed, fair traders have made important gains in Canada. In the decades following the Second World War, committed social justice groups were able to lay the groundwork for the fair trade network, which slowly, but steadily, expanded its reach. The development of TransFair Canada in the late 1990s and the introduction of the FLO system sparked growing sales and broader distribution for fair trade. Through buycotting campaigns, activists have compelled some of the largest coffee corporations in Canada and the world to participate in fair trade. Moreover, in addition to these direct gains, fair trade activists have also had a more general indirect impact on promoting social justice in Canada. NGOs like Oxfam Canada and Équiterre have used fair trade as an important rallying point to organize social justice activists and educate the public, not just around fair trade but around broader issues in international trade and food security (Kruger, presentation 2004; Bernier-Genest, presentation 2004; Conlon, presentation 2004a). In this sense, Ian Thomson (presentation 2004), a member of the 'no-sweat' group Maquila Solidarity Network (MSN), has commented that fair trade coffee is like a 'gateway drug' that leads the newly initiated into further activism in broader social justice campaigns.

Moreover, fair traders have had an impact on the coffee industry in Canada that transcends the direct involvement of corporations by setting a social justice bar for the industry and pressuring corporations to fall in line. It is as a result of pressure from fair trade groups that Starbucks has changed its overall purchasing policies in replication of fair trade standards; and it is in response to these same pressures that Kraft Foods has begun purchasing RA-certified coffee, which may not have standards as rigorous as TransFair but still represents a step above conventional trade practices (Iezzoni, presentation 2004). When added together, these gains translate into more farmers in the South gaining access to increased income and better social and environmental standards as a result of the fair trade network in Canada.

Nonetheless, the important gains that the fair trade network has made in Canada have continually come up against the limits imposed by the imperatives of the capitalist market. Not the least of these limits is the size of the fair trade market niche itself. While it has grown substantially over the past few years, the total size of fair trade coffee sales remains very small: in 2001 fair trade coffee sales represented only 0.2 per cent of Canada's total coffee imports for that year (UNCTAD 2004; TransFair Canada 2004). While it is impossible to predict the future growth of the fair trade coffee market in Canada, based on trends in Europe it is likely that sales will continue to grow to a more significant share of total coffee sales (perhaps 1 per cent or a bit higher), before levelling off and stagnating after their initial boom (EFTA 2001a: 33–6). These potential limits do not necessarily reflect an unwillingness on the part of a significant proportion of consumers to pay more for ethical reasons. Rather, they reflect a lack of resources on the part of the fair trade network. Expanding market share and stealing it from conventional companies requires massive advertising, marketing, and distributional resources, the same resources required for the original expansion of *conventional* coffee markets in North America in the first place (see chapter 3) (Dawson 2003). Without access to these resources on a massive scale, which seems highly unlikely, fair trade coffee in Canada will remain a relatively small market niche.

Perhaps more important than the limits to the size of the fair trade coffee market in Canada are the changes that the fair trade network has undergone as a result of the imperatives of the market and the need to gain access to conventional corporations. As described in this chapter, and, more broadly, in chapters 1 and 2, the emergence of the FLO system represented a major reorientation for the network towards a strategy based on voluntarism and mainstreaming. To curry favour with conventional corporations, the standards developed by FLO and TransFair Canada do not apply to Northern partners (which had previously consisted almost entirely of ATOs), and fair trade certification is granted to corporations regardless of how many of their total purchases are fair trade. For this reason, buycotting campaigns have met with some success because corporations have only had to meet the demands of fair traders for a tiny percentage of their total sales to gain positive publicity. (This would be the equivalent of the Nestlé boycott demanding that Nestlé change its exploitative marketing strategies for only 1 per cent of its customers while continuing to conduct business as usual with the remaining 99 per cent.)

Yet, while fair traders have made major concessions to gain the support of giant TNCs, these very TNCs likely threaten the long-term viability of fair trade and its principles. While TNCs represent increased fair trade coffee sales in the short term, their involvement in the long term threatens to overwhelm and significantly alter the fair trade network. This can be seen in the case of Starbucks, which continues to deny the majority of its workers, and Northern and Southern partners, the standards of fair trade while devoting mild attention to fair trade coffee, which it has employed as part of its CSR program to bolster its brand image as an 'ethical' company. At the same time, while increasing its influence within the network, Starbucks is also emerging as a major competitor to fair trade: both as a threat to small-scale fair trade ATOs that lack its marketing and financial resources and as a major developer of fair trade alternatives such as CI-certified coffee. While fair traders may have convinced Starbucks that an ethical consumer base exists that can be profitably tapped, Starbucks is clearly far more interested in doing this through corporate-friendly alternatives such as CI than through TransFair Canada.

All of this raises serious concerns about the future of fair trade coffee in Canada. As giant, profit-driven TNCs become increasingly major players in the network, the distinction between conventional trade and fair trade become less potent. If one can now purchase a pound of fair trade coffee sold by low-wage, non-unionized labour (and potentially packaged by prison labour) by a giant TNC that continues to deal in 'unfair' trade for the vast majority of its transactions, on what basis can this coffee truly be considered 'fair'? Such a scenario represents a major threat to the principles of fair trade and reveals the power of the imperatives of the capitalist market to gradually limit and erode these principles in action.

Yet, while the growing participation of TNCs is the dominant trend in the fair trade network today, it is not the only trend. Small-scale ATOs like Planet Bean continue to push forward with their agenda, which, echoing the original principles of fair trade, entails laying the basis for an alternative trading system designed to one day operate independently of the conventional international market and composed of local, democratically run organizations in the North and the South. These ATOs represent an important alternative vision to a fair trade network dominated by TNCs, and there are growing signs of antagonism between the two groups. In Canada, nothing as controversial as the group that recently broke with TransFair USA has occurred, but some ATOs are certainly concerned about the role of TNCs and frustrated with TransFair Canada's growing corporate orientation (Barrett, interview 2004). Either way, whether operating within the fair trade network or as part of a new fair trade organization that has split from the FLO system, these ATOs face an increasingly uphill battle against corporate competitors with vast financial and marketing resources. It is not at all clear that small-scale fair trade ATOs will be able to survive and thrive under these conditions. What is clear, however, is that the survival of the original vision of fair trade in the North depends on their ability to do so.

Conclusion: Fair Trade as Moral Economy

The great rewards of globalised trade have come to some, but not to others ... What is needed is to create conditions for a fuller and fairer sharing of the enormous benefits from trade. Can this be done without destroying the global market economy? The answer is very firmly yes.

Amartya Sen, in Oxfam International (2002b)

The goals of development envisaged by [new development] theories will depend on the actors for whom they are formulated and the scope for change that the theorist's preferred theory of world capitalism suggests exists for them. If, as I fear, it seems that not much scope for change exists – especially for small, severely underdeveloped countries – without a radical resubordination of capital to democratic control, development theory will have also to be about this, and agents capable of undertaking it.

Colin Leys (1996)

The above quotations from Amartya Sen and Colin Leys reveal significant differences in the long-term vision of development advanced by the capability expansion and historical materialist approaches. To Sen, the inventor of the capability expansion approach and the current honorary president of Oxfam International, development does not require a fundamental transformation of global capitalism. Rather, what is required is various state and non-state initiatives to distribute more fairly the 'great rewards' of the global market to poor workers and farmers. To Leys, a leading proponent of Marxist development theory, the prospect of Sen's vision happening, while welcome, does not appear highly probable, especially for the poorest regions in the South.

The structural imperatives of global capitalism drive exploitation and inequality on a world scale, and these outcomes cannot be overcome without a 'radical resubordination of capital to democratic control.' Yet, despite these important differences, the two do share one key fundamental assumption that places them both, to varying degrees, in opposition to the current international trade and development regime headed by rich Northern states, the World Bank, the International Monetary Fund, and the World Trade Organization: namely, that the global economy cannot and will not bring developmental benefits to the world's poor unless strategies are pursued which seek to counter or combat neoliberal policies and place the enhancement of human life, not merely economic growth, at the centre of development.

The fair trade network is one of these strategies, and its developmental vision contains aspects that match the descriptions and prescriptions of both Sen and Leys. While the fair trade vision is interpreted differently by diverse fair trade groups and has changed significantly over time, its core values have always centred on two key components. First, fair traders seek to provide immediate, tangible benefits to Southern partners, and, in the medium term, enhance their capabilities to survive and compete in the global capitalist economy. Second, fair traders seek to create an alternative model of international trade, and, in the long term, aspire to be part of a broader political movement that challenges the structural sources of exploitation and inequality, depicted as being either the institutions of neoliberal globalization, or, in more radical circles, the capitalist world system in general. Thus, the fair trade network has been constructed on both moderate and radical interpretations of social justice and development, which are apparent in the contemporary perspectives on fair trade critically analysed in chapter 2. These perspectives will now be reviewed in the light of the examination of fair trade coffee offered in the previous chapters.

Fair Trade as Shaped Advantage

Authors in the shaped advantage group describe the fair trade network as a development project designed to protect Southern partners from the worst effects of neoliberal globalization while enhancing their capabilities to gain greater access to its purported benefits (Page and Slater 2003; LeClair 2002; Simpson and Rapone 2000; Blowfield 1999; Renard 1999; Sick 1999; Littrell and Dickson 1999; Bird and Hughes

1997). Unión de Comunidades Indígenas del Región del Istmo (UCIRI) serves as an excellent example of the potential of the fair trade network in this regard. Through their participation in fair trade, UCIRI members have gained higher incomes and significantly better access to social programs (health care, education, training, home and community improvements) and economic infrastructure (coffee processing and transportation facilities, credit, technology, marketing skills), all of which have improved their capacity to combat extreme poverty, malnutrition, and environmental degradation, and enhanced their ability to survive and compete on the international market. In addition, UCIRI members have developed important international bonds of solidarity with Northern partners and have developed their sense of unity and collective identity, which has enhanced their ability to support community initiatives and lobby the government on their behalf. The fair trade network clearly has the potential to serve as an important initiator and supporter of local development in the South.

The fair trade network's success in helping to shape advantage for UCIRI, however, must be qualified by recognizing that significant limits exist to the network's potential to extend these benefits on a larger scale – a fact recognized by most authors in the shaped advantage group. In the North, where the social and environmental standards of Fairtrade Labelling Organizations International (FLO) do not apply, local capability expansion cannot even be considered a *general* goal of the network. Various *particular* organizations, such as Planet Bean, are concerned with promoting fair trade standards in the North but they face an increasingly uphill battle against conventional corporations that have become the focus of fair trade labelling. These corporations can hardly be said to be concerned with promoting local capacity building, as Starbuck's record of exploiting low-wage labour and its aggressive anti-union campaigning demonstrates.

In the South, the ability of the network to expand its benefits is limited by the size of fair trade markets, which, on the basis of historical patterns, seem unlikely to grow beyond a certain extent. In consequence, it appears likely that only organizations with particular historical advantages, like UCIRI, will be able to gain full access to the network's developmental benefits. Nonetheless, for those cooperatives that fair trade can help – there are currently over 670,000 coffee farmer families associated with FLO – the network has the ability to provide varying degrees of capability enhancement (FLO 2003b). This is the crux of the shaped advantage perspective: helping *specific groups* to survive and enter the global capitalist market on relatively better terms. Yet, as argued throughout this book, the fair trade network is based on a broader vision than this. Fair traders seek not just to provide immediate benefits to Southern partners but aspire in the long-term to promote an alternative model for international trade based on fair trade's moral standards.

Fair Trade as Alternative Globalization

The work of the alternative globalization group more adequately reflects the broad aims of fair trade organizations to lay the basis for the construction of an alternative model to a neoliberal global political-economic order (Jaffee, Kloppenburg, and Monroy 2004; Fisher 2004; Waridel 2002; Lappé and Lappé 2002; Raynolds 2002a; VanderHoff Boersma 2001). The notion of fair trade as an alternative model remains a concept that is central to the collective identity of fair traders. Nonetheless, the history of the fair trade network reveals that the ground upon which this claim can be made has significantly eroded over time. During its formative decades, the network was depicted as providing an alternative not just to neoliberalism but to the global capitalist system in general. This goal was abandoned with the development of fair trade labelling in the late 1980s, as fair traders sought to expand the fair trade market and followed the changing political-economic conditions ushered in by the emergence of neoliberal reforms internationally.

Since its reorientation, fair traders have modified their vision to depict the network as a challenge to neoliberal globalization. Yet, the success of the FLO system has not risen from the fact that it is a challenge to neoliberalism, but because it is a concession to it. The network's non-statist orientation and focus on voluntary commitments from corporations and consumers has made it highly compatible with neoliberal globalization. This fact has been recognized by international financial institutions, national and local public organizations, and transnational corporations that have increasingly thrown their support behind the network while continuing to push ahead with neoliberal reforms. To meet the demands of these organizations, fair traders have placed greater emphasis on the network's purported compatibility with the 'true' free trade *ideals* of the WTO, which has further eroded their alternative vision. In Mexico, UCIRI has over the years felt compelled to abandon its anti-capitalist discourse and place increasing emphasis on marketing strategies, productivity, and efficiency to gain the support of conventional corporations. Recently, UCIRI signed a deal with Carrefour, without FLO certification, essentially assisting the giant corporation in developing its own alternative to fair trade labelling. In Canada, TransFair has placed increasing emphasis on gaining the support of profit-driven transnational corporations that lack fair trade standards for their Northern employees. To gain further corporate support, FLO has recently begun to consider making amendments to its generic fair trade coffee standards to allow unionized plantations, not just smallholder cooperatives, to be certified for fair trade coffee. This represents a potentially significant step backwards on FLO's commitment to cooperative production in the South.

All of this is not to say that 'alternative' aspects of the fair trade network do not continue to exist. For example, cooperative processing and distribution methods, widespread within the network in the South and a tiny component of the network in the North, represent important alternatives to conventional capitalist enterprises – although support for cooperative methods is on the wane in both the South and North due to growing corporate involvement. The part of the network's alternative vision that remains most intact, however, is not its alternative political-economic vision, but its alternative moral vision. This moral alternative is expressed by Francisco VanderHoff Boersma (2001: 5), who states that while fair traders are compelled to accept the broad structures of the current global order, 'to give food to those that are hungry and drink to those who are thirsty is a work of protest, it is a fundamental reproach of neoliberalism and an economy that excludes the great majority.' Thus, the fair trade network today represents less an alternative to the underlying political-economic structures of neoliberalism and global capitalism than an alternative to a neoliberal *moral economy* that values profits and the rule of the market over the needs of the world's poor.

Fair Trade as Decommodification

Not only is moral force the key component of the fair trade network's alternative vision, but it is also central to the network's attempt to decommodify goods. To varying degrees, authors in the decommodification group suggest that the network's values of cooperation and solidarity represent a challenge to the capitalist imperatives of competition, accumulation, and profit-maximization, while its particular exchange conditions challenge the atomization, individualism, and anonymity characteristic of market exchanges under capitalism (Fisher 2004; Waridel 2002: 24–7, 100–13; Lappé and Lappé 2002: 199–203, 293–6; Elson 2002, 1988; Raynolds 2002a: 415–20; Simpson and Rapone 2000: 47–55). There are many indications of the positive outcome of fair traders' moral mission, such as UCIRI assisting other, smaller cooperatives in processing and selling its beans, or Planet Bean hosting Southern partners on a promotional tour of Canada. Through these actions, fair traders have been able to mitigate somewhat the competition, exploitation, and alienation inherent in capitalist production and trade. Nonetheless, there are significant structural limits to a predominantly moral approach, which, as David McNally (2002: 86) argues, 'ignores the fact that capitalism requires its dominant participants to behave in an exploitative and destructive fashion.'

As argued in chapter 3, the structural imperatives of capitalism have been key to exploitation and inequality in the coffee industry. Low wages, exploitative working conditions, and low prices have resulted from intense competitive pressures as market agents, large and small, have struggled to gain a share of oversaturated international coffee markets. These pressures have exacerbated the destructive boom and bust cycles of the coffee industry as farmers have followed fluctuations in supply and demand on the basis of rational individual decisions which have been completely irrational for the industry as a whole. Seeking some security and stability from the unpredictability of the market, giant monopolistic corporations have emerged in the North which have used their dominant positions to manipulate markets in the interest of corporate profitability, the effects of which have been to increase inequality between the North and South. Fair traders have not been immune to these structural imperatives. In the South, indications of growing competition have emerged between established fair trade cooperatives, newer fair trade cooperatives, and non-certified cooperatives as they battle for a share of a stagnating fair trade coffee market. In the North, giant, profit-driven TNCs have emerged as the dominant players in the fair trade network. These corporations threaten the moral mission of fair trade and many of them are more concerned with developing watered-down alternatives to the FLO system than they are in supporting it.

A similar case can be made for the network's impact on the commodification of goods. While fair traders have advanced important moral arguments against the alienation of producers and consumers, providing basic information on how a good is produced does not substantially alter this situation. While positive bonds of solidarity exist between Southern producers and Northern importers/distributors, the relationship between producer and consumer remains essentially the same. Producers relate to consumers as an abstract market for their goods, and consumers remain alienated, isolated, and, perhaps most importantly, disconnected from the political, social, and environmental consequences of their shopping decisions. The only way truly to bridge this gap would be for producers and consumers to engage in a *democratic political process* in which all are given equal input and equal responsibility for decisions concerning production and distribution. The global market does not represent such a democratic mechanism, as it imposes strict limitations on the capabilities assigned to participants: the consumer's role is confined to purchasing ethical products on the basis of advertising and marketing strategies; and the producer's role is limited to producing fair trade goods and then hoping that consumers will be willing to buy them. Under these circumstances, the link between producer and consumer is strictly a moral one, which is highly contingent and unpredictable, and not one based on direct connections between producers and consumers united in a politically regulated, democratic process.

What a truly democratic political process for the exchange of goods might look like is, of course, difficult to ascertain. I would argue, however, that the old statist prescriptions of the fair trade movement pointed in the right direction in pointing away from the market. This is not to say that these statist initiatives did not contain at times significant weaknesses, which are highlighted in chapter 4. Nonetheless, it has been one of the great ideological victories of neoliberal pundits to have convinced so many of those concerned with creating a fairer world system that the only solution to these weaknesses is to head in the opposite direction, roll back the state, and put increasing faith in the 'power' of isolated consumers. This despite the fact that the past two and one-half decades of market reforms have been a developmental failure in comparison to the previous decades of state-led development at national and international levels.

The statist projects of the fair trade movement provide the basis upon which to begin to consider what an alternative world system might look like. They were premised on the assertion that the market could not be relied upon to deliver fair exchanges, labour rights, and social welfare, but rather that these goals should be pursued by the state through regulation at both international (commodity and compensatory finance schemes, capital controls, the unrealized goal of internationally recognized labour rights) and national (state marketing boards, public welfare programs) levels. There is no reason to suppose that the shortcomings of these projects reveal the superiority of the market, as opposed to the need to further expand democratic participation within the state and to support state-led initiatives with more radical demands for a greater redistribution of wealth and resources at the local, national, and international levels. These actions could lay the basis for constructing a more democratic world system.

Beginning in the 1970s, however, rather than building upon the fair trade movement's vision of a new international economic order, governments in the North and South embarked upon the road of neoliberal restructuring. This was a result not primarily of uncontrollable market forces and technological changes, but of political decisions made by world leaders, especially those in the United States. Thus, whether or not national governments continue to pursue a neoliberal, market-driven path, or adopt a new state-driven one, is primarily a political decision which will ultimately be the outcome of political struggles. Within these struggles, the fair trade network occupies a somewhat contradictory position, appearing to be both in opposition to and highly compatible with the market-friendly reforms of neoliberal institutions. This ambiguous political position, I argue, is best captured through the concept of an international moral economy.

Fair Trade as Moral Economy

The above arguments raise two central contentions about the fair trade network, its vision, and its prospects and limitations. First, despite the widely held views of the alternative group and the decommodification group, the actual developmental impact of the fair trade network does not transcend that depicted by the shaped advantage group. Second, while the shaped advantage group effectively captures this developmental impact and its limits, it does not fully account for the political and ideological aspects of the network's moral mission. This is because there is within the network a discord between its developmental impact and its broader moral and political objectives.

This discord is best accounted for through the concept of a moral economy, which was developed by renowned social historian E.P. Thompson in the 1970s and based on his work on eighteenth-century

England. According to Thompson (1971: 131–2): 'It is not easy for us to conceive that there may have been a time, within a smaller and more integrated community, where it appeared to be "unnatural" that any man should profit from the necessities of others, and when it was assumed that, in time of dearth prices of "necessities" should remain at a customary level, even though there might be less all round.' Yet this conviction was common historically amongst local communities before the imperatives of industrial capitalism and the new ideology of political economy replaced the 'old moral economy of provision' (136). Thompson describes the moral economy of the poor during the transition to industrial capitalism in England, where notions of common well-being, often supported by paternalistic traditional authorities, imposed some limits on the free operations of the market. Premised on an eroded body of Statute law, common law, and local customs, the moral economy of provision asserted that farmers were not allowed to withhold their produce from local markets to wait for prices to increase, that the actions of middlemen were legally suspect and restricted, and that the poor had to be provided with opportunities to purchase grain, flour, or other basic foods in small parcels with properly supervised weights and measures.

If the moral economy were violated and the starving masses found themselves deprived of what they believed to be a 'fair price,' riots ensued, which often entailed the participants' attempting to forcibly set new prices for bread and other foods. The short-term political effectiveness of these riots were not always apparent, as they often provoked violent responses from the authorities and temporarily contributed to further dearth by scaring farmers from selling on the market at all. In the long term, however, the 'effect of the *expectation* of riot' had an impact on the general market situation (Thompson 1971: 120). Assessing this impact, Thompson states: 'While this moral economy cannot be described as "political" in any advanced sense, nevertheless it cannot be described as unpolitical either, since it supposed definite, and passionately held, notions of the common weal – notions which indeed, found some support in the paternalist tradition of the authorities; notions which the people re-echoed so loudly in their turn that the authorities were, in some measure, the prisoners of the people. Hence this moral economy impinged very generally upon the eighteenth-century government and thought, and did not only intrude at moments of disturbance' (79). According to Thompson, the nineteenth century saw the defeat of the old moral economy of provision and the victory of the new political economy of the free market, which, drawing on the work of Adam Smith, asserted that the 'natural' supply and demand of the free market would benefit everyone and maximize society's potential (Wood 1999: 58; Thompson 1971).

The concept of a moral economy fits well with the political objectives of the fair trade network, whose participants can be seen as attempting to take advantage of ethical market niches in the North to construct a new type of moral economy, one which crosses national boundaries and reasserts the notion of people's right to live taking precedence over the profit-driven aims of capital. Whereas the old moral economy in England described by Thompson asserted the right of poor consumers to gain access to the means of life, the new international moral economy of fair trade asserts the right of poor producers to get a fair price for what they sell on the market. Whereas the old moral economy of provision ultimately relied on the threat of the riot as its political force, the fair trade moral economy relies on activist and consumer pressure and the threat of bad publicity towards giant corporations that rely heavily on their brand image. Thus, while the fair trade network hardly has the capacity to make corporations and the state 'prisoners of the people,' it does have an impact on general market conditions.

The ideological basis of the fair trade moral economy is premised on a mixture of traditional and contemporary Christian values, the liberal human and labour rights embodied in the conventions of the International Labour Organization and the UN, and a radical interpretation of the Enlightenment values of social justice, all of which have been engaged with and analysed by Southern partners and appropriated and integrated with local and indigenous customs, both old and new (Hernández Castillo and Nigh 1998). The fair trade vision offered by Southern partners is very much consistent with the long history of peasant radicalism beginning with the emergence of industrial capitalism in England in the eighteenth and nineteenth centuries. In line with this tradition, social justice is interpreted as entailing equality of property for community members; liberty from outside sources of exploitation, such as local and international intermediaries; and fraternity within the community as a cooperative economic unit (Moore 1966: 497–505). Added to this is fraternity based on international solidarity – a value not traditionally emphasized in radical peasant imagery – with Northern partners and consumers. From the perspective of Northern fair traders, fraternity with Southern producers is the core aspect of their vision. Equality and liberty are central only to partners with alter-native projects like Planet Bean, which aspires for equality between members and liberty from the structural hierarchies of capitalism. The interplay between these values in the South and the North has been the driving force behind the fair trade network, whose impact over the years has been limited, but not insignificant.

The limits of the fair trade moral economy stem from its pro-market and non-statist orientation, both of which have been fundamental to its sales success in the medium term. Its pro-market orientation means that the price and message of fair trade goods, the size of fair trade market niches, and the social and political objectives of fair trade have, ultimately, been subject to the imperatives of global capitalism. These imperatives have imposed significant limits on the network, and have eroded, and will likely continue to erode, the fair trade program over time.

The network's non-statist orientation means that its ability to broaden its benefits has remained limited and unable to attain the more universal reach of state-driven development projects. The Inter-national Coffee Agreement reveals the ability of international regula-tory bodies to provide fairer prices to the majority of the world's coffee farmers, even while it did little to address gross inequalities within cof-fee countries. At the national level, the Costa Rican welfare state dem-onstrates the effectiveness of a state-managed program in promoting human development across broad sectors. This is not to say that these state-led models have not had their weaknesses. In both cases, their developmental potential has ultimately been constrained by the com-petitive pressures of the capitalist world system: the ICA eventually collapsed due to conflicts between signatory nations; and the Costa Rican welfare state, whose success stems partly from its ability to out-compete other coffee states, is difficult to replicate and is currently under threat from neoliberal reformers. Nonetheless, while these weaknesses reveal the limitations of state-managed capitalism, these limits cannot be overcome through the policy prescriptions of 'free' traders. Rather, what is needed is to formulate new projects that pro-mote greater democratization and the further empowerment of people through the state, not to abandon state-led development in favour of less democratic, and significantly less successful, pro-market models endorsed and imposed by neoliberal institutions.

The limits of the fair trade moral economy point to serious issues which are likely to lead to increasingly contentious debates between different organizations within the network in the near future. First, there is a need for fair traders to reconsider seriously the growing corporatization of the network and what this means not just in the short term – increasing sales – but in the long term as well – the erosion of fair trade principles and the final curtain for its alternative vision. Should corporations be certified for only purchasing 1 or 2 per cent of their beans under fair trade standards? Should FLO's principles continue to apply only to Southern partners, disregarding the prospect of building international solidarity on the basis of unity between workers and small farmers in the North and South? While corporations have been central to the network's growth over the past decade and a half, they have also emerged as fair trade's greatest threat: their massive marketing and distributional resources pose a threat to the competitiveness of small-scale, 100 per cent fair trade ATOs; their watered-down alternative, 'sustainable' products pose a threat to the prominence and effectiveness of the FLO seal; and their profit-driven motivations pose a threat to fair trade's organizational structure and moral principles. In consequence, fair traders currently run the risk of sacrificing the long-term feasibility of the network for short-term gain – a fact which has been recognized by the group of small fair trade ATOs that recently split with TransFair USA to develop their own association, the details of which have yet to be worked out (Rogers 2004).

Second, fair traders need to reconsider their non-statist vision and their growing support for 'true' free trade. While the network's market-friendly orientation has, to a certain extent, been imposed on fair traders by the changing international political-economic conditions ushered in by neoliberal globalization, it has equally been *embraced* by fair traders, who have all too quickly accepted neoliberal premises about the purported failures of state-led development and the alleged effectiveness of market reforms. Some fair traders have embraced the hegemonic concepts of neoliberal reformers to such an extent that they have referred to participants in the global justice movement as 'globaphobes,' preferring to align themselves with 'free trade' organizations like the WTO and the World Bank over international social justice activists (VanderHoff Boersma, interview 2002; Oxfam International 2002b). The effect of this political and ideological stance is to allow neoliberal institutions to proceed unchallenged in employing the fair trade network as an ethical fig leaf to justify neoliberal globalization, depicting the network not as a movement towards the broader macro-level reforms traditionally demanded by the fair trade movement but as an alternative to them. The outcome of this predicament is not just to narrow the impact of fair trade, but to limit significantly its vision of a future world.

Despite these limitations, the fair trade moral economy has had a significant positive impact in promoting social justice internationally, as can be seen with its effects on the global coffee industry. It has helped to enhance the capabilities of a relatively limited but nevertheless substantial number of poor and disadvantaged coffee farmers who desperately require better access to social and economic infrastructure to make their livelihoods more viable. On this basis alone, it is an important endeavour that should be supported by social justice activists worldwide. In broader terms, the fair trade moral economy has had a general impact on market conditions. Issues around labour and human rights and environmental sustainability are currently hot topics within the coffee industry, a matter which is in large part owing to the efforts of fair traders and their allies.

These efforts have not just sparked a growth in fair trade sales, but have prompted the emergence of increasing numbers of 'sustainable' alternatives and corporate codes of conduct. While these initiatives have been adopted by corporations to avoid the stricter standards and independent verification of the FLO system, they represent an upward movement of the bar of acceptable social and environmental standards. Thus, the fair trade moral economy has attained a mixture of victories – the expansion of sustainable coffee initiatives and increasing awareness of unfair trade – and defeat – the overall limiting of the fair trade network and its objectives.

Whether or not the fair trade moral economy will continue to be able to push the social justice bar forward in the coffee industry in the future is impossible to determine. Based on current trends, however, this does not appear likely. There are limits to the potential size of fair trade niche markets, and these markets are on the verge of being flooded with corporate-friendly alternatives – a barrage of competition that FLO and its allies lack the material and promotional resources to counter. Fair traders have made their impact on conventional markets, but are unlikely to be the direct, long-term beneficiaries of their work as corporations move in to 'free ride' off their initiatives. Under these conditions, fair traders can either maintain their current course, serving as moral leaders in ethical markets dominated by corporations, or they can begin to move the network forward by looking backward and recapturing key aspects of the fair trade vision of the past. Rather than continuing to entrench themselves in the marketing strategies of giant TNCs, fair traders, having made their positive impact on mainstream markets, can refocus their efforts on promoting real alternatives to the current international order.

There are several recommendations that can be put forward to potentially assist fair traders in staving off some of the mounting pressures from the global economy. A recent report on organic and fair trade coffee in Mexico by Muriel Calo and Timothy A. Wise (2005) shares many of the conclusions in this book on the prospects and limitations of fair trade, and offers solid policy recommendations on multiple levels. Within the fair trade network, Calo and Wise propose a higher fair trade premium, lower membership dues, coordinated labelling efforts with other 'sustainable' projects to reduce overall costs, and increasing efforts to promote long-term contracts and further expand the fair trade market. At the same time, they argue that the size of the fair trade market niche is likely to remain relatively small, and that the only way to expand fair trade standards broadly throughout the coffee industry would be through coordinated state action at the national and international levels. In line with the vision of fair trade typically advanced by Oxfam International (2002a; 2002b), Calo and Wise (2005: 43–8) propose a variety of measures directed towards small coffee producers, including state-provided credit, infrastructure, technology, agricultural inputs, and marketing and environmental services. At the international level, they call for renewed efforts to develop commodity control and diversification schemes, as well as preferential trade policies for poor Southern countries and transparency measures for TNCs.

Calo and Wise are correct to point out the need to combine the efforts of the fair trade network with broader reforms at national and international levels – reforms which run contra to the current prescriptions of neoliberal institutions. Nonetheless, as has been argued throughout this book, there is no *necessary* connection between the project of the fair trade network and broader demands for radical reforms to the international system such as those traditionally proposed by key players in the fair trade movement. Just as Oxfam International has held up the fair trade network as an important stepping stone towards broader demands for international market regulation in the interest of poor countries, so too has the World Bank held up the fair trade network as an alternative to market regulation that is compatible with neoliberal globalization. The extent to which the fair trade network will contribute towards promoting one vision over the other

is, ultimately, highly contingent and based in part on the political decisions made by fair traders in response to the pressures they face. Thus,
along with the recommendations provided by Calo and Wise, fair
traders must begin to pay greater attention to the network's *political
position*, and begin to develop future strategies with this in mind.

To steer the network away from the neoliberal camp and towards
promoting genuine alternatives, fair traders must revisit the old vision
of fair trade and the more radical proposals for an alternative trading
system, such as those advanced by Barratt Brown. Rather than accepting the demise of the old model and the triumph of the new on the
basis of the network's current marketing success (which itself has significant limitations), fair traders must begin to think about how they
can use their expanded popularity to revive and re-imagine the old
vision of fair trade and its distinctly non-neoliberal, and in many ways
anti-capitalist, objectives. To begin with, this would entail a renewed
focus on the necessary role of the state, instead of the purported benefits of 'free trade,' in their official statements. As a key goal of the network is to raise awareness about the injustices of the current order, fair
traders must resist efforts by powerful institutions to draw them into
accepting a 'free trade' discourse, thereby making them unintentional
conduits for the hegemony of neoliberal ideas.

Second, this would involve a new emphasis on supporting the cooperative efforts of Northern ATOs like Planet Bean, as opposed to profit-
driven TNCs like Starbucks. This might entail discussions within the
network on the possibility of developing new standards for Northern
licensees designed to ensure that they purchase a specified percentage
of their goods fair trade (well above 1 per cent) and adhere to labour
standards with their Northern employees that are more in line with
fair trade standards, which at a minimum should include a unionized
work force. Third, this would entail an emphasis on developing new
strategies to strengthen ties of solidarity with global justice activists
and Northern workers, as opposed to neoliberal institutions like the
World Bank. Fair traders must reconsider the political limits of align-
ing themselves too closely with neoliberal institutions, which ultimately seek to preserve the existing order, and look to strengthening
alliances with groups who share a common struggle. In the case of
CAW 3000, for example, fair traders should initiate discussions on the
possibility of coordinating their very similar efforts to attain workers'
rights and social justice from giant TNCs.

The above measures would open the door to reformulating a more radical vision of fair trade which pays greater attention to the eroding powers of capitalist imperatives. I have argued throughout this book, however, that the network's success since the late 1980s has been due to the participation of conventional TNCs and public institutions whose support for fair trade is contingent on the network remaining within the parameters of neoliberalism. It may well be that the network, having become dependent on ties with these organizations, has become locked into its current orientation and unable to pursue a more radical agenda. If this is indeed the case, then it would be indicative of the ultimate limits of the fair trade network – relegated to the confines of neoliberal constraints – and it would mean the end of the network's alternative vision and its long-term aspirations for a fairer world for everyone.

Notes

Introduction: Fair Trade and Global Capitalism

1 For examples of the capability expansion approach applied to fair trade, see
   Bird and Hughes (1997), EFTA (2001a), Littrell and Dickson (1999), and
   Oxfam International (2002b; 2002a). Other authors have employed a similar
   approach with a focus on cultural, social, or human 'capital'; see Sick (1999)
   and Simpson and Rapone (2000). The cultural, social, and human capital
   approach is located here within the broader concept of enhancing capabilities, following the work of Anthony Bebbington (1999), who asserts that
   capital ultimately involves 'assets that give [people] the capability to be and
   to act.' While the capability approach is employed (with qualifications) in
   this work, the social and human capital approach is rejected because it promotes the flawed notion that capital is a thing, as opposed to a social relation
   premised on class exploitation; see Fine (1999).
2 For example, in his latest book, Sen (1999) focuses on such capabilities as the
   freedom of the market (as opposed to the imperatives of the market), the
   freedom of wage employment (as opposed to workers' rights to own the
   products of their labor), and freedom to elect officials (as opposed to a more
   radical notion of participatory democracy).
3 For an assessment of Polanyi's compatibility with historical materialism
   and a critique of his technological determinism, see Wood (1999: 20–5) and
   Bernard (1997).

1: Historical and Theoretical Origins of the Fair Trade Network

1 Paul Prebisch is the former executive secretary of ECLA, and former secretary general of UNCTAD.

2 Paola Ghillani is FLO president, and director of Max Havelaar Switzerland.

3 An important exception to this is the work of Michael Barratt Brown (1993), discussed throughout this chapter, which gives a historical account of fair trade but says very little about the key reorientation of the network in the late 1980s. For some examples of works that give brief mention to the history of fair trade, see Laure Waridel (2002), Charles Simpson and Anita Rapone (2000), and Marie Christine Renard (1999).

4 For example, country 'A' might produce coffee and need oil, country 'B' might produce oil and need cars, and country 'C' might produce cars and need coffee. In such cases, a clearing house could make a multiple deal where direct exchanges between countries without a diverse trade base would not work. For more on this, see Barratt Brown (1993: 146–55).

5 Barratt Brown's vision of a decentralized economy and an alternative trade network is similar to the vision of a 'socialized market' expounded by Diane Elson (2002, 1988). She specifically cites Barratt Brown and gives reference to fair trade in her latter work. Elson's proposal was a response to a debate in the pages of *New Left Review* sparked by Ernest Mandel's defence of socialist planning and critique of Alec Nove's 'feasible' market socialism (Nove 1991, 1987; Mandel 1988, 1986). Elson attempts to offer a middle road between the two, asserting that the market must be tightly controlled to prevent monopoly and exploitation, but that some form of market mechanism is required to allow for decentralized planning. While providing strong arguments in favour of guaranteed wages and public services, Elson's argument exaggerates the extent to which consumer information can decommodify goods, and neglects the power of the market to ultimately overwhelm a socialist project if private enterprises and competition are allowed. For an excellent critique of Elson, see David McNally (1993: 213–17). This theme as it pertains to fair trade is addressed in greater detail in chapter 6.

6 This issue was first brought to my attention by sociologist Peter Vandergeest at a day-long workshop entitled 'Fair Trade: Economic Justice, Environmental Sustainability and Cultural Identity in the New Millennium' organized by the Centre for Research on Latin America and the Caribbean (CERLAC) at York University, Toronto, in February 2004 (Fridell and Jimenez 2004: 11).

7 This quote is translated from its original Spanish by the author.

8 This is also true in the North, where the Keynesian welfare state in the 1950s and 1960s brought about an unprecedented improvement in living standards for the majority of the population, a period referred to by historian Eric Hobsbawm (1994) as the 'Golden Years.'

9 One particularly stark example of this decline in progress is contained in a report by the Centre for Economic and Policy Research (CEPR). The authors indicates that people in the South with a life expectancy at birth of 44–53 in 1960 experienced an annual rate of increase of 0.56 per cent from 1960 to 1980. From 1980 to 2000, people in this same group experienced an annual increase of only 0.18 per cent, representing 'a reduction in life expectancy of approximately eight years measured against a scenario where the previous rate of improvement had been maintained in the years 1980 to 2000' (Weisbrot et al. 2001: 10).

2: Neoliberal Globalization and the Fair Trade Network

1 Francisco VanderHoff Boersma is co-founder of Max Havelaar Netherlands, and adviser to UCIRI Mexico. The quotation appears in VanderHoff Boersma (2000, 4). Translated from the original Spanish by the author.
2 Paul Rice is chief executive officer of Transfair USA. The quotation appears in Stecklow and White (2004).
3 For a more detailed discussion of FLO's organizational structure and certification mechanisms, see Renard (2005: 423–6).
4 Traditionally, the costs of fair trade certification by FLO initiatives have been borne entirely by Northern partners. In 2004, however, to raise additional funds FLO began charging Southern producer organizations an initial certification fee and an annual membership fee based on the previous year's fair trade sales (Calo and Wise 2005: 12–13).
5 Naomi Klein (2000: 428–36) provides an excellent critique of corporate codes of conduct which she asserts are driven by corporations' need to protect their brand image. However, she fails to properly distinguish these top-down codes from fair trade, which focuses on empowering workers and peasants from below (Bolscher, interview 2002). Corporate social responsibility is discussed in greater detail in chapter 6.
6 Recently, IFAT and its members have begun to seriously consider developing a labelling system similar to that of FLO. Under the proposed new system, IFAT would certify handicrafts and commodities that conventional corporations were willing to purchase under the conditions of IFAT's ethical code and from IFAT partners in the South (Frey, presentation 2004). If this is adopted, IFAT's operations would begin to look much more like those of FLO.
7 While there are no thorough statistics on fair trade prior to the late 1990s, Michael Barratt Brown (1993: 10) estimates that at the start of the 1990s the size of all alternative trade was around U.S.$50 million worth of exchanges

per year. It is on this basis that we can approximate an increase of around 400 per cent for the size of fair trade markets internationally.

8 This figure is difficult to calculate as the net retail value for importing organizations, worldshops, and label organizations tend to have significant overlap. One product may be recorded under all three categories. This estimate is based on EFTA's estimates of a total net retail turnover for fair trade goods in Europe in 2001 at 260 million Euros, minus a total net retail turnover for label organizations in 2001 at 208 million Euros. See EFTA 2001a: 33, 2001b: 73.

9 The tendency of Southern partners to sell to conventional intermediaries when they offer higher prices in the short term is a persistent difficulty for the network (FLO 2003b: 5–6; Renard 1999: 498). This does not stem primarily from a lack of loyalty by members, but from the survival needs of small producers. R.M. Wijesinge, the vice-president of the Small Organic Farmers Association (SOFA), a fair trade tea cooperative in Sri Lanka, stated during his visit to Canada that the immediate needs of SOFA members compel them to sell their product to whomever offers the highest prices, regardless of whether they are FLO-certified or not (Wijesinge, presentation 2005).

10 The use of the term 'globaphobe' in reference to global justice protestors was employed by Oxfam International in its 2002 trade report (Oxfam International 2002b), as well as by Francisco VanderHoff Boersma, co-founder of Max Havelaar Netherlands, in an interview with the author (VanderHoff Boersma, interview 2002). Walden Bello (2002b, 2002a) and Vandana Shiva (2002) have strongly criticized the Oxfam trade report for moving too close to the World Bank's neoliberal agenda and for adopting the World Bank's pejorative discourse around 'globaphobes,' which is both inaccurate and 'insulting' to Oxfam's allies in the global justice movement. As Bello (2002b) correctly points out, 'It has been the so-called "globaphobes" that have created the dynamic movement that has shaken the international financial and trade institutions and forced them to listen to the views of organizations like Oxfam.'

11 During the current global coffee crisis, when the prices for washed arabica coffee beans first dropped below $0.70 per pound on the New York exchange, Utz Kapeh began to 'strongly recommend' an additional price premium of $0.07 for its sustainable coffee (Giovannucci 2003: 57). Thus, at its highest price of $0.77, Utz Kapeh coffee is well below the current fair trade price for washed arabicas at $1.25 per pound.

12 Robbert Maseland and Albert de Vaal's (2002) article on fair trade does not fit into the three categories offered here. Maseland and de Vaal use abstract general equilibrium models of international trade and draw highly ques-

tionable conclusions. For example, they develop an abstract model that assumes that *all* manufacturing workers in the North buy *all* their agricultural products at fair trade prices. On this basis, they determine that fair trade could lead to an unfair outcome in which 'those that were worst off initially are not necessarily the ones who are worst off now' (Maseland and de Vaal 2002: 270). Such a conclusion ignores the historical and political-economic realities within which the fair trade network operates – which the authors themselves as much as acknowledge by stating that their arguments 'have little attention for the specific circumstances under which production by small-scale producers in Third World countries takes place' (270).

13 The use of the concept of 'shaped advantage' is drawn here from Gregory Albo (1996), who critiques social democratic strategies in the North for accepting that 'there is no alternative' to neoliberal globalization.

14 This price comparison is based on the FOB (free on board) price for conventional and fair trade green beans, which includes the cost of transporting the beans to port for export. In general, conventional farmers receive around 60 to 70 per cent of the FOB, while fair trade farmers receive around 80 per cent (Talbot 2004: 207–9; Scholer 2004). Thus, a direct comparison between fair trade and conventional FOB prices must be used with caution. Despite this fact, during many of the years stated in this paragraph, conventional prices were much higher than the current fair trade price, which resulted in conventional farmers receiving higher prices than today's current fair trade farmers. This is most apparent during the years of 1977, when prices for conventional arabicas reached $3.20 per pound; 1981, when prices reached $2.21 per pound; and 1986, when prices reached $3.06 per pound (UNCTAD 2004). This is discussed in greater detail in chapter 5.

15 Several media and NGO reports have claimed that the World Bank has directly funded the expansion of coffee production in Vietnam. In contrast to this, John Talbot (2004: 127–8) argues that no evidence exists to support this claim, and that in fact the World Bank has long officially discouraged increased coffee production. Nonetheless, Talbot states that the World Bank has imposed neoliberal structural adjustments on indebted poor countries and encouraged the general expansion of commodity exports to earn foreign exchange. As such, the policies of the World Bank have been a significant factor in indirectly prompting increased coffee exports and are in part responsible for the crisis that has occurred as a result.

16 The use of Polanyi's notions of 'embeddedness' has attained growing popularlity among grassroots movements like the fair trade network. However, as pointed out by Mitchell Bernard, these movements have generally accepted market society as a given, and as such do not envision the pros-

pect of 're-embedding' as Polanyi originally intended it. In Polanyian terms, the disembeddedness of the self-regulating market cannot be challenged without directly confronting the power of the state and capital that make this situation possible. As stated by Bernard (1997: 89), 'It is only through challenging the power relations and institutional frameworks that continue to sustain market society that Polanyi's goal is ultimately attainable.'

17 In some respects, fair traders' support of 'true' free trade is similar to the views expounded by neoliberal economist Jagdish Bhagwati (2002: 45–90), a fervent defender of globalization who criticizes the concept of 'fair trade' used by U.S. politicians and labour leaders to promote protectionism to preserve U.S. jobs, and social and environmental standards. Bhagwati believes that true free trade would benefit all stakeholders, rich and poor, and is a strong supporter of voluntary social and environmental codes. Unlike fair traders, however, Bhagwati believes in only a very minimal amount of market regulation. He asserts, for example, that international labour rights should be left in the hands of a slightly reformed ILO, which, although it lacks enforcement power, can offer 'a good tongue-lashing' which 'can push a country into better policies through shame, guilt, and the activities of NGOs that act on such findings' (79). In general terms, Bhagwati overlooks the negative impact of globalization, discussed throughout this work, and his focus on 'free trade' overlooks key aspects of neoliberal globalization – such as the removal of capital controls, the expansion of property rights, cuts to public spending, and the privatization of state assets (McNally 2002: 30–54; Gowan 1999; Helleiner 1994).

3: Coffee and the Capitalist Market

1 Eduard Douwes Dekker, who wrote under the famous pseudonym Multatuli, was a former member of the Dutch East India Civil Service. His work, *Max Havelaar*, was published in 1860. This quotation is from a 1987 reprint (my emphasis).

2 It is often stated in media and NGO reports that coffee is the 'second most valuable commodity in world trade,' or the 'second most valuable traded commodity.' John Talbot (2004: 44, 50n6) points out that neither of these assertions are accurate. Rather, he states that coffee is more precisely 'the second most valuable primary commodity *exported by developing countries*.'

3 Foundational UDT thinkers such as A.G. Frank (1972) and Immanuel Wallerstein (1974) were greatly influenced in their understanding of the emergence of capitalism by the work of Paul Sweezy. Sweezy argued that

the expansion of international trade resulted in the end of feudalism and the emergence of 'pre-capitalist commodity production' which laid the basis for the emergence of capitalism in the seventeenth and eighteenth centuries. His work criticized Maurice Dobb's assertion that capitalism emerged when peasant producers were 'freed' from the bonds of feudal production (see Hilton 1976). Ellen Meiksins Wood (1999: 27–41) asserts that both Sweezy and Dobb, in different ways, conform to the 'commercialization model' wherein capitalism is assumed to have emerged naturally out of the removal of feudal impediments. Her work is central to the historical account of capitalism presented here, along with the work of Robert Brenner (1985, 1977), who first accused Sweezy, Frank, and Wallerstein of being 'neo-Smithian Marxists.'

4 The history of the world system and the expansion of the capitalist mode of production and their impact on the South presented here relies significantly on Eric Wolf (1997), whose work draws on Polanyi (1944) and is highly compatible with those of Brenner (1985, 1977) and Wood (1999). Wolf relies for his account of industrial capitalism on Karl Polanyi (1944), who, like Wood and Brenner, asserted that capitalist imperatives were historically specific and not a natural propensity of human behaviour, as maintained by Adam Smith. For a critique of Polanyi's technological determinism, see Wood (1999: 20–5) and Bernard (1997).

5 The term 'semi-proletarian' refers to rural smallholders who provide a degree of their subsistence needs through home production (like the traditional 'peasantry') but must ultimately sell their labour power (like 'proletarians') to survive. Historically, this has allowed large-scale plantations owners to pay semi-proletarian workers below-subsistence wages that are in effect subsidized by home production, a situation Carmen Diana Deere and Alain de Janvry (1979) have referred to as 'functional dualism.'

6 Another negative environmental impact of this method is that the expulsion of high quantities of waste-water during processing leads to reduced oxygen levels in water, which can threaten many forms of aquatic life (UNCTAD and IISD 2003: 5–6).

7 Despite the fact that *Multinational Monitor* strives to avoid selecting repeat recipients, Philip Morris has the dubious distinction of having been on their 'Ten Worst Corporations' list in 1988, 1994, 1997, and 2001. See http://www.multinationalmonitor.org. For an assessment of the poor ethical and labour records of Procter & Gamble and Nestlé, see the *Corporate Watch* web site at http://www.corporatewatch.org.uk; and for Sara Lee see the *Responsible Shopper* web site at http://www.responsibleshopper.org/basic.cfm?cusip=803111.

8 E. Bradford Burns (1980) provides a thorough account of the attitudes of the nineteenth-century Latin American elite, who denigrated indigenous folk values and employed Westernized social Darwinist theories to justify the plunder and theft of indigenous land and the exploitation of indigenous and black people.

9 Patriarchal systems did not always result in a male-public/female-private sphere divide, although this was the dominant outcome. Elizabeth Dore (2003: 228–35) observes that the system of forced debt peonage in Nicaragua from 1885 to 1910 combined with patriarchal authority often resulted in males signing up their wives and children for debt peonage and appropriating their wages, while the men stayed home and took care of the 'domestic sphere' of self-provision.

4: Coffee and the 'Double Movement'

1 José Figueres Ferrer is the former president of Costa Rica, 1948–9, 1953–8. The quotation appears in Ferrer (1970).

2 Joseph Stiglitz was former chief economist and senior vice-president of the World Bank, 1997–2000. The quotation appears in Stiglitz (2002), 91.

3 While not specifically mentioned in Oxfam's proposals for addressing the coffee crisis (Oxfam International 2002a, 2001), Oxfam does give brief mention to the need for land redistribution in some countries in its general trade report (see Oxfam International 2002b: 243). Nonetheless, the report says very little about what sort of international and national political reforms would be required for this to happen and in general assigns a minimal role in its overall proposal to land redistribution.

4 U.S. officials' neglect of the economic realities that compel small farmers to participate in the growing of coca is apparent not only in Colombia. Joseph Stiglitz points out that in the 1990s Bolivia cooperated with the United States in nearly eradicating Bolivian coca production even though many poor farmers relied on coca income. Despite this, the United States refused to open its markets to alternative crops from Bolivia, such as sugar (Stiglitz 2002: 61).

5 At the start of the twentieth century, only 1 per cent of Costa Rica's population had an indigenous identity, compared to around 66 per cent in Guatemala, 33 per cent in Nicaragua, and nearly 20 per cent in Honduras and El Salvador (Samper 1994: 14).

6 John Weeks (1985: 13–17, 111–22) points out that, by the start of the 1980s, coffee land ownership in Costa Rica was just as concentrated as in other countries in Central America. Historically, however, highly unequal coffee

land concentration in Costa Rica did not begin to emerge until the late nineteenth century, well after other Central American countries and under a significantly different land tenure system based on wage labour as opposed to coercive labour. Thus, Costa Rica, has *historically* had a different concentration of land ownership than the rest of the region.

7 Not only was there a grossly unequal distribution of land in Guatemala, but the vast majority of land in private hands was not even being cultivated by the rural elite. In consequence, states Jim Handy (1994: 82), 'Guatemala suffered from a double-edged problem caused by its extremely inequitable structure of land tenure: large amounts of potentially productive land were left uncultivated on private estates while a land-hungry peasantry struggled for existence in the highlands.'

8 Gregory Albo (1996: 14–15) points out the difficulties of replicating the welfare-state models of advanced capitalist countries on an international scale within the competitive environment of global capitalism. The ability of rich states to maintain their welfare provisions is, in the final analysis, based on their ability to out-compete other countries, which are, in turn, deprived of the resources to fund their own welfare programs. He states: 'The world can stand only so many Swedens of competitive devaluations, Japans of import controls, or Germanys of austerity shaping advantage to prop up export surpluses and employment.'

9 As discussed in chapter 2, in 2003 FLO began to consider making amendments to its generic fair trade standards for coffee to allow for the certification of coffee plantations (Giovannucci 2003: 38n13). This move has likely been considered primarily to address the concerns of large TNCs that prefer to deal with large-scale plantations (Wong, presentation 2004).

5: Fair Trade in Mexico: The Case of UCIRI

1 The article cited as VanderHoff Boersma 2002 is drawn on throughout this chapter. It should be stated that while VanderHoff Boersma is officially credited as the author, the majority of the article is a dictation of statements made by a group of UCIRI members to a Peasant Festival in 2001. As such, the article is taken to represent the opinions not just of VanderHoff but of UCIRI members in general (see VanderHoff Boersma 2002: 17).

2 José E. Juárez Valera, advisor to the Unión de La Selva, Chiapas, Mexico, was decertified by the FLO after failing to fulfil a contract. The quotation appears in Gonzalas Cabanas (2002), p. 32.

3 The *qualitative* focus of the case study approach has frequently been criticized by *quantitative* methods proponents who argue, among other things,

that case studies lack objective scientific validity. This assertion, however, is highly questionable as the scientific validity of quantitative work is ultimately as constrained by the researcher's own subjectivity as is the case with qualitative work. Moreover, much quantitative work tends to suffer from 'tunnel vision' due to a tendency to look at a research object at a single point in time, detached from its social, political, physical, and historical context. This weakness can be effectively addressed through theoretically informed case studies which tend to be 'holistic' and examine objects 'as a whole' that are embedded in their particular context. For further arguments in defence of case studies and the comparative method, see Steinmetz (2004), Verschuren (2003), and Nissen (1998).

4 The PRI was originally founded in 1929 as the Partido Nacional Revolucionario (National Revolutionary Party, PNR). Its name was then changed to the Partido de la Revolución Mexicana (Party of the Mexican Revolution, PRM) in 1937, and then to the PRI in 1946, which remains its name to this day.

5 The reforms to the ejido sector announced by the Mexican government in 1991 permit and encourage the privatization of ejido land under a variety of regulations and restrictions. Ejidatarios can obtain individual certificates of title for their plots only if the entire ejidatario general assembly agrees, on the basis of a majority vote, to participate in the state's privatization program. If their ejido is participating, ejidatarios have the right to legally sell, rent, sharecrop, or mortgage their individual plots. Even then, some restrictions still apply: a two-thirds majority vote is required by the general assembly to authorize the sale of land to outsiders, individual ejido plots are limited in size to 5 per cent of the land of the total ejido, and foreign private investors are limited to owning 49 per cent of equity capital in joint ventures (Cornelius and Myhre 1998: 2–4).

6 This assertion is based on the author's own observation during a visit to UCIRI in October 2002.

7 This situation exists not only among coffee partners, but appears to be the case throughout the FLO system. For example, during his visit to Canada, R.M. Wijesinge, the vice-president of the Small Organic Farmers Association (SOFA), a FLO-certified tea cooperative in Sri Lanka, stated that his cooperative consisted of 765 members (by which he meant families), and that voting on the cooperative was based on one vote per household (Wijesinge, presentation 2005).

8 One must be careful not to over-romanticize the Jesuit philosophy as it relates to non-Christian groups during the colonial era, even when taking into account its relative progressiveness for its historical time period. For

example, throughout Latin America, Jesuit schools exploited African slaves on their large plantations in order to avoid enslaving local indigenous groups that were viewed as having greater potential for Chrisitan 'salvation' (Lacouture 1995: 242–3).

6: Fair Trade Coffee in Canada

1 An important exception to this is the work of Charles Simpson and Anita Rapone (2000), which explores fair trade in the North through an examination of Equal Exchange in the United States, and in the South through an examination of UCIRI in Mexico. Mary Ann Littrell and Marsha Ann Dickson (1999) provide an analysis of Northern fair trade ATOs in their work. The case studies they explore, however, are devoted primarily to cultural products.

2 Mark Pendergrast's history of coffee describes these general trends but has little to say about Canada specifically (1999: 304–424).

3 This price is converted from Canadian dollars based on the exchange rate on 30 June 1989. Unless otherwise stated, all prices in this chapter are in U.S. dollars.

4 This estimate is based on the prices of regular wholesale, freeze-dried, and ground coffee available for sale at Loblaws grocery store in Toronto on 28 June 2004, compared to the price of fair trade and other specialty coffees at Starbucks stores in Toronto on 28 June 2004, and the retail cost of Planet Bean fair trade coffee on sale online at Weekly Organic Wonder (WOW) Foods on 6 July 2004, at http://www.torontoorganics.com.

5 This price is based on the retail price of a pound of Planet Bean coffee on sale online at Weekly Organic Wonder (WOW) Foods on 6 July 2004, at http://www.torontoorganics.com. Regular coffee prices are based on the prices of regular wholesale, freeze-dried, and ground coffee available for sale at Loblaws grocery store in Toronto on 28 June 2004, which ranged from around $3.70 (CAD$5.00) to $4.80 (CAD$6.50).

6 Hosting Southern partners and taking them on community tours in the North is a fairly frequent activity among small fair trade organizations in general. The fair trade chocolate cooperative La Siembra in Ottawa, for example, has hosted partners from the cocoa cooperative CONACADO in the Dominican Republic and taken them to meet with people at local shops and churches (de Jong, interview 2004). La Siembra's members have also expressed an interest in Canadian fair traders expanding their efforts to promote more producer tours in the future (Loftsgard, presentation 2004).

7 The author's requests for interviews with official representatives from Star-

bucks Coffee Company about their corporate social responsibility and fair trade policies were refused.

8 The work of Darryl Reed (2002) provides an assessment of the changes in corporate governance structures in the South as a result of neoliberal restructuring, as well as a discussion on the differences between a 'shareholder' and a 'stakeholder' approach to corporate governance. Laura Westra (1995: 665) highlights the difficulties promoting environmentally ethical behaviour among corporations as many morally defensible actions are not '"economically feasible," within the present institutional setting.' Naomi Klein (2000: 334–436) provides an account of corporations' growing reliance on their brand image and the increasing disenchantment among the public over corporate behaviour along with an excellent critique of the limits of corporate social responsibility.

9 Starbucks is a major sponsor of *Business Ethics* magazine's Business Ethics Awards and has been on its '100 Best Corporate Citizens' list for four years in a row. Other major sponsors of the event include Procter & Gamble, Hewlett Packard, Intel, and National City Bank, all of which have at one time or another been on the magazine's top 100 list (Business Ethics 2004, 2003).

10 In July 2004, the South Asian Network for Secularism and Democracy (SANSAD) based in BC launched a petition against Starbucks for firing two women of South Asian origin who refused to remove their traditional nose studs at work. See http://www.PetitionOnline.com/sansadbc/petition.html.

11 CAW 3000 alleges that a human resources representative at a Starbucks management meeting stated that Starbucks was willing to pay the legal council for unionized employees that wished to decertify. This action is illegal under BC labour laws (Sobczak, interview 2005).

12 This price is based on the price of fair trade coffee at Starbucks stores in Toronto on June 28, 2004.

13 According to Starbucks, in 2001 farmers in the CI program were paid a 60 per cent price premium over 'local prices' (Starbucks 2004c). While it is unclear what this would be, it is likely to be well under $1.00 per pound as world prices for Brazilian arabicas ranged between $0.60 and $0.40 that year (UNCTAD 2004). This is significantly lower than the fair trade minimum price of $1.26 per pound.

14 The International Institute of Tropical Agriculture (ITTA), in conjunction with national researchers, USAID, the ILO, and other organizations documented 284,000 child labourers and 12,000 forced child labourers in the cocoa industry in West Africa (MacAdam 2004; IITA 2002).

15 During a workshop discussion, Marv Frey (executive director/CEO of Ten Thousand Villages in Canada) commented on the fact that nearly 80 per cent of TTV's customers were women, and stated that this meant that fair trade in the North was in many ways a 'women's movement' (Frey, presentation 2004). For an analysis of socially constructed gender differences, see Peterson and Runyan (1993). Elisabeth Gidengil (1995) has explored the influence of the gender gap among Canadians in their support for free trade with the United States, and determined that women tend to view trade issues as social ones, as opposed to strictly economic ones, and are more sceptical about the benefits of the market than men.

16 While Thorstein Veblen's concept of 'conspicuous consumption' is evoked in this passage to assess the consumer culture of the masses, Michael Dawson has convincingly argued that many have emphasized this perspective to the neglect of Veblen's analysis of class coercion. Of greater concern to Velben than the 'delusions of the masses' was how consumer habits were engineered by corporate marketing projects in the interests of the capitalist class (Dawson 2003: 11–15). Dawson has effectively drawn on Veblen's theories in his work on big-business marketing, which is drawn on in this section and throughout this book.

17 Lasch (1979: 72–5) points out that the earlier work of Eric Fromm missed this essential point about narcissism and tended to focus on narcissism as derived from self-love as opposed to stemming from self-hate, the latter of which is now commonly accepted among most contemporary psychoanalysts.

18 While both Lasch and Fromm offer critiques of alienation under capitalism, they have very different perspectives on human drives. Lasch critiques Fromm for placing too much emphasis on the social construction of human drives and neglecting basic instinctual drives, which Lasch sees as being fundamentally at odds with civilization (Lasch 1979: 124). This assertion is part of Herbert Marcuse's broader critique of Fromm and other neo-Freudian revisionists (Marcuse 1955: 217–51). Fromm's emphasis on society as the cause of human destructiveness does neglect 'the question as to how society becomes corrupt when human beings are naturally good' (Carveth 1996: 37). However, the instinctual emphasis of Lasch and Marcuse neglects the extent to which human beings are ultimately not instinct-driven but meaning- and metaphor-driven. For a discussion of this and an alternative view that 'resorts to an *existential* perspective that posits a uniquely human situation or predicament irreducible to heredity and environment,' see the work of Donald Carveth (1996: 43).

References

Select Internet Sources

Bridgehead: www.bridgehead.ca
Canadian AutoWorkers, Local 3000: www.cawlocal3000.ca
Equal Exchange: www.equalexchange.com
Équiterre: www.equiterre.qc.ca
European Fair Trade Association: www.eftafairtrade.org
Fairtrade Labelling Organizations International: www.fairtrade.net
Fairtrade News: www.fairtradenews.com
Fair Trade Research Group: www.colostate.edu/Depts/Sociology/
    FairTradeResearchGroup
Fair Trade Resource Network: www.fairtraderesource.org
Fair Trade@York: www.yorku.ca/cerlac/fairtrade
Global Exchange: wwww.globalexchange.org
International Coffee Organization: www.ico.org/historical.asp
International Federation for Alternative Trade: www.ifat.org
International Institute for Sustainable Development: www.iisd.org
JustUs! Coffee: www.justuscoffee.com
La Siembra: www.lasiembra.com/home.htm
Make Trade Fair (Oxfam Campaign): www.maketradefair.com/en/index.htm
Maquila Solidarity Network: www.maquilasolidarity.org
National Federation of Coffee Farmers (Colombia): www.juanvaldez.com
Network of European Worldshops: www.worldshops.org
Oxfam America: www.oxfamamerica.org
Oxfam Canada: www.oxfam.ca
Oxfam International: www.oxfam.org
Oxfam Québec: www.oxfam.qc.ca

Planet Bean: www.planetbeancoffee.com
Statewide Coordinating Network of Coffee Producers of Oaxaca.
    www.cepco.org.mx
Ten Thousand Villages: www.tenthousandvillages.com
TransFair Canada: www.transfair.ca
TransFair USA: www.transfairusa.org
Union of Indigenous Communities of the Isthmus Region: www.uciri.org
United Nations Conference on Trade and Development: www.unctad.org
United Nations Development Programme: www.undp.org
United Nations Economic Commission for Latin America: www.eclac.cl
United Students for Fair Trade: www.usft.org
United Students Against Sweatshops: www.studentsagainstsweatshops.org

Interviews, Workshop Presentations, and Personal Communications

Barrett, Bill (director and market manager, Planet Bean). 2004. Presentation on
    Planet Bean. Paper read at Fair Trade Workshop For Academic and Fair
    Trade/No Sweat Practitioners, 22 June, York University, Toronto.
– 2004. telephone interview with author. Guelph, ON, 28 May.
Bernier-Genest, Carle (Équiterre). 2004. Presentation on Équiterre. Paper read
    at Fair Trade Workshop for Academic and Fair Trade/No Sweat Practi-
    tioners, 22 June, York University, Toronto.
Bolscher, Hans (director, Max Havelaar Netherlands). 2002. Interview with
    author. Utrecht 18 February.
Cabrera Vázquez, Julissa (Teacher, CEC-UCIRI). 2002. Interview with author.
    San José el Paraíso, Oaxaca, Mexico, 13 October.
Conlon, Tina (Canadian programmer, Oxfam). 2004a. Presentation on Oxfam
    Canada. Paper read at Fair Trade Workshop for Academic and Fair Trade/
    No Sweat Practitioners, 22 June, York University, Toronto.
– 2004b. Presentation on Oxfam Canada. Paper read at Fair Trade Panel
    Discussion, 14 November, Glebe Presbyterian Church, Toronto.
Cowling, Adam (fair trade promotion intern, Falls Brook Centre, New Bruns-
    wick). 2002. Interview with author. San José el Paraíso, Oaxaca, Mexico,
    11 October.
de Jong, Jeff (co-executive director, La Siembra). 2004. Telephone interview
    with author. Ottawa, ON, 23 July.
Frey, Marv (executive director/CEO, Ten Thousand Villages, Canada). 2004.
    Presentation on Ten Thousand Villages. Paper read at Fair Trade Workshop
    for Academic and Fair Trade/No Sweat Practitioners, 22 June, York Univer-
    sity, Toronto.

Fried, Mark (communications and advocacy coordinator, Oxfam Canada). 2004. Can Advocacy Change the Rules? The OXFAM Make Trade Fair Campaign. Paper read at Colloquium on the Global South, at Toronto, 22 September.

Guzman Díaz, Anselmo (Quality Control, UCIRI). 2002. Interview with author. Lachiviza, Oaxaca, Mexico, 8 October.

Iezzoni, Dario (executive director, Oxfam Quebec). 2004. Presentation on Oxfam Quebec. Paper read at Fair Trade Workshop for Academic and Fair Trade/No Sweat Practitioners, 22 June, York University, Toronto.

Jurado Celis, Silvia Nuria (agricultural engineer intern, UNAM). 2002. Interview with author. San José el Paraíso, Oaxaca, Mexico, 10 October.

Kruger, Audra. 2004 (prairies regional coordinator, Oxfam Canada). Presentation on Oxfam Canada. Paper read at Fair Trade Workshop for Academic and Fair Trade/No Sweat Practitioners, 22 June, York University, Toronto.

Loftsgard, Tia. 2004 (director of sales, La Siembra). Presentation on La Siembra. Paper read at Fair Trade Workshop for Academic and Fair Trade/No Sweat Practitioners, 22 June, York University, Toronto.

Martínez Tapia, Nancy Carolina (dentist, UCIRI). 2002. Interview with author. Lachiviza, Oaxaca, Mexico, 8 October.

Nuñez Hernandez, Evanisto (production engineer, UCIRI). 2002. Interview with author. Lachiviza, Oaxaca, Mexico, 8 October.

Ramírez Guerrero, Jesús Antonio (general coordinator, CEC-UCIRI). 2002. Interview with author. San José el Paraíso, Oaxaca, Mexico, 9 October.

Roy, Normand (Équiterre). 2004. Personal communication, 5 March.

Smagge, Guy (Board of Directors, TransFair Canada). 2003. Presentation on TransFair Canada. Paper read at Fair Trade Day, organized by Resources for Environmental and Social Action (RESA), University of Toronto, Scarborough Campus, November.

Sobczak, Frank (president, CAW 3000). 2005. Telephone interview with author. Vancouver, BC, 22 April.

Starbucks Customer Relations. 2005. Personal communication, 24 March 24.

Thomson, Ian (Maquila Solidarity Network). 2004. No Sweat and Fair Trade. Paper read at Fair Trade: Economic Justice, Environmental Sustainability and Cultural Identity in the New Millennium, 5 February, York University, Toronto.

VanderHoff Boersma, Francisco (co-founder, Max Havelaar, and advisor to UCIRI). 2002. Interview with author. San José el Paraíso, Oaxaca, Mexico, 12 October.

– 2002. Lecture on fair trade coffee for students at Centro de Educación Campesina (CEC). San José el Paraíso, Oaxaca, Mexico, 11 October.

Vázquez Lucas, Elsa (health promoter, UCIRI). 2002. Interview with author. Lachiviza, Oaxaca, Mexico, 8 October.

Whitby, Caroline (managing director, TransFair Canada). 2004. Presentation on TransFair Canada. Paper read at Fair Trade Workshop for Academic and Fair Trade/No Sweat Practitioners, 22 June, York University, Toronto.

Wijesinge, R.M. (vice-president, SOFA). 2005. Fair Trade Tea in Sri Lanka: The Experience of SOFA. Paper read at event sponsored by TransFair Canada and Équiterre, 10 March, York University, Toronto.

Wong, John (board member, TransFair Canada). 2004. Presentation on Trans-Fair Canada. Paper read at Fair Trade Panel Discussion, 14 November, at Glebe Presbyterian Church, Toronto.

Primary Reports and Secondary Sources

ACP Group. 2000. Cotonou Agreement. Brussels: Secretariat of the African, Caribbean and Pacific Group of States (ACP Group).

Adam, Barry D. 1997. Post-Marxism and the New Social Movements. In *Organizing Dissent: Contemporary Social Movements in Theory and Practice*, edited by W.K. Carroll. Toronto: Garamond Press.

Albo, Gregory. 1996. The World Economy, Market Imperatives and Alternatives. *Monthly Review* 48 (7): 6–22.

Alternative Grounds. 2004. Homepage, http://www.alternativegrounds.com/. Accessed 17 February 2004.

Alvarez, Sonia E., Evelina Dagnino, and Arturo Escobar. 1998. Introduction: The Cultural and the Political in Latin American Social Movements. In *Cultures of Politics, Politics of Cultures: Re-visioning Latin American Social Movements*, edited by S.E. Alvarez, E. Dagnino and A. Escobar. Boulder, CO: Westview Press.

Amin, Samir. 1977. *Imperialism and Unequal Development: Essays by Samir Amin*. New York: Monthly Review Press.

Appendini, Kirsten. 1998. Changing Agrarian Institutions: Interpreting the Contradictions. In *The Transformation of Rural Mexico: Reforming the Ejido Sector*, edited by W.A. Cornelius and D. Myhre. San Diego: Center for U.S.–Mexican Studies, University of California.

Aranda, Josefina, and Carmen Morales. 2002. Poverty Alleviation through Participation in Fair Trade Coffee Networks: The Case of CEPCO, Oaxaca, Mexico. New York: Fair Trade Research Group / Colorado State University / Ford Foundation.

Arias Sánchez, Oscar. 2004. Gem in a World of Rocks. *New Internationalist* (January-February): 364.

Baby Milk Action. 2002. Nestlé's Public Relations Machine Exposed. Cambridge, UK: Baby Milk Action.

Baer, Werner. 1972. Import Substitution and Industrialization in Latin America: Experiences and Interpretations. *Latin American Research Review* 7 (1): 95–122.

Barnett, Erica C. 2002. Prison Coffee. *Organic Consumers Association*, 27 December–2 January. www.organicconsumers.org/starbucks/prison.cfm.

Barratt Brown, Michael. 1993. *Fair Trade: Reform and Realities in the International Trading System*. London: Zed Books.

Bebbington, Anthony. 1999. Capitals and Capabilities: A Framework for Analyzing Peasant Viability, Rural Livelihoods and Poverty. *World Development* 27 (12): 2021–44.

Bello, Walden. 2002a. The Oxfam Debate: From Controversy to Common Strategy. *Focus on Trade* 78: 1–4.

– 2002b. What's Wrong with the Oxfam Trade Campaign? *Focus on Trade* 77.

– 2003. The Meaning of Cancun. *Focus on Trade* 93.

– 2004. *Deglobalization: Ideas for a New World Economy*. London: Zed Books.

Benjamin, Medea. 2000. Toil and Trouble: Student Activism in the Fight against Sweatshops. In *Campus, Inc.*, edited by G.D. White. New York: Prometheus Books.

Bernard, Mitchell. 1997. Ecology, Political Economy and the Counter-Movement: Karl Polanyi and the Second Great Transformation. In *Innovation and Transformation in International Studies*, edited by S. Gill and J.H. Mittelman. Cambridge: Cambridge University Press.

Bhagwati, Jagdish. 2002. *Free Trade Today*. Princeton: Princeton University Press.

Bird, Kate, and David R. Hughes. 1997. Ethical Consumerism: The Case of 'Fairly-Traded' Coffee. *Business Ethics: A European Review* 6 (3): 159–67.

Blount, Sally. 1997. Whoever Said that Markets Were Fair? *Negotiation Journal* 16 (3): 237–52.

Blowfield, Mick. 1999. Ethical Trade: A Review of Developments and Issues. *Third World Quarterly* 20 (4): 753–70.

Bohman, Mary, Lovell Jarvis, and Richard Barichello. 1996. Rent Seeking and International Commodity Agreements: The Case of Coffee. *Economic Development and Cultural Change* 44 (2): 378–404.

Booth, John A. 1988. Costa Rica: The Roots of Democratic Stability. In *Democracy in Developing Countries: Latin America*, edited by L. Diamond, J.J. Linz, and S.M. Lipset. Boulder, CO: Lynne Rienner.

Brenner, Robert. 1977. The Origins of Capitalist Development: A Critique of Neo-Smithian Marxism. *New Left Review* 104: 25–93.

– 1985. The Social Basis of Economic Development. In *Analytical Marxism*, edited by J. Roemer. Cambridge: Cambridge University Press.

Brewer, Anthony. 1990. *Marxist Theories of Imperialism: A Critical Survey.* 2d ed. London: Routledge.

Bridgehead. 2004. *Our History,* http://www.bridgehead.ca/en/aboutus/history.asp?SID=2534198892124 60890101639621301125457049043450039405 236789311&LangID=1&.

BRIDGES. 2000. ACP, EU Sign 'Cotonu Agreement' on Trade, Aid and Sustainable Development to Replace Lomé. *BRIDGES Weekly Trade News Digest* 4 (25).

– 2001. EC-ACP Cotonou Waiver Finally Granted. *BRIDGES Weekly Trade News Digest* 5 (39).

Bullard, Nicola. 2004. The G20: Their Power Is Not Ours. *Focus on Trade* 98: 7–10.

Bulmer-Thomas, Victor. 1987. *The Political Economy of Central America since 1920.* Cambridge: Cambridge University Press.

– ed. 2001. *Regional Integration in Latin Ameriica and the Caribbean: The Political Economy of Open Regionalism.* London: Institute of Latin America Studies.

Burke, Mike, and John Shields. 2000. Tracking Inequality in the New Canadian Labour Market. In *Restructuring and Resistance: Canadian Public Policy in an Age of Global Capitalism*, edited by M. Burke, C. Mooers, and J. Shields. Halifax: Fernwood Books.

Burns, E. Bradford. 1980. *The Poverty of Progress: Latin America in the Nineteenth Century.* Berkeley: University of California Press.

Business Ethics. 2003. 15th Annual Business Ethics Awards. *Business Ethics: Corporate Social Responsiblity Report* 17(4).

– 2004. 100 Best Corporate Citizens of 2003. *Business Ethics: Corporate Social Responsibility Report*, www.business-ethics.com.

Calo, Muriel, and Timothy A. Wise. 2005. Revaluing Peasant Coffee Production: Organic and Fair Trade Markets in Mexico. Medford, MA: Global Development and Environment Institute, Tufts University.

Cardoso, Fernando Henrique, and Enzo Faletto. 1979. *Dependency and Development in Latin America.* Berkeley and Los Angeles: University of California Press.

Carpenter, David. 2003. Kraft, Activist Groups Still Differ on 'Fair-Trade' Coffee. *Miami Herald*, 8 October.

Carroll, William K. 1997. Social Movements and Counterhegemony: Canadian Contexts and Social Theories. In *Organizing Dissent: Contemporary Social Movements in Theory and Practice*, edited by W.K. Carroll. Toronto: Garamond Press.

Carveth, Donald L. 1996. Psychoanalytic Conceptions of the Passions. In *Freud and the Passions*, edited by J. O'Neill. University Park: Pennsylvania State University Press.

CAW. 2002. CAW Starbucks UnStrike for Justice and Dignity. CAW press release, 9 May.

CAW Starbucks Unstrikers. 2002. CAW Starbucks UnStrike for Justice and Dignity. *Organic Consumers Association*, 1 June. www.orgarnicopnsumers.org/starbucks/unstrike.cfm.

CBC. 2002. Starbucks Changes Its Brew. Canadian Broadcasting Corporation, 21 May.

Chianello, Joanne. 2002. Bridgehead Bounces Back. *Ottawa Citizen*, 4 May.

Chibber, Vivek. 1999. Building a Developmental State: The Korean Case Reconsidered. *Politics and Society* 27 (3): 309–46.

Chossudovsky, Michel. 1995a. IMF-World Bank Policies and the Rwandan Holocaust. *Third World Network Features*, 24 January, www.twnside.org.sg/twnf.htm.

– 1995b. Rwandan Tragedy Not Just Due to Tribal Enmity. *Third World Network Features*, 24 January, www.twnside.org.sg/twnf.htm.

– 1997. *The Globalisation of Poverty*. Penang, Malaysia: Third World Network.

Choudry, Aziz. 2003. Beware the Wolf at the Door. *Seedling (GRAIN)*, October.

Cobridge, Stuart. 1993. Ethics in Development Studies: The Example of Debt. In *Beyond the Impasse: New Directions in Development Theory*, edited by F. Schuurman. London: Zed Books.

Cockcroft, James D. 1998. *Mexico's Hope: An Encounter with Politics and History*. New York: Monthly Review Press.

Cohen, Leonard. 1993. *Stranger Music: Selected Poems and Songs*. Toronto: McClelland & Stewart.

Conservation International, Consumer's Choice Council, Rainforest Alliance, Smithsonian Migratory Bird Center, and Summit Foundation. 2001. *Conservation Principles for Coffee Production, Final Version*: http://www.celb.org/xp/CELB/programs/agriculture-fisheries/conservation_principles.xml

Cornelius, Wayne A. , and David Myhre, eds. 1998. *The Transformation of Rural Mexico: Reforming the Ejido Sector*. San Diego: Center for U.S.–Mexican Studies at the University of California.

Crawshaw, Caitlin. 2006. Would You Spare a Dime for a Cup of (Fair Trade) Coffee? *Express News* (University of Alberta), 23 April.

Curwin, Kelly. 2002. McMaster Is First Canadian University. Hamilton: *McMaster University Daily News*. 31 July.

Dawson, Michael. 2003. *The Consumer Trap: Big Business Marketing in American Life*. Urbana: University of Illinois Press.

Deere, Carmen Diana, and Alain de Janvry. 1979. A Conceptual Framework for the Empirical Analysis of Peasants. *American Journal of Agricultural Economics* 61: 602–11.

Devlin, Robert, and Antoni Estevadeordal. 2001. What's New in the New Regionalism in the Americas? In *Regional Integration in Latin America and the Caribbean: The Political Economy of Open Regionalism*, edited by V. Bulmer-Thomas. London: Institute of Latin America Studies.

Dicum, Gregory, and Nina Luttinger. 1999. *The Coffee Book: Anatomy of an Industry from Crop to the Last Drop*. New York: New Press.

Dore, Elizabeth. 2003. Patriarchy from Above, Patriarchy from Below: Debt Peonage on Nicaraguan Coffee Estates, 1870–1930. In *The Global Coffee Economy in Africa, Asia, and Latin America, 1500–1989*, edited by W.G. Clarence Smith and S.C. Topik. Cambridge: Cambridge University Press.

Dugger, Ronnie. 2000. Introduction: The Struggle That Matters the Most. In *Campus, Inc.*, edited by G.D. White. New York: Prometheus Books.

ECLAC. 2004. *A Decade of Social Development in Latin America, 1990–1999*. Santiago, Chile: Economic Commission for Latin America and the Caribbean.

Edelman, Marc. 1999. *Peasants against Globalization: Rural Social Movements in Costa Rica*. Stanford: Stanford University Press.

EFTA. 1995. *Fair Trade in Europe 1995: Facts and Figures on the Fair Trade Sector in 14 European Countries*. Maastricht, Netherlands: European Fair Trade Association.

– 2001a. *EFTA Yearbook: Challenges of Fair Trade, 2001–2003*. Maastricht, Netherlands: European Fair Trade Association.

– 2001b. *Fair Trade in Europe 2001: Facts and Figures on the Fair Trade Sector in 18 European Countries*. Maastricht, Netherlands: European Fair Trade Association.

– 2001c. *Making Fair Trade Effective and Efficient*. European Fair Trade Association, http://www.eftafairtrade.org/efta.asp.

Elson, Diane. 1988. Market Socialism or Socialization of the Market? *New Left Review* 172: 1–44.

– 2002. Socializing Markets, Not Market Socialism. In *Socialist Register 2002: Necessary and Unnecessary Utopias*, edited by L. Panitch and C. Leys. Black Point, NS: Fernwood Books.

Escobar, Arturo. 1995. Imagining a Post-Development Era. In *Power of Development*, edited by J. Crush. London: Routledge.

Escobar, Arturo, and Sonia E. Alvarez. 1992. Introduction: Theory and Protest in Latin America Today. In *The Making of Social Movements in Latin America: Identity, Strategy and Democracy*, edited by A. Escobar and S.E. Alvarez. oulder: Westview Press.

Esteva, Gustavo. 2003. The Meaning and Scope of the Struggle for Autonomy. In *Mayan Lives, Mayan Utopias: The Indigenous Peoples of Chiapas and the Zapatista Rebellion*, edited by J. Rus, R.A. Hernández Castillo, and S.L. Mattiace. Lanham, MD: Rowman & Littlefield.

Evans, Peter. 1987. Class, State, and Dependence in East Asia: Lessons for Latin Americanists. In *The Political Economy of the New Asian Industrialism*, edited by F.C. Deyo. Ithaca, NY: Cornell University Press.

Fair Trade Declaration - UNCTAD XI. 2004. Sao Paulo, Brazil, www. worldshops.org/activities/advoc/FAIR_TRADE_DECLARATION_ with_signatures.doc.

Featherstone, Mike. 1990. Perspectives on Consumer Culture. *Sociology* 24 (1): 5–22.

Figueres Ferrer, José. 1970. Oral History Interview with Jose Figueres Ferrer: President of Costa Rica, 1948–9, 1953–8. By Donald R. McCoy and Richard D. McKinzie, 8 July, Harry S. Truman Library, www.elespiritudel48.org/docre/ h_103.htm

Fine, Ben. 1999. The Developmental State Is Dead – Long Live Social Capital. *Development and Change* 30: 1–19.

Fisher, Carolyn. 2004. Report from the Field: Fair Trade and the Idea of the Market. *North American Dialogue* 7 (2): 15–18.

Fisher, Eleanor. 1997. Beekeepers in the Global 'Fair Trade' Market: A Case from Tabora Region, Tanzania. *International Journal of Sociology of Agriculture and Food* 6: 109–59.

FLO. 2001. *Report 2000–2001: Developing Fairtrade's Labelling*. Bonn: Fairtrade Labelling Organizations International.

– 2003a. *Fairtrade Standards in General*. Bonn: Fairtrade Labelling Organizations International.

– 2003b. *Report 2002–2003: Cum Laude*. Bonn: Fairtrade Labelling Organizations International.

Follesdal, Andreas. 2004. Political Consumerism as Chance and Challenge. In *Politics, Products, and Markets: Exploring Ethical Consumerism Past and Present*, edited by M. Micheletti, A. Follesdal, and D. Stolle. Piscatawny, NJ: Transaction.

Fowler-Salamini, Heather. 2002. Women Coffee Sorters Confront the Mill Owners and the Veracruz Revolutionary State, 1915–1918. *Journal of Women's History* 14 (1): 34–65.

Fox, Jonathon. 1997. The Difficult Transition from Clientelism to Citizenship:

Lessons from Mexico. In *Participation, Inequality, and the Whereabouts of Democracy,* edited by D.A. Chalmers, C.M. Vilas, K. Hite, S.B. Martin, K. Piester, and M. Segarra. New York: Oxford University Press.

Frank, A.G. 1972. *Lumpenbourgeoisie: Lumpendevelopment.* New York: Monthly Review Press.

French, Michelle. 2001. Fair Trade Coffee Is Close Enough to Taste: Can You Handle It? *Manitoban,* 12 September.

Fridell, Gavin. 2004a. The Fair Trade Network in Historical Perspective. *Canadian Journal of Development Studies* 25 (3): 411–28.

Fridell, Gavin. 2004b. The University and the Moral Imperative of Fair Trade Coffee. *Journal of Academic Ethics* 2 (1): 141–59.

Fridell, Gavin, and Vivian Jimenez. 2004. Fair Trade: Economic Justice, Environmental Sustainability and Cultural Identity in the New Millennium: CERLAC Colloquia Paper. Toronto: Centre for Research on Latin America and the Caribbean (CERLAC – York University).

Friedman, Thomas L. 2000. *The Lexus and the Olive Tree.* New York: Anchor Books.

Fromm, Erich. 1941. *Escape from Freedom.* New York: Holt, Rinehart and Winston.

Furtado, Celso. 1976. *Economic Development of Latin America.* 2d ed. Cambridge: Cambridge University Press.

Gerber, Jurg. 1990. Enforced Self-Regulation in the Infant Formula Industry: A Radical Extension of an "Impractical" Proposal. *Social Justice* 17 (1): 98–112.

Gereffi, Gary, and Miguel Korzeniewicz, eds. 1994. *Commodity Chains and Global Capitalism.* Westport, CT: Praeger.

Gidengil, Elisabeth. 1995. Economic Man–Social Woman? The Case of the Gender Gap in Support for the Canada–United States Free Trade Agreement. *Comparative Political Studies* 28 (3): 384–408.

Giovannucci, Daniele. 2001. *Sustainable Coffee Survey of the North American Specialty Coffee Industry.* Washington: North American Commission for Environmental Cooperation (CEC) and Specialty Coffee Association of America (SCAA).

– 2003, and F.J. Koekoek. *The State of Sustainable Coffee: A Study of Twelve Major Markets.* London: International Coffee Organization.

Global Exchange. 2000. Consumers' Wish for a Proven Alternative to Sweatshop Coffee Will Come True When Starbucks Launches 'Fair Trade Certified' Coffee October. San Francisco: Global Exchange, 22 September, www. globalexchange.org/economy/coffee/pressrelease092200 .html.

– 2001. Squeezing Coffee Farmers to the Last Drop. San Francisco: Global Exchange.

– 2003. Advocacy Groups and Shareholders Persuade Procter & Gamble to Offer Fair Trade Coffee. San Francisco: Global Exchange.

Golub, Stephen S. 1997. Are International Labor Standards Needed to Prevent Social Dumping? *Finance and Development* 34 (4).

Gonzalez Cabanas, Alma Amalia. 2002. Evaluation of the Current and Potential Poverty Alleviation Benefits of Participation in the Fair Trade Market: The Case of Unión La Selva, Chiapas, Mexico. San Cristóbal de las Casas, Chiapas: Union of Societies of La Selva / Federation of Social Solidarity Societies.

Gowan, Peter. 1999. *The Global Gamble: Washington's Faustian Bid for World Dominance*. London: Verso.

Greider, William. 1997. *One World, Ready or Not: The Manic Logic of Global Capitalism*. New York: Touchstone.

Grigg, Heather, Tina Puchalski, and Don Wells. 2003. Ethical Trade and University Purchasing Policies: McMaster University's 'No Sweat' and 'Fair Trade' Purchasing Codes. Unpublished article.

Grinspun, Ricardo. 2003. Exploring the Links among Global Trade, Industrial Agriculture, and Rural Development. In *Rural Progress, Rural Decay: Neoliberal Adjustment Policies and Local Initiatives*, edited by L.L. North and J.D. Cameron. Bloomfield, CT: Kumarian Press.

Gruner, Stephanie L. 1998. Masters in Business. *Inc. Magazine*, July.

Hamerschlag, Kari, Glayson Ferrari, and Rebeca Monteiro. 2004. Report on Fair Trade Activities at UNCTAD XI. Minneapolis, MN: Institute for Agriculture and Trade Policy (IATP), World Vision/FACES Brasil. Available at www.iatp.org.

Handy, Jim. 1984. *Gift of the Devil: A History of Guatemala*. Boston: South End Press.

– 1994. *Revolution in the Countryside: Rural Conflict and Agrarian Reform in Guatemala, 1944–1954*. Chapel Hill: University of North Carolina Press.

Harvey, David. 2003. *The New Imperialism*. Oxford: Oxford University Press.

Harvey, Neil. 1998. *The Chiapas Rebellion: The Struggle for Land and Democracy*. Durham, NC: Duke University Press.

Held, David, A. McGrew, D. Goldblatt, and J. Perraton. 1999. *Global Transformations: Politics, Economics, Culture*. Stanford, CA: Stanford University Press.

Helleiner, Eric. 1994. *States and the Reemergence of Global Finance: From Bretton Woods to the 1990s*. Ithaca, NY: Cornell University Press.

Hellman, Judith Adler. 1988. *Mexico in Crisis*. 2d ed. London: Holmes & Meier.

– 1994. Mexican Popular Movements, Clientelism, and the Process of Democratization. *Latin American Perspectives* 81 (21): 124–42.

Hernández Castillo, Rosalva Aída. 2003. Between Civil Disobedience and Silent Rejection: Differing Responses by Mam Peasants to the Zapitista Rebellion. In *Mayan Lives, Mayan Utopias: The Indigenous Peoples of Chiapas and the Zapatista Rebellion*, edited by J. Rus, R.A. Hernández Castillo, and S.L. Mattiace. Lanham, MD: Rowman & Littlefield.

Hernández Castillo, Rosalva Aída, and Ronald Nigh. 1998. Global Processes and Local Identity among Mayan Coffee Growers in Chiapas, Mexico. *American Anthropologist* 100 (1): 136–47.

Hernández Díaz, Jorge. 1999. The New Top-Down Organizing: Campesino Coffee Growers in the Chatino Region of Oaxaca. In *Institutional Adaptation and Innovation in Rural Mexico*, edited by R. Synder. San Diego: Center for U.S.–Mexican Studies, University of California.

Hernández Navarro, Luis. 2001. Dreams of Coffee. In *Café Organico / Organic Coffee*, edited by E. Poniatowska. Mexico City: Sedesol Fonaes, CEPCO, UCIRI, MAJOMUT.

Hilton, Rodney, ed. 1976. *The Transition from Feudalism to Capitalism*. London: Verso.

Hirschman, Albert O. 1961. Ideologies of Economic Development in Latin America. In *Latin American Issues: Essays and Comments*, edited by A.O. Hirschman. New York: Twentieth Century Fund.

Hobsbawm, Eric. 1994. *Age of Extremes: The Short Twentieth Century, 1914–1991*. London: Abacus.

Hoogvelt, Ankie. 2001. *Globalization and the Postcolonial World: The New Political Economy of Development*. 2d ed. Baltimore, MD: Johns Hopkins University Press.

Hudson, Ian, and Mark Hudson. 2003. Removing the Veil? Commodity Fetishism, Fair Trade, and the Environment. *Organization and Environment* 16 (10): 413–30.

Human Capital Development Sub-committee. 2003. Human Capital Development in Canada: Closing the Gaps. Canadian CED Network, www.ccednet-rcdec.ca/en/docs/pubs/Human_capital_Development.pdf.

Hunt, Diana. 1989. *Economic Theories of Development: An Analysis of Competing Paradigms*. Savage, MD: Barnes & Noble.

Hussain, A. 1987. Commodity Fetishism. In *The New Palgrave: Marxian Economics*, edited by J. Eatwell, M. Milgate, and P. Newman. New York: W.W. Norton.

IFAT. 2001. *What Is IFAT?* International Federation for Alternative Trade, http://www.ifat.org. Accessed on 17 February 2004.

IITA. 2002. Summary of Findings from the Child Labor Surveys in the Cocoa Sector of West Africa: Cameroon, Côte d'Ivoire, Ghana, and Nigeria, Ibadan, Nigeria. www.iita.org/news/chlab-rpt.htm.

Jackson, Andrew. 2003a. From Leaps of Faith to Hard Landings: Fifteen Years of 'Free Trade': Research paper #28. Canadian Labour Congress, www.clc-ctc.ca.

– 2003b. 'Good Jobs in Good Workplaces': Reflections on Medium-Term Labour Market Challenges. Research paper #21. Canadian Labour Congress, www.clc-ctc.ca.

Jaffee, Daniel, Jack R. Kloppenburg, Jr., and Mario B. Monroy. 2004. Bringing the "Moral Charge" Home: Fair Trade within the North and within the South. *Rural Sociology* 69 (2): 169–96.

James, Deborah. 2000. Justice and Java: Coffee in a Fair Trade Market. *North American Congress on Latin America (NACLA)*. September/October, www.globalexchange.org/economy/coffee.

Just US! 2004. Homepage, http://www.justuscoffee.com/. Accessed 17 February 2004.

Killing for Coca-Cola in Colombia. 2001. *Hamilton Spectator*, 11 December.

Klein, Naomi. 2000. *No Logo: Taking Aim at the Brand Bullies*. Toronto: Vintage Canada.

Kniffin, Kevin. 2000. The Goods at Their Worst: Campus Procurement in the Global Pillage. In *Campus, Inc.*, edited by G.D. White. New York: Prometheus Books.

Knight, Franklin W. 1990. *The Caribbean: The Genesis of a Fragmented Nationalism*. 2d. ed. New York: Oxford Press.

Kolko, Gabriel. 1988. *Confronting the Third World: United States Foreign Policy, 1945–1980*. New York: Pantheon Books.

Kurian, Rachel. 2003. Labour, Race, and Gender on the Coffee Plantations in Ceylon (Sri Lanka), 1834–1880. In *The Global Coffee Economy in Africa, Asia, and Latin America, 1500–1989*, edited by W.G. Clarence Smith and S.C. Topik. Cambridge: Cambridge University Press.

La Siembra. 2004. Homepage, http://www.lasiembra.com/home.htm. Accessed 17 February 2004.

Laclau, Ernesto, and Chantal Mouffe. 1985. *Hegemony and Socialist Strategy: Toward a Radical Democratic Politics*. London: Verso.

Lacouture, Jean. 1995. *Jesuits: A Multibiography*. Washington, DC: Counterpoint.

Lappé, Frances Moore, and Anna Lappé. 2002. *Hope's Edge: The Next Diet for a Small Planet*. New York: Jeremy P. Tarcher/Putnam.

Lasch, Christopher. 1979. *The Culture of Narcissism: American Life in An Age of Diminishing Expectations*. New York: W.W. Norton.

LeClair, Mark S. 2002. Fighting the Tide: Alternative Trade Organizations in the Era of Global Free Trade. *World Development* 30 (6): 949–58.

Lewin, Bryan, Daniele Giovannucci, and Panos Varangis. 2004. Coffee Markets: New Paradigms in Global Supply and Demand. Agriculture and Rural Development Discussion Paper 3. New York: World Bank, Agriculture and Rural Development Department.

Leys, Colin. 1996. *The Rise and Fall of Development Theory.* Bloomington and Indianapolis: Indiana University Press.

Littrell, Mary Ann, and Marsha Ann Dickson. 1999. *Social Responsibility in the Global Market: Fair Trade of Cultural Products.* London: Sage.

Lyon, Sarah. 2002. Evaluation of the Actual and Potential Benefits for the Alleviation of Poverty through the Participation in Fair Trade Coffee Networks: Guatemalan Case Study. New York: Fair Trade Research Group / Colorado State University/Ford Foundation.

– 2003. Fantasies of Social Justice and Equality: Market Relations and the Future of Fair Trade. Paper read at the 2003 meeting of Latin American Studies Association (LASA), Dallas, Texas.

MacAdam, Murray. 2004. Bittersweet Chocolate. *Sustainable Times,* 8 March.

Mandel, Ernest. 1986. In Defense of Socialist Planning. *New Left Review* 159: 5–37.

– 1988. The Myth of Market Socialism. *New Left Review* 169: 108–20.

Maniates, Michael. 2002. In Search of Consumptive Resistance: The Voluntary Simplicity Movement. In *Confronting Consumption,* edited by T. Princen, M. Maniates, and K. Conca. Boston: MIT Press.

Marcuse, Herbert. 1955. *Eros and Civilization: A Philosophical Inquiry into Freud.* New York: Vintage Books.

Martinez, Maria Elena. 2002. Poverty Alleviation through Participation in Fair Trade Coffee Networks: The Case of the Tzotzilotic Tzobolotic Coffee Coop, Chiapas, Mexico. New York: Fair Trade Research Group / Colorado State University/Ford Foundation.

Marx, Karl. 1978. Capital. Volume 1. In *The Marx–Engels Reader,* edited by R.C. Tucker. New York: W.W. Norton.

Maseland, Robbert, and Albert de Vaal. 2002. How Fair Is Fair Trade? *De Economist* 150 (3): 251–72.

McCreery, David. 2003. Coffee and Indigenous Labour in Guatemala, 1871–1980. In *The Global Coffee Economy in Africa, Asia, and Latin America, 1500–1989,* edited by W.G. Clarence Smith and S.C. Topik. Cambridge: Cambridge University Press.

McMaster Ad Hoc Code of Labour Practices Development Committee. 2002.

Fair Trade Purchasing Policy for University Suppliers and Retailers. Hamilton, ON: McMaster University.

McNally, David. 1993. *Against the Market: Political Economy, Market Socialism and the Marxist Critique*. London: Verso.

– 2002. *Another World Is Possible: Globalization and Anti-Capitalism*. Winnipeg: Arbeiter Ring.

Méndez, V. Ernesto. 2002. Fair Trade Networks in Two Coffee Cooperatives of Western El Salvador: An Analysis of Insertion Through a Second Level Organization. New York: Fair Trade Research Group / Colorado State University/Ford Foundation.

Mendoza, Ronald, and Chandrika Bahadur. 2002. Toward Free and Fair Trade: A Global Public Good Perspective. *Challenge* 45 (4): 21–62.

Micheletti, Michele. 2004. Why More Women? Issues of Gender and Political Consumerism. In *Politics, Products, and Markets: Exploring Ethical Consumerism Past and Present*, edited by M. Micheletti, A. Follesdal, and D. Stolle. Piscatawny, NJ: Transaction.

Micheletti, Michele, Andreas Follesdal, and Dietlind Stolle, eds. 2004. *Politics, Products, and Markets: Exploring Ethical Consumerism Past and Present*. Piscatawny, NJ: Transaction.

Mikesell, Raymond F. 1961. The Movement toward Regional Trading Groups in Latin America. In *Latin American Issues: Essays and Comments*, edited by A.O. Hirschman. New York: Twentieth Century Fund.

Million-Dollar Club. 2003. *Seattle Times*, 6 June.

Mintz, Sidney W. 1985. *Sweetness and Power: The Place of Sugar in Modern History*. New York: Penguin.

Moguel, Patricia, and Victor M. Toledo. 1999. Biodiversity Conservation in Traditional Coffee Systems of Mexico. *Conservation Biology* 13 (1): 11–21.

Moore, Barrington, Jr. 1966. *Social Origins of Dictatorship and Democracy: Lord and Peasant in the Making of the Modern World*. Boston: Beacon Press.

Multatuli. 1987. *Max Havelaar: Or the Coffee Auctions of the Dutch Trading Company*. London: Penguin.

Myhre, David. 1998. The Achilles' Heel of the Reforms: The Rural Finance System. In *The Transformation of Rural Mexico: Reforming the Ejido Sector*, edited by W.A. Cornelius and D. Myhre. San Diego: Center for U.S.–Mexican Studies, University of California.

Nederveen Pieterse, Jan. 1992. Emancipations, Modern and Postmodern. In *Emancipations, Modern and Postmodern*, edited by J. Nederveen Pieterse. London: Sage.

NEWS. 2004. *NEWS – Network of European Worldshops: Facts at a Glance*. Network of European Worldshops, http://www.worldshops.org/news.html. Accessed 15 February 2004.

Newton, Seth. 2000. Pocket Change or Social Change? University Investment Responsibility and Activism. In *Campus, Inc.*, edited by G.D. White. New York: Prometheus Books.

Nissen, Sylke. 1998. The Case of Case Studies: On the Methodological Discussion in Comparative Political Science. *Quality and Quantity* 32: 399–418.

North, Liisa L. 1985. *Bitter Grounds: Roots of Revolt in El Salvador*. 2d ed. Westport, CT: Lawrence Hill.

North, Liisa L., and John D. Cameron. 2000. Grassroots-Based Rural Development Strategies: Ecuador in Comparative Perspective. *World Development* 28 (10): 1751–66.

Noticias. 2002. La Crisis que Afecta a los Productos Básicos y el Café. *Noticias* (September): 2–3.

Nove, Alec. 1987. Markets and Socialism. *New Left Review* 161: 98–104.

– 1991. *The Economics of Feasible Socialism: Revisited*. 2d ed. London: Unwin Hyman.

Olsen, Gregg M. 2002. *The Politics of the Welfare State: Canada, Sweden, and the United States*. Oxford: Oxford University Press.

Oxfam America. 2003. *Campus Case Studies*. Oxfam America, www. oxfamamerica.org/campaigncoffee/art3506.html.

Oxfam International. 2001. Bitter Coffee: How the Poor Are Paying for the Slump in Coffee Prices. UK: Oxfam International, www.maketradefair.org.

– 2002a. Mugged: Poverty in Your Coffee Cup. UK: Oxfam International, www.maketradefair.org.

– 2002b. *Rigged Rules and Double Standards: Trade, Globalization, and the Fight Against Poverty (Oxfam trade report)*. UK: Oxfam International, www.maketradefair.org.

– 2004. Trading Away Our Rights: Women Working in Global Supply Chains. UK: Oxfam International, www.oxfam.org/eng/pdfs/report_042008_labor. pdf.

Oxford Policy Management, and International Institute for Environment and Development. 2000. Fair Trade: Overview, Impact, Challenges. Study to Inform DFID's Support to Fair Trade. Oxford: Oxford Policy Management / Sustainable Markets Group, International Institute for Environment and Development.

Page, Sheila, and Rachel Slater. 2003. Small Producers Participation in Global Food Systems: Policy Opportunities and Constraints. *Development Policy Review* 21 (5–6): 641–54.

Paige, Jeffery M. 1997. *Coffee and Power: Revolution and the Rise of Democracy in Central America*. Cambridge: Harvard University Press.

Pearson, Ruth. 1994. Gender Relations, Capitalism and Third World Industrialization. In *Capitalism and Development*, edited by L. Sklair. London: Routledge.

Pendergrast, Mark. 1999. *Uncommon Grounds: The History of Coffee and How It Transformed Our World*. New York: Basic Books.

– 2002. The Starbucks Experience Going Global. *Tea and Coffee Trade Online* 176 (2).

Pérez-Grovas, Víctor, and Edith Cervantes Trejo. 2002. Poverty Alleviation through Participation in Fair Trade Coffee Networks: The Case of Unión Majomut, Chiapas, Mexico. New York: Fair Trade Research Group / Colorado State University/Ford Foundation.

Pérez-Grovas, Victor, Cervantes Trejo, and John Burstein. 2001. Case Study of the Coffee Sector in Mexico. Research paper for Oxfam Coffee Report 'Mugged,' www.maketradefair.com.

Peterson, V. Spike, and Anne Sisson Runyan. 1993. *Global Gender Issues*. Boulder, CO: Westview Press.

Petras, James. 1997. Imperialism and NGOs in Latin America. *Monthly Review* 49 (7): 10–27.

Planet Bean. 2004a. The Difference Alternative Trade Makes, http://www.planetbeancoffee.com/Fairtrade. Accessed 12 May 2004.

– 2004b. Homepage, http://www.planetbeancoffee.com/. Accessed May 2004.

– 2004c. Investing in a Co-operative Economy, http://www.planetbeancoffee.com/investment. Accessed 12 May 2004.

– 2004d. Planet Bean Philosophy, http://www.planetbeancoffee.com/Mission. Accessed 12 May 2004.

Polanyi, Karl. 1944. *The Great Transformation: The Political and Economic Origins of Our Time*. Boston: Beacon Press.

Prebisch, Raúl. 1950. *The Economic Development of Latin America and Its Principal Problems*. New York: United Nations.

– 1980. The Dynamics of Peripheral Capitalism. In *Democracy and Development in Latin America*, edited by L. Lefeber and L.L. North. Toronto: Centre for Research on Latin America and the Caribbean–Latin American Research Unit (CERLAC–LARU).

Princen, Thomas. 2002. Distancing: Consumption and the Severing of Feedback. In *Confronting Consumption*, edited by T. Princen, M. Maniates, and K. Conca. Boston: MIT Press.

Princen, Thomas, Michael Maniates, and Ken Conca. 2002a. Conclusion: To

Confront Consumption. In *Confronting Consumption*, edited by T. Princen, M. Maniates, and K. Conca. Boston: MIT Press.

– 2002b. Confronting Consumption. In *Confronting Consumption*, edited by T. Princen, M. Maniates, and K. Conca. Boston: MIT Press.

Quijandría, Benjamín, Aníbal Monares, and Raquel Ugarte de Peña Montenegro. 2001. Assessment of Rural Poverty Latin America and the Caribbean. Rome: International Fund for Agricultural Development (IFAD).

Rainforest Alliance. 2003. Kraft Foods Makes Unprecedented Commitment to Taking Sustainable Coffee Mainstream, http://www.rainforest-alliance.org/news/archives/news/news77.html. Accessed 12 May 2004.

Ranger, Terence. 1983. The Invention of Tradition in Colonial Africa. In *The Invention of Tradition*, edited by E. Hobsbawm and T. Ranger. Cambridge: Cambridge University Press.

Ransom, David. 2001. *The No-Nonsense Guide to Fair Trade*. Toronto: New Internationalist and Between the Lines.

Raynolds, Laura T. 2002a. Consumer/Producer Links in Fair Trade Coffee Networks. *Sociologia Ruralis* 42 (4): 404–24.

– 2002b. Poverty Alleviation through Participation in Fair Trade Coffee Networks: Existing Research and Critical Issues. New York: Fair Trade Research Group / Colorado State University/Ford Foundation.

Raynolds, Laura T., Douglas Murray, and Peter Leigh Taylor. 2004. Fair Trade Coffee: Building Producer Capacity Via Global Networks. *Journal of International Development* 16: 1109–21.

Reed, Darryl. 2002. Corporate Governance Reforms in Developing Countries. *Journal of Business Ethics* 37: 223–47.

Renard, Marie-Christine. 1999. The Interstices of Globalization: The Example of Fair Coffee. *Sociologia Ruralis* 39 (4): 484–500.

– 2005. Quality Certification, Regulation and Power in Fair Trade. *Journal of Rural Studies* 21: 419–31.

Renner, Miriam, and Wiktor Adamowicz. 1998. The Effects of Alternative Agriculture and Fair Trade on the Development of Producer Groups and Their Members: Case Studies from Northern Thailand (staff paper). Edmonton: Department of Rural Economy, University of Alberta.

Rice, Robert A. 1998. A Rich Brew from the Shade. *Americas* 50 (2): 52–9.

Robinson, William I. 2002. Remapping Development in Light of Globalisation: From a Territorial to a Social Cartography. *Third World Quarterly* 23 (6).

Rodney, Walter. 1972. *How Europe Underdeveloped Africa*. Rev. ed. London: Bogle L'Ouverture Publications.

Rogers, Tim. 2004. Small Coffee Brewers Try to Redefine Fair Trade. *Christian Science Monitor*, 13 April.

Roozen, Niko, and Francisco VanderHoff Boersma. 2002. App. 1: Excerpt from Fair Trade: An Adventure in the Fair Trade Market. In *Poverty Alleviation through Participation in Fair Trade Coffee Networks: The Case of UCIRI, Oaxaca, Mexico*, edited by F. VanderHoff Boersma and UCIRI. New York: Fair Trade Research Group, funded by the Community and Resource Development Program, the Ford Foundation.

Ross, John. 2002. In the Midst of a Lacerating Coffee Crises, Starbucks, the World's Largest Over-the-Counter Drug Dealer, Comes to Mexico. *Mexico Barbaro*, 340.

Rus, Jan. 2003. Coffee and the Recolonization of Highland Chiapas, Mexico: Indian Communities and Plantation Labour, 1892–1912. In *The Global Coffee Economy in Africa, Asia, and Latin America, 1500–1989*, edited by W.G. Clarence Smith and S.C. Topik. Cambridge: Cambridge University Press.

Rus, Jan, and George A. Collier. 2003. A Generation of Crisis in the Central Highlands of Chiapas: The Cases of Chamula and Zinacantán, 1974–2000. In *Mayan Lives, Mayan Utopias: The Indigenous Peoples of Chiapas and the Zapatista Rebellion*, edited by J. Rus, R.A. Hernández Castillo, and S.L. Mattiace. Lanham, MD: Rowman & Littlefield.

Rus, Jan, Rosalva Aída Hernández Castillo, and Shannan L. Mattiace, eds. 2003. *Mayan Lives, Mayan Utopias: The Indigenous Peoples of Chiapas and the Zapatista Rebellion*. Lanham, MD: Rowman & Littlefield.

Samper, Mario K. 1994. Café, trabajo y sociedad en Centroamérica (1870–1930): Una historia común y divergente. In *Las Repúblicas agroexportadoras*. Volume 4. Historía General de Centroamérica, edited by V. H. Acuña Ortega. Costa Rica: FLACSO – Programa Costa Rica.

Sarukhán, José, and Jorge Larson. 2001. When the Commons Become Less Tragic: Land Tenure, Social Organization, and Fair Trade in Mexico. In *Protecting the Commons: A Framework for Resource Management in the Americas*, edited by J. Burger, E. Ostrom, R.B. Norgaard, D. Policansky and B.D. Goldstein. Washington, DC: Island Press.

Scholer, Morten. 2004. Bitter or Better Future for Coffee Producers? *International Trade Forum* 2.

Scott, Catherine. 1995. *Gender and Development: Rethinking Modernization and Dependency Theory*. Boulder, CO: Lynne Rienner.

Seligman, Paul. 2002. Protestors Can Tell You the Next Consumer Trend. *Marketing*, 11 July.

Sen, Amartya. 1990. Development as Capability Expansion. In *Human Development and the International Development Strategy for the 1990s*, edited by K. Griffin and J. Knight. London: Macmillan.

– 1999. *Development as Freedom*. New York: Anchor Books.

Shiva, Vandana. 2002. *Export at Any Cost: Oxfam's Free Trade Recipe for the Third World*. http://maketradefair.org. Accessed 2002.

Shuurman, Frans, ed. 1993. *Beyond the Impasse: New Directions in Development Theory*. London: Zed Books.

Sick, Deborah. 1999. *Farmers of the Golden Bean: Costa Rican Households and the Global Coffee Economy*. DeKalb: Northern Illinois University Press.

Simpson, Charles R., and Anita Rapone. 2000. Community Development from the Ground Up: Social-Justice Coffee. *Human Ecology Review* 7 (1): 46–57.

Slater, David. 1994. Power and Social Movements in the Other Occident: Latin America in an International Context. *Latin American Perspectives* 81 (21): 11–37.

Smith, Adam. 1776. *The Wealth of Nations: Books I–III*, edited by A. Skinner. London: Penguin Books.

Soley, Lawrence C. 2000. The Tricks of Academe. In *Campus, Inc.*, edited by G.D. White. New York: Prometheus Books.

Starbucks. 2002. Your Special Blend. Seattle: Starbucks Coffee Company.

– 2003. Corporate Social Responsibility: Annual Report Fiscal 2002. Seattle: Starbucks Coffee Company.

– 2004a. Awards and Accolades, http://www.starbucks.com/aboutus/recognition.asp. Accessed 12 March 2004.

– 2004b. Coffee Sourcing Guidelines, http://www.starbucks.com/aboutus/sourcingcoffee.asp. Accessed 12 March 2004.

– 2004c. Corporate Social Responsibility, http://www.starbucks.com/aboutus/csr.asp. Accessed 12 March 2004.

– 2004d. Environmental Mission Statement, //www.starbucks.com/aboutus/environment.asp. Accessed 12 March 2004.

– 2004e. Starbucks Fact Sheet: GE-Free Ingredients, Fair Trade and Cocoa Sourcing, http://www.starbucks.com/aboutus/progress_report.asp. Accessed 12 March 2004.

– 2004f. Starbucks Mission Statement, //www.starbucks.com/aboutus/environment.asp. Accessed 12 March 2004.

– 2004g. Starbucks Timeline and History, //www.starbucks.com/aboutus/timeline.asp. Accessed 12 March 2004.

Statistics Canada. 2003. Food Expenditure in Canada 2001. Ottawa: Minister of Industry.

Stavrianos, L.S. 1981. *Global Rift: The Third World Comes of Age*. New York: William Morrow.

Stecklow, Steve, and Erin White. 2004. Farmers Not Always Winners as 'Good Corporate Citizen' Retailers Are Found Charging Huge Markups on 'Fair Trade' Food. *Wall Street Journal*, 8 June.

Steinmetz, George. 2004. Odious Comparisons: Incommensurability, the Case Study, and 'Small N's' in Sociology. *Sociological Theory* 22 (3): 371–400.

Stiglitz, Joseph. 2000. The Insider: What I Learned at the World Economic Crisis. *New Republic Online* (17 April): 1–9.

– 2002. *Globalization and Its Discontents*. New York: W.W. Norton.

– 2003. Whither Reform? Towards a New Agenda for Latin America. *CEPAL Review* 80 (August): 7–37.

Synder, Richard. 1999. Reconstructing Institutions for Market Governance: Participatory Policy Regimes in Mexico's Coffee Sector. In *Institutional Adaptation and Innovation in Rural Mexico*, edited by R. Synder. San Diego: Center for U.S.–Mexican Studies, University of California.

Talbot, John M. 1997. The Struggle for Control of a Commodity Chain: Instant Coffee From Latin America. *Latin American Research Review* 32 (2): 117–35.

– 2002. Tropical Commodity Chains, Forward Integration Strategies and International Inequality: Coffee, Cocoa and Tea. *Review of International Political Economy* 9 (4): 701–34.

– 2004. *Grounds for Agreement: The Political Economy of the Coffee Commodity Chain*. Oxford: Rowman & Littlefield.

Tallontire, Anne. 2002. Challenges Facing Fair Trade: Which Way Now? Kent, UK: Natural Resources and Ethical Trade Programme, Natural Resources Institute, University of Greenwich, Chatham Maritime.

Taylor, Peter. 2002. Poverty Alleviation through Participation in Fair Trade Coffee Networks: Synthesis of Case Study Research Question Findings. New York: Fair Trade Research Group/Colorado State University/Ford Foundation.

Taylor, Peter Leigh. 2005. In the Market but Not of It: Fair Trade Coffee and Forest Stewardship Council Certification as Market-Based Social Change. *World Development* 33: 129–47.

Tea & Coffee. 2003. Sustainable Coffee Goes Mainstream. *Tea & Coffee Trade Online* 177 (11).

Teeple, Gary. 2000. *Globalization and the Decline of Social Reform: Into the Twenty-First Century*. 2d ed. Aurora, ON: Garamond Press.

Ten Thousand Villages Canada. 2003. Ten Thousand Villages Canada Annual Report, 1 March 2002 – 28 February 2003. New Hamburg, ON: Ten Thousand Villages Canada.

– 2004. Our History, http://www.villages.ca/.

Thompson, E.P. 1971. The Moral Economy of the English Crowd in the Eighteenth Century. *Past and Present* 5: 76–136.

Thorp, Rosemary. 1991. *Economic Management and Economic Development in Peru and Colombia*. Pittsburgh: University of Pittsburgh Press.

Topik, Steven C. 1998. Coffee. In *The Second Conquest of Latin America: Coffee, Henequen, and Oil during the Export Boom*, edited by S.C. Topik and A. Wells. Austin: University of Texas Press.

TransFair Canada. 2003. Press release. Fair Trade: How It Works and Who It Benefits. Ottawa: TransFair Canada.

– 2004. Homepage, http://www.transfair.ca/. Accessed 17 February 2004.

TransFair Canada and Timothy's World Coffee. 2004. Media release. Timothy's World Coffee Launches Fair Trade Certified Coffees.

UCIRI. 1985. Educacion: Paso 2. Santa Maria Guienagati, Tehuantepec, Oaxaca: Unión de Comunidades Indígenas de la Región del Istmo.

– 1986. El Centro de Educacion Campesina: Paso. 3. Santa Maria Guienagati, Tehuantepec, Oaxaca: Unión de Comunidades Indígenas de la Región del Istmo.

– 1987a. El Primer Encuentro de los diferentes comites de UCIRI: Paso 15. Santa Maria Guienagati, Tehuantepec, Oaxaca: Unión de Comunidades Indígenas de la Región del Istmo.

– 1987b. Preparación y Aplicación del Abono Orgánico: Paso 16. Santa Maria Guienagati, Tehuantepec, Oaxaca: Unión de Comunidades Indígenas de la Región del Istmo.

– 1989. Vamos al CEC. Centro de Educacion Campesina (CEC), San Jose El Paraiso, Tehuantepec, Oaxaca: Unión de Comunidades Indígenas de la Región del Istmo.

– 1991. Manual de Prestamos F.A.C.: Paso 29. Santa Maria Guienagati, Tehuantepec, Oaxaca: Unión de Comunidades Indígenas de la Región del Istmo.

– 1994. Los estatutos de fondo de ahorro y credito: Paso 42. Santa Maria Guienagati, Tehuantepec, Oaxaca: Unión de Comunidades Indígenas de la Región del Istmo.

– 2004a. *Centre of Rural Studies for Organic and Sustainable Development of the Communities (CEC)*. Unión de Comunidades Indígenas de la Región del Istmo (UCIRI), www.uciri.org. Accessed December 2004.

– 2004b. *Communally Organized Work (COW)*. Unión de Comunidades Indígenas de la Región del Istmo, www.uciri.org. Accessed December 2004.

– 2004c. *Health*. Unión de Comunidades Indígenas de la Región del Istmo, www.uciri.org. Accessed December 2004.

– 2004d. *Housing*. Unión de Comunidades Indígenas de la Región del Istmo, www.uciri.org. Accessed December 2004.

– 2004e. *Lachinavani Hardware Store*. Unión de Comunidades Indígenas de la Región del Istmo, www.uciri.org. Accessed December 2004.

– 2004f. *Marmalades, Juices, and Concentrates*. Unión de Comunidades

Indígenas de la Región del Istmo, www.uciri.org. Accessed December 2004.

- 2004g. *Organic.* Unión de Comunidades Indígenas de la Región del Istmo, www.uciri.org. Accessed December 2004.

- 2004h. *Organizational Structure.* Unión de Comunidades Indígenas de la Región del Istmo, www.uciri.org. Accessed December 2004.

- 2004i. *Our History.* Unión de Comunidades Indígenas de la Región del Istmo, www.uciri.org. Accessed December 2004.

- 2004j. *Short Portrait of UCIRI.* Unión de Comunidades Indígenas de la Región del Istmo, www.uciri.org. Accessed December 2004.

- 2004k. *UCIRI's Basic Rules.* Unión de Comunidades Indígenas de la Región del Istmo, www.uciri.org. Accessed December 2004.

- 2004l. *What We Defend and Strive For.* Unión de Comunidades Indígenas de la Región del Istmo, www.uciri.org. Accessed December 2004.

- 2004m. *Who Are We?* Unión de Comunidades Indígenas de la Región del Istmo, www.uciri.org. Accessed December 2004.

UNCTAD. 2004. UNCTAD Handbook of Statistics On-Line: United Nations Conference on Trade and Development.

UNCTAD and IISD. 2003. Sustainability in the Coffee Sector: Exploring Opportunities for International Cooperation. United Nations Conference on Trade and Development and the International Institute for Sustainable Development.

UNDP. 2004. Human Development Report 2004: Cultural Liberty in Today's Diverse World. New York: United National Development Programme.

US/LEAP. 2001. Starbucks Issues New Sourcing Guidelines: US/LEAP.

- 2004. *The Starbucks Campaign,* http://www.usleap.org/Coffee/coffeetemp.html. Accessed December 2004.

VanderHoff Boersma, Francisco. 2001. Economía y Reino de Dios: Neoliberalismo y dignidad opuestos que viven juntos. *Christus* 723.

- 2002. Poverty Alleviation through Participation in Fair Trade Coffee Networks: The Case of UCIRI, Oaxaca, Mexico. New York: Fair Trade Research Group / Colorado State University / Ford Foundation.

Veblen, Thorstein. 1953. *The Theory of the Leisure Class.* New York: Mentor Books.

Verschuren, Piet J. M. 2003. Case Study as a Research Strategy: Some Ambiguities and Opportunities. *International Journal of Social Research Methodology* 6 (2): 121–39.

Vilas, Carlos M. 1997. Participation, Inequality, and the Whereabouts of Democracy. In *The New Politics of Inequality in Latin America: Rethinking Participation and Representation,* edited by D.A. Chalmers, C.M. Vilas, K. Hite,

S.B. Martin, K. Piester, and M. Segarra. New York: Oxford University Press.

Wallerstein, Immanuel. 1974. The Rise and Future Demise of the World Capitalist System: Concepts for Comparative Analysis. *Comparative Studies and History* 15: 387–415.

Waridel, Laure. 2002. *Coffee with Pleasure: Just Java and World Trade*. Montreal: Black Rose Books.

Weeks, John. 1985. *The Economies of Central America*. New York: Holmes & Meier.

Weisbrot, Mark, Dean Baker, Egor Kraev, and Judy Chen. 2001. The Scorecard on Globalization, 1980–2000: Twenty Years of Diminished Progress. Washington, DC: Center for Economic and Policy Research.

Weisbrot, Mark, Dean Baker, Robert Naiman, and Gila Neta. 2000. Growth May Be Good for the Poor – But Are IMF and World Bank Policies Good for Growth? A Closer Look at the World Bank's Most Recent Defense of Its Policies. Washington, DC: Center for Economic and Policy Research.

Westra, Laura. 1995. The Corporation and the Environment. *Business Ethics Quarterly* 5 (4): 661–73.

Wignaraja, Ponna. 1993. Rethinking Development and Democracy. In *New Social Movements in the South: Empowering the People*, edited by P. Wignaraja. London: Zed Books.

Williams, Eric. 1964. *Capitalism and Slavery*. London: Andre Deutsch.

Winson, Anthony. 1989. *Coffee and Democracy in Modern Costa Rica*. Toronto: Between the Lines.

Wirpsa, Leslie. 1997. Economics Fuels Return of La Violencia. *National Catholic Reporter*, 24 October.

Wolf, Eric R. 1997. *Europe and the People without History*. Berkeley: University of California Press.

Wood, Ellen Meiksins. 1999. *The Origin of Capitalism*. New York: Monthly Review Press.

Workforce Management. 2003. Workforce Optimas Awards 2003. *Workforce Management*, March.

World Bank. 2001. World Development Report, 2000/2001. New York: World Bank.

– 2002a. *Colombia Poverty Report*. Volume 1. *Main Report*. New York: World Bank.

– 2002b. *Toward More Sustainable Coffee*, http://lnweb18.worldbank.org/ESSD/essdext.nsf/11ByDocName/TowardMoreSustainableCoffee/$FILE/AgTech30.pdf.

– 2003a. *Nicaragua Poverty Assessment: Raising Welfare and Reducing Vulnerability.* New York: World Bank.
– 2003b. *Poverty in Guatemala.* New York: World Bank.
– 2004. World Development Index On-Line: World Bank.
Zonneveld, Luuk. 2003. *2001–2002: The Year in Review.* Bonn: Fairtrade Labelling Organizations International (FLO).

Index

Studies in Comparative Political Economy and Public Policy